Urantia 2025 Part 2

Urantia 2025 Part 2

The Local Universe

A Revised Urantia Book

Joel F. Covey

The Parts of the Urantia 2025 Book

PART 1

THE CENTRAL AND SUPERUNIVERSES

Sponsored by a Uversa Corps of Super-universe Personalities acting by authority of the Orvonton Ancients of Days

PART 2

THE LOCAL UNIVERSE

Sponsored by a Nebadon Corps of Local Universe Personalities acting by authority of Gabriel of Salvington

PART 3

THE HISTORY OF URANTIA

These papers were sponsored by a Corps of Local Universe Personalities acting by authority of Gabriel of Salvington

PART 4

THE LIFE AND TEACHINGS OF JESUS

This group of papers was sponsored by a commission of twelve Urantia midwayers acting under the supervision of a Melchizedek revelatory director.

The basis of this narrative was supplied by the superhuman watch-care of the Apostle Andrew.

Contents

PART II
THE LOCAL UNIVERSE

~

Sponsored by a Nebadon Corps of Local Universe
Personalities acting by authority of
Gabriel of Salvington.

PAPER 32
THE EVOLUTION OF LOCAL UNIVERSES

A LOCAL UNIVERSE is the handiwork of a Creator Son of the Paradise order of Michael. Most universes are four dimensional (three spatial and one time dimension) hyper-surfaces (or what you call M-branes in String Theory) and exist within the larger (10 or more) dimensional space-time of the super-universes. Each universe contains enormous numbers of major sectors of giant galactic superclusters. Each major sector contains large numbers of minor sectors, which are composed of smaller clusters or groups of galaxies. Each galaxy comprises approximately one hundred constellations depending on its size, each embracing around one hundred systems of inhabited worlds. Each system will eventually contain about one thousand inhabited spheres.

These universes of time and space are all evolutionary. The creative plan of the Paradise Michaels always proceeds along the path of gradual evolvement and progressive development of the physical, intellectual, and spiritual natures and capacities of the manifold creatures who inhabit the varied orders of spheres comprising such a local universe.

Urantia belongs to a local universe whose sovereign is the God-man of Nebadon, Jesus of Nazareth and Michael of Salvington. And all of Michael's plans for this local universe were fully approved by the Paradise Trinity before he ever embarked upon the supreme adventure of space.

The Sons of God may choose the realms of their creator activities, but the foundations for these material creations were originally projected and planned by the Paradise Architects of the Master Universe.

1. PHYSICAL EMERGENCE OF UNIVERSES

The pre-universe manipulations of space-force and the primordial energies are the work of the Paradise Master Force Organizers; but in the superuniverse domains, when emergent energy becomes responsive to local or linear gravity, they retire in favor of the power directors of the superuniverse concerned.

These power directors function alone in the pre-material and post-force phases of a local universe creation. There is no opportunity for a Creator Son to begin universe organization until the power directors have effected the mobilization of the basic space-time dimensional structure of the preuniverse and the space-energies sufficiently to provide a material foundation , a "Big Bang" of energy release which ultimately produces literal suns and material spheres for the emerging universe.

The local universes are all approximately of the same energy potential, though they differ greatly in physical dimensions and may vary in visible-matter content. The power charge and potential-matter endowment of a local universe are determined by the manipulations of the power directors and their predecessors as well as by the Creator Son's activities and by the endowment of the inherent physical control possessed by his creative associate.

The energy charge of a local universe, used for the "Big Bang", is approximately one one-hundred-thousandth of the force endowment of its super-universe. In the case of Nebadon, your local universe, the mass materialization is a trifle less. Physically speaking, Nebadon possesses all of the physical endowment of energy and matter that may be found in any of the Orvonton local creations. The only physical limitation upon the developmental expansion of the Nebadon universe consists in the quantitative charge of space-energy held captive by the gravity control of the associated powers and personalities of the combined universe mechanism.

When energy-matter has attained a certain stage in mass materialization, a Paradise Creator Son appears upon the scene, accompanied by a Creative Daughter of the Infinite Spirit. Simultaneously with the arrival of the Creator Son, work is begun upon the architectural sphere which is to become the headquarters world of the projected local universe. For long ages such a local creation evolves, suns become stabilized, the suns form galaxies, planets form and swing into their orbits, while the work of creating the architectural worlds which are to serve as headquarters and capitals for the major and minor sectors, the galaxies, constellations, and systems continues.

2. UNIVERSE ORGANIZATION

The Creator Sons are preceded in universe organization by the power directors and other beings originating in the Third Source and Center. From the energies of space, thus previously organized, Michael, your Creator Son, established the inhabited realms of the universe of Nebadon and ever since has been painstakingly devoted to their administration. From pre-existent energy these divine Sons materialize visible matter, project living creatures, and with the co-operation of the universe presence of the Infinite Spirit, create a diverse retinue of spirit personalities.

These power directors and energy controllers who long preceded the Creator Son in the preliminary physical work of universe organization later serve in magnificent liaison with this Universe Son, forever remaining in associated control of those energies which they originally organized and circuitized. On Salvington there now function the same large group of power centers who co-operated with your Creator Son in the original formation of this local universe.

The first completed act of physical creation in Nebadon consisted in the organization of the headquarters world, the architectural sphere of Salvington, with its satellites. From the time of the initial moves of the power centers and physical controllers to the arrival of the living staff on the completed spheres of Salvington, there intervened a little over one billion years of your present planetary time. The construction of Salvington was immediately followed by the creation of the headquarters worlds of all of the planned major and minor sector capitals. Next, as time progressed and the galaxies began to stabilize, the architectural headquarters spheres for each galaxy and its roughly one hundred constellations were built. Finally, the ten thousand headquarters spheres of each of the projected local systems of planetary control and administration, together with their architectural satellites, were constructed. Such architectural worlds are designed to accommodate both physical and spiritual personalities as well as the intervening morontia or transition stages of being.

Salvington is the personal headquarters of Michael of Nebadon, but he will not always be found there. While the smooth functioning of your local universe no longer requires the fixed presence of the Creator Son at the capital sphere, this was not true of the earlier epochs of physical organization. A Creator Son is unable to leave his headquarters world until such a time as gravity stabilization of the realm has been effected through the materialization of sufficient energy to enable the various circuits and systems to counterbalance one another by mutual material attraction.

Presently, the physical plan of a universe is completed, and the Creator Son, in association with the Creative Spirit, projects his plan of life creation; whereupon does this representation of the Infinite Spirit begin her universe function as a distinct creative personality. When this first creative act is formulated and executed, there springs into being the Bright and Morning Star, the personification of this initial creative concept of identity and ideal of divinity. This is the chief executive of the universe, the personal associate of the Creator Son, one like him in all aspects of character, though markedly limited in the attributes of divinity.

And now that the right-hand helper and chief executive of the Creator Son has been provided, there ensues the bringing into existence of a vast and wonderful array of diverse creatures. The sons and daughters of the local universe are forthcoming, and soon thereafter the government of such a creation is provided, extending from the supreme councils of the universe to the fathers of the constellations and the sovereigns of the local systems — the aggregations of those worlds which are designed subsequently to become the homes of the varied mortal races of will creatures; and each of these worlds will be presided over by a Planetary Prince.

And then, when such a universe has been so completely organized and so repletely manned, does the Creator Son enter into the Father's proposal to create mortal man in their divine image.

The organization of planetary abodes is still progressing in Nebadon, for this universe is, indeed, one of the newer universes in Orvonton. Your local system of Satania is not a uniform physical system, a single astronomic unit or organization. Its 619 inhabited worlds are located in over five hundred different physical systems. Only five have more than two inhabited worlds, and of these only one has four peopled planets, while there are forty-six having two inhabited worlds.

Viewed from the higher dimensional space-time of the super-universe, the universe of Nebadon now swings far to the south and east in the super-universe circuit of Orvonton. The nearest neighboring universes are: Avalon, Henselon, Sanselon, Portalon, Wolvering, Fanoving, and Alvoring.

But the evolution of a local universe is a long narrative. Papers dealing with the super-universe introduce this subject, those of this section, treating of the local creations, continue it, while those to follow, touching upon the history and destiny of Urantia, complete the story. But you can adequately comprehend the destiny of the mortals of such a local creation only by a perusal of the narratives of the life and teachings of your Creator Son as he once lived the life of man, in the likeness of mortal flesh, on your own evolutionary world.

3. THE EVOLUTIONARY IDEA

The only creation that is perfectly settled is Havona, the central universe, which was made directly by the thought of the Universal Father and the word of the Eternal Son. Havona is an existential, perfect, and replete universe, surrounding the home of the eternal Deities, the center of all things. The creations of the seven super-universes are finite, evolutionary, and consistently progressive.

The physical systems of time and space are all evolutionary in origin. They are not even physically stabilized until they are swung into the settled circuits of their super-universes. Neither is a local universe settled in light and life until its physical possibilities of expansion and development have been exhausted, and until the spiritual status of all its inhabited worlds has been forever settled and stabilized.

Except in the central universe, perfection is a progressive attainment. In the central creation we have a pattern of perfection, but all other realms must attain that perfection by the methods established for the advancement of those particular worlds or universes. And an almost infinite variety characterizes the plans of the Creator Sons for organizing, evolving, disciplining, and settling their respective local universes.

With the exception of the deity presence of the Father, every local universe is, in a certain sense, a duplication of the administrative organization of the central or pattern creation. Although the Universal Father is personally present in the residential universe, he does not indwell the minds of the beings originating in that universe as he does literally dwell with the souls of the mortals of time and space. There seems to be an all-wise compensation in the adjustment and regulation of the spiritual affairs of the far-flung creation. In the central universe the Father is personally present as such but absent in the minds of the children of that perfect creation; in the universes of space the Father is absent in person, being represented by his Sovereign Sons, while he is intimately present in the minds of his mortal children, being spiritually represented by the pre-personal presence of the Mystery Monitors that reside in the minds of these will creatures.

On the headquarters of a local universe there reside all those creator and creative personalities who represent self-contained authority and administrative autonomy except the personal presence of the Universal Father. In the local universe there are to be found something of everyone and someone of almost every class of intelligent beings existing in the central universe except the Universal Father. Although the Universal Father is not personally present in a local universe, he is personally represented by its Creator Son, sometime vicegerent of God and subsequently supreme and sovereign ruler in his own right.

The farther down the scale of life we go, the more difficult it becomes to locate, with the eye of faith, the invisible Father. The lower creatures — and sometimes even the higher personalities — find it difficult always to envisage the Universal Father in his Creator Sons. And so, pending the time of their spiritual exaltation, when perfection of development will enable them to see God in person, they grow weary in progression, entertain spiritual doubts, stumble into confusion, and thus isolate themselves from the progressive spiritual aims of their time and universe. In this way they lose the ability to see the Father when beholding the Creator Son. The surest safeguard for the creature throughout the long struggle to attain the Father, during this time when inherent conditions make such attainment impossible, is tenaciously to hold on to the truth-fact of the Father's presence in his Sons. Literally and figuratively, spiritually and personally, the Father and the Sons are one. It is a fact: He who has seen a Creator Son has seen the Father.

The personalities of a given universe are settled and dependable, at the start, only in accordance with their degree of kinship to Deity. When creature origin departs sufficiently far from the original and divine Sources, whether we are dealing with the Sons of God or the creatures of ministry belonging to the Infinite Spirit, there is an increase in the possibility of disharmony, confusion, and sometimes rebellion — sin.

Excepting perfect beings of Deity origin, all will creatures in the super-universes are of evolutionary nature, beginning in lowly estate and climbing ever upward, in reality inward. Even highly spiritual personalities continue to ascend the scale of life by progressive translations from life to life and from sphere to sphere. And in the case of those who entertain the Mystery Monitors, there is indeed no limit to the possible heights of their spiritual ascent and universe attainment.

The perfection of the creatures of time, when finally achieved, is wholly an acquirement, a bona fide personality possession. While the elements of grace are freely admixed, nevertheless, the creature attainments are the result of individual effort and actual living, personality reaction to the existing environment.

The fact of animal evolutionary origin does not attach stigma to any personality in the sight of the universe as that is the exclusive method of producing one of the two basic types of finite intelligent will creatures. When the heights of perfection and eternity are attained, all the more honor to those who began at the bottom and joyfully climbed the ladder of life, round by round, and who, when they do reach the heights of glory, will have gained a personal experience which embodies an actual knowledge of every phase of life from the bottom to the top.

In all this is shown the wisdom of the Creators. It would be just as easy for the Universal Father to make all mortals perfect beings, to impart perfection by his divine word. But that would deprive them of the wonderful experience of the adventure and training associated with the long and gradual inward climb, an experience to be had only by those who are so fortunate as to begin at the very bottom of living existence.

In the universes encircling Havona there are provided only a sufficient number of perfect creatures to meet the need for pattern teacher guides for those who are ascending the evolutionary scale of life. The experiential nature of the evolutionary type of personality is the natural cosmic complement of the ever-perfect natures of the Paradise-Havona creatures. In reality, both perfect and perfected creatures are incomplete as regards finite totality. But in the complemental association of the existentially perfect creatures of the Paradise-Havona system with the experientially perfected finaliters ascending from the evolutionary universes, both types find release from inherent limitations and thus may conjointly attempt to reach the sublime heights of the ultimate of creature status.

These creature transactions are the universe repercussions of actions and reactions within the Sevenfold Deity, wherein the eternal divinity of the Paradise Trinity is conjoined with the evolving divinity of the Supreme Creators of the time-space universes in, by, and through the power-actualizing Deity of the Supreme Being.

The divinely perfect creature and the evolutionary perfected creature are equal in degree of divinity potential, but they differ in kind. Each must depend on the other to attain supremacy of service. The evolutionary superuniverses depend on perfect Havona to provide the final training for their ascending citizens, but so does the perfect central universe require the existence of the perfecting super-universes to provide for the full development of its descending inhabitants.

The two prime manifestations of finite reality, innate perfection and evolved perfection, be they personalities or universes, are co-ordinate, dependent, and integrated. Each requires the other to achieve completion of function, service, and destiny.

4. GOD'S RELATION TO A LOCAL UNIVERSE

Do not entertain the idea that, since the Universal Father has delegated so much of himself and his power to others, he is a silent or inactive member of the Deity partnership. Aside from personality domains and Adjuster bestowal, he is apparently the least active of the Paradise Deities in that he allows his Deity co-ordinates, his Sons, and numerous created intelligences to perform so much in the carrying out of his eternal purpose. He is the silent member of the creative trio only in that he never does aught which any of his co-ordinate or subordinate associates can do.

God has full understanding of the need of every intelligent creature for function and experience, and therefore, in every situation, be it concerned with the destiny of a universe or the welfare of the humblest of his creatures, God retires from activity in favor of the galaxy of creature and Creator personalities who inherently intervene between himself and any given universe situation or creative event. But notwithstanding this retirement, this exhibition of infinite co-ordination, there is on God's part an actual, literal, and personal participation in these events by and through these ordained agencies and personalities. The Father is working in and through all these channels for the welfare of all his far-flung creation.

As regards the policies, conduct, and administration of a local universe, the Universal Father acts in the person of his Creator Son. In the interrelationships of the Sons of God, in the group associations of the personalities of origin in the Third Source and Center, or in the relationship between any other creatures, such as human beings — as concerns such associations the Universal Father never intervenes. The law of the Creator Son, the rule of the Constellation Fathers, the System Sovereigns, and the Planetary Princes — the ordained policies and procedures for that universe — always prevail. There is no division of authority; never is there a cross working of divine power and purpose. The Deities are in perfect and eternal unanimity.

The Creator Son rules supreme in all matters of ethical associations, the relations of any division of creatures to any other class of creatures or of two or more individuals within any given group; but such a plan does not mean that the Universal Father may not in his own way intervene and do aught that pleases the divine mind with any *individual creature* throughout all creation, as pertains to that individual's present status or future prospects and as concerns the Father's eternal plan and infinite purpose.

In the mortal will creatures the Father is actually present in the indwelling Adjuster, a fragment of his pre-personal spirit; and the Father is also the source of the personality of such a mortal will creature.

These Thought Adjusters, the bestowals of the Universal Father, are comparatively isolated; they indwell human minds but have no discernible connection with the ethical affairs of a local creation. They are not directly co-ordinated with the seraphic service nor with the administration of systems, constellations, or a local universe, not even with the rule of a Creator Son, whose will is the supreme law of his universe.

The indwelling Adjusters are one of God's separate but unified modes of contact with the creatures of his all but infinite creation. Thus does he who is invisible to mortal man manifest his presence, and could he do so, he would show himself to us in still other ways, but such further revelation is not divinely possible.

We can see and understand the mechanism whereby the Sons enjoy intimate and complete knowledge regarding the universes of their jurisdiction; but we cannot fully comprehend the methods whereby God is so fully and personally conversant with the details of the universe of universes, although we at least can recognize the avenue whereby the Universal Father can receive information regarding, and manifest his presence to, the beings of his immense creation. Through the personality circuit the Father is cognizant — has personal knowledge — of all the thoughts and acts of all the beings in all the systems of all the universes of all creation. Though we cannot fully grasp this technique of God's communion with his children, we can be strengthened in the assurance that the "Lord knows his children," and that of each one of us "he takes note where we were born."

In your universe and in your heart the Universal Father is present, spiritually speaking, by one of the Seven Master Spirits of central abode and, specifically, by the divine Adjuster who lives and works and waits in the depths of the mortal mind.

God is not a self-centered personality; the Father freely distributes himself to his creation and to his creatures. He lives and acts, not only in the Deities, but also in his Sons, whom he intrusts with the doing of everything that it is divinely possible for them to do. The Universal Father has truly divested himself of every function which it is possible for another being to perform. And this is just as true of mortal man as of the Creator Son who rules in God's stead at the headquarters of a local universe. Thus we behold the outworking of the ideal and infinite love of the Universal Father.

In this universal bestowal of himself we have abundant proof of both the magnitude and the magnanimity of the Father's divine nature. If God has withheld aught of himself from the universal creation, then of that residue he is in lavish generosity bestowing the Thought Adjusters upon the mortals of the realms, the Mystery Monitors of time, who so patiently indwell the mortal candidates for life everlasting.

The Universal Father has poured out himself, as it were, to make all creation rich in personality possession and potential spiritual attainment. God has given us himself that we may be like him, and he has reserved for himself of power and glory only that which is necessary for the maintenance of those things for the love of which he has thus divested himself of all things else.

5. THE ETERNAL AND DIVINE PURPOSE

There is a great and glorious purpose in the march of the universes through space. All of your mortal struggling is not in vain. We are all part of an immense plan, a gigantic enterprise, and it is the vastness of the undertaking that renders it impossible to see very much of it at any one time and during any one life. We are all a part of an eternal project which the Gods are supervising and outworking. The whole marvelous and universal mechanism moves on majestically through space to the music of the meter of the infinite thought and the eternal purpose of the First Great Source and Center.

The eternal purpose of the eternal God is a high spiritual ideal. The events of time and the struggles of material existence are but the transient scaffolding which bridges over to the other side, to the promised land of spiritual reality and supernal existence. Of course, you mortals find it difficult to grasp the idea of an eternal purpose; you are virtually unable to comprehend the thought of eternity, something never beginning and never ending. Everything familiar to you has an end.

As regards an individual life, the duration of a realm, or the chronology of any connected series of events, it would seem that we are dealing with an isolated stretch of time; everything seems to have a beginning and an end. And it would appear that a series of such experiences, lives, ages, or epochs, when successively arranged, constitutes a straightaway drive, an isolated event of time flashing momentarily across the infinite face of eternity. But when we look at all this from behind the scenes, a more comprehensive view and a more complete understanding suggest that such an explanation is inadequate, disconnected, and wholly unsuited properly to account for, and otherwise to correlate, the transactions of time with the underlying purposes and basic reactions of eternity.

To me it seems more fitting, for purposes of explanation to the mortal mind, to conceive of eternity as a cycle and the eternal purpose as an endless circle, a cycle of eternity in some way synchronized with the transient material cycles of time. As regards the sectors of time connected with, and forming a part of, the cycle of eternity, we are forced to recognize that such temporary epochs are born, live, and die just as the temporary beings of time are born, live, and die. Most human beings die because, having failed to achieve the spirit level of Adjuster fusion, the metamorphosis of death constitutes the only possible procedure whereby they may escape the fetters of time and the bonds of material creation, thereby being enabled to strike spiritual step with the progressive procession of eternity. Having survived the trial life of time and material existence, it becomes possible for you to continue on in touch with, even as a part of, eternity, swinging on forever with the worlds of space around the circle of the eternal ages.

The sectors of time are like the flashes of personality in temporal form; they appear for a season, and then they are lost to human sight, only to reappear as new actors and continuing factors in the higher life of the endless swing around the eternal circle. Eternity can hardly be conceived as a straightaway drive, in view of our belief in a delimited universe moving over a vast, elongated circle around the central dwelling place of the Universal Father.

Frankly, eternity is incomprehensible to the finite mind of time. You simply cannot grasp it; you cannot comprehend it. I do not completely visualize it, and even if I did, it would be impossible for me to convey my concept to the human mind. Nevertheless, I have done my best to portray something of our viewpoint, to tell you somewhat of our understanding of things eternal. I am endeavoring to aid you in the crystallization of your thoughts about these values which are of infinite nature and eternal import.

There is in the mind of God a plan which embraces every creature of all his vast domains, and this plan is an eternal purpose of boundless opportunity, unlimited progress, and endless life. And the infinite treasures of such a matchless career are yours for the striving!

The goal of eternity is ahead! The adventure of divinity attainment lies before you! The race for perfection is on! whosoever will may enter, and certain victory will crown the efforts of every human being who will run the race of faith and trust, depending every step of the way on the leading of the indwelling Adjuster and on the guidance of that good spirit of the Universe Son, which so freely has been poured out upon all flesh.

[Presented by a Mighty Messenger temporarily attached to the Supreme Council of Nebadon and assigned to this mission by Gabriel of Salvington.]

PAPER 33
ADMINISTRATION OF THE LOCAL UNIVERSE

WHILE THE UNIVERSAL Father most certainly rules over his vast creation, he functions in a local universe administration through the person of the Creator Son. The Father does not otherwise personally function in the administrative affairs of a local universe. These matters are intrusted to the Creator Son and to the local universe Mother Spirit and to their manifold children. The plans, policies, and administrative acts of the local universe are formed and executed by this Son, who, in conjunction with his Spirit associate, delegates executive power to Gabriel and jurisdictional authority down to the major and minor sectors, to the galaxies, and down to the Constellation Fathers, System Sovereigns, and Planetary Princes.

1. MICHAEL OF NEBADON

Our Creator Son is the personification of the 611,121st original concept of infinite identity of simultaneous origin in the Universal Father and the Eternal Son. The Michael of Nebadon is the "only-begotten Son" personalizing this 611,121st universal concept of divinity and infinity. His headquarters is in the threefold mansion of light on Salvington. And this dwelling is so ordered because Michael has experienced the living of all three phases of intelligent creature existence: spiritual, morontial, and material. Because of the name associated with his seventh and final bestowal on Urantia, he is sometimes spoken of as Christ Michael.

Our Creator Son is not the Eternal Son, the existential Paradise associate of the Universal Father and the Infinite Spirit. Michael of Nebadon is not a member of the Paradise Trinity. Nevertheless our Master Son possesses in his realm all of the divine attributes and powers that the Eternal Son himself would manifest were he actually to be present on Salvington and functioning in Nebadon. Michael possesses even additional power and authority, for he not only personifies the Eternal Son but also fully represents and actually embodies the personality presence of the Universal Father to and in this local universe. He even represents the Father-Son. These relationships constitute a Creator Son the most powerful, versatile, and influential of all divine beings who are capable of direct administration of evolutionary universes and of personality contact with immature creature beings.

Our Creator Son exerts the same spiritual drawing power, spirit gravity, from the headquarters of the local universe that the Eternal Son of Paradise would exert if he were personally present on Salvington, and *more*; this Universe Son is also the personification of the Universal Father to the universe of Nebadon. Creator Sons are personality centers for the spiritual forces of the Paradise Father-Son. Creator Sons are the final power-personality focalizations of the mighty time-space attributes of God the Sevenfold.

The Creator Son is the vicegerent personalization of the Universal Father, the divinity co-ordinate of the Eternal Son, and the creative associate of the Infinite Spirit. To our universe and all its inhabited worlds the Sovereign Son is, to all practical intents and purposes, God. He personifies all of the Paradise Deities which evolving mortals can discerningly comprehend. This Son and his Spirit associate *are* your creator parents. To you, Michael, the Creator Son, is the supreme personality; to you, the Eternal Son is super-supreme — an infinite Deity personality.

In the person of the Creator Son we have a ruler and divine parent who is just as mighty, efficient, and beneficent as would be the Universal Father and the Eternal Son if both were present on Salvington and engaged in the administration of the affairs of the universe of Nebadon.

2. THE SOVEREIGN OF NEBADON

Observation of Creator Sons discloses that some resemble more the Father, some the Son, while others are a blend of both their infinite parents. Our Creator Son very definitely manifests traits and attributes which more resemble the Eternal Son.

Michael elected to organize this local universe, and herein he now reigns supreme. His personal power is limited by the pre-existent gravity circuits centering at Paradise and by the reservation on the part of the Ancients of Days of the super-universe government of all final executive judgments regarding the extinction of personality. Personality is the sole bestowal of the Father, but the Creator Sons, with the approval of the Eternal Son, do initiate new creature designs, and with the working co-operation of their Spirit associates they may attempt new transformations of energy-matter.

Michael is the personification of the Paradise Father-Son to and in the local universe of Nebadon; therefore, when the Creative Mother Spirit, the local universe representation of the Infinite Spirit, subordinated herself to Christ Michael upon the return from his final bestowal on Urantia, the Master Son thereby acquired jurisdiction over "all power in heaven and on earth."

This subordination of the Divine Ministers to the Creator Sons of the local universes constitutes these Master Sons the personal repositories of the finitely manifestable divinity of the Father, Son, and Spirit, while the creature-bestowal experiences of the Michaels qualify them to portray the experiential divinity of the Supreme Being. No other beings in the universes have thus personally exhausted the potentials of present finite experience, and no other beings in the universes possess such qualifications for solitary sovereignty.

Although Michael's headquarters is officially located on Salvington, the capital of Nebadon, he spends much of his time visiting the major and minor sectors, the various galaxies, and the constellation and system headquarters, and even the individual planets. Periodically he journeys to Paradise and often to Uversa, where he counsels with the Ancients of Days. When he is away from Salvington, his place is assumed by Gabriel, who then functions as regent of the universe of Nebadon.

3. THE UNIVERSE SON AND SPIRIT

While pervading all the universes of time and space, the Infinite Spirit functions from the headquarters of each local universe as a specialized focalization acquiring full personality qualities by the technique of creative co-operation with the Creator Son. As concerns a local universe, the administrative authority of a Creator Son is supreme; the Infinite Spirit, as the Divine Minister, is wholly co-operative though perfectly co-ordinate.

The Universe Mother Spirit of Salvington, the associate of Michael in the control and administration of Nebadon, is of the sixth group of Supreme Spirits, being the 611,121st of that order. She volunteered to accompany Michael on the occasion of his liberation from Paradise obligations and has ever since functioned with him in creating and governing his universe.

The Master Creator Son is the personal sovereign of his universe, but in all the details of its management the Universe Spirit is codirector with the Son. While the Spirit ever acknowledges the Son as sovereign and ruler, the Son always accords the Spirit a co-ordinate position and equality of authority in all the affairs of the realm. In all his work of love and life bestowal the Creator Son is always and ever perfectly sustained and ably assisted by the all-wise and ever-faithful Universe Spirit and by all of her diversified retinue of angelic personalities. Such a Divine Minister is in reality the mother of spirits and spirit personalities, the ever-present and all-wise adviser of the Creator Son, a faithful and true manifestation of the Paradise Infinite Spirit.

The Son functions as a father in his local universe. The Spirit, as mortal creatures would understand, enacts the role of a mother, always assisting the Son and being everlastingly indispensable to the administration of the universe. In the face of insurrection only the Son and his associated Sons can function as deliverers. Never can the Spirit undertake to contest rebellion or defend authority, but ever does the Spirit sustain the Son in all of everything he may be required to experience in his efforts to stabilize government and uphold authority on worlds tainted with evil or dominated by sin. Only a Son can retrieve the work of their joint creation, but no Son could hope for final success without the incessant co-operation of the Divine Minister and her vast assemblage of spirit helpers, the daughters of God, who so faithfully and valiantly struggle for the welfare of mortal men and the glory of their divine parents.

Upon the completion of the Creator Son's seventh and final creature bestowal, the uncertainties of periodic isolation terminate for the Divine Minister, and the Son's universe helper becomes forever settled in surety and control. It is at the enthronement of the Creator Son as a Master Son, at the jubilee of jubilees, that the Universe Spirit, before the assembled hosts, first makes public and universal acknowledgment of subordination to the Son, pledging fidelity and obedience. This event occurred in Nebadon at the time of Michael's return to Salvington after the Urantian bestowal. Never before this momentous occasion did the Universe Spirit acknowledge subordination to the Universe Son, and not until after this voluntary relinquishment of power and authority by the Spirit could it be truthfully proclaimed of the Son that "all power in heaven and on earth has been committed to his hand."

After this pledge of subordination by the Creative Mother Spirit, Michael of Nebadon nobly acknowledged his eternal dependence on his Spirit companion, constituting the Spirit coruler of his universe domains and requiring all their creatures to pledge themselves in loyalty to the Spirit as they had to the Son; and there issued and went forth the final "Proclamation of Equality." Though he was the sovereign of this local universe, the Son published to the worlds the fact of the Spirit's equality with him in all endowments of personality and attributes of divine character. And this becomes the transcendent pattern for the family organization and government of even the lowly creatures of the worlds of space. This is, in deed and in truth, the high ideal of the family and the human institution of voluntary marriage.

The Son and the Spirit now preside over the universe much as a father and mother watch over, and minister to, their family of sons and daughters. It is not altogether out of place to refer to the Universe Spirit as the creative companion of the Creator Son and to regard the creatures of the realms as their sons and daughters — a grand and glorious family but one of untold responsibilities and endless watch-care.

The Son initiates the creation of certain of the universe children, while the Spirit is solely responsible for bringing into existence the numerous orders of spirit personalities who minister and serve under the direction and guidance of this selfsame Mother Spirit. In the creation of other types of universe personalities, both the Son and the Spirit function together, and in no creative act does the one do aught without the counsel and approval of the other.

4. GABRIEL — THE CHIEF EXECUTIVE

The Bright and Morning Star is the personalization of the first concept of identity and ideal of personality conceived by the Creator Son and the local universe manifestation of the Infinite Spirit. Going back to the early days of the local universe, before the union of the Creator Son and the Mother Spirit in the bonds of creative association, back to the times before the beginning of the creation of their versatile family of sons and daughters, the first conjoint act of this early and free association of these two divine persons results in the creation of the highest spirit personality of the Son and the Spirit, the Bright and Morning Star.

Only one such being of wisdom and majesty is brought forth in each local universe. The Universal Father and the Eternal Son can, in fact do, create an unlimited number of Sons in divinity equal to themselves; but such Sons, in union with the Daughters of the Infinite Spirit, can create only one Bright and Morning Star in each universe, a being like themselves and partaking freely of their combined natures but not of their creative prerogatives. Gabriel of Salvington is like the Universe Son in divinity of nature though considerably limited in the attributes of Deity.

This first-born of the parents of a new universe is a unique personality possessing many wonderful traits not visibly present in either ancestor, a being of unprecedented versatility and unimagined brilliance. This supernal personality embraces the divine will of the Son combined with the creative imagination of the Spirit. The thoughts and acts of the Bright and Morning Star will ever be fully representative of both the Creator Son and the Creative Spirit. Such a being is also capable of a broad understanding of, and sympathetic contact with, both the spiritual seraphic hosts and the material evolutionary will creatures.

The Bright and Morning Star is not a creator, but he is a marvelous administrator, being the personal administrative representative of the Creator Son. Aside from creation and life impartation the Son and the Spirit never confer upon important universe procedures without Gabriel's presence.

Gabriel of Salvington is the chief executive of the universe of Nebadon and the arbiter of all executive appeals respecting its administration. This universe executive was created fully endowed for his work, but he has gained experience with the growth and evolution of our local creation.

Gabriel is the chief officer of execution for super-universe mandates relating to non-personal affairs in the local universe. Most matters pertaining to mass judgment and dispensational resurrections, adjudicated by the Ancients of Days, are also delegated to Gabriel and his staff for execution. Gabriel is thus the combined chief executive of both the super- and the local universe rulers. He has at his command an able corps of administrative assistants, created for their special work, who are unrevealed to evolutionary mortals. In addition to these assistants, Gabriel may employ any and all of the orders of celestial beings functioning in Nebadon, and he is also the commander in chief of "the armies of heaven" — the celestial hosts.

Gabriel and his staff are not teachers; they are administrators. They were never known to depart from their regular work except when Michael was incarnated on a creature bestowal. During such bestowals Gabriel was ever attendant on the will of the incarnated Son, and with the collaboration of the Union of Days, he became the actual director of universe affairs during the later bestowals. Gabriel has been closely identified with the history and development of Urantia ever since the mortal bestowal of Michael.

Aside from meeting Gabriel on the bestowal worlds and at the times of general- and special-resurrection roll calls, mortals will seldom encounter him as they ascend through the local universe until they are inducted into the administrative work of the local creation. As administrators, of whatever order or degree, you will come under the direction of Gabriel.

5. THE TRINITY AMBASSADORS

The administration of Trinity-origin personalities ends with the government of the super-universes. The local universes are characterized by dual supervision, the beginning of the father-mother concept. The universe father is the Creator Son; the universe mother is the Divine Minister, the local universe Creative Spirit. Every local universe is, however, blessed with the presence of certain personalities from the central universe and Paradise. At the head of this Paradise group in Nebadon is the ambassador of the Paradise Trinity — Immanuel of Salvington — the Union of Days assigned to the local universe of Nebadon. In a certain sense this high Trinity Son is also the personal representative of the Universal Father to the court of the Creator Son; hence his name, Immanuel.

Immanuel of Salvington, number 611,121 of the sixth order of Supreme Trinity Personalities, is a being of sublime dignity and of such superb condescension that he refuses the worship and adoration of all living creatures. He bears the distinction of being the only personality in all Nebadon who has never acknowledged subordination to his brother Michael. He functions as adviser to the Sovereign Son but gives counsel only on request. In the absence of the Creator Son he might preside over any high universe council but would not otherwise participate in the executive affairs of the universe except as requested.

This ambassador of Paradise to Nebadon is not subject to the jurisdiction of the local universe government. Neither does he exercise authoritative jurisdiction in the executive affairs of an evolving local universe except in the supervision of his liaison brethren, the Perfections of Days serving in the major sectors, the Recents of Days serving in the minor sectors and on the galaxies, and the Faithfuls of Days, serving on the headquarters of the constellations.

All of these Paradise Sons, like the Union of Days, never proffer advice or offer assistance to the local universe rulers unless it is asked for. These Paradise ambassadors represent the final personal presence of the Stationary Sons of the Trinity functioning in advisory roles in the local universes. Constellations are thus more closely related to the super-universe administration than local systems, which are administered exclusively by personalities native to the local universe.

6. GENERAL ADMINISTRATION

Gabriel is the chief executive and actual administrator of Nebadon. Michael's absence from Salvington in no way interferes with the orderly conduct of universe affairs. During the absence of Michael, as recently on the mission of reunion of Orvonton Master Sons on Paradise, Gabriel is the regent of the universe. At such times Gabriel always seeks the counsel of Immanuel of Salvington regarding all major problems.

The Father Melchizedek is Gabriel's first assistant. When the Bright and Morning Star is absent from Salvington, his responsibilities are assumed by this original Melchizedek Son.

The various sub-administrations of the universe have assigned to them certain special domains of responsibility. While, in general, a system government looks after the welfare of its planets, it is more particularly concerned with the physical status of living beings, with biologic problems. In turn, the constellation rulers pay especial attention to the social and governmental conditions prevailing on the different planets and systems. A constellation government is chiefly exercised over unification and stabilization. Still higher up, the universe rulers are more occupied with the spiritual status of the realms.

Ambassadors are appointed by judicial decree and represent galaxies to other galaxies. Consuls are representatives of constellations to one another and to the galaxy headquarters; they are appointed by legislative decree and function only within the confines of the local galaxy. Observers are commissioned by executive decree of a System Sovereign to represent that system to other systems and at the constellation capital, and they function only within the confines of the local constellation.

From Salvington, broadcasts are simultaneously directed down through the major and minor sectors, to the galaxies, the constellation headquarters, the system headquarters, and to individual planets. All higher orders of celestial beings are able to utilize this service for communication with their fellows scattered throughout the universe. The universe broadcast is extended to all inhabited worlds regardless of their spiritual status. Planetary intercommunication is denied only those worlds under spiritual quarantine.

Broadcasts are also sent out from the major and minor capitals, as well as from each galaxy headquarters to their component constellations. Constellation broadcasts are periodically sent out from the headquarters of the constellation by the chief of the Constellation Fathers.

Chronology is reckoned, computed, and rectified by a special group of beings on Salvington. The standard day of Nebadon is equal to eighteen days and six hours of Urantia time, plus two and one-half minutes. The Nebadon year consists of a segment of the time of universe swing in relation to the Uversa circuit and is equal to one hundred days of standard universe time, about five years of Urantia time.

Nebadon time, broadcast from Salvington, is the standard for this local universe. Each administrative unit down to the constellations conducts its affairs by Nebadon time, but the systems maintain their own chronology, as do the individual planets.

The day in Satania, as reckoned on Jerusem, is a little less (1 hour, 4 minutes, 15 seconds) than three days of Urantia time. These times are generally known as Salvington or universe time, and Satania or system time. Standard time is universe time.

7. THE COURTS OF NEBADON

The Master Son, Michael, is supremely concerned with but three things:

creation, sustenance, and ministry. He does not personally participate in the judicial work of the universe. Creators never sit in judgment on their creatures; that is the exclusive function of creatures of high training and actual creature experience.

The entire judicial mechanism of Nebadon is under the supervision of Gabriel. The high courts, located on Salvington, are occupied with problems of general universe import and with the appellate cases coming up from the lower tribunals. There are seventy branches of these universe courts, and they function in seven divisions of ten sections each. In all matters of adjudication there presides a dual magistracy consisting of one judge of perfection antecedents and one magistrate of ascendant experience.

As regards jurisdiction, the local universe courts are limited in the following matters:

1. The administration of the local universe is concerned with creation, evolution, maintenance, and ministry. The universe tribunals are, therefore, denied the right to pass upon those cases involving the question of eternal life and death. This has no reference to natural death as it obtains on Urantia, but if the question of the right of continued existence, life eternal, comes up for adjudication, it must be referred to the tribunals of Orvonton, and if decided adversely to the individual, all sentences of extinction are carried out upon the orders, and through the agencies, of the rulers of the super-government.

2. The default or defection of any of the Local Universe Sons of God which jeopardizes their status and authority as Sons is never adjudicated in the tribunals of a Son; such a misunderstanding would be immediately carried to the super-universe courts.

3. The question of the readmission of any constituent part of a local universe — such as a local system — to the fellowship of full spiritual status in the local creation subsequent to spiritual isolation must be concurred in by the high assembly of the super-universe.

In all other matters the courts of Salvington are final and supreme. There is no appeal and no escape from their decisions and decrees.

However unfairly human contentions may sometimes appear to be adjudicated on Urantia, in the universe justice and divine equity do prevail. You are living in a well-ordered universe, and sooner or later you may depend upon being dealt with justly, even mercifully.

8. THE LEGISLATIVE AND EXECUTIVE FUNCTIONS

On Salvington, the headquarters of Nebadon, there are no true legislative bodies. The universe headquarters worlds are concerned largely with adjudication. The legislative assemblies of the local universe are located on the headquarters of the major and minor sectors, the galaxies, and the constellations. The systems are chiefly concerned with the executive and administrative work of the local creations. The System Sovereigns and their associates enforce the legislative mandates of the constellation rulers and execute the judicial decrees of the high courts of the universe.

While true legislation is not enacted at the universe headquarters, there do function on Salvington a variety of advisory and research assemblies, variously constituted and conducted in accordance with their scope and purpose. Some are permanent; others disband upon the accomplishment of their objective.

The supreme council of the local universe is made up of three members from each minor sector and seven representatives from each major sector.

The one hundred councils of supreme sanction are also situated on Salvington. The presidents of these councils constitute the immediate working cabinet of Gabriel.

All findings of the high universe advisory councils are referred either to the Salvington judicial bodies or to the legislative assemblies of the major or minor sectors, or to the galaxy or constellation concerned. These high councils are without authority or power to enforce their recommendations. If their advice is founded on the fundamental laws of the universe, then will the Nebadon courts issue rulings of execution; but if their recommendations have to do with local or emergency conditions, they must pass these down to the legislative assemblies for deliberative enactment and then to the system authorities for execution. These high councils are, in reality, the universe super-legislatures, but they function without the authority of enactment and without the power of execution.

While we speak of universe administration in terms of "courts" and "assemblies," it should be understood that these spiritual transactions are very different from the more primitive and material activities of Urantia which bear corresponding names.

[Presented by the Chief of the Archangels of Nebadon.]

PAPER 34
THE LOCAL UNIVERSE MOTHER SPIRIT

WHEN A CREATOR SON is personalized by the Universal Father and the Eternal Son, then does the Infinite Spirit individualize a new and unique representation of himself to accompany this Creator Son to the realms of space, there to be his companion, first, in physical organization and, later, in creation and ministry to the creatures of the newly projected universe.

A Creative Spirit reacts to both physical and spiritual realities; so does a Creator Son; and thus are they co-ordinate and associate in the administration of a local universe of time and space.

These Daughter Spirits are of the essence of the Infinite Spirit, but they cannot function in the work of physical creation and spiritual ministry simultaneously. In physical creation the Universe Son provides the pattern while the Universe Spirit initiates the materialization of physical realities. The Son operates in the power designs, but the Spirit transforms these energy creations into physical substances. Although it is somewhat difficult to portray this early universe presence of the Infinite Spirit as a person, nevertheless, to the Creator Son the Spirit associate is personal and has always functioned as a distinct individual.

1. PERSONALIZATION OF THE CREATIVE SPIRIT

After the completion of the physical organization of a local universe and the establishment of the energy circuits by the super-universe power centers, subsequent to this preliminary work of creation by the agencies of the Infinite Spirit, operating through, and under the direction of, his local universe creative focalization, there goes forth the proclamation of the Michael Son that life is next to be projected in the newly organized universe. Upon the Paradise recognition of this declaration of intention, there occurs a reaction of approval in the Paradise Trinity, followed by the disappearance in the spiritual shining of the Deities of the Master Spirit in whose super-universe this new creation is organizing. Meanwhile the other Master Spirits draw near this central lodgment of the Paradise Deities, and subsequently, when the Deity-embraced Master Spirit emerges to the recognition of his fellows, there occurs what is known as a "primary eruption." This is a tremendous spiritual flash, a phenomenon clearly discernible as far away as the head-quarters of the super-universe concerned; and simultaneously with this little-understood Trinity manifestation there occurs a marked change in the nature of the creative spirit presence and power of the Infinite Spirit resident in the local universe concerned. In response to these Paradise phenomena there immediately personalizes, in the very presence of the Creator Son, a new personal representation of the Infinite Spirit. This is the Divine Minister. The individualized Creative Spirit helper of the Creator Son has become his personal creative associate, the local universe Mother Spirit.

From and through this new personal segregation of the Conjoint Creator there proceed the established currents and the ordained circuits of spirit power and spiritual influence destined to pervade all the worlds and beings of that local universe. In reality, this new and personal presence is but a transformation of the pre-existent and less personal associate of the Son in his earlier work of physical universe organization.

This is the relation of a stupendous drama in few words, but it represents about all that can be told regarding these momentous transactions. They are instantaneous, inscrutable, and incomprehensible; the secret of the technique and procedure resides in the bosom of the Paradise Trinity. Of only one thing are we certain: The Spirit presence in the local universe during the time of purely physical creation or organization was incompletely differentiated from the spirit of the Paradise Infinite Spirit; whereas, after the reappearance of the supervising Master Spirit from the secret embrace of the Gods and following the flash of spiritual energy, the local universe manifestation of the Infinite Spirit suddenly and completely changes to the personal likeness of that Master Spirit who was in transmuting liaison with the Infinite Spirit. The local universe Mother Spirit thus acquires a personal nature tinged by that of the Master Spirit of the super-universe of astronomic jurisdiction.

This personalized presence of the Infinite Spirit, the Creative Mother Spirit of the local universe, is known in Satania as the Divine Minister. To all practical intents and spiritual purposes this manifestation of Deity is a divine individual, a spirit person. And she is so recognized and regarded by the Creator Son. It is through this localization and personalization of the Third Source and Center in our local universe that the Spirit could subsequently become so fully subject to the Creator Son that of this Son it was truly said, "All power in heaven and on earth has been intrusted to him."

2. NATURE OF THE DIVINE MINISTER

Having undergone marked personality metamorphosis at the time of life creation, the Divine Minister thereafter functions as a person and co-operates in a very personal manner with the Creator Son in the planning and management of the extensive affairs of their local creation. To many universe types of being, even this representation of the Infinite Spirit may not appear to be wholly personal during the ages preceding the final Michael bestowal; but subsequent to the elevation of the Creator Son to the sovereign authority of a Master Son, the Creative Mother Spirit becomes so augmented in personal qualities as to be personally recognized by all contacting individuals.

From the earliest association with the Creator Son the Universe Spirit possesses all the physical-control attributes of the Infinite Spirit, including the full endowment of antigravity. Upon the attainment of personal status the Universe Spirit exerts just as full and complete control of mind gravity, in the local universe, as would the Infinite Spirit if personally present.

In each local universe the Divine Minister functions in accordance with the nature and inherent characteristics of the Infinite Spirit as embodied in one of the Seven Master Spirits of Paradise. While there is a basic uniformity of character in all Universe Spirits, there is also a diversity of function, determined by their origin through one of the Seven Master Spirits. This differential of origin accounts for the diverse techniques in the function of the local universe Mother Spirits in different super-universes. But in all essential spiritual attributes these Spirits are identical, equally spiritual and wholly divine, irrespective of super-universe differentiation.

The Creative Spirit is coresponsible with the Creator Son in producing the creatures of the worlds and never fails the Son in all efforts to uphold and conserve these creations. Life is ministered and maintained through the agency of the Creative Spirit. "You send forth your Spirit, and they are created. You renew the face of the earth."

In the creation of a universe of intelligent creatures the Creative Mother Spirit functions first in the sphere of universe perfection, collaborating with the Son in the production of the Bright and Morning Star. Subsequently the offspring of the Spirit increasingly approach the order of created beings on the planets, even as the Sons grade downward from the Melchizedeks to the Material Sons, who actually contact with the mortals of the realms. In the later evolution of mortal creatures the Life Carrier Sons provide the physical body, fabricated out of the existing organized material of the realm, while the Universe Spirit contributes the "breath of life."

While the seventh segment of the grand universe may, in many respects, be tardy in development, thoughtful students of our problems look forward to the evolution of an extraordinarily well-balanced creation in the ages to come. We predict this high degree of symmetry in Orvonton because the presiding Spirit of this super-universe is the chief of the Master Spirits on high, being a spirit intelligence embodying the balanced union and perfect co-ordination of the traits and character of all three of the eternal Deities. We are tardy and backward in comparison with other sectors, but there undoubtedly awaits us a transcendent development and an unprecedented achievement sometime in the eternal ages of the future.

3. THE SON AND SPIRIT IN TIME AND SPACE

Neither the Eternal Son nor the Infinite Spirit is limited or conditioned by either time or space, but most of their offspring are.

The Infinite Spirit pervades all space and indwells the circle of eternity. Still, in their personal contact with the children of time, the personalities of the Infinite Spirit must often reckon with temporal elements, though not so much with space. Many mind ministries ignore space but suffer a time lag in effecting co-ordination of diverse levels of universe reality. A Solitary Messenger is virtually independent of space except that time is actually required in traveling from one location to another; and there are similar entities unknown to you.

In personal prerogatives a Creative Spirit is wholly and entirely independent of space, but not of time. There is no specialized personal presence of such a Universe Spirit on any of the major or minor sectors, the galaxies, constellations, or system headquarters. She is equally and diffusely present throughout her entire local universe and is, therefore, just as literally and personally present on one world as on any other.

Only as regards the element of time is a Creative Spirit ever limited in her universe ministrations. A Creator Son acts instantaneously throughout his universe; but the Creative Spirit must reckon with time in the ministration of the universal mind except as she consciously and designedly avails herself of the personal prerogatives of the Universe Son. In pure-spirit function the Creative Spirit also acts independently of time as well as in her collaboration with the mysterious function of universe reflectivity.

Though the spirit-gravity circuit of the Eternal Son operates independently of both time and space, all functions of the Creator Sons are not exempt from space limitations. If the transactions of the evolutionary worlds are excepted, these Michael Sons seem to be able to operate relatively independent of time. A Creator Son is not handicapped by time, but he is conditioned by space; he cannot personally be in two places at the same time. Michael of Nebadon acts timelessly within his own universe and by reflectivity practically so in the super-universe. He communicates timelessly with the Eternal Son directly.

The Divine Minister is the understanding helper of the Creator Son, enabling him to overcome and atone for his inherent limitations regarding space, for when these two function in administrative union, they are practically independent of time *and* space within the confines of their local creation. Therefore, as practically observed throughout a local universe, the Creator Son and the Creative Spirit usually function independently of both time and space since there is always available to each the time and the space liberation of the other.

Only absolute beings are independent of time and space in the absolute sense. The majority of the subordinate persons of both the Eternal Son and the Infinite Spirit are subject to both time and space.

When a Creative Spirit becomes "space conscious," she is preparing to recognize a circumscribed "space domain" as hers, a realm in which to be space free in contradistinction to all other space by which she would be conditioned. One is free to choose and act only within the realm of one's consciousness.

4. THE LOCAL UNIVERSE CIRCUITS

There are three distinct spirit circuits in the local universe of Nebadon:

1. The bestowal spirit of the Creator Son, the Comforter, the Spirit of Truth.
2. The spirit circuit of the Divine Minister, the Holy Spirit.
3. The intelligence-ministry circuit, including the more or less unified activities but diverse functioning of the seven adjutant mind-spirits.

The Creator Sons are endowed with a spirit of universe presence in many ways analogous to that of the Seven Master Spirits of Paradise. This is the Spirit of Truth which is poured out upon a world by a bestowal Son after he receives spiritual title to such a sphere. This bestowed Comforter is the spiritual force which ever draws all truth seekers towards Him who is the personification of truth in the local universe. This spirit is an inherent endowment of the Creator Son, emerging from his divine nature just as the master circuits of the grand universe are derived from the personality presences of the Paradise Deities.

The Creator Son may come and go; his personal presence may be in the local universe or elsewhere; yet the Spirit of Truth functions undisturbed, for this divine presence, while derived from the personality of the Creator Son, is functionally centered in the person of the Divine Minister.

The Universe Mother Spirit, however, never leaves the local universe headquarters world. The spirit of the Creator Son may and does function independently of the personal presence of the Son, but not so with her personal spirit. The Holy Spirit of the Divine Minister would become nonfunctional if her personal presence should be removed from Salvington. Her spirit presence seems to be fixed on the universe headquarters world, and it is this very fact that enables the spirit of the Creator Son to function independently of the whereabouts of the Son. The Universe Mother Spirit acts as the universe focus and center of the Spirit of Truth as well as of her own personal influence, the Holy Spirit.

The Creator Father-Son and the Creative Mother Spirit both contribute variously to the mind endowment of their local universe children. But the Creative Spirit does not bestow mind until she is endowed with personal prerogatives.

The super-evolutionary orders of personality in a local universe are endowed with the local universe type of the super-universe pattern of mind. The human and the subhuman orders of evolutionary life are endowed with the adjutant spirit types of mind ministration.

The seven adjutant mind-spirits are the creation of the Divine Minister of a local universe. These mind-spirits are similar in character but diverse in power, and all partake alike of the nature of the Universe Spirit, although they are hardly regarded as personalities apart from their Mother Creator. The seven adjutants have been given the following names: the spirit of *wisdom*, the spirit of *worship*, the spirit of *counsel*, the spirit of *knowledge*, the spirit of *courage*, the spirit of *understanding*, the spirit of *intuition* — of quick perception. After intelligent life develops the ability to respond to these seven adjutant spirits, they begin to become capable of responding to the higher aspects of these spirits. The higher aspects of the seven adjutant mind spirits are called the seven ray energies.

[JFC Note: for more information, and a slightly different perspective, on these seven ray energies, see the five volume set of books by Alice A. Bailey "A Treatise on the Seven Rays".]

These are the "seven spirits of God," "like lamps burning before the throne," which the prophet saw in the symbols of vision. But he did not see the seats of the four and twenty sentinels about these seven adjutant mind-spirits. This record represents the confusion of two presentations, one pertaining to the universe headquarters and the other to the system capital. The seats of the four and twenty elders are on Jerusem, the headquarters of your local system of inhabited worlds.

But it was of Salvington that John wrote: "And out of the throne proceeded lightnings and thunderings and voices" — the universe broadcasts to the local systems. He also envisaged the directional control creatures of the local universe, the living compasses of the headquarters world. This directional control in Nebadon is maintained by the four control creatures of Salvington, who operate over the universe currents and are ably assisted by the first functioning mind-spirit, the adjutant of intuition, the spirit of "quick understanding." But the description of these four creatures — called beasts — has been sadly marred; they are of unparalleled beauty and exquisite form.

5. THE MINISTRY OF THE SPIRIT

The Divine Minister co-operates with the Creator Son in the formulation of life and the creation of new orders of beings up to the time of his seventh bestowal and, subsequently, after his elevation to the full sovereignty of the universe, continues to collaborate with the Son and the Son's bestowed spirit in the further work of world ministry and planetary progression.

On the inhabited worlds the Spirit begins the work of evolutionary progression, starting with the lifeless material of the realm, first endowing vegetable life, then the animal organisms, then the first orders of human existence; and each succeeding impartation contributes to the further unfolding of the evolutionary potential of planetary life from the initial and primitive stages to the appearance of will creatures. This labor of the Spirit is largely effected through the seven adjutants, the spirits of promise, the unifying and co-ordinating spirit-mind of the evolving planets, ever and unitedly leading the races of men towards higher ideas and spiritual ideals.

Mortal man first experiences the ministry of the Spirit in conjunction with mind when the purely animal mind of evolutionary creatures develops reception capacity for the adjutants of worship and of wisdom. This ministry of the sixth and seventh adjutants indicates mind evolution crossing the threshold of spiritual ministry. And immediately are such minds of worship- and wisdom-function included in the spiritual circuits of the Divine Minister.

When mind is thus endowed with the ministry of the Holy Spirit, it possesses the capacity for (consciously or unconsciously) choosing the spiritual presence of the Universal Father — the Thought Adjuster. But it is not until a bestowal Son has liberated the Spirit of Truth for planetary ministry to all mortals that all normal minds are automatically prepared for the reception of the Thought Adjusters. The Spirit of Truth works as one with the presence of the spirit of the Divine Minister. This dual spirit liaison hovers over the worlds, seeking to teach truth and to spiritually enlighten the minds of men, to inspire the souls of the creatures of the ascending races, and to lead the peoples dwelling on the evolutionary planets ever towards their Paradise goal of divine destiny.

Though the Spirit of Truth is poured out upon all flesh, this spirit of the Son is almost wholly limited in function and power by man's personal reception of that which constitutes the sum and substance of the mission of the bestowal Son. The Holy Spirit is partly independent of human attitude and partially conditioned by the decisions and co-operation of the will of man. Nevertheless, the ministry of the Holy Spirit becomes increasingly effective in the sanctification and spiritualization of the inner life of those mortals who the more fully *obey* the divine leadings.

As individuals you do not personally possess a segregated portion or entity of the spirit of the Creator Father-Son or the Creative Mother Spirit; these ministries do not contact with, nor indwell, the thinking centers of the individual's mind as do the Mystery Monitors. Thought Adjusters are definite individualizations of the pre-personal reality of the Universal Father, actually indwelling the mortal mind as a very part of that mind, and they ever work in perfect harmony with the combined spirits of the Creator Son and Creative Spirit.

The presence of the Holy Spirit of the Universe Daughter of the Infinite Spirit, of the Spirit of Truth of the Universe Son of the Eternal Son, and of the Adjuster-spirit of the Paradise Father in or with an evolutionary mortal, denotes symmetry of spiritual endowment and ministry and qualifies such a mortal consciously to realize the faith-fact of sonship with God.

6. THE SPIRIT IN MAN

With the advancing evolution of an inhabited planet and the further spiritualization of its inhabitants, additional spiritual influences may be received by such mature personalities, including response to the seven ray energies. As mortals progress in mind control and spirit perception, these multiple spirit ministries become more and more co-ordinate in function; they become increasingly blended with the over-ministry of the Paradise Trinity.

Although Divinity may be plural in manifestation, in human experience Deity is singular, always *one*. Neither is spiritual ministry plural in human experience. Regardless of plurality of origin, all spirit influences are one in function. Indeed they are one, being the spirit ministry of God the Sevenfold in and to the creatures of the grand universe; and as creatures grow in appreciation of, and receptivity for, this unifying ministry of the spirit, it becomes in their experience the ministry of God the Supreme.

From the heights of eternal glory the divine Spirit descends, by a long series of steps, to meet you as you are and where you are and then, in the partnership of faith, lovingly to embrace the soul of mortal origin and to embark on the sure and certain retracement of those steps of condescension, never stopping until the evolutionary soul is safely exalted to the very heights of bliss from which the divine Spirit originally sallied forth on this mission of mercy and ministry.

Spiritual forces unerringly seek and attain their own original levels. Having gone out from the Eternal, they are certain to return thereto, bringing with them all those children of time and space who have espoused the leading and teaching of the indwelling Adjuster, those who have been truly "born of the Spirit," the faith sons of God.

The divine Spirit is the source of continual ministry and encouragement to the children of men. Your power and achievement is "according to his mercy, through the renewing of the Spirit." Spiritual life, like physical energy, is consumed. Spiritual effort results in relative spiritual exhaustion. The whole ascendant experience is real as well as spiritual; therefore, it is truly written, "It is the Spirit that quickens." "The Spirit gives life."

The dead theory of even the highest religious doctrines is powerless to transform human character or to control mortal behavior. What the world of today needs is the truth which your teacher of old declared: "Not in word only but also in power and in the Holy Spirit." The seed of theoretical truth is dead, the highest moral concepts without effect, unless and until the divine Spirit breathes upon the forms of truth and quickens the formulas of right-eousness.

Those who have received and recognized the indwelling of God have been born of the Spirit. "You are the temple of God, and the spirit of God dwells in you." It is not enough that this spirit be poured out upon you; the divine Spirit must dominate and control every phase of human experience.

It is the presence of the divine Spirit, the water of life, that prevents the consuming thirst of mortal discontent and that indescribable hunger of the unspiritualized human mind. Spirit-motivated beings "never thirst, for this spiritual water shall be in them a well of satisfaction springing up into life everlasting." Such divinely watered souls are all but independent of material environment as regards the joys of living and the satisfactions of earthly existence. They are spiritually illuminated and refreshed, morally strength-ened and endowed.

In every mortal there exists a dual nature: the inheritance of animal tendencies and the high urge of spirit endowment. During the short life you live on Urantia, these two diverse and opposing urges can seldom be fully reconciled; they can hardly be harmonized and unified; but throughout your lifetime the combined Spirit ever ministers to assist you in subjecting the flesh more and more to the leading of the Spirit. Even though you must live your material life through, even though you cannot escape the body and its necessities, nonetheless, in purpose and ideals you are empowered increasingly to subject the animal nature to the mastery of the Spirit. There truly exists within you a conspiracy of spiritual forces, a confederation of divine powers, whose exclusive purpose is to effect your final deliverance from material bondage and finite handicaps.

The purpose of all this ministration is, "That you may be strengthened with power through His spirit in the inner man." And all this represents but the preliminary steps to the final attainment of the perfection of faith and service, that experience wherein you shall be "filled with all the fullness of God," "for all those who are led by the spirit of God are the sons of God."

The Spirit never *drives*, only leads. If you are a willing learner, if you want to attain spirit levels and reach divine heights, if you sincerely desire to reach the eternal goal, then the divine Spirit will gently and lovingly lead you along the pathway of sonship and spiritual progress. Every step you take must be one of willingness, intelligent and cheerful co-operation. The domination of the Spirit is never tainted with coercion nor compromised by compulsion.

And when such a life of spirit guidance is freely and intelligently accepted, there gradually develops within the human mind a positive consciousness of divine contact and assurance of spirit communion; sooner or later "the Spirit bears witness with your spirit (the Adjuster) that you are a child of God." Already has your own Thought Adjuster told you of your kinship to God so that the record testifies that the Spirit bears witness "*with* your spirit," not *to* your spirit.

The consciousness of the spirit domination of a human life is presently attended by an increasing exhibition of the characteristics of the Spirit in the life reactions of such a spirit-led mortal, "for the fruits of the spirit are love, joy, peace, long-suffering, gentleness, goodness, faith, meekness, and temperance." Such spirit-guided and divinely illuminated mortals, while they yet tread the lowly paths of toil and in human faithfulness perform the duties of their earthly assignments, have already begun to discern the lights of eternal life as they glimmer on the faraway shores of another world; already have they begun to comprehend the reality of that inspiring and comforting truth, "The kingdom of God is not meat and drink but righteousness, peace, and joy in the Holy Spirit." And throughout every trial and in the presence of every hardship, spirit-born souls are sustained by that hope which transcends all fear because the love of God is shed abroad in all hearts by the presence of the divine Spirit.

7. THE SPIRIT AND THE FLESH

The flesh, the inherent nature derived from the animal-origin races, does not naturally bear the fruits of the divine Spirit. When the mortal nature has been up stepped by the addition of the nature of the Material Sons of God, as Urantians were in a measure advanced by the bestowal of Adam, then is the way better prepared for the Spirit of Truth to co-operate with the indwelling Adjuster to bring forth the beautiful harvest of the character fruits of the spirit. If you do not reject this spirit, even though eternity may be required to fulfill the commission, "he will guide you into all truth."

Evolutionary mortals inhabiting normal worlds of spiritual progress do not experience the acute conflicts between the spirit and the flesh which characterize the present-day Urantians. But even on the most ideal planets, pre-Adamic man must put forth positive efforts to ascend from the purely animalistic plane of existence up through successive levels of increasingly intellectual meanings and higher spiritual values.

The mortals of a normal world do not experience constant warfare between their physical and spiritual natures. They are confronted with the necessity of climbing up from the animal levels of existence to the higher planes of spiritual living, but this ascent is more like undergoing an educational training when compared with the intense conflicts of Urantia mortals in this realm of the divergent material and spiritual natures.

The Urantia peoples are suffering the consequences of a double deprivation of help in this task of progressive planetary spiritual attainment. The Caligastia upheaval precipitated world-wide confusion and robbed all subsequent generations of the moral assistance which a well-ordered society would have provided. But even more disastrous was the Adamic default in that it deprived Urantians of that superior type of physical nature which would have been more consonant with spiritual aspirations.

Urantia mortals are compelled to undergo such marked struggling between the spirit and the flesh because their remote ancestors were not more fully Adamized by the Edenic bestowal. It was the divine plan that the mortals of Urantia should have had physical natures more naturally spirit responsive.

Notwithstanding this double disaster to man's nature and his environment, present-day mortals would experience less of this apparent warfare between the flesh and the spirit if they would enter the spirit kingdom, wherein the faith sons of God enjoy comparative deliverance from the slave-bondage of the flesh in the enlightened and liberating service of whole-hearted devotion to doing the will of the Father in heaven. Jesus showed mankind the new way of mortal living whereby human beings may very largely escape the dire consequences of the Caligastic rebellion and most effectively compensate for the deprivations resulting from the Adamic default. "The spirit of the life of Christ Jesus has made us free from the law of animal living and the temptations of evil and sin." "This is the victory that overcomes the flesh, even your faith."

Those God-knowing men and women who have been born of the Spirit experience no more conflict with their mortal natures than do the inhabitants of the most normal of worlds, planets which have never been tainted with sin nor touched by rebellion. Faith sons work on intellectual levels and live on spiritual planes far above the conflicts produced by unrestrained or unnatural physical desires. The normal urges of animal beings and the natural appetites and impulses of the physical nature are not in conflict with even the highest spiritual attainment except in the minds of ignorant, mistaught, or unfortunately overconscientious persons.

Having started out on the way of life everlasting, having accepted the assignment and received your orders to advance, do not fear the dangers of human forgetfulness and mortal inconstancy, do not be troubled with doubts of failure or by perplexing confusion, do not falter and question your status and standing, for in every dark hour, at every crossroad in the forward struggle, the Spirit of Truth will always speak, saying, "This is the way."

[Presented by a Mighty Messenger temporarily assigned to service on Urantia.]

PAPER 35
THE LOCAL UNIVERSE SONS OF GOD

THEW SONS of God previously introduced have had a Paradise origin. They are the offspring of the divine Rulers of the universal domains. Of the first Paradise order of sonship, the Creator Sons, there is in Nebadon only one, Michael, the universe father and sovereign. Of the second order of Paradise sonship, the Avonal or Magisterial Sons, Nebadon has its full quota . And these "lesser Christs" are just as effective and all-powerful in their planetary bestowals as was the Creator and Master Son on Urantia. The third order, being of Trinity origin, do not register in a local universe. These Paradise Daynals are neither magistrates nor administrators; they are super-teachers.

The types of Sons about to be considered are of local universe origin; they are the offspring of a Paradise Creator Son in varied association with the complemental Universe Mother Spirit. The following orders of local universe sonship find mention in these narratives:

1. Melchizedek Sons.
2. Vorondadek Sons.
3. Lanonandek Sons.
4. Life Carrier Sons.

Triune Paradise Deity functions for the creation of three orders of sonship: the Michaels, the Avonals, and the Daynals. Dual Deity in the local universe, the Son and the Spirit, also functions in the creation of three high orders of Sons: the Melchizedeks, the Vorondadeks, and the Lanonandeks; and having achieved this threefold expression, they collaborate with the next level of God the Sevenfold in the production of the versatile order of Life Carriers. These beings are classified with the descending Sons of God, but they are a unique and original form of universe life. Their consideration will occupy the whole of the next paper.

1. THE FATHER MELCHIZEDEK

After bringing into existence the beings of personal aid, such as the Bright and Morning Star and other administrative personalities, in accordance with the divine purpose and creative plans of a given universe, there occurs a new form of creative union between the Creator Son and the Creative Spirit, the local universe Daughter of the Infinite Spirit. The personality offspring resulting from this creative partnership is the original Melchizedek — the Father Melchizedek — that unique being who subsequently collaborates with the Creator Son and the Creative Spirit to bring into existence the entire group of that name.

In the universe of Nebadon the Father Melchizedek acts as the first executive associate of the Bright and Morning Star. Gabriel is occupied more with universe policies, Melchizedek with practical procedures. Gabriel presides over the regularly constituted tribunals and councils of Nebadon, Melchizedek over the special, extraordinary, and emergency commissions and advisory bodies. Gabriel and the Father Melchizedek are never away from Salvington at the same time, for in Gabriel's absence the Father Melchizedek functions as the chief executive of Nebadon.

The Melchizedeks of our universe were all created within one millennial period of standard time by the Creator Son and the Creative Spirit in liaison with the Father Melchizedek. Being an order of sonship wherein one of their own number functioned as co-ordinate creator, Melchizedeks are in constitution partly of self-origin and therefore candidates for the realization of a supernal type of self-government. They periodically elect their own administrative chief for a term of seven years of standard time and otherwise function as a self-regulating order, though the original Melchizedek does exercise certain inherent coparental prerogatives. From time to time this Father Melchizedek designates certain individuals of his order to function as special Life Carriers to the midsonite worlds, a type of inhabited planet not heretofore revealed on Urantia.

The Melchizedeks do not function extensively outside the local universe except when they are called as witnesses in matters pending before the tribunals of the super-universe, and when designated special ambassadors, as they sometimes are, representing one universe to another in the same super-universe. The original or first-born Melchizedek of each universe is always at liberty to journey to the neighboring universes or to Paradise on missions having to do with the interests and duties of his order.

2. THE MELCHIZEDEK SONS

The Melchizedeks are the first order of divine Sons to approach sufficiently near the lower creature life to be able to function directly in the ministry of mortal uplift, to serve the evolutionary races without the necessity of incarnation. These Sons are naturally at the mid-point of the great personality descent, by origin being just about midway between the highest Divinity and the lowest creature life of will endowment. They thus become the natural intermediaries between the higher and divine levels of living existence and the lower, even the material, forms of life on the evolutionary worlds. The seraphic orders, the angels, delight to work with the Melchizedeks; in fact, all forms of intelligent life find in these Sons understanding friends, sympathetic teachers, and wise counselors.

The Melchizedeks are a self-governing order. With this unique group we encounter the first attempt at self-determination on the part of local universe beings and observe the highest type of true self-government. These Sons organize their own machinery for their group and home-planet administration, as well as that for the six associated spheres and their tributary worlds. And it should be recorded that they have never abused their prerogatives; not once throughout all the super-universe of Orvonton have these Melchizedek Sons ever betrayed their trust. They are the hope of every universe group which aspires to self-government; they are the pattern and the teachers of self-government to all the spheres of Nebadon. All orders of intelligent beings, superiors from above and subordinates from below, are wholehearted in their praise of the government of the Melchizedeks.

The Melchizedek order of sonship occupies the position, and assumes the responsibility, of the eldest son in a large family. Most of their work is regular and somewhat routine, but much of it is voluntary and altogether self-imposed. A majority of the special assemblies which, from time to time, convene on Salvington are called on motion of the Melchizedeks. On their own initiative these Sons patrol their native universe. They maintain an autonomous organization devoted to universe intelligence, making periodical reports to the Creator Son independent of all information coming up to universe headquarters through the regular agencies concerned with the routine administration of the realm. They are by nature unprejudiced observers; they have the full confidence of all classes of intelligent beings.

The Melchizedeks function as mobile and advisory review courts of the realms; these universe Sons go in small groups to the worlds to serve as advisory commissions, to take depositions, to receive suggestions, and to act as counselors, thus helping to compose the major difficulties and settle the serious differences which arise from time to time in the affairs of the evolutionary domains.

These eldest Sons of a universe are the chief aids of the Bright and Morning Star in carrying out the mandates of the Creator Son. When a Melchizedek goes to a remote world in the name of Gabriel, he may, for the purposes of that particular mission, be deputized in the name of the sender and in that event will appear on the planet of assignment with the full authority of the Bright and Morning Star. Especially is this true on those spheres where a higher Son has not yet appeared in the likeness of the creatures of the realm.

When a Creator Son enters upon the bestowal career on an evolutionary world, he goes alone; but when one of his Paradise brothers, an Avonal Son, enters upon a bestowal, he is accompanied by the Melchizedek supporters, twelve in number, who so efficiently contribute to the success of the bestowal mission. They also support the Paradise Avonals on magisterial missions to the inhabited worlds, and in these assignments the Melchizedeks are visible to mortal eyes if the Avonal Son is also thus manifest.

There is no phase of planetary spiritual need to which they do not minister. They are the teachers who so often win whole worlds of advanced life to the final and full recognition of the Creator Son and his Paradise Father.

The Melchizedeks are well-nigh perfect in wisdom, but they are not infallible in judgment. When detached and alone on planetary missions, they have sometimes erred in minor matters, that is, they have elected to do certain things which their supervisors did not subsequently approve. Such an error of judgment temporarily disqualifies a Melchizedek until he goes to Salvington and, in audience with the Creator Son, receives that instruction which effectually purges him of the disharmony which caused disagreement with his fellows; and then, following the correctional rest, reinstatement to service ensues on the third day. But these minor misadaptations in Melchizedek function have rarely occurred in Nebadon.

3. THE MELCHIZEDEK WORLDS

The Melchizedeks occupy a world of their own near Salvington, the universe headquarters. This sphere, by name Melchizedek, is the pilot world of the Salvington circuit of seventy primary spheres, each of which is encircled by six tributary spheres devoted to specialized activities. These marvelous spheres — seventy primaries and 420 tributaries — are often spoken of as the Melchizedek University. Ascending mortals from all over the local universe pass through for training on these 490 worlds in the acquirement of residential status on Salvington. But the education of ascenders is only one phase of the manifold activities taking place on the Salvington cluster of architectural spheres.

The 490 spheres of the Salvington circuit are divided into ten groups, each containing seven primary and forty-two tributary spheres. Each of these groups is under the general supervision of some one of the major orders of universe life. The first group, embracing the pilot world and the next six primary spheres in the encircling planetary procession, is under the supervision of the Melchizedeks.

These Melchizedek worlds are:

1. The pilot world — the home world of the Melchizedek Sons.
2. The world of the physical-life schools and the laboratories of living energies.
3. The world of morontia life.
4. The sphere of initial spirit life.
5. The world of mid-spirit life.
6. The sphere of advancing spirit life.
7. The domain of co-ordinate and supreme self-realization.

The six tributary worlds of each of these Melchizedek spheres are devoted to activities germane to the work of the associated primary sphere.

The pilot world, the sphere *Melchizedek*, is the common meeting ground for all beings who are engaged in educating and spiritualizing the ascending mortals of time and space. To an ascender this world is probably the most interesting place in all Nebadon. All evolutionary mortals who graduate from their major sector training are destined to land on Melchizedek, where they are initiated into the regime of the disciplines and spirit progression of the Salvington educational system. And never will you forget your reactions to the first day of life on this unique world, not even after you have reached your Paradise destination.

Ascending mortals maintain residence on the Melchizedek world while pursuing their training on the six encircling planets of specialized education. And this same method is adhered to throughout their sojourn on the seventy cultural worlds, the primary spheres of the Salvington circuit.

Many diverse activities occupy the time of the numerous beings who reside on the six tributary worlds of the Melchizedek sphere, but as concerns the ascending mortals, these satellites are devoted to the following special phases of study:

1. Sphere number one is occupied with the review of the initial planetary life of the ascending mortals. This review has, of course, been done before (possibly many times) but this time from a greater spiritual perspective. This work is carried on in classes composed of those who hail from a given world of mortal origin. Those from Urantia pursue such an experiential review together.

2. The special work of sphere number two consists in a similar review of the experiences passed through on the mansion worlds encircling the premier satellite of the local system headquarters.

3. The reviews of this sphere pertain to the sojourn on the capital of the local system and embrace the activities of the remainder of the architectural worlds of the system headquarters cluster.

4. The fourth sphere is occupied with a review of the experiences of the seventy tributary worlds of the constellation and of their associated spheres, along with a review of the ascendant sojourn on the constellation headquarters world.

5. On the fifth sphere there is conducted the review of the ascendant sojourn on the galaxy headquarters world, and the experiences of the minor and major sector headquarter worlds.

6. The time on sphere number six is devoted to an attempt to correlate these five epochs and thus achieve co-ordination of experience preparatory to entering the Melchizedek primary schools of universe training.

The schools of universe administration and spiritual wisdom are located on the Melchizedek home world, where also are to be found those schools devoted to a single line of research, such as energy, matter, organization, communication, records, ethics, and comparative creature existence.

In the Melchizedek College of Spiritual Endowment all orders — even the Paradise orders — of the Sons of God co-operate with the Melchizedek and the seraphic teachers in training the hosts who go forth as evangels of destiny, proclaiming spiritual liberty and divine sonship even to the remote worlds of the universe. This particular school of the Melchizedek University is an exclusive universe institution; student visitors are not received from other realms.

The highest course of training in universe administration is given by the Melchizedeks on their home world. This College of High Ethics is presided over by the original Father Melchizedek. It is to these schools that the various universes send exchange students. While the young universe of Nebadon stands low in the scale of universes as regards spiritual achievement and high ethical development, nevertheless, our administrative troubles have so turned the whole universe into a vast clinic for other near-by creations that the Melchizedek colleges are thronged with student visitors and observers from other realms. Besides the immense group of local registrants there are an enormous number of foreign students in attendance upon the Melchizedek schools, for the order of Melchizedeks in Nebadon is renowned throughout Orvonton.

4. SPECIAL WORK OF THE MELCHIZEDEKS

A highly specialized branch of Melchizedek activities has to do with the supervision of the progressive morontia career of the ascending mortals. Much of this training is conducted by the patient and wise seraphic ministers, assisted by mortals who have ascended to relatively higher levels of universe attainment, but all of this educational work is under the general supervision of the Melchizedeks in association with the Trinity Teacher Sons.

While the Melchizedek orders are chiefly devoted to the vast educational system and experiential training regime of the local universe, they also function in unique assignments and in unusual circumstances. In an evolving universe eventually embracing such a near infinite number of inhabited worlds, many things out of the ordinary are destined to happen, and it is in such emergencies that the Melchizedeks act. On Edentia, your constellation headquarters, they are known as emergency Sons. They are always ready to serve in all exigencies — physical, intellectual, or spiritual — whether on a planet, in a system, in a constellation, or in the universe. Whenever and wherever special help is needed, there you will find one or more of the Melchizedek Sons.

When failure of some feature of the Creator Son's plan is threatened, forthwith will go a Melchizedek to render assistance. But not often are they summoned to function in the presence of sinful rebellion, such as occurred in Satania.

The Melchizedeks are the first to act in all emergencies of whatever nature on all worlds where will creatures dwell. They sometimes act as temporary custodians on wayward planets, serving as receivers of a defaulting planetary government. In a planetary crisis these Melchizedek Sons serve in many unique capacities. It is easily possible for such a Son to make himself visible to mortal beings, and sometimes one of this order has even incarnated in the likeness of mortal flesh. Seven times in Nebadon has a Melchizedek served on an evolutionary world in the similitude of mortal flesh, and on numerous occasions these Sons have appeared in the likeness of other orders of universe creatures. They are indeed the versatile and volunteer emergency ministers to all orders of universe intelligences and to all the worlds and systems of worlds.

The Melchizedek who lived on Urantia during the time of Abraham was locally known as Prince of Salem because he presided over a small colony of truth seekers residing at a place called Salem. He volunteered to incarnate in the likeness of mortal flesh and did so with the approval of the Melchizedek receivers of the planet, who feared that the light of life would become extinguished during that period of increasing spiritual darkness. And he did foster the truth of his day and safely pass it on to Abraham and his associates.

5. THE VORONDADEK SONS

After the creation of the personal aids and the first group of the versatile Melchizedeks, the Creator Son and the local universe Creative Spirit planned for, and brought into existence, the second great and diverse order of universe sonship, the Vorondadeks.

Each Vorondadek Son is unique and original and they all have qualities derived from both of their co-creator parents, but each also was found to be slightly more like either their mother, the Creative Spirit (thus more resembling of the Infinite Spirit), their father, the Creative Son (and thus more resembling the Eternal Son), or resembling more God the Father, the First Great Source and Center. They were thus classified into three groups: the smallest group, the more Father like, was designated as Primary Vorondadeks; the next largest group were designated as Secondary Vorondadeks and are more like the Eternal Son; while the most numerous group, the Tertiary Vorondadeks, are more like the Creative Spirit.

The Vorondadek Sons are assigned duty depending on their type:

1. *Primary Vorondadeks*. These are the Sons designated as the Sovereigns of the major and minor sectors of a universe, and as counselors in the higher universe administrative work. A large reserve is maintained on the Vorondadek worlds of Salvington.

2. *Secondary Vorondadeks*. They are assigned as Galaxy Fathers, and as assistants, as needed, to the Primary Vorondadeks in the major and minor universe sectors, and to the reserves of their order.

3. *Tertiary Vorondadeks*. They are assigned as Constellation Fathers in all of the galaxies of the local universe, and to the reserves of their order.

The number of Vorondadeks varies in each local universe. These Sons, like their co-ordinates, the Melchizedeks, possess no power of reproduction, but they were created in such numbers that there are enough Vorondadeks to not only maintain large groups of reserves, but also to fulfill all current and possible future universe needs.

In many respects these Sons are a self-governing body; as individuals and as groups, even as a whole, they are largely self-determinative, much as are the Melchizedeks, but Vorondadeks do not function through such a wide range of activities. They do not equal their Melchizedek brethren in brilliant versatility, but they are even more reliable and efficient as rulers and farseeing administrators. Neither are they quite the administrative peers of their subordinates, the Lanonandek System Sovereigns, but they excel all orders of universe sonship in stability of purpose and in divinity of judgment.

Although the decisions and rulings of this order of Sons are always in accordance with the spirit of divine sonship and in harmony with the policies of the Creator Son, they have been cited for error to the Creator Son, and in details of technique their decisions have sometimes been reversed on appeal to the superior tribunals of the universe. But these Sons rarely fall into error, and they have never gone into rebellion; never in all the history of Nebadon has a Vorondadek been found in contempt of the universe government.

The service of the Vorondadeks in the local universes is extensive and varied. They serve as ambassadors to other universes and as consuls representing constellations within their native universe. Of all orders of local universe sonship they are the most often intrusted with the full delegation of sovereign powers to be exercised in critical universe situations.

On those worlds segregated in spiritual darkness, those spheres which have, through rebellion and default, suffered planetary isolation, an observer Vorondadek is usually present pending the restoration of normal status. In certain emergencies this Most High observer could exercise absolute and arbitrary authority over every celestial being assigned to that planet. It is of record on Salvington that the Vorondadeks have sometimes exercised such authority as Most High regents of such planets. And this has also been true even of inhabited worlds that were untouched by rebellion.

Often a corps of twelve or more Vorondadek Sons sits en banc as a high court of review and appeal concerning special cases involving the status of a planet or a system. But their work more largely pertains to the legislative functions indigenous to the constellation governments. As a result of all these services, the Vorondadek Sons have become the historians of the local universes; they are personally familiar with all the political struggles and the social upheavals of the inhabited worlds.

6. THE CONSTELLATION FATHERS

At least three Tertiary Vorondadeks are assigned to the rulership of each of the constellations of a local galaxy. These Sons are selected by the Creator Son and are commissioned by Gabriel as the *Most Highs* of the constellations for service during one dekamillennium — 10,000 standard years, about 50,000 years of Urantia time. The reigning Most High, the Constellation Father, has two associates, a senior and a junior. At each change of administration the senior associate becomes the head of the government, the junior assumes the duties of the senior, while the unassigned Tertiary Vorondadeks resident on the Salvington worlds nominate one of their number as candidate for selection to assume the responsibilities of junior associate. Thus each of the Most High rulers, in accordance with present policy, has a period of service on the headquarters of a constellation of three dekamillenniums, about 150,000 Urantia years.

The Constellation Fathers, the actual presiding heads of the constellation governments, in addition to the ruling Vorondadek Sons of the galaxies and the minor and major sectors of the universe, constitute the supreme advisory cabinet of the Creator Son. This council is in frequent session at universe headquarters and is unlimited in the scope and range of its deliberations but is chiefly concerned with the welfare and unification of the administration of the entire local universe.

When a Constellation Father is in attendance upon duties at the universe headquarters, as he frequently is, the senior associate becomes acting director of constellation affairs. The normal function of the senior associate is the oversight of spiritual affairs, while the junior associate is personally occupied with the physical welfare of the constellation. No major policy, however, is ever carried out in a constellation unless all three of the Most Highs are agreed upon all the details of its execution.

The entire mechanism of spirit intelligence and communication channels is at the disposal of the constellation Most Highs. They are in perfect touch with their superiors on the headquarters of their local galaxy and with their direct subordinates, the sovereigns of the local systems. They frequently convene in council with these System Sovereigns to deliberate upon the state of the constellation.

The Most Highs surround themselves with a corps of counselors, which varies in number and personnel from time to time in accordance with the presence of the various groups at constellation headquarters and also as the local requirements vary. During times of stress they may ask for, and will quickly receive, additional Sons of the Vorondadek order to assist with the administrative work. Norlatiadek, your own constellation, is at present administered by twelve Tertiary Vorondadek Sons.

7. THE VORONDADEK WORLDS

The second group of seven worlds in the circuit of seventy primary spheres surrounding Salvington comprise the Vorondadek planets. Each of these spheres, with its six encircling satellites, is devoted to a special phase of Vorondadek activities. On these forty-nine realms the ascending mortals secure the acme of their education respecting universe legislation.

The ascending mortals have observed the legislative assemblies as they functioned on the headquarters worlds of the constellations, galaxies, and the minor and major sectors, but here on these Vorondadek worlds they participate in the enactment of the actual general legislation of the local universe under the tutelage of the senior Vorondadeks. Such enactments are designed to co-ordinate the varied pronouncements of the autonomous legislative assemblies of the universe. The instruction to be had in the Vorondadek schools is unexcelled even on Uversa. This training is progressive, extending from the first sphere, with supplemental work on its six satellites, on up through the remaining six primary spheres and their associated satellite groups.

The ascending pilgrims will be introduced to numerous new activities on these worlds of study and practical work. We are not forbidden to undertake the revelation of these new and undreamed-of pursuits, but we despair of being able to portray these undertakings to the material mind of mortal beings. We are without words to convey the meanings of these supernal activities, and there are no analogous human engagements which might be utilized as illustrations of these new occupations of the ascending mortals as they pursue their studies on these forty-nine worlds. And many other activities, not a part of the ascendant regime, are centered on these Vorondadek worlds of the Salvington circuit.

8. THE LANONANDEK SONS

After the creation of the Vorondadeks, the Creator Son and the Universe Mother Spirit unite for the purpose of bringing into existence the third order of universe sonship, the Lanonandeks. Although occupied with varied tasks connected with the system administrations, they are best known as System Sovereigns, the rulers of the local systems, and as Planetary Princes, the administrative heads of the inhabited worlds.

Being a later and lower — as concerns divinity levels — order of sonship creation, these beings were required to pass through certain courses of training on the Melchizedek worlds in preparation for subsequent service. They were the first students in the Melchizedek University and were classified and certified by their Melchizedek teachers and examiners according to ability, personality, and attainment.

When they had passed through the Melchizedek sphere, they were divided in the final tests into three classes:

1. *Primary Lanonandeks*. These are the Sons designated as System Sovereigns and assistants to the supreme councils of the constellations and as counselors in the higher administrative work of the universe.

2. *Secondary Lanonandeks*. They are assigned as Planetary Princes and to the reserves of that order.

3. *Tertiary Lanonandeks*. These Sons function as subordinate assistants, messengers, custodians, commissioners, observers, and prosecute the miscellaneous duties of a system and its component worlds.

It is not possible, as it is with evolutionary beings, for these Sons to progress from one group to another. When subjected to the Melchizedek training, when once tested and classified, they serve continuously in the rank assigned. Neither do these Sons engage in reproduction; their number in the universe is stationary.

The Lanonandek order of Sons is classified on Salvington as, and function in, the following positions of responsibility: Universe Coordinators and

Constellation Counselors; System Sovereigns and Assistants; Planetary Princes; the Messenger Corps; Custodians and Recorders; and the various reserves of their order.

Since Lanonandeks are a somewhat lower order of sonship than the Melchizedeks and the Vorondadeks, they are of even greater service in the subordinate units of the universe, for they are capable of drawing nearer the lower creatures of the intelligent races. They also stand in greater danger of going astray, of departing from the acceptable technique of universe government. But these Lanonandeks, especially the primary order, are the most able and versatile of all local universe administrators. In executive ability they are excelled only by Gabriel and his unrevealed associates.

9. THE LANONANDEK RULERS

The Lanonandeks are the continuous rulers of the planets and the rotating sovereigns of the systems. Such a Son now rules on Jerusem, the headquarters of your local system of inhabited worlds.

The System Sovereigns rule in commissions of two or three on the headquarters of each system of inhabited worlds. The Constellation Father names one of these Lanonandeks as chief every dekamillennium. Sometimes no change in the head of the trio is made, the matter being entirely optional with the constellation rulers. System governments do not suddenly change in personnel unless a tragedy of some sort occurs.

When System Sovereigns or assistants are recalled, their places are filled by selections made by the supreme council located on the constellation headquarters from the reserves of that order, a group which is larger on Edentia than the average indicated.

The supreme Lanonandek councils are stationed on the various constellation headquarters. Such a body is presided over by the senior Most High associate of the Constellation Father, while the junior associate supervises the reserves of the secondary order.

The System Sovereigns are true to their names; they are well-nigh sovereign in the local affairs of the inhabited worlds. They are almost paternal in their direction of the Planetary Princes, the Material Sons, and the ministering spirits. The personal grasp of the sovereign is all but complete. These rulers are not supervised by Trinity observers from the central universe. They are the executive division of the local universe, and as custodians of the enforcement of legislative mandates and as executives for the application of judicial verdicts, they present the one place in all universe administration where personal disloyalty to the will of the Michael Son could most easily and readily intrench itself and seek to assert itself.

Our local universe has been unfortunate in that over seven hundred Sons of the Lanonandek order have rebelled against the universe government, thus precipitating confusion in several systems and on numerous planets. Of this entire number of failures only three were System Sovereigns; practically all of these Sons belonged to the second and third orders, Planetary Princes and tertiary Lanonandeks.

The large number of these Sons who have lapsed from integrity does not indicate any fault in creator-ship. They could have been made divinely perfect, but they were so created that they might better understand, and draw near to, the evolutionary creatures dwelling on the worlds of time and space.

Of all the local universes in Orvonton, our universe has, with the exception of Henselon, lost the largest number of this order of Sons. On Uversa it is the consensus that we have had so much administrative trouble in Nebadon because our Sons of the Lanonandek order have been created with such a large degree of personal liberty in choosing and planning. I do not make this observation by way of criticism. The Creator of our universe has full authority and power to do this. It is the contention of our high rulers that, while such free-choosing Sons make excessive trouble in the earlier ages of the universe, when things are fully sifted and finally settled, the gains of higher loyalty and fuller volitional service on the part of these thoroughly tested Sons will far more than compensate for the confusion and tribulations of earlier times.

In the event of rebellion on a system headquarters, a new sovereign is usually installed within a comparatively short time, but not so on the individual planets. They are the component units of the material creation, and creature free will is a factor in the final adjudication of all such problems. Successor Planetary Princes are designated for isolated worlds, planets whose princes of authority may have gone astray, but they do not assume active rulership of such worlds until the results of insurrection are partially overcome and removed by the remedial measures adopted by the Melchizedeks and other ministering personalities. Rebellion by a Planetary Prince instantly isolates his planet; the local spiritual circuits are immediately severed. Only a bestowal Son can re-establish interplanetary lines of communication on such a spiritually isolated world.

There exists a plan for saving these wayward and unwise Sons, and many have availed themselves of this merciful provision; but never again may they function in those positions wherein they defaulted. After rehabilitation they are assigned to custodial duties and to departments of physical administration.

10. THE LANONANDEK WORLDS

The third group of seven worlds in the Salvington circuit of seventy planets, with their respective forty-two satellites, constitute the Lanonandek cluster of administrative spheres. On these realms the experienced Lanonandeks belonging to the ex-System Sovereign corps officiate as administrative teachers of the ascending pilgrims and the seraphic hosts. The evolutionary mortals observe the system administrators at work on the system capitals, but here they participate in the actual co-ordination of the administrative pronouncements of the local systems.

These administrative schools of the local universe are supervised by a corps of Lanonandek Sons who have had long experience as System Sovereigns and as constellation counselors.

While serving as training spheres for ascending mortals, the Lanonandek worlds are the centers for extensive undertakings having to do with the normal and routine administrative operations of the universe. All the way in to Paradise the ascending pilgrims pursue their studies in the practical schools of applied knowledge — actual training in really doing the things they are being taught. The universe educational system sponsored by the Melchizedeks is practical, progressive, meaningful, and experiential. It embraces training in things material, intellectual, morontial, and spiritual.

It is in connection with these administrative spheres of the Lanonandeks that most of the salvaged Sons of that order serve as custodians and directors of planetary affairs. And these defaulting Planetary Princes and their associates in rebellion who choose to accept the proffered rehabilitation will continue to serve in these routine capacities, at least until the universe of Nebadon is settled in light and life.

Many of the Lanonandek Sons in the older systems, however, have established wonderful records of service, administration, and spiritual achievement. They are a noble, faithful, and loyal group, notwithstanding their tendency to fall into error through fallacies of personal liberty and fictions of self-determination.

[Sponsored by the Chief of Archangels acting by authority of Gabriel of Salvington.]

PAPER 36
THE LIFE CARRIERS

LIFE DOES NOT ORIGINATE SPONTANEOUSLY. Life is constructed according to plans formulated by the (unrevealed) Architects of Being and appears on the inhabited planets either by direct importation or as a result of the operations of the Life Carriers of the local universes. These carriers of life are among the most interesting and versatile of the diverse family of universe Sons. They are intrusted with designing and carrying creature life to the planetary spheres. And after planting this life on such new worlds, they remain there for long periods to foster its development.

1. ORIGIN AND NATURE OF LIFE CARRIERS

Though the Life Carriers belong to the family of divine sonship, they are a peculiar and distinct type of universe Sons, being the only group of intelligent life in a local universe in whose creation the rulers of a super-universe participate. The Life Carriers are the offspring of three pre-existent personalities: the Creator Son, the Universe Mother Spirit, and, by designation, one of the three Ancients of Days presiding over the destinies of the super-universe concerned. These Ancients of Days, who alone can decree the extinction of intelligent life, participate in the creation of the Life Carriers, who are intrusted with establishing physical life on the evolving worlds.

This efficient corps of life disseminators is not a truly self-governing group. They are directed by the life-determining trio, consisting of Gabriel, the Father Melchizedek, and Nambia, the original and first-born Life Carrier of Nebadon. But in all phases of their divisional administration they are self-governing.

Life Carriers are graded into three grand divisions: The first division is the senior Life Carriers, the second, assistants, and the third, custodians. The primary division is subdivided into twelve groups of specialists in the various forms of life manifestation. The segregation of these three divisions was effected by the Melchizedeks, who conducted tests for such purposes on the Life Carriers' headquarters sphere. The Melchizedeks have ever since been closely associated with the Life Carriers and always accompany them when they go forth to establish life on a new planet.

When an evolutionary planet is finally settled in light and life, the Life Carriers are organized into the higher deliberative bodies of advisory capacity to assist in the further administration and development of the world and its glorified beings. In the later and settled ages of an evolving universe these Life Carriers are intrusted with many new duties.

2. THE LIFE CARRIER WORLDS

The Melchizedeks have the general oversight of the fourth group of seven primary spheres in the Salvington circuit. These worlds of the Life Carriers are designated as follows:

1. The Life Carrier headquarters.
2. The life-planning sphere.
3. The life-conservation sphere.
4. The sphere of life evolution.
5. The sphere of life associated with mind.
6. The sphere of mind and spirit in living beings.
7. The sphere of unrevealed life.

Each of these primary spheres is surrounded by six satellites, on which the special phases of all the Life Carrier activities in the universe are centered.

World Number One, the headquarters sphere, together with its six tributary satellites, is devoted to the study of universal life, life in all of its known phases of manifestation. Here is located the college of life planning, wherein function teachers and advisers from Uversa and Havona, even from Paradise. And I am permitted to reveal that the seven central emplacements of the adjutant mind-spirits are situated on this world of the Life Carriers.

The number ten — the decimal system — is inherent in the physical universe but not in the spiritual. The domain of life is characterized by three, seven, and twelve or by multiples and combinations of these basic numbers. There are three primal and essentially different life plans, after the order of the three Paradise Sources and Centers, and in the universe of Nebadon these three basic forms of life are segregated on three different types of planets. There were, originally, twelve distinct and divine concepts of transmissible life. This number twelve, with its subdivisions and multiples, runs throughout all basic life patterns of all seven super-universes. There are also seven architectural types of life design, fundamental arrangements of the reproducing configurations of living matter. The Orvonton life patterns are usually configured in multiples of twelve inheritance carriers. The differing orders of will creatures are thus normally configured with 12, 24, 48, 96, 192, 384, and 768 trait determiners in the sex cells of human reproduction. However, there are many life experiment planets which deviate from this series, as on Urantia where human beings have 46 chromosomes, units of pattern control.

The Second World is the life-designing sphere; here all new modes of life organization are worked out. While the original life designs are provided by the Creator Son, the actual outworking of these plans is intrusted to the Life Carriers and their associates. When the general life plans for a new world have been formulated, they are transmitted to the headquarters sphere, where they are minutely scrutinized by the supreme council of the senior Life

Carriers in collaboration with a corps of consulting Melchizedeks. If the plans are a departure from previously accepted formulas, they must be passed upon, and endorsed by, the Creator Son. The chief of Melchizedeks often represents the Creator Son in these deliberations.

Planetary life, therefore, while similar in some respects, differs in many ways on each evolutionary world. Even in a uniform life series in a single family of worlds, life is not exactly the same on any two planets; there is always a planetary type, for the Life Carriers work constantly in an effort to improve the vital formulas committed to their keeping.

There are over one million fundamental or cosmic chemical formulas which constitute the parent patterns and the numerous basic functional variations of life manifestations. Satellite number one of the life-planning sphere is the realm of the universe physicists and electrochemists who serve as technical assistants to the Life Carriers in the work of capturing, organizing, and manipulating the essential units of energy which are employed in building up the material vehicles of life transmission, the so-called germ plasm.

The planetary life-planning laboratories are situated on the second satellite of this world number two. In these laboratories the Life Carriers and all their associates collaborate with the Melchizedeks in the effort to modify and possibly improve the life designed for implantation on the *decimal planets* of Nebadon. The life now evolving on Urantia was planned and partially worked out on this very world, for Urantia is a decimal planet, a life-experiment world. On one world in each ten a greater variance in the standard life designs is permitted than on the other (non-experimental) worlds.

World Number Three is devoted to the conservation of life. Here various modes of life protection and preservation are studied and developed by the assistants and custodians of the Life Carrier corps. The life plans for every new world always provide for the early establishment of the life-conservation commission, consisting of custodian specialists in the expert manipulation of the basic life patterns.

Sphere Number Four and its tributary satellites are devoted to the study of the evolution of creature life in general and to the evolutionary antecedents of any one life level in particular. The original life plasm of an evolutionary world must contain the full potential for all future developmental variations and for all subsequent evolutionary changes and modifications. The provision for such far-reaching projects of life metamorphosis may require the appearance of many apparently useless forms of animal and vegetable life. Such by-products of planetary evolution, foreseen or unforeseen, appear upon the stage of action only to disappear, but in and through all this long process there runs the thread of the wise and intelligent formulations of the original designers of the planetary life plan and species scheme. The manifold by-products of biologic evolution are all essential to the final and full function of the higher intelligent forms of life, notwithstanding that great outward disharmony may prevail from time to time in the long upward struggle of the higher creatures to effect the mastery of the lower forms of life, many of which are sometimes so antagonistic to the peace and comfort of the evolving will creatures.

Number Five World is concerned wholly with life associated with mind. Each of its satellites is devoted to the study of a single phase of creature mind correlated with creature life. Mind such as man comprehends is an endowment of the seven adjutant mind-spirits superimposed on the nonteachable or mechanical levels of mind by the agencies of the Infinite Spirit. The life patterns are variously responsive to these adjutants and to the different spirit ministries operating throughout the universes of time and space. The capacity of material creatures to affect spirit response is entirely dependent on the associated mind endowment, which, in turn, has directionized the course of the biologic evolution of these same mortal creatures.

World Number Six is dedicated to the correlation of mind with spirit as they are associated with living forms and organisms. This world and its six tributaries embrace the schools of creature co-ordination, wherein teachers from both the central universe and the super-universe collaborate with the Nebadon instructors in presenting the highest levels of creature attainment in time and space.

The Seventh Sphere of the Life Carriers is dedicated to the unrevealed domains of evolutionary creature life as it is related to the cosmic philosophy of the expanding factualization of the Supreme Being.

3. LIFE TRANSPLANTATION

Life does not spontaneously appear in the universes; the Life Carriers must initiate it on the barren planets. They are the carriers, disseminators, and guardians of life as it appears on the evolutionary worlds of space. All life of the order and forms known on Urantia arises with these Sons, though not all forms of planetary life are existent on Urantia.

The corps of Life Carriers commissioned to plant life upon a new world usually consists of one hundred senior carriers, one hundred assistants, and one thousand custodians. The Life Carriers often carry actual life plasm to a new world, but not always. They sometimes organize the life patterns after arriving on the planet of assignment in accordance with formulas previously approved for a new adventure in life establishment. Such was the origin of the planetary life of Urantia.

When, in accordance with approved formulas, the physical patterns have been provided, then do the Life Carriers catalyze this lifeless material, imparting through their persons the vital spirit spark; and forthwith do the inert patterns become living matter.

The vital spark — the mystery of life — is bestowed through the Life Carriers, not by them. They do indeed supervise such transactions, they formulate the life plasm itself, but it is the Universe Mother Spirit who supplies the essential factor of the living plasm. From the Creative Daughter of the Infinite Spirit comes that energy spark which enlivens the body and presages the mind.

In the bestowal of life the Life Carriers transmit nothing of their personal natures, not even on those spheres where new orders of life are projected. At such times they simply initiate and transmit the spark of life, start the required revolutions of matter in accordance with the physical, chemical, and electrical specifications of the ordained plans and patterns. Life Carriers are living catalytic presences which agitate, organize, and vitalize the otherwise inert elements of the material order of existence.

The Life Carriers of a planetary corps are given a certain period in which to establish life on a new world, approximately one-half million years of the time of that planet. At the termination of this period, indicated by certain developmental attainments of the planetary life, they cease implantation efforts, and they may not subsequently add any thing new or supplemental to the life of that planet.

During the ages intervening between life establishment and the emergence of human creatures of moral status, the Life Carriers are permitted to manipulate the life environment and otherwise favorably directionize the course of biologic evolution. And this they do for long periods of time.

When the Life Carriers operating on a new world have once succeeded in producing a being with will, with the power of moral decision and spiritual choice, then and there their work terminates — they are through; they may manipulate the evolving life no further. From this point forward the evolution of living things must proceed in accordance with the endowment of the inherent nature and tendencies which have already been imparted to, and established in, the planetary life formulas and patterns. The Life Carriers are not permitted to experiment or to interfere with will; they are not allowed to dominate or arbitrarily influence moral creatures.

Upon the arrival of a Planetary Prince they prepare to leave, though two of the senior carriers and twelve custodians may volunteer, by taking temporary renunciation vows, to remain indefinitely on the planet as advisers in the matter of the further development and conservation of the life plasm. Two such Sons and their twelve associates are now serving on Urantia.

4. MELCHIZEDEK LIFE CARRIERS

In every local system of inhabited worlds throughout Nebadon there is a single sphere whereon the Melchizedeks have functioned as life carriers. These abodes are known as the system *midsonite* worlds, and on each of them a materially modified Melchizedek Son has mated with a selected Daughter of the material order of sonship. The Mother Eves of such midsonite worlds are dispatched from the system headquarters of jurisdiction, having been chosen by the designated Melchizedek life carrier from among the numerous volunteers who respond to the call of the System Sovereign addressed to the Material Daughters of his sphere.

The progeny of a Melchizedek life carrier and a Material Daughter are known as *midsoniters*. The Melchizedek father of such a race of supernal creatures eventually leaves the planet of his unique life function, and the Mother Eve of this special order of universe beings also departs upon the appearance of the seventh generation of planetary offspring. The direction of such a world then devolves upon her eldest son.

The midsonite creatures live and function as reproducing beings on their magnificent worlds until they are one thousand standard years of age; whereupon they are translated by seraphic transport. Midsoniters are non-reproducing beings thereafter because the technique of dematerialization which they pass through in preparation for enseraphiming forever deprives them of reproductive prerogatives.

The present status of these beings can hardly be reckoned as either mortal or immortal, neither can they be definitely classified as human or divine. These creatures are not Adjuster indwelt, hence hardly immortal. But neither do they seem to be mortal; no midsoniter has experienced death. All midsoniters ever born in Nebadon are alive today, functioning on their native worlds, on some intervening sphere, or on the Salvington midsonite sphere in the finaliters' group of worlds.

The Salvington Worlds of the Finaliters. The Melchizedek life carriers, as well as the associated Mother Eves, go from the system midsonite spheres to the finaliters' worlds of the Salvington circuit, where their offspring are also destined to forgather.

It should be explained in this connection that the fifth group of seven primary worlds in the Salvington circuit are the Nebadon worlds of the finaliters. The children of the Melchizedek life carriers and the Material Daughters are domiciled on the seventh world of the finaliters, the Salvington midsonite sphere.

The satellites of the seven primary worlds of the finaliters are the rendezvous of the personalities of the super- and central universes who may be executing assignments in Nebadon. While the ascending mortals go about freely on all of the cultural worlds and training spheres of the 490 worlds comprising the Melchizedek University, there are certain special schools and numerous restricted zones which they are not permitted to enter. This is especially true of the forty-nine spheres under the jurisdiction of the finaliters.

The purpose of the midsonite creatures is not at present known, but it would appear that these personalities are forgathering on the seventh finaliter world in preparation for some future eventuality in universe evolution. Our inquiries concerning the midsonite races are always referred to the finaliters, and always do the finaliters decline to discuss the destiny of their wards. Regardless of our uncertainty as to the future of the midsoniters, we do know that every local universe in Orvonton harbors such an accumulating corps of these mysterious beings. It is the belief of the Melchizedek life carriers that their midsonite children will some day be endowed with the transcendental and eternal spirit of absonity by God the Ultimate.

5. THE SEVEN ADJUTANT MIND-SPIRITS

It is the presence of the seven adjutant mind-spirits on the primitive worlds that conditions the course of organic evolution; that explains why evolution is purposeful and not accidental. These adjutants represent that function of the mind ministry of the Infinite Spirit which is extended to the lower orders of intelligent life through the operations of a local universe Mother Spirit. The adjutants are the children of the Universe Mother Spirit and constitute her personal ministry to the material minds of the realms. Wherever and whenever such mind is manifest, these spirits are variously functioning.

The seven adjutant mind-spirits are called by names which are the equivalents of the following designations: intuition, understanding, courage, knowledge, counsel, worship, and wisdom. These mind-spirits send forth their influence into all the inhabited worlds as a differential urge, each seeking receptivity capacity for manifestation quite apart from the degree to which its fellows may find reception and opportunity for function.

The central lodgments of the adjutant spirits on the Life Carrier headquarters world indicate to the Life Carrier supervisors the extent and quality of the mind function of the adjutants on any world and in any given living organism of intellect status. These life-mind emplacements are perfect indicators of living mind function for the first five adjutants. But with regard to the sixth and seventh adjutant spirits — worship and wisdom — these central lodgments record only a qualitative function. The quantitative activity of the adjutant of worship and the adjutant of wisdom is registered in the immediate presence of the Divine Minister on Salvington, being a personal experience of the Universe Mother Spirit.

The seven adjutant mind-spirits always accompany the Life Carriers to a new planet, but they should not be regarded as entities; they are more like circuits. The spirits of the seven universe adjutants do not function as personalities apart from the universe presence of the Divine Minister; they are in fact a level of consciousness of the Divine Minister and are always subordinate to the action and presence of their creative mother.

We are handicapped for words adequately to designate these seven adjutant mind-spirits. They are ministers of the lower levels of experiential mind, and they may be described, in the order of evolutionary attainment, as follows:

1. *The spirit of intuition* — quick perception, the primitive physical and inherent reflex instincts, the directional and other self-preservative endowments of all mind creations; the only one of the adjutants to function so largely in the lower orders of animal life and the only one to make extensive functional contact with the non-teachable levels of mechanical mind.

2. *The spirit of understanding* — the impulse of co-ordination, the spontaneous and apparently automatic association of ideas. This is the gift of the co-ordination of acquired knowledge, the phenomenon of quick reasoning, rapid judgment, and prompt decision.

3. *The spirit of courage* — the fidelity endowment — in personal beings, the basis of character acquirement and the intellectual root of moral stamina and spiritual bravery. When enlightened by facts and inspired by truth, this becomes the secret of the urge of evolutionary ascension by the channels of intelligent and conscientious self-direction.

4. *The spirit of knowledge* — the curiosity-mother of adventure and discovery, the scientific spirit; the guide and faithful associate of the spirits of courage and counsel; the urge to direct the endowments of courage into useful and progressive paths of growth.

5. *The spirit of counsel* — the social urge, the endowment of species co-operation; the ability of will creatures to harmonize with their fellows; the origin of the gregarious instinct among the more lowly creatures.

6. *The spirit of worship* — the religious impulse, the first differential urge separating mind creatures into the two basic classes of mortal existence. The spirit of worship forever distinguishes the animal of its association from the soulless creatures of mind endowment. Worship is the badge of spiritual-ascension candidacy.

7. *The spirit of wisdom* — the inherent tendency of all moral creatures towards orderly and progressive evolutionary advancement. This is the highest of the adjutants, the spirit co-ordinator and articulator of the work of all the others. This spirit is the secret of that inborn urge of mind creatures which initiates and maintains the practical and effective program of the ascending scale of existence; that gift of living things which accounts for their inexplicable ability to survive and, in survival, to utilize the co-ordination of all their past experience and present opportunities for the acquisition of all of everything that all of the other six mental ministers can mobilize in the mind of the organism concerned. Wisdom is the acme of intellectual performance. Wisdom is the goal of a purely mental and moral existence.

The adjutant mind-spirits experientially grow, but they never become personal. They evolve in function, and the function of the first five in the animal orders is to a certain extent essential to the function of all seven as human intellect. This animal relationship makes the adjutants more practically effective as human mind; hence animals are to a certain extent indispensable to man's intellectual as well as to his physical evolution. The higher aspects of the adjutant mind-spirits are known as the seven ray energies, and these begin to find response once intelligent life has evolved to the point where it has made contact with the spirit of wisdom. These seven ray energies will be discussed in a later paper dealing with the planetary mortal epochs.

These mind-adjutants of a local universe Mother Spirit are related to creature life of intelligence status much as the power centers and physical controllers are related to the nonliving forces of the universe. They perform invaluable service in the mind circuits on the inhabited worlds and are effective collaborators with the Master Physical Controllers, who also serve as controllers and directors of the pre-adjutant mind levels, the levels of non-teachable or mechanical mind.

Living mind, prior to the appearance of capacity to learn from experience, is the ministry domain of the Master Physical Controllers. Creature mind, before acquiring the ability to recognize divinity and worship Deity, is the exclusive domain of the adjutant spirits. With the appearance of the spiritual response of the creature intellect, such created minds at once become responsive to the seven ray energies and develop the capability to become super-minded, being instantly encircuited in the spirit cycles of the local universe Mother Spirit.

The adjutant mind-spirits are in no manner directly related to the diverse and highly spiritual function of the spirit of the personal presence of the Divine Minister, the Holy Spirit of the inhabited worlds; but they are functionally antecedent to, and preparatory for, the appearance of this very spirit in evolutionary man. The adjutants afford the Universe Mother Spirit a varied contact with, and control over, the material living creatures of a local universe, but they do not repercuss in the Supreme Being when acting on pre-personality levels.

Nonspiritual mind is either a spirit-energy manifestation or a physical-energy phenomenon. Even human mind, personal mind, has no survival qualities apart from spirit identification. Mind is a divinity bestowal, but it is not immortal when it functions without spirit insight, and when it is devoid of the ability to worship and crave survival.

6. LIVING FORCES

Life is both mechanistic and vitalistic — material and spiritual. Ever will Urantia physicists and chemists progress in their understanding of the protoplasmic forms of vegetable and animal life. Animal mind and human mind are gifts of the local universe Mother Spirit, functioning through the seven adjutant mind-spirits.

When the Life Carriers have designed the patterns of life, after they have organized the energy systems, there must occur an additional phenomenon; the "breath of life" must be imparted to these lifeless forms. The Sons of God can construct the forms of life, but it is the Spirit of God who really contributes the vital spark. And when the life thus imparted is spent, then again the remaining material body becomes dead matter. When the bestowed life is exhausted, the body returns to the bosom of the material universe from which it was borrowed by the Life Carriers to serve as a transient vehicle for that life endowment which they conveyed to such a visible association of energy-matter.

We speak of life as "energy" and as "force," but it is really neither. Force-energy is variously gravity responsive; life is not. Pattern is also non-responsive to gravity, being a configuration of energies that have already fulfilled all gravity-responsive obligations. Life, as such, constitutes the animation of some pattern-configured or otherwise segregated system of energy — material, mindal, or spiritual.

There are some things connected with the elaboration of life on the evolutionary planets which are not altogether clear to us. We fully comprehend the physical organization of the electrochemical formulas of the Life Carriers, but we do not wholly understand the nature and source of the *life-activation spark*. We know that life flows from the Father through the Son and *by* the Spirit. It is more than possible that the Master Spirits are the sevenfold channel of the river of life which is poured out upon all creation. But we do not comprehend the technique whereby the supervising Master Spirit participates in the initial episode of life bestowal on a new planet. The Ancients of Days, we are confident, also have some part in this inauguration of life on a new world, but we are wholly ignorant of the nature thereof. We do know that the Universe Mother Spirit actually vitalizes the lifeless patterns and imparts to such activated plasm the prerogatives of organismal reproduction. We observe that these three are the levels of God the Sevenfold, sometimes designated as the Supreme Creators of time and space; but otherwise we know little more than Urantia mortals — simply that concept is inherent in the Father, expression in the Son, and life realization in the Spirit.

[Indited by a Vorondadek Son stationed on Urantia as an observer and acting in this capacity by request of the Melchizedek Chief of the Supervising Revelatory Corps.]

PAPER 37
PERSONALITIES OF THE LOCAL UNIVERSE

AT THE HEAD of all personality in Nebadon stands the Creator and Master Son, Michael, the universe father and sovereign. Co-ordinate in divinity and complemental in creative attributes is the local universe Mother Spirit, the Divine Minister of Salvington. And these creators are in a very literal sense the Father-Son and the Spirit-Mother of all the native creatures of Nebadon.

Preceding papers have dealt with the created orders of sonship; succeeding narratives will portray the ministering spirits and the ascending orders of sonship. This paper is chiefly concerned with an intervening group, the Universe Aids, but it will also give brief consideration to certain of the higher spirits stationed in Nebadon and to certain of the orders of permanent citizenship in the local universe.

1. THE UNIVERSE AIDS

Many of the unique orders generally grouped in this category are unrevealed, but as presented in these papers, the Universe Aids include the following seven orders:

1. Bright and Morning Stars.
2. Brilliant Evening Stars.
3. Archangels.
4. Most High Assistants.
5. High Commissioners.
6. Celestial Overseers.
7. Mansion World Teachers.

Of the first order of Universe Aids, the Bright and Morning Stars, there is just one in each local universe, and he is the first-born of all creatures native to a local universe. The Bright and Morning Star of our universe is known as Gabriel of Salvington. He is the chief executive of all Nebadon, functioning as the personal representative of the Sovereign Son and as spokesman for his creative consort.

During the earlier times of Nebadon, Gabriel worked quite alone with Michael and the Creative Spirit. As the universe grew and administrative problems multiplied, he was provided with a personal staff of unrevealed assistants, and eventually this group was augmented by the creation of the Nebadon corps of Evening Stars.

2. THE BRILLIANT EVENING STARS

These brilliant creatures were planned by the Melchizedeks and were then brought into being by the Creator Son and the Creative Spirit. They serve in many capacities but chiefly as liaison officers of Gabriel, the local universe chief executive. One or more of these beings function as his representatives at the capitals of the major and minor sectors, all galaxies, and every constellation and system in Nebadon.

As chief executive of Nebadon, Gabriel is ex officio chairman of, or observer at, most of the Salvington conclaves, and as many as one thousand of these are often in session simultaneously. The Brilliant Evening Stars represent Gabriel on these occasions; he cannot be in two places at the same time, and these super-angels compensate for this limitation. They perform an analogous service for the corps of the Trinity Teacher Sons.

Though personally occupied with administrative duties, Gabriel maintains contact with all other phases of universe life and affairs through the Brilliant Evening Stars. They always accompany him on his planetary tours and frequently go on special missions to the individual planets as his personal representatives. On such assignments they have sometimes been known as "the angel of the Lord." They frequently go to Uversa to represent the Bright and Morning Star before the courts and assemblies of the Ancients of Days, but they seldom journey beyond the confines of Orvonton.

The Brilliant Evening Stars are a unique twofold order, embracing some of created dignity and others of attained service. Many of these ascendant Evening Stars started their universe careers as seraphim; others have ascended from unrevealed levels of creature life. As an attainment goal this high corps is never closed to ascension candidates so long as a universe is not settled in light and life.

Both types of Brilliant Evening Stars are easily visible to morontia personalities and certain types of super-mortal material beings. The created beings of this interesting and versatile order possess a spirit force which can be manifested independently of their personal presence.

The head of these super-angels is Gavalia, the first-born of this order in Nebadon. Since the return of Christ Michael from his triumphant bestowal on Urantia, Gavalia has been assigned to the ascendant mortal ministry, and for the last two thousand Urantia years his associate, Galantia, has maintained headquarters on Jerusem, where he spends about half of his time. Galantia is the first of the ascendant super-angels to attain this high estate.

No grouping or company organization of the Brilliant Evening Stars exists other than their customary association in pairs on many assignments. They are not extensively assigned on missions pertaining to the ascendant career of mortals, but when thus commissioned, they never function alone. They always work in pairs — one a created being, the other an ascendant Evening Star.

One of the high duties of the Evening Stars is to accompany the Avonal bestowal Sons on their planetary missions, even as Gabriel accompanied Michael on his Urantia bestowal. The two attending super-angels are the ranking personalities of such missions, serving as cocommanders of the archangels and all others assigned to these undertakings. It is the senior of these super-angel commanders who, at the significant time and age, bids the Avonal bestowal Son, "Be about your brother's business."

Similar pairs of these super-angels are assigned to the planetary corps of Trinity Teacher Sons that functions to establish the post-bestowal or dawning spiritual age of an inhabited world. On such assignments the Evening Stars serve as liaisons between the mortals of the realm and the invisible corps of Teacher Sons.

The Worlds of the Evening Stars. The sixth group of seven Salvington worlds and their forty-two tributary satellites are assigned to the administration of the Brilliant Evening Stars. The seven primary worlds are presided over by the created orders of these super-angels, while the tributary satellites are administered by ascendant Evening Stars.

The satellites of the first three worlds are devoted to the schools of the Teacher Sons and the Evening Stars dedicated to the spirit personalities of the local universe. The next three groups are occupied by similar joint schools devoted to the training of ascending mortals. The seventh-world satellites are reserved for the triune deliberations of the Teacher Sons, the Evening Stars, and the finaliters. During recent times these super-angels have been closely identified with the local universe work of the Corps of the Finality, and they have long been associated with the Teacher Sons. There exists a liaison of tremendous power and import between the Evening Stars and the Gravity Messengers attached to the finaliter working groups. The seventh primary world itself is reserved for those unrevealed matters which pertain to the future relationship that will obtain between the Teacher Sons, the finaliters, and the Evening Stars consequent upon the completed emergence of the super-universe manifestation of the personality of God the Supreme.

3. THE ARCHANGELS

Archangels are the offspring of the Creator Son and the Universe Mother Spirit. They are the highest type of high spirit being produced in large numbers in a local universe.

Archangels are one of the few groups of local universe personalities who are not normally under the jurisdiction of Gabriel. They are not in any manner concerned with the routine administration of the universe, being dedicated to the work of creature survival and to the furtherance of the ascending career of the mortals of time and space. While not ordinarily subject to the direction of the Bright and Morning Star, the archangels do sometimes function by his authority. They also collaborate with others of the Universe Aids, such as the Evening Stars, as is illustrated by certain transactions depicted in the narrative of life transplantation on your world.

The archangel corps of Nebadon is directed by the first-born of this order, and in more recent times a divisional headquarters of the archangels has been maintained on Urantia. It is this unusual fact that soon arrests the attention of extra-Nebadon student visitors. Among their early observations of intrauniverse transactions is the discovery that many ascendant activities of the Brilliant Evening Stars are directed from the capital of a local system, Satania. On further examination they discover that certain archangel activities are directed from a small and apparently insignificant inhabited world called Urantia. And then ensues the revelation of Michael's bestowal on Urantia and their immediately quickened interest in you and your lowly sphere.

Do you grasp the significance of the fact that your lowly and confused planet has become a divisional headquarters for the universe administration and direction of certain archangel activities having to do with the Paradise ascension scheme? This undoubtedly presages the future concentration of other ascendant activities on the bestowal world of Michael and lends a tremendous and solemn import to the Master's personal promise, "I will come again."

In general, the archangels are assigned to the service and ministry of the Avonal order of sonship, but not until they have passed through extensive preliminary training in all phases of the work of the various ministering spirits. A corps of one hundred accompanies every Paradise bestowal Son to an inhabited world, being temporarily assigned to him for the duration of such a bestowal. If the Magisterial Son should become temporary ruler of the planet, these archangels would act as the directing heads of all celestial life on that sphere.

Two senior archangels are always assigned as the personal aids of a Paradise Avonal on all planetary missions, whether involving judicial actions, magisterial missions, or bestowal incarnations. When this Paradise Son has finished the judgment of a realm and the dead are called to record (the so-called resurrection), it is literally true that the seraphic guardians of the slumbering personalities respond to "the voice of the archangel." The roll call of a dispensation termination is promulgated by an attendant archangel. This is the archangel of the resurrection, sometimes referred to as the "archangel of Michael."

The Worlds of the Archangels. The seventh group of the encircling Salvington worlds, with their associated satellites, is assigned to the archangels. Sphere number one and all of its six tributary satellites are occupied by the personality record keepers. This enormous corps of recorders busy themselves with keeping straight the record of each mortal of time from the moment of birth up through the universe career until such an individual either leaves Salvington for the super-universe regime or is "blotted out of recorded existence" by the mandate of the Ancients of Days.

It is on these worlds that personality records and identification sureties are classified, filed, and preserved during that time which intervenes between mortal death and the hour of repersonalization, the resurrection from death.

4. MOST HIGH ASSISTANTS

The Most High Assistants are a group of volunteering beings, of origin outside the local universe, who are temporarily assigned as central and super-universe representatives to, or observers of, the local creations.

From time to time we thus benefit from the ministry and assistance of such Paradise-origin beings as Perfectors of Wisdom, Divine Counselors, Universal Censors, Inspired Trinity Spirits, Trinitized Sons, Solitary Messengers, supernaphim, seconaphim, tertiaphim, and other gracious ministers, who sojourn with us for the purpose of helping our native personalities in the effort to bring all Nebadon into fuller harmony with the ideas of Orvonton and the ideals of Paradise.

Any of these beings may be voluntarily serving in Nebadon and hence be technically outside our jurisdiction, but when functioning by assignment, such personalities of the super- and central universes are not wholly exempt from the regulations of the local universe of their sojourn, though they continue to function as representatives of the higher universes and to work in accordance with the instructions which constitute their mission in our realm. Their general headquarters is situated in the Salvington sector of the Union of Days, and they operate in Nebadon subject to the oversupervision of this ambassador of the Paradise Trinity. When serving in unattached groups, these personalities from the higher realms are usually self-directing, but when serving on request, they often voluntarily place themselves wholly under the jurisdiction of the supervising directors of the realms of assigned function.

Most High Assistants serve in local universe, sector, galaxy, and in constellation capacities but are not directly attached to the system or planetary governments. They may, however, function anywhere in the local universe and may be assigned to any phase of Nebadon activity — administrative, executive, educational, and others.

Most of this corps is enlisted in assisting the Nebadon Paradise personalities — the Union of Days, the Creator Son, Perfections of Days, Recents of Days, Faithfuls of Days, the Magisterial Sons, and the Trinity Teacher Sons. Now and then in the transaction of the affairs of a local creation it becomes wise to withhold certain details, temporarily, from the knowledge of practically all of the native personalities of that local universe. Certain advanced plans and complex rulings are also better grasped and more fully understood by the more mature and farseeing corps of Most High Assistants, and it is in such situations, and many others, that they are so highly serviceable to the universe rulers and administrators.

5. HIGH COMMISSIONERS

The High Commissioners are Spirit-fused ascendant mortals; they are not Adjuster fused. You quite well understand about the universe-ascension career of a mortal candidate for Adjuster fusion, that being the high destiny in prospect for all Urantia mortals since the bestowal of Christ Michael. But this is not the exclusive destiny of all mortals in the pre-bestowal ages of worlds like yours, and there is another type of world whose inhabitants are never permanently indwelt by Thought Adjusters. Such mortals are never permanently joined in union with a Mystery Monitor of Paradise bestowal; nevertheless, the Adjusters do transiently indwell them, serving as guides and patterns for the duration of the life in the flesh. During this temporary sojourn they foster the evolution of an immortal soul just as in those beings with whom they hope to fuse, but when the mortal race is run, they take eternal leave of the creatures of temporary association.

Surviving souls of this order attain immortality by eternal fusion with an individualized fragment of the spirit of the local universe Mother Spirit. They are not a numerous group, at least not in Nebadon. On the mansion worlds you will meet and fraternize with these Spirit-fused mortals as they ascend the Paradise path with you as far as Salvington, where they stop. Some of them may subsequently ascend to higher universe levels, but the majority will forever remain in the service of the local universe; as a class they are not destined to attain Paradise.

Not being Adjuster fused, they never become finaliters, but they do eventually become enrolled in the local universe Corps of Perfection. They have in spirit obeyed the Father's command, "Be you perfect."

After attaining the Nebadon Corps of Perfection, Spirit-fused ascenders may accept assignment as Universe Aids, this being one of the avenues of continuing experiential growth which is open to them. Thus do they become candidates for commissions to the high service of interpreting the viewpoints of the evolving creatures of the material worlds to the celestial authorities of the local universe.

The High Commissioners begin their service on the planets as race commissioners. In this capacity they interpret the viewpoints and portray the needs of the various planetary races. They are supremely devoted to the welfare of the mortal races whose spokesmen they are, ever seeking to obtain for them mercy, justice, and fair treatment in all relationships with other peoples. Race commissioners function in an endless series of planetary crises and serve as the articulate expression of whole groups of struggling mortals.

After long experience in problem solving on the inhabited worlds, these race commissioners are advanced to the higher levels of function, eventually attaining the status of High Commissioners of and in the local universe. These beings are not finaliters, but they are ascendant beings of long experience and of great service to their native realm.

We invariably find these commissioners in all the tribunals of justice, from the lowest to the highest. Not that they participate in the proceedings of justice, but they do act as friends of the court, advising the presiding magistrates respecting the antecedents, environment, and inherent nature of those concerned in the adjudication.

High Commissioners are attached to the various messenger hosts of space and always to the ministering spirits of time. They are encountered on the programs of various universe assemblies, and these same mortal-wise commissioners are always attached to the missions of the Sons of God to the worlds of space.

Whenever fairness and justice require an understanding of how a contemplated policy or procedure would affect the evolutionary races of time, these commissioners are at hand to present their recommendations; they are always present to speak for those who cannot be present to speak for themselves.

The Worlds of the Spirit-fused Mortals. The eighth group of seven primary worlds and tributary satellites in the Salvington circuit are the exclusive possession of the Spirit-fused mortals of Nebadon. Ascending Adjuster-fused mortals are not concerned with these worlds except to enjoy many pleasant and profitable sojourns as the invited guests of the Spirit-fused residents.

Except for those few who attain Uversa and Paradise, these worlds are the permanent residence of the Spirit-fused survivors. Such designed limitation of mortal ascent reacts to the good of the local universes by insuring the retention of a permanent evolved population whose augmenting experience will continue to enhance the future stabilization and diversification of the local universe administration. These beings may not attain Paradise, but they achieve an experiential wisdom in the mastery of Nebadon problems that utterly surpasses anything attained by the transient ascenders. And these surviving souls continue as unique combinations of the human and the divine, being increasingly able to unite the viewpoints of these two widely separate levels and to present such a dual viewpoint with ever-heightening wisdom.

6. CELESTIAL OVERSEERS

The Nebadon educational system is jointly administered by the Trinity Teacher Sons and the Melchizedek teaching corps, but much of the work designed to effect its maintenance and upbuilding is carried on by the Celestial Overseers. These beings are a recruited corps embracing all types of individuals connected with the scheme of educating and training the ascending mortals. They are all volunteers who have qualified by experience to serve as educational advisers to the entire realm. From their headquarters on the Salvington worlds of the Melchizedeks, these overseers range the local universe as inspectors of the Nebadon school technique designed to effect the mind training and the spirit education of the ascending creatures.

This training of mind and education of spirit is carried on from the worlds of human origin up through the system mansion worlds and the other spheres of progress associated with Jerusem, on the seventy socializing realms attached to Edentia, and on the four hundred and ninety spheres of spirit progress encircling Salvington. On the universe headquarters itself are numerous Melchizedek schools, the colleges of the Universe Sons, the seraphic universities, and the schools of the Teacher Sons and the Union of Days. Every possible provision is made to qualify the various personalities of the universe for advancing service and improving function. The entire universe is one vast school.

The methods employed in many of the higher schools are beyond the human concept of the art of teaching truth, but this is the keynote of the whole educational system: character acquired by enlightened experience. The teachers provide the enlightenment; the universe station and the ascender's status afford the opportunity for experience; the wise utilization of these two augments character.

Fundamentally, the Nebadon educational system provides for your assignment to a task and then affords you opportunity to receive instruction as to the ideal and divine method of best performing that task. You are given a definite task to perform, and at the same time you are provided with teachers who are qualified to instruct you in the best method of executing your assignment. The divine plan of education provides for the intimate association of work and instruction. We teach you how best to execute the things we command you to do.

The purpose of all this training and experience is to prepare you for admission to the higher and more spiritual training spheres of the super-universe. Progress within a given realm is individual, but transition from one phase to another is usually by classes.

The progression of eternity does not consist solely in spiritual development. Intellectual acquisition is also a part of universal education. The experience of the mind is broadened equally with the expansion of the spiritual horizon. Mind and spirit are afforded like opportunities for training and advancement. But in all this superb training of mind and spirit you are forever free from the handicaps of mortal flesh. No longer must you constantly referee the conflicting contentions of your divergent spiritual and material natures. At last you are qualified to enjoy the unified urge of a glorified mind long since divested of primitive animalistic trends towards things material.

Before leaving the universe of Nebadon, most Urantia mortals will be afforded opportunity to serve for a longer or shorter time as members of the Nebadon corps of Celestial Overseers.

7. MANSION WORLD TEACHERS

The Mansion World Teachers are recruited and glorified cherubim. Like most other instructors in Nebadon they are commissioned by the Melchizedeks. They function in most of the educational enterprises of the morontia life, and their number is quite beyond the comprehension of mortal mind.

As an attainment level of cherubim and sanobim, the Mansion World Teachers will receive further consideration in the next paper, while as teachers playing an important part in the morontia life, they will be more extensively discussed in the paper of that name.

8. HIGHER SPIRIT ORDERS OF ASSIGNMENT

Besides the power centers and the physical controllers, certain of the higher-origin spirit beings of the family of the Infinite Spirit are of permanent assignment to the local universe. Of the higher spirit orders of the family of the Infinite Spirit the following are so assigned:

The Solitary Messengers, when functionally attached to the local universe administration, render invaluable service to us in our efforts to overcome the handicaps of time and space. When they are not thus assigned, we of the local universes have absolutely no authority over them, but even then these unique beings are always willing to help us with the solution of our problems and with the execution of our mandates.

Andovontia is the name of the secondary *Universe Circuit Supervisor* stationed in our local universe. He is concerned only with spirit and morontia circuits, not with those under the jurisdiction of the power directors. It was he who isolated Urantia at the time of the Caligastia betrayal of the planet during the testing seasons of the Lucifer rebellion. In sending greetings to the mortals of Urantia, he expresses pleasure in the anticipation of your sometime restoration to the universe circuits of his supervision.

The Nebadon *Census Director*, Salsatia, maintains headquarters within the Gabriel sector of Salvington. He is automatically cognizant of the birth and death of will and currently registers the exact number of will creatures functioning in the local universe. He works in close association with the personality recorders domiciled on the record worlds of the archangels.

An *Associate Inspector* is resident on Salvington. He is the personal representative of the Supreme Executive of Orvonton. His associates, the *Assigned Sentinels* in the local systems, are also representatives of the Supreme Executive of Orvonton.

The *Universal Conciliators* are the traveling courts of the universes of time and space, functioning from the evolutionary worlds up through every section of the local universe and on beyond. These referees are registered on Uversa; the exact number operating in Nebadon is not of record.

Of the *Technical Advisers*, the legal minds of the realm, we have our quota. These beings are the living and circulating experiential law libraries of all space.

Of the *Celestial Recorders*, the ascendant seraphim, we have in Nebadon large numbers of senior or supervising recorders. In addition, we have enormous numbers of advanced students of this order in training.

The ministry of the *Morontia Companions* in Nebadon is described in those narratives dealing with the transition planets of the pilgrims of time.

Each universe has its own native angelic corps; nevertheless, there are occasions on which it is very helpful to have the assistance of those higher spirits of origin outside the local creation. Supernaphim perform certain rare and unique services; the present chief of Urantia seraphim is a primary supernaphim of Paradise. The reflective seconaphim are encountered wherever the super-universe personnel is functioning, and a great many tertiaphim are of temporary service as Most High Assistants.

9. PERMANENT CITIZENS OF THE LOCAL UNIVERSE

As with the super- and central universes, the local universe has its orders of permanent citizenship. These include the following created types:

1. Susatia.
2. Univitatia.
3. Material Sons.
4. Midway Creatures.

These natives of the local creation, together with the Spirit-fused ascenders and the spironga (who are otherwise classified), constitute a relatively permanent citizenship. These orders of beings are by and large neither ascending nor descending. They are all experiential creatures, but their enlarging experience continues to be available to the universe on their level of origin. While this is not wholly true of the Adamic Sons and midway creatures, it is relatively true of these orders.

The Susatia. These marvelous beings reside and function as permanent citizens on Salvington, the headquarters of this local universe, as well as on the capitals of the major and minor sectors. They are the brilliant offspring of the Creator Son and Creative Spirit and are closely associated with the ascendant citizens of the local universe, the Spirit-fused mortals of the Nebadon Corps of Perfection.

The Univitatia. Each galactic capital and all of the constellation head-quarters clusters of architectural spheres enjoys the continuous ministry of a residential order of beings known as the univitatia. These children of the Creator Son and the Creative Spirit constitute the permanent population of the galaxy and constellation headquarters worlds. They are non-reproducing beings existing on a plane of life about halfway between the semi-material status of the Material Sons domiciled on the system headquarters and the more definitely spiritual plane of the Spirit-fused mortals and the susatia of Salvington; but the univitatia are not morontia beings. They accomplish for ascending mortals during the traversal of the galaxy and constellation spheres what the Havona natives contribute to the pilgrim spirits passing through the central creation.

The Material Sons of God. When a creative liaison between the Creator Son and the universe representative of the Infinite Spirit, the Universe Mother Spirit, has completed its cycle, when no more offspring of the combined nature are forthcoming, then does the Creator Son personalize in dual form his last concept of being, thus finally confirming his own and original dual origin. In and of himself he then creates the beautiful and superb Sons and Daughters of the material order of universe sonship. This is the origin of the original Adam and Eve of each local system of Nebadon. They are a reproducing order of sonship, being created male and female. Their progeny function as the relatively permanent citizens of a system capi-tal, though some are commissioned as Planetary Adams.

On a planetary mission the Material Son and Daughter are commissioned to found the Adamic race of that world, a race designed eventually to amalgamate with the mortal inhabitants of that sphere. Planetary Adams are both descending and ascending Sons, but we ordinarily class them as ascending.

The Midway Creatures. In the early days of most inhabited worlds, certain superhuman but materialized beings are of assignment, but they usually retire upon the arrival of the Planetary Adams. The transactions of such beings and the efforts of the Material Sons to improve the evolutionary races often result in the appearance of a limited number of creatures who are difficult to classify. These unique beings are often midway between the Material Sons and the evolutionary creatures; hence their designation, midway creatures. In a comparative sense these midwayers are the permanent citizens of the evolutionary worlds. From the early days of the arrival of a Planetary Prince to the far-distant time of the settling of the planet in light and life, they are the only group of intelligent beings to remain continuously on the sphere. On Urantia the midway ministers are in reality the actual custodians of the planet; they are, practically speaking, the citizens of Urantia. Mortals are indeed the physical and material inhabitants of an evolutionary world, but you are all so short-lived; you tarry on your nativity planet such a short time. You are born, live, die, and pass on to other worlds of evolutionary progression. Even the superhuman beings who serve on the planets as celestial ministers are of transient assignment; few of them are long attached to a given sphere. The midway creatures, however, provide continuity of planetary administration in the face of ever-changing celestial ministries and constantly shifting mortal inhabitants. Throughout all of this never-ceasing changing and shifting, the midway creatures remain on the planet uninterruptedly carrying on their work.

In like manner, all divisions of the administrative organization of the local universes and super-universes have their more or less permanent populations, inhabitants of citizenship status. As Urantia has its midwayers, Jerusem, your system capital, has the Material Sons and Daughters; Edentia, your constellation headquarters, and Zion, your galactic capital both have the univitatia; while the citizens of Salvington, and the major and minor sectors, are twofold with the created susatia and the evolved Spirit-fused mortals. The Uversa headquarters spheres are continuously fostered by an amazing group of beings known as the *abandonters*, the creation of the unrevealed agents of the Ancients of Days and the seven Reflective Spirits resident on the capital of Orvonton. These residential citizens on Uversa are at present administering the routine affairs of their world under the immediate supervision of the Uversa corps of the Son-fused mortals. Even Havona has its native beings, and the central Isle of Light and Life is the home of the various groups of Paradise Citizens.

10. OTHER LOCAL UNIVERSE GROUPS

Besides the seraphic and mortal orders, who will be considered in later papers, there are numerous additional beings concerned in the maintenance and perfecting of such a gigantic organization as the universe of Nebadon. The various Nebadon types of life are much too numerous to be catalogued in this paper, but there are two unusual orders that function extensively on the architectural spheres of the local universe, that may be mentioned.

The *Spironga* are the spirit offspring of the Bright and Morning Star and the Father Melchizedek. They are exempt from personality termination but are not evolutionary or ascending beings. Neither are they functionally concerned with the evolutionary ascension regime. They are the spirit helpers of the local universe, executing the routine spirit tasks of Nebadon.

The *Spornagia*. The architectural headquarters worlds of the local universe are real worlds — physical creations. There is much work connected with their physical upkeep, and herein we have the assistance of a group of physical creatures called spornagia. They are devoted to the care and culture of the material phases of these headquarters worlds, from Jerusem to Salvington. Spornagia are neither spirits nor persons; they are an animal order of existence, but if you could see them, you would agree that they seem to be perfect animals.

The various *courtesy colonies* are domiciled on Salvington and elsewhere. We especially profit from the ministry of the celestial artisans on the constellations and benefit from the activities of the reversion directors, who operate chiefly on the capitals of the local systems.

Always there is attached to the universe service a corps of ascending mortals, including the glorified midway creatures. These ascenders, after attaining Salvington, are used in an almost endless variety of activities in the conduct of universe affairs. From each level of achievement these advancing mortals reach back and down to extend a helping hand to their fellows who follow them in the upward climb. Such mortals of temporary sojourn on Salvington are assigned on requisition to practically all corps of celestial personalities as helpers, students, observers, and teachers.

There are still other types of intelligent life concerned with the administration of a local universe, but the plan of this narrative does not provide for the further revelation of these orders of creation. Enough of the life and administration of this universe is being herewith portrayed to afford the mortal mind a grasp of the reality and grandeur of the survival existence. Further experience in your advancing careers will increasingly reveal these interesting and charming beings. This narrative cannot be more than a brief outline of the nature and work of the manifold personalities who throng the universes of space administering these creations as enormous training schools, schools wherein the pilgrims of time advance from life to life and from world to world until they are lovingly dispatched from the borders of the universe of their origin to the higher educational regime of the superuniverse and thence on to the spirit-training worlds of Havona and eventually to Paradise and the high destiny of the finaliters — the eternal assignment on missions not yet revealed to the universes of time and space.

[Dictated by a Brilliant Evening Star of Nebadon, Number 1,146 of the Created Corps.]

PAPER 38
MINISTERING SPIRITS OF THE LOCAL UNIVERSE

THERE ARE three distinct orders of the personalities of the Infinite Spirit. The impetuous apostle understood this when he wrote respecting Jesus, "who has gone to heaven and is on the right hand of God, angels and authorities and powers being made subject to him." Angels are the ministering spirits of time; authorities, the messenger hosts of space; powers, the higher personalities of the Infinite Spirit.

As the supernaphim in the central universe and the seconaphim in a super-universe, so the seraphim, with the associated cherubim and sanobim, constitute the angelic corps of a local universe.

The seraphim are all fairly uniform in design. From universe to universe, throughout all seven of the super-universes, they show a minimum of variation; they are the most nearly standard of all spirit types of personal beings. Their various orders constitute the corps of the skilled and common ministers of the local creations.

1. ORIGIN OF SERAPHIM

Seraphim are created by the Universe Mother Spirit and have been projected in unit formation — 41,472 at a time — ever since the creation of the "pattern angels" and certain angelic archetypes in the early times of Nebadon. The Creator Son and the universe representation of the Infinite Spirit collaborate in the creation of a large number of Sons and other universe personalities. Following the completion of this united effort, the Son engages in the creation of the Material Sons, the first of the sex creatures, while the Universe Mother Spirit concurrently engages in her initial solitary effort at spirit reproduction. Thus begins the creation of the seraphic hosts of a local universe.

These angelic orders are projected at the time of planning for the evolution of mortal will creatures. The creation of seraphim dates from the attainment of relative personality by the Universe Mother Spirit, not as the later co-ordinate of the Master Son, but as the early creative helper of the Creator Son. Previous to this event the seraphim on duty in Nebadon were temporarily loaned by a neighboring universe.

Seraphim are still being periodically created; the universe of Nebadon is still in the making. The Universe Mother Spirit never ceases creative activity in a growing and perfecting universe.

2. ANGELIC NATURES

Angels do not have material bodies, but they are definite and discrete beings; they are of spirit nature and origin. Though invisible to mortals, they perceive you as you are in the flesh without the aid of transformers or translators; they intellectually understand the mode of mortal life, and they share all of man's non-sensuous emotions and sentiments. They appreciate and greatly enjoy your efforts in music, art, and real humor. They are fully cognizant of your moral struggles and spiritual difficulties. They love human beings, and only good can result from your efforts to understand and love them.

Though seraphim are very affectionate and sympathetic beings, they are not sex-emotion creatures. They are much as you will be on the mansion worlds, where you will "neither marry nor be given in marriage but will be as the angels of heaven." For all who "shall be accounted worthy to attain the mansion worlds neither marry nor are given in marriage; neither do they die any more, for they are equal to the angels." Nevertheless, in dealing with sex creatures it is our custom to speak of those beings of more direct descent from the Father and the Son as the sons of God, while referring to the children of the Spirit as the daughters of God. Angels are, therefore, commonly designated by feminine pronouns on the sex planets.

The seraphim are so created as to function on both spiritual and literal levels. There are few phases of morontia or spirit activity which are not open to their ministrations. While in personal status angels are not so far removed from human beings, in certain functional performances seraphim far transcend them. They possess many powers far beyond human comprehension. For example: You have been told that the "very hairs of your head are numbered," and it is true they are, but a seraphim does not spend her time counting them and keeping the number corrected up to date. Angels possess inherent and automatic (that is, automatic as far as you could perceive) powers of knowing such things; you would truly regard a seraphim as a mathematical prodigy. Therefore, numerous duties which would be tremendous tasks for mortals are performed with exceeding ease by seraphim.

Angels are superior to you in spiritual status, but they are not your judges or accusers. No matter what your faults, "the angels, although greater in power and might, bring no accusation against you." Angels do not sit in judgment on mankind, neither should individual mortals prejudge their fellow creatures.

You do well to love them, but you should not adore them; angels are not objects of worship. The great seraphim, Loyalatia, when your seer "fell down to worship before the feet of the angel," said: "See that you do it not; I am a fellow servant with you and with your races, who are all enjoined to worship God."

In nature and personality endowment the seraphim are just a trifle ahead of mortal races in the scale of creature existence. Indeed, when you are delivered from the flesh, you become very much like them. On the mansion worlds you will begin to appreciate the seraphim, on the constellation spheres to enjoy them, while on Salvington they will share their places of rest and worship with you. Throughout the whole morontia and subsequent spirit ascent, your fraternity with the seraphim will be ideal; your companionship will be superb.

3. UNREVEALED ANGELS

Numerous orders of spirit beings function throughout the domains of the local universe that are unrevealed to mortals because they are in no manner connected with the evolutionary plan of Paradise ascension. In this paper the word "angel" is purposely limited to the designation of those seraphic and associated offspring of the Universe Mother Spirit who are so largely concerned with the operation of the plans of mortal survival. There serve in the local universe six other orders of related beings, the unrevealed angels, who are not in any specific manner connected with those universe activities pertaining to the Paradise ascent of evolutionary mortals. These six groups of angelic associates are never called seraphim, neither are they referred to as ministering spirits. These personalities are wholly occupied with the administrative and other affairs of Nebadon, engagements which are in no way related to man's progressive career of spiritual ascent and perfection attainment.

4. THE SERAPHIC WORLDS

The ninth group of seven primary spheres in the Salvington circuit are the worlds of the seraphim. Each of these worlds has six tributary satellites, whereon are the special schools devoted to all phases of seraphic training. While the seraphim have access to all forty-nine worlds comprising this group of Salvington spheres, they exclusively occupy only the first cluster of seven. The remaining six clusters are occupied by the six orders of angelic associates unrevealed on Urantia; each such group maintains headquarters on one of these six primary worlds and carries on specialized activities on the six tributary satellites. Each angelic order has free access to all the worlds of these seven diverse groups.

These headquarters worlds are among the magnificent realms of Nebadon; the seraphic estates are characterized by both beauty and vastness. Here each seraphim has a real home, and "home" means the domicile of two seraphim; they live in pairs.

Though not male and female as are the Material Sons and the mortal races, seraphim are negative and positive. In the majority of assignments it requires two angels to accomplish the task. When they are not encircuited, they can work alone; neither do they require complements of being when stationary. Ordinarily they retain their original complements of being, but not necessarily. Such associations are primarily necessitated by function; they are not characterized by sex emotion, though they are exceedingly personal and truly affectionate.

Besides designated homes, seraphim also have group, company, battalion, and unit headquarters. They forgather for reunions every millennium and are all present in accordance with the time of their creation. If a seraphim bears responsibilities which forbid absence from duty, she alternates attendance with her complement, being relieved by a seraphim of another birth date. Each seraphic partner is thereby present at least every other reunion.

5. SERAPHIC TRAINING

Seraphim spend their first millennium as noncommissioned observers on Salvington and its associated world schools. The second millennium is spent on the seraphic worlds of the Salvington circuit. Their central training school is now presided over by the first one hundred thousand Nebadon seraphim, and at their head is the original or first-born angel of this local universe. The first created group of Nebadon seraphim were trained by a corps of one thousand seraphim from Avalon; subsequently our angels have been taught by their own seniors. The Melchizedeks also have a large part in the education and training of all local universe angels — seraphim, cherubim, and sanobim.

At the termination of this period of training on the seraphic worlds of Salvington, seraphim are mobilized in the conventional groups and units of the angelic organization and are assigned to some one of the constellations. They are not yet commissioned as ministering spirits, although they have well entered upon the pre-commissioned phases of angelic training.

Seraphim are initiated as ministering spirits by serving as observers on the lowest of the evolutionary worlds. After this experience they return to the associate worlds of the headquarters of the assigned constellation to begin their advanced studies and more definitely to prepare for service in some particular local system. Following this general education they are advanced to the service of some one of the local systems. On the architectural worlds associated with the capital of some Nebadon system our seraphim complete their training and are commissioned as ministering spirits of time.

When once seraphim are commissioned, they may range all Nebadon, even Orvonton, on assignment. Their work in the universe is without bounds and limitations; they are closely associated with the material creatures of the worlds and are ever in the service of the lower orders of spiritual personalities, making contact between these beings of the spirit world and the mortals of the material realms.

6. SERAPHIC ORGANIZATION

After the second millennium of sojourn at seraphic headquarters the seraphim are organized under chiefs into groups of twelve (12 pairs, 24 seraphim), and twelve such groups constitute a company (144 pairs, 288 seraphim), which is commanded by a leader. Twelve companies under a commander constitute a battalion (1,728 pairs or 3,456 seraphim), and twelve battalions under a director equal a seraphic unit (20,736 pairs or 41,472 individuals), while twelve units, subject to the command of a supervisor, constitute a legion numbering 248,832 pairs or 497,664 individuals.

Jesus alluded to such a group of angels that night in the garden of Gethsemane when he said: "I can even now ask my Father, and he will presently give me more than twelve legions of angels."

Twelve legions of angels comprise a host numbering 2,985,984 pairs or 5,971,968 individuals, and twelve such hosts (35,831,808 pairs or 71,663,616 individuals) make up the largest operating organization of seraphim, an angelic army. A seraphic host is commanded by an archangel or by some other personality of co-ordinate status, while the angelic armies are directed by the Brilliant Evening Stars or by other immediate lieutenants of Gabriel. And Gabriel is the "supreme commander of the armies of heaven," the chief executive of the Sovereign of Nebadon, "the Lord God of hosts."

Though serving under the direct supervision of the Infinite Spirit as personalized on Salvington, since the bestowal of Michael on Urantia, seraphim and all other local universe orders have become subject to the sovereignty of the Master Son. Even when Michael was born of the flesh on Urantia, there issued the super-universe broadcast to all Nebadon which proclaimed, "And let all the angels worship him." All ranks of angels are subject to his sovereignty; they are a part of that group which has been denominated "his mighty angels."

7. CHERUBIM AND SANOBIM

In all essential endowments cherubim and sanobim are similar to seraphim. They have the same origin but not always the same destiny. They are wonderfully intelligent, marvelously efficient, touchingly affectionate, and almost human. They are the lowest order of angels, hence all the nearer of kin to the more progressive types of human beings on the evolutionary worlds.

Cherubim and sanobim are inherently associated, functionally united. One is an energy positive personality; the other, energy negative. The right-hand deflector, or positively charged angel, is the cherubim — the senior or controlling personality. The left-hand deflector, or negatively charged angel, is the sanobim — the complement of being. Each type of angel is very limited in solitary function; hence they usually serve in pairs. When serving independently of their seraphic directors, they are more than ever dependent on mutual contact and always function together.

Cherubim and sanobim are the faithful and efficient aids of the seraphic ministers, and all seven orders of seraphim are provided with these subordinate assistants. Cherubim and sanobim serve for ages in these capacities, but they do not accompany seraphim on assignments beyond the confines of the local universe.

The cherubim and sanobim are the routine spirit workers on the individual worlds of the systems. On a non-personal assignment and in an emergency, they may serve in the place of a seraphic pair, but they never function, even temporarily, as attending angels to human beings; that is an exclusive seraphic privilege.

When assigned to a planet, cherubim enter the local courses of training, including a study of planetary usages and languages. The ministering spirits of time are all bilingual, speaking the language of the local universe of their origin and that of their native super-universe. By study in the schools of the realms they acquire additional tongues. Cherubim and sanobim, like seraphim and all other orders of spirit beings, are continuously engaged in efforts at self-improvement. Only such as the subordinate beings of power control and energy direction are incapable of progression; all creatures having actual or potential personality volition seek new achievements.

Cherubim and sanobim are by nature very near the morontia level of existence, and they prove to be most efficient in the borderland work of the physical, morontial, and spiritual domains. These children of the local universe Mother Spirit are characterized by "fourth creatures" much as are the Havona Servitals and the conciliating commissions. Every fourth cherubim and every fourth sanobim are quasi-material, very definitely resembling the morontia level of existence.

These angelic fourth creatures are of great assistance to the seraphim in the more literal phases of their universe and planetary activities. Such morontia cherubim also perform many indispensable borderline tasks on the morontia training worlds and are assigned to the service of the Morontia Companions in large numbers. They are to the morontia spheres about what the midway creatures are to the evolutionary planets. On the inhabited worlds these morontia cherubim frequently work in liaison with the midway creatures. Cherubim and midway creatures are distinctly separate orders of beings; they have dissimilar origins, but they disclose great similarity in nature and function.

8. EVOLUTION OF CHERUBIM AND SANOBIM

Numerous avenues of advancing service are open to cherubim and sanobim leading to an enhancement of status, which may be still further augmented by the embrace of the Divine Minister. There are three great classes of cherubim and sanobim with regard to evolutionary potential:

1. *Ascension Candidates*. These beings are by nature candidates for seraphic status. Cherubim and sanobim of this order are brilliant, though not by inherent endowment equal to the seraphim; but by application and experience it is possible for them to attain full seraphic standing.

2. *Mid-phase Cherubim*. All cherubim and sanobim are not equal in ascension potential, and these are the inherently limited beings of the angelic creations. Most of them will remain cherubim and sanobim, although the more gifted individuals may achieve limited seraphic service.

3. *Morontia Cherubim*. These "fourth creatures" of the angelic orders always retain their quasi-material characteristics. They will continue on as cherubim and sanobim, together with a majority of their mid-phase brethren, pending the completed factualization of the Supreme Being.

While the second and third groups are somewhat limited in growth potential, the ascension candidates may attain the heights of universal seraphic service. Many of the more experienced of these cherubim are attached to the seraphic guardians of destiny and are thus placed in direct line for advancement to the status of Mansion World Teachers when deserted by their seraphic seniors. Guardians of destiny do not have cherubim and sanobim as helpers when their mortal wards attain the morontia life. And when other types of evolutionary seraphim are granted clearance for Seraphington and Paradise, they must forsake their former subordinates when they pass out of the confines of Nebadon. Such deserted cherubim and sanobim are usually embraced by the Universe Mother Spirit, thus achieving a level equivalent to that of a Mansion World Teacher in the attainment of seraphic status.

When, as Mansion World Teachers, the once-embraced cherubim and sanobim have long served on the morontia spheres, from the lowest to the highest, and when their corps on Salvington is over-recruited, the Bright and Morning Star summons these faithful servants of the creatures of time to appear in his presence. The oath of personality transformation is administered; and thereupon, in groups of seven thousand, these advanced and senior cherubim and sanobim are re-embraced by the Universe Mother Spirit. From this second embrace they emerge as full-fledged seraphim. Henceforth, the full and complete career of a seraphim, with all of its Paradise possibilities, is open to such reborn cherubim and sanobim. Such angels may be assigned as guardians of destiny to some mortal being, and if the mortal ward attains survival, then do they become eligible for advancement to Seraphington and the seven circles of seraphic attainment, even to Paradise and the Corps of the Finality.

9. THE MIDWAY CREATURES

The midway creatures have a threefold classification: They are properly classified with the ascending Sons of God; they are factually grouped with the orders of permanent citizenship, while they are functionally reckoned with the ministering spirits of time because of their intimate and effective association with the angelic hosts in the work of serving mortal man on the individual worlds of space.

These unique creatures appear on the majority of the inhabited worlds and are always found on the decimal or life-experiment planets, such as Urantia. Midwayers are of two types — primary and secondary — and they appear by the following techniques:

1. *Primary Midwayers*, the more spiritual group, are a somewhat stan-

dardized order of beings who are uniformly derived from the modified ascendant-mortal staffs of the Planetary Princes. The number of primary midway creatures is always fifty thousand, and no planet enjoying their ministry has a larger group.

2. *Secondary Midwayers*, the more material group of these creatures, vary greatly in numbers on the different worlds, though the average is around fifty thousand. They are variously derived from the planetary biologic uplifters, the Adams and Eves, or from their immediate progeny. There are no less than twenty-four diverse techniques involved in the production of these secondary midway creatures on the evolutionary worlds of space. The mode of origin for this group on Urantia was unusual and extraordinary.

Neither of these groups is an evolutionary accident; both are essential features in the predetermined plans of the universe architects, and their appearance on the evolving worlds at the opportune juncture is in accordance with the original designs and developmental plans of the supervising Life Carriers.

Primary midwayers are energized intellectually and spiritually by the angelic technique and are uniform in intellectual status. The seven adjutant mind-spirits make no contact with them; and only the sixth and the seventh, the spirit of worship and the spirit of wisdom, are able to minister to the secondary group.

Secondary midwayers are physically energized by the Adamic technique, spiritually encircuited by the seraphic, and intellectually endowed with the morontia transition type of mind. They are divided into four physical types, seven orders spiritually, and twelve levels of intellectual response to the joint ministry of the last two adjutant spirits and the morontia mind. These diversities determine their differential of activity and of planetary assignment.

Primary midwayers resemble angels more than mortals; the secondary orders are much more like human beings. Each renders invaluable assistance to the other in the execution of their manifold planetary assignments. The primary ministers can achieve liaison co-operation with both morontia- and spirit-energy controllers and mind circuiters. The secondary group can establish working connections only with the physical controllers and the material-circuit manipulators. But since each order of midwayer can establish perfect synchrony of contact with the other, either group is thereby able to achieve practical utilization of the entire energy gamut extending from the gross physical power of the material worlds up through the transition phases of universe energies to the higher spirit-reality forces of the celestial realms.

The gap between the material and spiritual worlds is perfectly bridged by the serial association of mortal man, secondary midwayer, primary midwayer, morontia cherubim, mid-phase cherubim, and seraphim. In the personal experience of an individual mortal these diverse levels are undoubtedly more or less unified and made personally meaningful by the unobserved and mysterious operations of the divine Thought Adjuster.

On normal worlds the primary midwayers maintain their service as the intelligence corps and as celestial entertainers in behalf of the Planetary Prince, while the secondary ministers continue their co-operation with the Adamic regime of furthering the cause of progressive planetary civilization. In case of the defection of the Planetary Prince and the failure of the Material Son, as occurred on Urantia, the midway creatures become the wards of the System Sovereign and serve under the directing guidance of the acting custodian of the planet. But on only three other worlds in Satania do these beings function as one group under unified leadership as do the united midway ministers of Urantia.

The planetary work of both primary and secondary midwayers is varied and diverse on the numerous individual worlds of a universe, but on the normal and average planets their activities are very different from the duties which occupy their time on isolated spheres, such as Urantia.

The primary midwayers are the planetary historians who, from the time of the arrival of the Planetary Prince to the age of settled light and life, formulate the pageants and design the portrayals of planetary history for the exhibits of the planets on the system headquarters worlds.

Midwayers remain for long periods on an inhabited world, but if faithful to their trust, they will eventually and most certainly be recognized for their agelong service in maintaining the sovereignty of the Creator Son; they will be duly rewarded for their patient ministry to the material mortals on their world of time and space. Sooner or later all accredited midway creatures will be mustered into the ranks of the ascending Sons of God and will be duly initiated into the long adventure of the Paradise ascent in company with those very mortals of animal origin, their earth brethren, whom they so jealously guarded and so effectively served during the long planetary sojourn.

[Presented by a Melchizedek acting by request of the Chief of the Seraphic Hosts of Nebadon.]

PAPER 39
THE SERAPHIC HOSTS

As far as we are cognizant, the Infinite Spirit, as personalized on the local universe headquarters, intends to produce uniformly perfect seraphim, but for some unknown reason these seraphic offspring are very diverse. This diversity may be a result of the unknown interposition of evolving experiential Deity; if so, we cannot prove it. But we do observe that, when seraphim have been subjected to educational tests and training discipline, they unfailingly and distinctly classify into the following seven groups:

1. Supreme Seraphim.
2. Superior Seraphim.
3. Supervisor Seraphim.
4. Administrator Seraphim.
5. Planetary Helpers.
6. Transition Ministers.
7. Seraphim of the Future.

To say that any one seraphim is inferior to an angel of any other group would hardly be true. Nevertheless every angel is at first service-limited to the group of original and inherent classification. My seraphic associate in the preparation of this statement, Manotia, is a supreme seraphim and onetime functioned only as a supreme seraphim. By application and devoted service she has, one by one, achieved all seven of the seraphic services, having functioned in well-nigh every avenue of activity open to a seraphim, and now holds the commission of associate chief of seraphim on Urantia.

Human beings sometimes find it hard to understand that a created capacity for higher-level ministry does not necessarily imply ability to function on relatively lower service levels. Man begins life as a helpless infant; hence every mortal attainment must embrace all experiential prerequisites; seraphim have no such pre-adult life — no childhood. They are, however, experiential creatures, and by experience and through additional education they can augment their divine and inherent endowment of ability by the experiential acquirement of functional skill in one or more of the seraphic services.

After being commissioned, seraphim are assigned to the reserves of their inherent group. Those of planetary and administrator status often serve for long periods as originally classified, but the higher the inherent function level, the more persistently do the angelic ministers seek assignment to the lower orders of universe service. Especially do they desire assignment to the reserves of the planetary helpers, and if successful they enroll in the celestial schools attached to the headquarters of the Planetary Prince of some evolutionary world. Here they begin the study of the languages, history, and local habits of the races of mankind. Seraphim must acquire knowledge and gain experience much as do human beings. They are not far removed from you in certain personality attributes. And they all crave to start at the bottom, on the lowest possible level of ministry; thus may they hope to achieve the highest possible level of experiential destiny.

1. SUPREME SERAPHIM

These seraphim are the highest of the seven revealed orders of local universe angels. They function in seven groups, each of which is closely associated with the angelic ministers of the Seraphic Corps of Completion.

1. *Son-Spirit Ministers.* The first group of the supreme seraphim are assigned to the service of the high Sons and Spirit-origin beings resident and

functioning in the local universe. This group of angelic ministers also serve the Universe Son and the Universe Spirit and are closely affiliated with the intelligence corps of the Bright and Morning Star, the universe chief executive of the united wills of the Creator Son and the Creative Spirit.

Being of assignment to the high Sons and Spirits, these seraphim are naturally associated with the far-flung services of the Paradise Avonals, the divine offspring of the Eternal Son and the Infinite Spirit. The Paradise Avonals are always attended on all magisterial and bestowal missions by this high and experienced order of seraphim, who are at such times devoted to organizing and administering the special work connected with the termination of one planetary dispensation and the inauguration of a new age. But they are not concerned in the work of adjudication which might be incidental to such a change in dispensations.

Bestowal Attendants. Paradise Avonals, but not Creator Sons, when on a bestowal mission are always accompanied by a corps of 144 bestowal attendants. These 144 angels are the chiefs of all other Son-Spirit ministers who may be associated with a bestowal mission. There might possibly be legions of angels subject to the command of an incarnated Son of God on a planetary bestowal, but all these seraphim would be organized and directed by the 144 bestowal attendants. Higher orders of angels, supernaphim and seconaphim, might also form a part of the attending host, and though their missions are distinct from those of the seraphim, all these activities would be co-ordinated by the bestowal attendants.

These bestowal attendants are completion seraphim; they have all traversed the circles of Seraphington and have attained the Seraphic Corps of Completion. And they have been further especially trained to meet the difficulties and to cope with the emergencies associated with the bestowals of the Sons of God for the advancement of the children of time. Such seraphim have all achieved Paradise and the personal embrace of the Second Source and Center, the Eternal Son.

Seraphim equally crave assignment to the missions of the incarnated Sons and attachment as destiny guardians to the mortals of the realms; the latter is the surest seraphic passport to Paradise, while the bestowal attendants have achieved the highest local universe service of the completion seraphim of Paradise attainment.

2. *Court Advisers*. These are the seraphic advisers and helpers attached to all orders of adjudication, from the conciliators up to the highest tribunals of the realm. It is not the purpose of such tribunals to determine punitive sentences but rather to adjudicate honest differences of opinion and to decree the everlasting survival of ascending mortals. Herein lies the duty of the court advisers: to see that all charges against mortal creatures are stated in justice and adjudicated in mercy. In this work they are closely associated with the High Commissioners, Spirit-fused ascendant mortals serving in the local universe.

The seraphic court advisers serve extensively as defenders of mortals. Not that there ever exists any disposition to be unfair to the lowly creatures of the realms, but while justice demands the adjudication of every default in the climb towards divine perfection, mercy requires that every such misstep be fairly adjudged in accordance with the creature nature and the divine purpose. These angels are the exponents and exemplification of the element of mercy inherent in divine justice — of fairness based on the knowledge of the underlying facts of personal motives and the struggle against lower tendencies.

This order of angels serves from the councils of the Planetary Princes to the highest tribunals of the local universe, while their associates of the Seraphic Corps of Completion function in the higher realms of Orvonton, even to the courts of the Ancients of Days on Uversa.

3. *Universe Orientators*. These are the true friends and postgraduate counselors of all those ascending creatures who are pausing for the last time on Salvington, in their universe of origin, as they stand on the brink of the spirit adventure stretching out before them in the vast super-universe of Orvonton. And at such a time many an ascender has a feeling which mortals could understand only by comparison with the human emotion of nostalgia. Behind lie the realms of achievement, realms grown familiar by long service and morontia attainment; ahead lies the challenging mystery of a greater and vaster universe.

It is the task of the universe orientators to facilitate the passage of the ascending pilgrims from the attained to the unattained level of universe service, to help these pilgrims in making those kaleidoscopic adjustments in the comprehension of meanings and values inherent in the realization that a first-stage spirit being stands, not at the end and climax of the local universe morontia ascent, but rather at the very bottom of the long ladder of spiritual ascent to the Universal Father on Paradise.

Many of the Seraphington graduates, members of the Seraphic Corps of Completion who are associated with these seraphim, engage in extensive teaching in certain Salvington schools concerned with the preparation of the creatures of Nebadon for the relationships of the next universe age.

4. *The Teaching Counselors*. These angels are the invaluable assistants of the spiritual teaching corps of the local universe. Teaching counselors are secretaries to all orders of teachers, from the Melchizedeks and the Trinity Teacher Sons down to the morontia mortals who are assigned as helpers to those of their kind who are just behind them in the scale of ascendant life. You will first *see* these associate teaching seraphim on some one of the seven mansion worlds surrounding Jerusem.

These seraphim become associates of the division chiefs of the numerous educational and training institutions of the local universes, and they are attached in large numbers to the faculties of the seven training worlds of the local systems, of the seventy educational spheres of the constellations, and the universities and training facilities of the galaxy and the minor and major sectors. These ministrations even extend on down to the individual worlds. Even the true and consecrated teachers of time are assisted, and often attended, by these counselors of the supreme seraphim.

The fourth creature bestowal of the Creator Son was in the likeness of a teaching counselor of the supreme seraphim of Nebadon.

5. *Directors of Assignment*. A body of 144 supreme seraphim is elected from time to time by the angels serving on the evolutionary and on the architectural spheres of creature habitation. This is the highest angelic council on any sphere, and it co-ordinates the self-directed phases of seraphic service and assignment. These angels preside over all seraphic assemblies pertaining to the line of duty or the call to worship.

6. *The Recorders*. These are the official recorders for the supreme seraphim. Many of these high angels were born with their gifts fully developed; others have qualified for their positions of trust and responsibility by

diligent application to study and faithful performance of similar duties while attached to lower or less responsible orders.

7. *Unattached Ministers*. Large numbers of unattached seraphim of the supreme order are self-directed servers on the architectural spheres and on the inhabited planets. Such ministers voluntarily meet the differential of demand for the service of the supreme seraphim, thus constituting the general reserve of this order.

2. SUPERIOR SERAPHIM

Superior seraphim receive their name, not because they are in any sense qualitatively superior to other orders of angels, but because they are in charge of the higher activities of a local universe. Very many of the first two groups of this seraphic corps are attainment seraphim, angels who have served in all phases of training and have returned to a glorified assignment as directors of their kind in the spheres of their earlier activities. Being a young universe, Nebadon does not have many of this order.

The superior seraphim function in the following seven groups:

1. *The Intelligence Corps*. These seraphim belong to the personal staff of Gabriel, the Bright and Morning Star. They range the local universe gathering the information of the realms for his guidance in the councils of Nebadon. They are the intelligence corps of the mighty hosts over which Gabriel presides as vicegerent of the Master Son. These seraphim are not directly affiliated with either the systems, constellations, galaxies, minor or major sectors; their information pours in direct to Salvington upon a continuous, direct, and independent circuit.

The intelligence corps of the various local universes can and do intercommunicate but only within a given super-universe. There is a differential of energy which effectively segregates the business and transactions of the various super-governments. One super-universe can ordinarily communicate with another super-universe only through the provisions and facilities of the Paradise clearinghouse.

2. *The Voice of Mercy*. Mercy is the keynote of seraphic service and angelic ministry. It is therefore fitting that there should be a corps of angels who, in a special manner, portray mercy. These seraphim are the real mercy ministers of the local universes. They are the inspired leaders who foster the higher impulses and holier emotions of men and angels. The directors of these legions are now always completion seraphim who are also graduate guardians of mortal destiny; that is, each angelic pair has guided at least one soul of animal origin during the life in the flesh and has subsequently traversed the circles of Seraphington and has been mustered into the Seraphic Corps of Completion.

3. *Spirit Co-ordinators*. The third group of superior seraphim are based on Salvington but function in the local universe anywhere they can be of fruitful service. While their tasks are essentially spiritual and therefore beyond the real understanding of human minds, you will perhaps grasp something of their ministry to mortals if it is explained that these angels are intrusted with the task of preparing the ascendant sojourners on Salvington for their last transition in the local universe — from the highest morontia level to the status of newborn spirit beings. As the mind planners on the mansion worlds help the surviving creature to adjust to, and make effective use of, the potentials of morontia mind, so do these seraphim instruct the morontia graduates on Salvington regarding the newly attained capacities of the mind of the spirit. And they serve the ascendant mortals in many other ways.

4. *Assistant Teachers*. The assistant teachers are the helpers and associates of their fellow seraphim, the teaching counselors. They are also individually connected with the extensive educational enterprises of the local universe, especially with the sevenfold scheme of training operative on the mansion worlds of the local systems. A marvelous corps of this order of seraphim functions on Urantia for the purpose of fostering and furthering the cause of truth and righteousness.

5. *The Transporters*. All groups of ministering spirits have their transport corps, angelic orders dedicated to the ministry of transporting those personalities who are unable, of themselves, to journey from one sphere to another.

The fifth group of the superior seraphim are headquartered on Salvington and serve as space traversers to and from the headquarters of the local universe. Like other subdivisions of the superior seraphim, some were created as such while others have risen from the lower or less endowed groups.

The "energy range" of seraphim is wholly adequate for local universe and even for super-universe requirements, but they could never withstand the energy demands entailed by such a long journey as that from Uversa to Havona. Such an exhaustive journey requires the special powers of a primary seconaphim of transport endowments. Transporters take on energy for flight while in transit and recuperate personal power at the end of the journey.

Even on Salvington ascending mortals do not possess personal transit forms. Ascenders must depend upon seraphic transport in advancing from world to world until after the last rest of sleep on the inner circle of Havona and the eternal awakening on Paradise. Subsequently you will not be dependent on angels for transport from universe to universe.

The process of being enseraphimed is not unlike the experience of death or sleep except that there is an automatic time element in the transit slumber. You are consciously unconscious during seraphic rest. But the Thought Adjuster is wholly and fully conscious, in fact, exceptionally efficient since you are unable to oppose, resist, or otherwise hinder creative and transforming work.

When enseraphimed, you go to sleep for a specified time, and you will awake at the designated moment. The length of a journey when in transit sleep is immaterial. You are not directly aware of the passing of time. It is as if you went to sleep on a transport vehicle in one city and, after resting in peaceful slumber all night, awakened in another and distant metropolis. You journeyed while you slumbered. And so you take flight through space, enseraphimed, while you rest — sleep. The transit sleep is induced by the liaison between the Adjusters and the seraphic transporters.

The angels cannot transport combustion bodies — flesh and blood — such as you now have, but they can transport all others, from the lowest morontia to the higher spirit forms. They do not function in the event of natural death. When you finish your earthly career, your body remains on this planet. Your Thought Adjuster proceeds to the bosom of the Father, and these angels are not directly concerned in your subsequent personality reassembly on the identification mansion world. There your new body is a morontia form, one that can enseraphim. You "sow a mortal body" in the grave; you "reap a morontia form" on the mansion worlds.

6. *The Recorders*. These personalities are especially concerned with the reception, filing, and redispatch of the records of Salvington and its associated worlds. They also serve as special recorders for resident groups of super-universe and higher personalities and as clerks of the courts of Salvington and secretaries to the rulers thereof.

Broadcasters — receivers and dispatchers — are a specialized subdivision of the seraphic recorders, being concerned with the dispatch of records and with the dissemination of essential information. Their work is of a high order, being so multi-circuited that an incredible number of messages can simultaneously traverse the same lines of energy. They adapt the higher ideographic techniques of the superaphic chief recorders and with these common symbols maintain reciprocal contact with both the intelligence co-ordinators of the tertiary supernaphim and the glorified intelligence co-ordinators of the Seraphic Corps of Completion.

Seraphic recorders of the superior order thus effect a close liaison with the intelligence corps of their own order and with all subordinate recorders, while the broadcasts enable them to maintain constant communication with the higher recorders of the super-universe and, through this channel, with the recorders of Havona and the custodians of knowledge on Paradise. Many of the superior order of recorders are seraphim ascended from similar duties in lower sections of the universe.

7. *The Reserves*. Large reserves of all types of the superior seraphim are held on Salvington, instantly available for dispatch to the farthermost worlds of Nebadon as they are requisitioned by the directors of assignment or upon the request of the universe administrators. The reserves of superior seraphim also furnish messenger aids upon requisition by the chief of the Brilliant

Evening Stars, who is intrusted with the custody and dispatch of all personal communications. A local universe is fully provided with adequate means of intercommunication, but there is always a residue of messages which requires dispatch by personal messengers.

The basic reserves for the entire local universe are held on the seraphic worlds of Salvington. This corps includes all types of all groups of angels.

3. SUPERVISOR SERAPHIM

This versatile order of universe angels is assigned to the exclusive service of the constellations. These able ministers make their headquarters on the constellation capitals but function throughout all Nebadon in the interests of their assigned realms.

1. *Supervising Assistants.* The first order of the supervising seraphim are assigned to the collective work of the Constellation Fathers, and they are the ever-efficient helpers of the Most Highs. These seraphim are primarily concerned with the unification and stabilization of a whole constellation.

2. *Law Forecasters.* The intellectual foundation of justice is law, and in a local universe law originates in the legislative assemblies of the constellations. These deliberative bodies codify and formally promulgate the basic laws of Nebadon, laws designed to afford the greatest possible co-ordination of a whole constellation consistent with the fixed policy of non-infringement of the moral free will of personal creatures. It is the duty of the second order of supervisor seraphim to place before the constellation lawmakers a forecast of how any proposed enactment would affect the lives of freewill creatures. This service they are well qualified to perform by virtue of long experience in the local systems and on the inhabited worlds. These seraphim seek no special favors for one group or another, but they do appear before the celestial lawmakers to speak for those who cannot be present to speak for themselves. Even mortal man may contribute to the evolution of universe law, for these very seraphim do faithfully and fully portray, not necessarily man's transient and conscious desires, but rather the true longings of the

inner man, the evolving morontia soul of the material mortal on the worlds of space.

3. *Social Architects*. From the individual planets up through the morontia training worlds, these seraphim labor to enhance all sincere social contacts and to further the social evolution of universe creatures. These are the angels who seek to divest the associations of intelligent beings of all artificiality while endeavoring to facilitate the inter-association of will creatures on a basis of real self-understanding and genuine mutual appreciation.

Social architects do everything within their province and power to bring together suitable individuals that they may constitute efficient and agreeable working groups on earth; and sometimes such groups have found themselves reassociated on the mansion worlds for continued fruitful service. But not always do these seraphim attain their ends; not always are they able to bring together those who would form the most ideal group to achieve a given purpose or to accomplish a certain task; under these conditions they must utilize the best of the material available.

These angels continue their ministry on the mansion and higher morontia worlds. They are concerned with any undertaking having to do with progress on the morontia worlds and which concerns three or more persons. Two beings are regarded as operating on the mating, complemental, or partnership basis, but when three or more are grouped for service, they constitute a social problem and therefore fall within the jurisdiction of the social architects. These efficient seraphim are organized in seventy divisions on Edentia, and these divisions minister on the seventy morontia progress worlds encircling the headquarters sphere.

4. *Ethical Sensitizers*. It is the mission of these seraphim to foster and to promote the growth of creature appreciation of the morality of interpersonal relationships, for such is the seed and secret of the continued and purposeful growth of society and government, human or superhuman. These enhancers of ethical appreciation function anywhere and everywhere they may be of service, as volunteer counselors to the planetary rulers and as exchange teachers on the system training worlds. You will not, however, come under their full guidance until you reach the brotherhood schools on Edentia, where they will quicken your appreciation of those very truths of fraternity

which you will even then be so earnestly exploring by the actual experience of living with the univitatia in the social laboratories of Edentia, the seventy satellites of the Norlatiadek capital.

5. *The Transporters*. The fifth group of supervisor seraphim operate as personality transporters, carrying beings to and from the headquarters of the constellations. Such transport seraphim, while in flight from one sphere to another, are fully conscious of their velocity, direction, and astronomic whereabouts. They are not traversing space as would an inanimate projectile. They may pass near one another during space flight without the least danger of collision. They are fully able to vary speed of progression and to alter direction of flight, even to change destinations if their directors should so instruct them at any space junction of the universe intelligence circuits.

These transit personalities are so organized that they can simultaneously utilize all three of the universally distributed lines of energy, each having a clear space velocity of 186,280 miles per second. These transporters are thus able to superimpose velocity of energy upon velocity of power until they attain an average speed on their long journeys varying anywhere from 555,000 to almost 559,000 of your miles per second of your time. The velocity is affected by the mass and proximity of neighboring matter and by the strength and direction of the near-by main circuits of universe power. There are numerous types of beings, similar to the seraphim, who are able to traverse space, and who also are able to transport other beings who have been properly prepared.

6. *The Recorders*. The sixth order of supervising seraphim act as the special recorders of constellation affairs. A large and efficient corps functions on Edentia, the headquarters of the constellation of Norlatiadek, to which your system and planet belong.

7. *The Reserves*. General reserves of the supervisor seraphim are held on the headquarters of the constellations. Such angelic reservists are in no sense inactive; many serve as messenger aids to the constellation rulers; others are attached to the Salvington reserves of unassigned Vorondadeks; still others may be attached to Vorondadek Sons on special assignment, such as the Vorondadek observer, and sometimes Most High regent, of Urantia.

4. ADMINISTRATOR SERAPHIM

The fourth order of seraphim are assigned to the administrative duties of the local systems. They are indigenous to the system capitals but are stationed in large numbers on the mansion and morontia spheres and on the inhabited worlds. Fourth-order seraphim are by nature endowed with unusual administrative ability. They are the able assistants of the directors of the lower divisions of the universe government of a Creator Son and are mainly occupied with the affairs of the local systems and their component worlds. They are organized for service as follows:

1. *Administrative Assistants.* These able seraphim are the immediate assistants of a System Sovereign, a primary Lanonandek Son. They are invaluable aids in the execution of the intricate details of the executive work of the system headquarters. They also serve as the personal agents of the system rulers, journeying back and forth in large numbers to the various transition worlds and to the inhabited planets, executing many commissions for the welfare of the system and in the physical and biologic interests of its inhabited worlds.

These same seraphic administrators are also attached to the governments of the world rulers, the Planetary Princes. The majority of planets in a given universe are under the jurisdiction of a secondary Lanonandek Son, but on certain worlds, such as Urantia, there has been a miscarriage of the divine plan. In the event of the defection of a Planetary Prince, these seraphim become attached to the Melchizedek receivers and their successors in planetary authority. The present acting ruler of Urantia is assisted by a corps of one thousand of this versatile order of seraphim.

2. *Justice Guides.* These are the angels who present the summary of evidence concerning the eternal welfare of men and angels when such matters come up for adjudication in the tribunals of a system or a planet. They prepare the statements for all preliminary hearings involving mortal survival, statements which are subsequently carried with the records of such cases to the higher tribunals of the universe and the super-universe. The defense of all cases of doubtful survival is prepared by these seraphim, who

have a perfect understanding of all the details of every feature of every count in the indictments drawn by the administrators of universe justice.

It is not the mission of these angels to defeat or to delay justice but rather to insure that unerring justice is dealt out with generous mercy in fairness to all creatures. These seraphim often function on the local worlds, commonly appearing before the referee trios of the conciliating commissions — the courts for minor misunderstandings. Many who at one time served as justice guides in the lower realms later appear as Voices of Mercy in the higher spheres and on Salvington.

In the Lucifer rebellion in Satania very few of the justice guides were lost, but more than one quarter of the other administrator seraphim and of the lower orders of seraphic ministers were misled and deluded by the sophistries of unbridled personal liberty.

3. *Interpreters of Cosmic Citizenship*. When ascending mortals have completed the mansion world training, the first student apprenticeship in the universe career, they are permitted to enjoy the transient satisfactions of relative maturity — citizenship on the system capital. While the attainment of each ascendant goal is a factual achievement, in the larger sense such goals are simply milestones on the long ascending path to Paradise. But however relative such successes may be, no evolutionary creature is ever denied the full though transient satisfaction of goal attainment. Ever and anon there is a pause in the Paradise ascent, a short breathing spell, during which universe horizons stand still, creature status is stationary, and the personality tastes the sweetness of goal fulfillment.

The first of such periods in the career of a mortal ascender occurs on the capital of a local system. During this pause you will, as a citizen of Jerusem, attempt to express in creature life those things which you have acquired during the eight preceding life experiences — embracing Urantia and the seven mansion worlds.

The seraphic interpreters of cosmic citizenship guide the new citizens of the system capitals and quicken their appreciation of the responsibilities of universe government. These seraphim are also closely associated with the Material Sons in the system administration, while they portray the responsibility and morality of cosmic citizenship to the material mortals on the inhabited worlds.

4. *Quickeners of Morality*. On the mansion worlds you begin to learn self-government for the benefit of all concerned. Your mind learns co-operation, learns how to plan with other and wiser beings. On the system headquarters the seraphic teachers will further quicken your appreciation of cosmic morality — of the interactions of liberty and loyalty.

What is loyalty? It is the fruit of an intelligent appreciation of universe brotherhood; one could not take so much and give nothing. As you ascend the personality scale, first you learn to be loyal, then to love, then to be filial, and then may you be free; but not until you are a finaliter, not until you have attained perfection of loyalty, can you self-realize finality of liberty.

These seraphim teach the fruitfulness of patience: That stagnation is certain death, but that over-rapid growth is equally suicidal; that as a drop of water from a higher level falls to a lower and, flowing onward, passes ever downward through a succession of short falls, so ever upward is progress in the morontia and spirit worlds — and just as slowly and by just such gradual stages.

To the inhabited worlds the quickeners of morality portray mortal life as an unbroken chain of many links. Your short sojourn on Urantia, on this sphere of mortal infancy, is only a single link, the very first in the long chain that is to stretch across universes and through the eternal ages. It is not so much what you learn in this first life; it is the experience of living this life that is important. Even the *work* of this world, paramount though it is, is not nearly so important as the *way* in which you do this work. There is no material reward for righteous living, but there is profound satisfaction — consciousness of achievement — and this transcends any conceivable material reward.

The keys of the kingdom of heaven are: sincerity, more sincerity, and more sincerity. All men have these keys. Men use them — advance in spirit status — by decisions, by more decisions, and by more decisions. The highest moral choice is the choice of the highest possible value, and always — in any sphere, in all of them — this is to choose to do the will of God. If man thus chooses, he *is* great, though he be the humblest citizen of Jerusem or even the least of mortals on Urantia.

5. *The Transporters*. These are the transport seraphim who function in the local systems. In Satania, your system, they carry passengers back and forth from Jerusem and otherwise serve as interplanetary transporters. Seldom does a day pass in which a transport seraphim of Satania does not deposit some student visitor or some other traveler of spirit or semi-spirit nature on the shores of Urantia. These very space traversers will sometime carry you to and from the various worlds of the system headquarters group, and when you have finished the Jerusem assignment, they will carry you forward to Edentia. But under no circumstances will they carry you backward to the world of human origin. A mortal never returns to his native planet during the dispensation of his temporal existence, and if he should return during a subsequent dispensation, he would be escorted by a transport seraphim of the universe headquarters group.

6. *The Recorders*. These seraphim are the keepers of the threefold records of the local systems. The temple of records on a system capital is a unique structure, one third material, constructed of luminous metals and crystals; one third morontial, fabricated of the liaison of spiritual and material energy but beyond the range of mortal vision; and one third spiritual. The recorders of this order preside over and maintain this threefold system of records. Ascending mortals will at first consult the material archives, Material Sons and the higher transition beings consult those of the morontia halls, while seraphim and the higher spirit personalities of the realm peruse the records of the spirit section.

7. *The Reserves*. The reserve corps of administrator seraphim on Jerusem spend much of their waiting time in visiting, as spirit companions, with the newly arrived ascending mortals from the various worlds of the system — the accredited graduates of the mansion worlds. One of the delights of your sojourn on Jerusem will be to talk and visit, during recess periods, with these much-traveled and many-experienced seraphim of the waiting reserve corps.

It is just such friendly relationships as these that so endear a system capital to the ascending mortals. On Jerusem you will find the first intermingling of Material Sons, angels, and ascending pilgrims. Here fraternize beings who are wholly spiritual and semi-spiritual and individuals just emerging from material existence. Mortal forms are there so modified and human ranges of light reaction so extended that all are able to enjoy mutual recognition and sympathetic personality understanding.

5. PLANETARY HELPERS

These seraphim maintain headquarters on the system capitals and, though closely associated with the resident Adamic citizens, are primarily assigned to the service of the Planetary Adams, the biologic or physical uplifters of the material races on the evolutionary worlds. The ministering work of angels becomes of increasing interest as it nears the inhabited worlds, as it nears the actual problems faced by the men and women of time who are preparing themselves for the attempt to attain the goal of eternity.

On Urantia the majority of the planetary helpers were removed upon the collapse of the Adamic regime, and the seraphic supervision of your world devolved to a greater extent upon the administrators, the transition ministers, and the guardians of destiny. But these seraphic aids of your defaulting Material Sons still serve Urantia in the following groups:

1. *The Voices of the Garden.* When the planetary course of human evolution is attaining its highest biologic level, there always appear the Material Sons and Daughters, the Adams and Eves, to augment the further evolution of the races by an actual contribution of their superior life plasm. The planetary headquarters of such an Adam and Eve is usually denominated the Garden of Eden, and their personal seraphim are often known as the "voices of the Garden." These seraphim are of invaluable service to the Planetary Adams in all their projects for the physical and intellectual up-stepping of the evolutionary races. After the Adamic default on Urantia, some of these seraphim were left on the planet and were assigned to Adam's successors in authority.

2. *The Spirits of Brotherhood.* It should be apparent that, when an Adam and Eve arrive on an evolutionary world, the task of achieving harmony and social co-operation among its diverse peoples is one of considerable proportions. Seldom do the inhabitants take kindly to the plan of human brotherhood. These primitive men only come to realize the wisdom of peaceful

inter-association as a result of ripened human experience and through the faithful ministry of the seraphic spirits of brotherhood. Without the work of these seraphim the efforts of the Material Sons to harmonize and advance the citizens of an evolving world would be greatly delayed. And had your Adam adhered to the original plan for the advancement of Urantia, by this time these spirits of brotherhood would have worked unbelievable transformations in the human race. In view of the Adamic default, it is indeed remarkable that these seraphic orders have been able to foster and bring to realization even as much of brotherhood as you now have on Urantia.

3. *The Souls of Peace*. The early millenniums of the upward strivings of evolutionary men are marked by many a struggle. Peace is not the natural state of the material realms. The worlds first realize "peace on earth and good will among men" through the ministry of the seraphic souls of peace. Although these angels were largely thwarted in their early efforts on Urantia, Vevona, chief of the souls of peace in Adam's day, was left on Urantia and is now attached to the staff of the resident governor general. And it was this same Vevona who, when Michael was born, heralded to the worlds, as the leader of the angelic host, "Glory to God in Havona and on earth peace and good will among men."

In the more advanced epochs of planetary evolution these seraphim are instrumental in supplanting the atonement idea by the concept of divine attunement as a philosophy of mortal survival.

4. *The Spirits of Trust*. Suspicion is the inherent reaction of primitive men; the survival struggles of the early ages do not naturally breed trust. Trust is a new human acquisition brought about by the ministry of these planetary seraphim of the Adamic regime. It is their mission to inculcate trust into the minds of evolving men. The Gods are very trustful; the Universal Father is willing freely to trust himself — the Adjuster — to man's association.

This entire group of seraphim was transferred to the new regime after the Adamic miscarriage, and they have ever since continued their labors on Urantia. And they have not been wholly unsuccessful since a civilization is now evolving which embodies much of their ideals of confidence and trust.

In the more advanced planetary ages these seraphim enhance man's appreciation of the truth that uncertainty is the secret of contented continuity. They help the mortal philosophers to realize that, when ignorance is essential to success, it would be a colossal blunder for the creature to know the future. They heighten man's taste for the sweetness of uncertainty, for the romance and charm of the indefinite and unknown future.

5. *The Transporters*. The planetary transporters serve the individual worlds. The majority of enseraphimed beings brought to this planet are in transit; they merely stop over; they are in custody of their own special seraphic transporters; but there are a large number of such seraphim stationed on Urantia. These are the transport personalities operating from the local planets, as from Urantia to Jerusem.

Your conventional idea of angels has been derived in the following way: During moments just prior to physical death a reflective phenomenon sometimes occurs in the human mind, and this dimming consciousness seems to visualize something of the form of the attending angel, and this is immediately translated into terms of the habitual concept of angels held in that individual's mind.

The erroneous idea that angels possess wings is not wholly due to olden notions that they must have wings to fly through the air. Human beings have sometimes been permitted to observe seraphim that were being prepared for transport service, and the traditions of these experiences have largely determined the Urantian concept of angels. In observing a transport seraphim being made ready to receive a passenger for interplanetary transit, there may be seen what are apparently double sets of wings extending from the head to the foot of the angel. In reality these wings are energy insulators — friction shields.

When celestial beings are to be enseraphimed for transfer from one world to another, they are brought to the headquarters of the sphere and, after due registry, are inducted into the transit sleep. Meantime, the transport seraphim moves into a horizontal position immediately above the universe energy pole of the planet. While the energy shields are wide open, the sleeping personality is skillfully deposited, by the officiating seraphic assistants, directly on top of the transport angel. Then both the upper and lower pairs of shields are carefully closed and adjusted.

And now, under the influence of the transformers and the transmitters, a strange metamorphosis begins as the seraphim is made ready to swing into the energy currents of the universe circuits. To outward appearance the seraphim grows pointed at both extremities and becomes so enshrouded in a queer light of amber hue that very soon it is impossible to distinguish the enseraphimed personality. When all is in readiness for departure, the chief of transport makes the proper inspection of the carriage of life, carries out the routine tests to ascertain whether or not the angel is properly encircuited, and then announces that the traveler is properly enseraphimed, that the energies are adjusted, that the angel is insulated, and that everything is in readiness for the departing flash. The mechanical controllers, two of them, next take their positions. By this time the transport seraphim has become an almost transparent, vibrating, torpedo-shaped outline of glistening luminosity. Now the transport dispatcher of the realm summons the auxiliary batteries of the living energy transmitters, usually one thousand in number; as he announces the destination of the transport, he reaches out and touches the near point of the seraphic carriage, which shoots forward with lightninglike speed, leaving a trail of celestial luminosity as far as the planetary atmospheric investment extends. In less than ten minutes the marvelous spectacle will be lost even to reinforced seraphic vision.

While planetary space reports are received at noon at the meridian of the designated spiritual headquarters, the transporters are dispatched from this same place at midnight. That is the most favorable time for departure and is the standard hour when not otherwise specified.

6. *The Recorders.* These are the custodians of the major affairs of the planet as it functions as a part of the system, and as it is related to, and concerned in, the universe government. They function in the recording of planetary affairs but are not concerned with matters of individual life and existence.

7. *The Reserves.* The Satania reserve corps of the planetary seraphim is maintained on Jerusem in close association with the reserves of the Material

Sons. These abundant reserves repletely provide for every phase of the manifold activities of this seraphic order. These angels are also the personal message bearers of the local systems. They serve transition mortals, angels, and the Material Sons as well as others domiciled on the system headquarters. While Urantia is, at present, outside the spiritual circuits of Satania and Norlatiadek, you are otherwise in intimate touch with interplanetary affairs, for these messengers from Jerusem frequently come to this world as to all the other spheres of the system.

6. TRANSITION MINISTERS

As their name might suggest, seraphim of transitional ministry serve wherever they can contribute to creature transition from the material to the spiritual estate. These angels serve from the inhabited worlds to the system capitals, but those in Satania at present direct their greatest efforts toward the education of the surviving mortals on the seven mansion worlds. This ministry is diversified in accordance with the following seven orders of assignment:

1. Seraphic Evangels.
2. Racial Interpreters.
3. Mind Planners.
4. Morontia Counselors.
5. Technicians.
6. Recorder-Teachers.
7. Ministering Reserves.

More about these seraphic ministers to transitional ascenders you will learn in connection with the narratives dealing with the mansion worlds and the morontia life.

7. SERAPHIM OF THE FUTURE

These angels do not minister extensively except in older realms and on the more advanced planets of Nebadon. Large numbers of them are held in reserve on the seraphic worlds near Salvington, where they are engaged in pursuits relevant to the sometime dawning of the age of light and life in Nebadon. These seraphim do function in connection with the ascendant-mortal career but minister almost exclusively to those mortals who survive by some one of the modified orders of ascension.

Inasmuch as these angels are not now directly concerned with either Urantia or Urantians, it is deemed best to withhold the description of their fascinating activities.

8. SERAPHIC DESTINY

Seraphim are of origin in the local universes, and in these very realms of their nativity some achieve service destiny. With the help and counsel of the senior archangels some seraphim may be elevated to the exalted duties of Brilliant Evening Stars, while others attain the status and service of the unrevealed co-ordinates of the Evening Stars. Still other adventures in local universe destiny may be attempted, but Seraphington ever remains the eternal goal of all angels. Seraphington is the angelic threshold to Paradise and Deity attainment, the transition sphere from the ministry of time to the exalted service of eternity.

Seraphim may attain Paradise in scores — hundreds — of ways, but the most important as elaborated in these narratives are the following:

1. To gain admission to the Paradise seraphic abode in a personal capacity by achieving perfection of specialized service as a celestial artisan, a Technical Adviser, or a Celestial Recorder. To become a Paradise Companion and, having thus attained the center of all things, perhaps then to become an eternal minister and adviser to the seraphic orders and others.

2. To be summoned to Seraphington. Under certain conditions seraphim are commanded on high; in other circumstances angels sometimes achieve Paradise in a much shorter time than mortals. But no matter how fitted any seraphic pair may be, they cannot initiate departure for Seraphington or elsewhere. None but successful destiny guardians can be sure of proceeding to Paradise by a progressive path of evolutionary ascent. All others must patiently await the arrival of the Paradise messengers of the tertiary supernaphim who come with the summons commanding them to appear on high.

3. To attain Paradise by the evolutionary mortal technique. The supreme choice of seraphim in the career of time is the post of guardian angel in order that they may attain the career of finality and be qualified for assignment to the eternal spheres of seraphic service. Such personal guides of the children of time are called guardians of destiny, signifying that they guard mortal creatures in the path of divine destiny, and that in so doing they are determining their own high destiny.

Guardians of destiny are drawn from the ranks of the more experienced angelic personalities of all orders of seraphim who have qualified for this service. All surviving mortals of Adjuster-fusion destiny have temporary guardians assigned, and these associates may become permanently attached when mortal survivors attain the requisite intellectual and spiritual development. Before mortal ascenders leave the mansion worlds, they all have permanent seraphic associates. This group of ministering spirits is discussed in connection with the Urantia narratives.

It is not possible for angels to attain God from the human level of origin, for they are created a "little higher than you"; but it has been wisely arranged that, while they cannot possibly start up from the very bottom, the spiritual lowlands of mortal existence, they may go down to those who do start from the bottom and pilot such creatures, step by step, world by world, to the portals of Havona. When mortal ascenders leave Uversa to begin the circles of Havona, those guardians of attachment subsequent to the life in the flesh will bid their pilgrim associates a temporary farewell while they journey to Seraphington, the angelic destination of the grand universe. Here will these guardians attempt, and undoubtedly achieve, the seven circles of seraphic light.

Many, but not all, of those seraphim assigned as destiny guardians during the material life accompany their mortal associates through the Havona circles, and certain other seraphim pass through the circuits of the central universe in a way that is wholly different from the mortal ascent. But irrespective of the route of ascent, all evolutionary seraphim traverse Seraphington, and the majority pass through this experience instead of the Havona circuits.

Seraphington is the destiny sphere for angels, and their attainment of this world is quite different from the experiences of the mortal pilgrims on Ascendington. Angels are not absolutely sure of their eternal future until they have attained Seraphington. No angel attaining Seraphington has ever been known to go astray; sin will never find response in the heart of a seraphim of completion.

The graduates of Seraphington are variously assigned: Destiny guardians of Havona-circle experience usually enter the Mortal Finaliter Corps. Other guardians, having passed their Havona separation tests, frequently rejoin their mortal associates on Paradise, and some become the everlasting associates of the mortal finaliters, while others enter the various non-mortal finaliter corps, and many are mustered into the Corps of Seraphic Completion.

9. THE CORPS OF SERAPHIC COMPLETION

After attainment of the Father of spirits and admission to the seraphic service of completion, angels are sometimes assigned to the ministry of worlds settled in light and life. They gain attachment to the high trinitized beings of the universes and to the exalted services of Paradise and Havona. These seraphim of the local universes have experientially compensated the differential in divinity potential formerly setting them apart from the ministering spirits of the central and super-universes. Angels of the Seraphic Corps of Completion serve as associates of the super-universe seconaphim and as assistants to the high Paradise-Havona orders of supernaphim. For such angels the career of time is finished; henceforth and forever they are the servants of God, the consorts of divine personalities, and the peers of the Paradise finaliters.

Large numbers of the completion seraphim return to their native universes, there to complement the ministry of divine endowment by the ministry of experiential perfection. Nebadon is, comparatively speaking, one of the younger universes and therefore does not have so many of these returned Seraphington graduates as would be found in an older realm; nonetheless our local universe is adequately supplied with the completion seraphim, for it is significant that the evolutionary realms disclose increasing need for their services as they near the status of light and life. Completion seraphim now serve more extensively with the supreme orders of seraphim, but some serve with each of the other angelic orders. Even your world enjoys the extensive ministry of twelve specialized groups of the Seraphic Corps of Completion; these master seraphim of planetary supervision accompany each newly commissioned Planetary Prince to the inhabited worlds.

Many fascinating avenues of ministry are open to the completion seraphim, but just as they all craved assignment as destiny guardians in the pre-Paradise days, so in the post-Paradise experience they most desire to serve as bestowal attendants of the incarnated Paradise Sons. They are still supremely devoted to that universal plan of starting the mortal creatures of the evolutionary worlds out upon the long and enticing journey towards the Paradise goal of divinity and eternity. Throughout the whole mortal adventure of finding God and of achieving divine perfection, these spirit ministers of seraphic completion, together with the faithful ministering spirits of time, are always and forever your true friends and unfailing helpers.

[Presented by a Melchizedek acting by request of the Chief of the Seraphic Hosts of Nebadon.]

PAPER 40
THE ASCENDING SONS OF GOD

As in many of the major groups of universe beings, seven general classes of the Ascending Sons of God have been revealed:

1. Father-fused Mortals.
2. Son-fused Mortals.
3. Spirit-fused Mortals.
4. Evolutionary Seraphim.
5. Ascending Material Sons.
6. Translated Midwayers.
7. Personalized Adjusters.

The story of these beings, from the lowly animal-origin mortals of the evolutionary worlds to the Personalized Adjusters of the Universal Father, presents a glorious recital of the unstinted bestowal of divine love and gracious condescension throughout all time and in all universes of the far-flung creation of the Paradise Deities.

These presentations began with a description of the Deities, and group by group, the narrative has descended the universal scale of living beings until it has reached the lowest order of life endowed with the potential of immortality; and now am I dispatched from Salvington — onetime a mortal of origin on an evolutionary world of space — to elaborate and continue the recital of the eternal purpose of the Gods respecting the ascending orders of sonship, more particularly with regard to the mortal creatures of time and space.

Since the greater part of this narrative will be devoted to a discussion of the three basic orders of ascending mortals, consideration will first be given to the non-mortal ascending orders of sonship — seraphic, Adamic, midwayer, and Adjuster.

1. EVOLUTIONARY SERAPHIM

Mortal creatures of animal origin are not the only beings privileged to enjoy sonship; the angelic hosts also share the supernal opportunity to attain Paradise. Guardian seraphim, through experience and service with the ascending mortals of time, also achieve the status of ascendant sonship. Such angels attain Paradise through Seraphington, and many are even mustered into the Corps of Mortal Finality.

To climb to the supernal heights of finaliter sonship with God is a masterly achievement for an angel, an accomplishment far transcending your attainment of eternal survival through the plan of the Eternal Son and the ever-present help of the indwelling Adjuster; but the guardian seraphim, and occasionally others, do actually effect such ascensions.

2. ASCENDING MATERIAL SONS

The Material Sons of God are created in the local universe along with the Melchizedeks and their associates, who are all classified as descending Sons. And indeed, the Planetary Adams — the Material Sons and Daughters of the evolutionary worlds — are descending Sons, coming down to the inhabited worlds from their spheres of origin, the capitals of the local systems.

When such an Adam and Eve are wholly successful in their joint planetary mission as biologic uplifters, they share the destiny of the inhabitants of their world. When such a world is settled in the advanced stages of light and life, this faithful Material Son and Daughter are permitted to resign all planetary administrative duties, and after being thus liberated from the descending adventure, they are permitted to register themselves as perfected Material Sons on the records of the local universe. Likewise, when planetary assignment is long delayed, may the Material Sons of stationary status — the citizens of the local systems — withdraw from the activities of their status spheres and similarly register as perfected Material Sons. After these formalities such liberated Adams and Eves are accredited as ascending Sons of God and may immediately begin the long journey to Havona and Paradise, starting at the exact point of their then present status and spiritual attainment. And they make this journey in company with the mortal and other ascending Sons, continuing until they have found God and have achieved the Corps of Mortal Finality in the eternal service of the Paradise Deities.

3. TRANSLATED MIDWAYERS

Although deprived of the immediate benefits of the planetary bestowals of the descending Sons of God, though the Paradise ascent is long deferred, nevertheless, soon after an evolutionary planet has attained the intermediate epochs of light and life (if not before), both groups of midway creatures are released from planetary duty. Sometimes the majority of them are translated, along with their human cousins, on the day of the descent of the temple of light and the elevation of the Planetary Prince to the dignity of Planetary Sovereign. Upon being relieved of planetary service, both orders are registered in the local universe as ascending Sons of God and immediately begin the long Paradise ascent by the very routes ordained for the progression of the mortal races of the material worlds. The primary group are destined to various finaliter corps, but the secondary or Adamic midwayers are all routed for enrollment in the Mortal Corps of Finality.

4. PERSONALIZED ADJUSTERS

When the mortals of time fail to achieve the eternal survival of their souls in planetary association with the spirit gifts of the Universal Father, such failure is never in any way due to neglect of duty, ministry, service, or devotion on the part of the Adjuster. At mortal death, such deserted Monitors return to Divinington, and subsequently, following the adjudication of the non-survivor, they may be reassigned to the worlds of time and space. Sometimes, after repeated services of this sort or following some unusual experience, such as functioning as the indwelling Adjuster of an incarnated bestowal Son, these efficient Adjusters are personalized by the Universal Father.

Personalized Adjusters are beings of a unique and unfathomable order. Originally of existential pre-personal status, they have experientialized by participation in the lives and careers of the lowly mortals of the material worlds. And since the personality bestowed upon these experienced Thought Adjusters takes origin, and has its wellspring, in the Universal Father's personal and continuing ministry of the bestowals of experiential personality upon his creature creation, these Personalized Adjusters are classified as ascending Sons of God, the highest of all such orders of sonship.

5. MORTALS OF TIME AND SPACE

Mortals represent the last link in the chain of those beings who are called sons of God. The personal touch of the Original and Eternal Son passes on down through a series of decreasingly divine and increasingly human personalizations until there arrives a being much like yourselves, one you can see, hear, and touch. And then you are made spiritually aware of the great truth which your faith may grasp — sonship with the eternal God!

Likewise does the Original and Infinite Spirit, by a long series of decreasingly divine and increasingly human orders, draw nearer and nearer to the struggling creatures of the realms, reaching the limit of expression in the angels — than whom you were created but a little lower — who personally guard and guide you in the life journey of the mortal career of time.

God the Father does not, cannot, thus downstep himself to make such near personal contact with the almost limitless number of ascending creatures throughout the universe of universes. But the Father is not deprived of personal contact with his lowly creatures; you are not without the divine presence. Although God the Father cannot be with you by direct personality manifestation, he is in you and of you in the identity of the indwelling

Thought Adjusters, the divine Monitors. Thus does the Father, who is the farthest from you in personality and in spirit, draw the nearest to you in the personality circuit and in the spirit touch of inner communion with the very souls of his mortal sons and daughters.

Spirit identification constitutes the secret of personal survival and determines the destiny of spiritual ascension. And since the Thought Adjusters are the only spirits of fusion potential to be identified with man during the life in the flesh, the mortals of time and space are primarily classified in accordance with their relation to these divine gifts, the indwelling Mystery Monitors. This classification is as follows:

1. Mortals of the transient or experiential Adjuster sojourn.
2. Mortals of the non-Adjuster-fusion types.
3. Mortals of Adjuster-fusion potential.

Series one — mortals of the transient or experiential Adjuster sojourn. This series designation is temporary for any evolving planet, being used during the early stages of all inhabited worlds except those of the second series.

Mortals of series one inhabit the worlds of space during the earlier epochs of the evolution of mankind and embrace the most primitive types of human minds. On many worlds like pre-Adamic Urantia great numbers of the higher and more advanced types of primitive men acquire survival capacity but fail to attain Adjuster fusion. For ages upon ages, before man's ascent to the level of higher spiritual volition, the Adjusters occupy the minds of these struggling creatures during their short lives in the flesh, and the moment such will creatures are indwelt by Adjusters, the group guardian angels begin to function. While these mortals of the first series do not have personal guardians, they do have group custodians.

An experiential Adjuster remains with a primitive human being throughout his entire lifetime in the flesh. The Adjusters contribute much to the advancement of primitive men but are unable to form eternal unions with such mortals. This transient ministry of the Adjusters accomplishes two things: First, they gain valuable and actual experience in the nature and working of the evolutionary intellect, an experience which will be invaluable in connection with later contacts on other worlds with beings of higher development. Second, the transient sojourn of the Adjusters contributes much towards preparing their mortal subjects for possible subsequent Spirit fusion. All God-seeking souls of this type achieve eternal life through the spiritual embrace of the Mother Spirit of the local universe, thus becoming ascending mortals of the local universe regime. Many persons from pre-Adamic Urantia were thus advanced to the mansion worlds of Satania.

The Gods who ordained that mortal man should climb to higher levels of spiritual intelligence through long ages of evolutionary trials and tribulations, take note of his status and needs at every stage of the ascent; and always are they divinely fair and just, even charmingly merciful, in the final judgments of these struggling mortals of the early days of the evolving races.

Series two — mortals of the non-Adjuster-fusion types. These are specialized types of human beings who are not able to effect eternal union with their indwelling Adjusters. Type classification among the one-, two-, and three-brained races is not a factor in Adjuster fusion; all such mortals are akin, but these non-Adjuster-fusion types are a wholly different and markedly modified order of will creatures. Many of the non-breathers belong to this series, and there are numerous other groups who do not ordinarily fuse with Adjusters.

Like series number one, each member of this group enjoys the ministry of a single Adjuster during lifetime in the flesh. During temporal life these Adjusters do everything for their subjects of temporary indwelling that is done on other worlds where the mortals are of fusion potential. The mortals of this second series are often indwelt by virgin Adjusters, but the higher human types are often in liaison with masterful and experienced Monitors.

In the ascendant plan for up-stepping the animal-origin creatures, these beings enjoy the same devoted service of the Sons of God as is extended to the Urantia type of mortals. Seraphic co-operation with Adjusters on the non-fusion planets is just as fully provided as on the worlds of fusion potential; the guardians of destiny minister on such spheres just as on Urantia and similarly function at the time of mortal survival, at which time the surviving soul becomes Spirit fused.

When you encounter these modified mortal types on the mansion worlds, you will find no difficulty in communicating with them. There they speak the same system language but by a modified technique. These beings are identical with your order of creature life in spirit and personality manifestations, differing only in certain physical features and in the fact that they are non-fusible with Thought Adjusters.

As to just why this type of creature is never able to fuse with the Adjusters of the Universal Father, I am unable to say. Some of us incline to the belief that the Life Carriers, in their efforts to formulate beings capable of maintaining existence in an unusual planetary environment, are confronted with the necessity of making such radical modifications in the universe plan of intelligent will creatures that it becomes inherently impossible to bring about permanent union with the Adjusters. Often have we asked: Is this an intended or an unintended part of the ascension plan? but we have not found the answer.

Series three — mortals of Adjuster-fusion potential. All Father-fused mortals are of animal origin, just like all Urantians. They embrace mortals of the one-brained, two-brained, and three-brained types of Adjuster-fusion potential. Urantians are of the intermediate or two-brained type, being in many ways humanly superior to the one-brained groups but definitely limited in comparison with the three-brained orders. These three types of physical-brain endowment are not factors in Adjuster bestowal, in seraphic service, or in any other phase of spirit ministry. The intellectual and spiritual differential between the three brain types characterizes individuals who are otherwise quite alike in mind endowment and spiritual potential, being greatest in the temporal life and tending to diminish as the mansion worlds are traversed one by one. From the system headquarters on, the progression of these three types is the same, and their eventual Paradise destiny is identical.

The unnumbered series. These narratives cannot possibly embrace all of the fascinating variations in the evolutionary worlds. You know that every tenth world is a decimal or experimental planet, but you know nothing of the other variables that punctuate the processional of the evolutionary spheres. There are differences too numerous to narrate even between the revealed orders of living creatures as between planets of the same group, but this presentation makes clear the essential differences in relation to the ascension career. And the ascension career is the most important factor in any consideration of the mortals of time and space.

As to the chances of mortal survival, let it be made forever clear: All souls of every possible phase of mortal existence will survive provided they manifest willingness to co-operate with their indwelling Adjusters and exhibit a desire to find God and to attain divine perfection, even though these desires be but the first faint flickers of the primitive comprehension of that "true light which lights every man who comes into the world."

6. THE FAITH SONS OF GOD

The mortal races stand as the representatives of the lowest order of intelligent and personal creation. You mortals are divinely beloved, and every one of you may choose to accept the certain destiny of a glorious experience, but you are not yet by nature of the divine order; you are wholly mortal. You will be reckoned as ascending sons the instant fusion takes place, but the status of the mortals of time and space is that of faith sons prior to the event of the final amalgamation of the surviving mortal soul with some type of eternal and immortal spirit.

It is a solemn and supernal fact that such lowly and material creatures as Urantia human beings are the sons of God, faith children of the Highest. "Behold, what manner of love the Father has bestowed upon us that we should be called the sons of God." "As many as received him, to them gave he the power to recognize that they are the sons of God." While "it does not yet appear what you shall be," even now "you are the faith sons of God"; "for you have not received the spirit of bondage again to fear, but you have received the spirit of sonship, whereby you cry, `our Father.'" Spoke the prophet of old in the name of the eternal God: "Even to them will I give in my house a place and a name better than sons; I will give them an everlasting name, one that shall not be cut off." "And because you are sons, God has sent forth the spirit of his Son into your hearts."

All evolutionary worlds of mortal habitation harbor these faith sons of God, sons of grace and mercy, mortal beings belonging to the divine family and accordingly called the sons of God. Urantia mortals are entitled to regard themselves as being the sons of God because:

1. You are sons of spiritual promise, faith sons; you have accepted the status of sonship. You believe in the reality of your sonship, and thus does your sonship with God become eternally real.
2. A Creator Son of God became one of you; he is your elder brother in fact; and if in spirit you become truly related brothers of Christ, the victorious Michael, then in spirit must you also be sons of that Father which you have in common — even the Universal Father of all.
3. You are sons because the spirit of a Son has been poured out upon you, has been freely and certainly bestowed upon all Urantians. This spirit ever draws you toward the divine Son, who is its source, and toward the Paradise Father, who is the source of that divine Son.
4. Of his divine free-wiliness, the Universal Father has given you your creature personalities. You have been endowed with a measure of that divine spontaneity of freewill action, which God shares with all who may become his sons.
5. There dwells within you a fragment of the Universal Father, and you are thus directly related to the divine

Father of all the Sons of God.

7. FATHER-FUSED MORTALS

The sending of Adjusters, their indwelling, is indeed one of the unfathomable mysteries of God the Father. These fragments of the divine nature of the Universal Father carry with them the potential of creature immortality. Adjusters are immortal spirits, and union with them confers eternal life upon the soul of the fused mortal.

Your own races of surviving mortals belong to this group of the ascending Sons of God. You are now planetary sons, evolutionary creatures derived from the Life Carrier implantations and modified by the Adamic-life infusion, hardly yet ascending sons; but you are indeed sons of ascension potential — even to the highest heights of glory and divinity attainment — and this spiritual status of ascending sonship you may attain by faith and by freewill co-operation with the spiritualizing activities of the indwelling Adjuster. When you and your Adjusters are finally and forever fused, when you two are made one, even as in Christ Michael the Son of God and the Son of Man are one, then in fact have you become the ascending sons of God.

The details of the Adjuster career of indwelling ministry on a probationary and evolutionary planet are not a part of my assignment; the elaboration of this great truth embraces your whole career. I include the mention of certain Adjuster functions in order to make a replete statement regarding Adjuster-fused mortals. These indwelling fragments of God are with your order of being from the early days of physical existence through all of the ascending career in Nebadon and Orvonton and on through Havona to Paradise itself. Thereafter, in the eternal adventure, this same Adjuster is one with you and of you.

These are the mortals who have been commanded by the Universal Father, "Be you perfect, even as I am perfect." The Father has bestowed himself upon you, placed his own spirit within you; *therefore* does he demand ultimate perfection of you. The narrative of human ascent from the mortal spheres of time to the divine realms of eternity constitutes an intriguing recital not included in my assignment, but this supernal adventure should be the supreme study of mortal man.

Fusion with a fragment of the Universal Father is equivalent to a divine validation of eventual Paradise attainment, and such Adjuster-fused mortals are the only class of human beings who all traverse the Havona circuits and find God on Paradise. To the Adjuster-fused mortal the career of universal service is wide open. What dignity of destiny and glory of attainment await every one of you! Do you fully appreciate what has been done for you? Do you comprehend the grandeur of the heights of eternal achievement which are spread out before you? — even you who now trudge on in the lowly path of life through your so-called "vale of tears"?

8. SON-FUSED MORTALS

While practically all surviving mortals are fused with their Adjusters on one of the mansion worlds or immediately upon their arrival on the higher morontia spheres, there are certain cases of delayed fusion, some not experiencing this final surety of survival until they reach the last educational worlds of the universe headquarters; and a few of these mortal candidates for never-ending life utterly fail to attain identity fusion with their faithful Adjusters.

Such mortals have been deemed worthy of survival by the adjudicational authorities, and even their Adjusters, by returning from Divinington, have concurred in their ascension to the mansion worlds. Such beings have ascended through a system, a constellation, a galaxy, up through the minor and major sectors, and through the educational worlds of the Salvington circuit; they have enjoyed the "seventy times seven" opportunities for fusion and still have been unable to attain oneness with their Adjusters.

When it becomes apparent that some synchronizing difficulty is inhibiting Father fusion, the survival referees of the Creator Son are convened. And when this court of inquiry, sanctioned by a personal representative of the Ancients of Days, finally determines that the ascending mortal is not guilty of any discoverable cause for failure to attain fusion, they so certify on the records of the local universe and duly transmit this finding to the Ancients of Days. Thereupon does the indwelling Adjuster return forthwith to Divinington for confirmation by the Personalized Monitors, and upon this leave-taking the morontia mortal is immediately fused with an individualized gift of the spirit of the Creator Son.

Much as the morontia spheres of Nebadon are shared with the Spirit-fused mortals, so do these Son-fused creatures share the services of Orvonton with their Adjuster-fused brethren who are journeying inward towards the far-distant Isle of Paradise. They are truly your brethren, and you will greatly enjoy their association as you pass through the training worlds of the super-universe.

Son-fused mortals are not a numerous group. Aside from residential destiny on Paradise they are in every way the equals of their Adjuster-fused associates. They frequently journey to Paradise on super-universe assignment but seldom permanently reside there, being, as a class, confined to the super-universe of their nativity.

9. SPIRIT-FUSED MORTALS

Ascending Spirit-fused mortals are not Third Source personalities; they are included in the Father's personality circuit, but they have fused with individualizations of the pre-mind spirit of the Third Source and Center. Such Spirit fusion never occurs during the span of natural life; it takes place only at the time of mortal reawakening in the morontia existence on the mansion worlds. In the fusion experience there is no overlapping; the will creature is either Spirit fused, Son fused, or Father fused. Those who are Adjuster or Father fused are never Spirit or Son fused.

The fact that these types of mortal creatures are not Adjuster-fusion candidates does not prevent the Adjusters from indwelling them during the life in the flesh. Adjusters do work in the minds of such beings during the span of material life but never become everlastingly one with their pupil souls. During this temporary sojourn the Adjusters effectively build up the same spirit counterpart of mortal nature — the soul — that they do in the candidates for Adjuster fusion. Up to the time of mortal death the work of the Adjusters is wholly akin to their function in your own races, but upon mortal dissolution the Adjusters take eternal leave of these Spirit-fusion candidates and, proceeding directly to Divinington, the headquarters of all divine Monitors, there to await the new assignments of their order.

When such sleeping survivors are repersonalized on the mansion worlds, the place of the departed Adjuster is filled by an individualization of the spirit of the Divine Minister, the representative of the Infinite Spirit in the local universe concerned. This spirit infusion constitutes these surviving creatures Spirit-fused mortals. Such beings are in every way your equals in mind and spirit; and they are indeed your contemporaries, sharing the mansion and morontia spheres in common with your order of fusion candidates and with those who are to be Son fused.

There is, however, one particular in which Spirit-fused mortals differ from their ascendant brethren: Mortal memory of human experience on the material worlds of origin survives death in the flesh because the indwelling Adjuster has acquired a spirit counterpart, or transcript, of those events of human life which were of spiritual significance. But with Spirit-fused mortals there exists no such mechanism whereby human memory may persist. The Adjuster transcripts of memory are full and intact, but these acquisitions are experiential possessions of the departed Adjusters and are not available to the creatures of their former indwelling, who therefore awaken in the resurrection halls of the morontia spheres of Nebadon as if they were newly created beings, creatures without consciousness of former existence.

Such children of the local universe are enabled to repossess themselves of much of their former human memory experience through having it retold by the associated seraphim and cherubim and by consulting the records of the mortal career filed by the recording angels. This they can do with undoubted assurance because the surviving soul, of experiential origin in the material and mortal life, while having no memory of mortal events, does have a residual experiential-recognition-response to these unremembered events of past experience.

When a Spirit-fused mortal is told about the events of the unremembered past experience, there is an immediate response of experiential recognition within the soul (identity) of such a survivor which instantly invests the narrated event with the emotional tinge of reality and with the intellectual quality of fact; and this dual response constitutes the reconstruction, recognition, and validation of an unremembered facet of mortal experience.

Even with Adjuster-fusion candidates, only those human experiences which were of spiritual value are common possessions of the surviving mortal and the returning Adjuster and hence are immediately remembered subsequent to mortal survival. Concerning those happenings which were not of spiritual significance, even these Adjuster-fusers must depend upon the attribute of recognition-response in the surviving soul. And since any one event may have a spiritual connotation to one mortal but not to another, it becomes possible for a group of contemporary ascenders from the same planet to pool their store of Adjuster-remembered events and thus to reconstruct any experience which they had in common, and which was of spiritual value in the life of any one of them.

While we understand such techniques of memory reconstruction fairly well, we do not grasp the technique of personality recognition. Personalities of onetime association mutually respond quite independently of the operation of memory, albeit, memory itself and the techniques of its reconstruction are necessary to invest such mutual personality response with the fullness of recognition.

A Spirit-fused survivor is also able to learn much about the life he lived in the flesh by revisiting his nativity world subsequent to the planetary dispensation in which he lived. Such children of Spirit fusion are enabled to enjoy these opportunities for investigating their human careers since they are in general confined to the service of the local universe. They do not share your high and exalted destiny in the Paradise Corps of the Finality; only Adjuster-fused mortals or other especially embraced ascendant beings are mustered into the ranks of those who await the eternal Deity adventure. Spirit-fused mortals are the permanent citizens of the local universes; they may aspire to Paradise destiny, but they cannot be sure of it. In Nebadon their universe home is the eighth group of worlds encircling Salvington, a destiny-heaven of nature and location much like the one envisioned by the planetary traditions of Urantia.

10. ASCENDANT DESTINIES

Spirit-fused mortals are, generally speaking, confined to a local universe; Son-fused survivors are restricted to a super-universe; Adjuster-fused mortals are destined to penetrate the universe of universes. The spirits of mortal fusion always ascend to the level of origin; such spirit entities unfailingly return to the sphere of primal source.

Spirit-fused mortals are of the local universe; they do not, ordinarily, ascend beyond the confines of their native realm, beyond the boundaries of the space range of the spirit that pervades them. Son-fused ascenders likewise rise to the source of spirit endowment, for much as the Truth Spirit of a

Creator Son focalizes in the associated Divine Minister, so is his "fusion spirit" implemented in the Reflective Spirits of the higher universes. Such spirit relationship between the local and the super-universe levels of God the Sevenfold may be difficult of explanation but not of discernment, being unmistakably revealed in those children of the Reflective Spirits — the secoraphic Voices of the Creator Sons. The Thought Adjuster, hailing from the Father on Paradise, never stops until the mortal son stands face to face with the eternal God.

The mysterious variable in associative technique whereby a mortal being does not or cannot become eternally fused with the indwelling Thought Adjuster may seem to disclose a flaw in the ascension scheme; Son and Spirit fusion do, superficially, resemble compensations of unexplained failures in some detail of the Paradise-attainment plan; but all such conclusions stand in error; we are taught that all these happenings unfold in obedience to the established laws of the Supreme Universe Rulers.

We have analyzed this problem and have reached the undoubted conclusion that the consignment of all mortals to an ultimate Paradise destiny would be unfair to the time-space universes inasmuch as the courts of the Creator Sons and of the Ancients of Days would then be wholly dependent on the services of those who were in transit to higher realms. And it does seem to be no more than fitting that the local and the super-universe governments should each be provided with a permanent group of ascendant citizenship; that the functions of these administrations should be enriched by the efforts of certain groups of glorified mortals who are of permanent status, evolutionary complements of the abandonters and of the susatia. Now it is quite obvious that the present ascension scheme effectively provides the time-space administrations with just such groups of ascendant creatures; and we have many times wondered: Does all this represent an intended part of the all-wise plans of the Architects of the Master Universe designed to provide the Creator Sons and the Ancients of Days with a permanent ascendant population? with evolved orders of citizenship that will become increasingly competent to carry forward the affairs of these realms in the universe ages to come?

That mortal destinies do thus vary in no wise proves that one is necessarily greater or lesser than another, merely that they differ. Adjuster-fused ascenders do indeed have a grand and glorious career as finaliters spread out before them in the eternal future, but this does not mean that they are preferred above their ascendant brethren. There is no favoritism, nothing arbitrary, in the selective operation of the divine plan of mortal survival.

While the Adjuster-fused finaliters obviously enjoy the widest service opportunity of all, the attainment of this goal automatically shuts them off from the chance to participate in the agelong struggle of some one universe or super-universe, from the earlier and less settled epochs to the later and established eras of relative perfection attainment. Finaliters acquire a marvelous and far-flung experience of transient service in all seven segments of the grand universe, but they do not ordinarily acquire that intimate knowledge of any one universe which even now characterizes the Spirit-fused veterans of the Nebadon Corps of Completion. These individuals enjoy an opportunity to witness the ascending processional of the planetary ages as they unfold one by one on an enormous number of inhabited worlds. And in the faithful service of such local universe citizens, experience superimposes upon experience until the fullness of time ripens that high quality of wisdom which is engendered by focalized experience — *authoritative* wisdom — and this in itself is a vital factor in the settling of any local universe.

As it is with the Spirit fusers, so is it with those Son-fused mortals who have achieved residential status on Uversa. Some of these beings hail from the earliest epochs of Orvonton, and they represent a slowly accumulating body of insight-deepening wisdom which is making ever-augmenting service contributions to the welfare and eventual settlement of the seventh super-universe.

What the ultimate destiny of these stationary orders of local and of super-universe citizenship will be we do not know, but it is quite possible that, when the Paradise finaliters are pioneering the expanding frontiers of divinity in the planetary systems of the first outer space level, their Son- and Spirit-fused brethren of the ascendant evolutionary struggle will be acceptably contributing to the maintenance of the experiential equilibrium of the perfected super-universes while they stand ready to welcome the incoming stream of Paradise pilgrims who may, at that distant day, pour in through Orvonton and its sister creations as a vast spirit-questing torrent from these now uncharted and uninhabited new space-time universes of outer space.

While the majority of Spirit fusers serve permanently as citizens of the local universes, all do not. If some phase of their universe ministry should require their personal presence in the super-universe, then would such transformations of being be wrought in these citizens as would enable them to ascend to the higher universe; and upon the arrival of the Celestial Guardians with orders to present such Spirit-fused mortals at the courts of the Ancients of Days, they would so ascend, never to return. They become wards of the super-universe, serving as assistants to the Celestial Guardians and permanently, save for those few who are in turn summoned to the service of Paradise and Havona.

Like their Spirit-fused brethren, the Son fusers neither traverse Havona nor attain Paradise unless they have undergone certain modifying transformations. For good and sufficient reasons, such changes have been wrought in certain Son-fused survivors, and these beings are to be encountered ever and anon on the seven circuits of the central universe. Thus it is that certain numbers of both the Son- and the Spirit-fused mortals do actually ascend to Paradise, do attain a goal in many ways equal to that which awaits the Father-fused mortals.

Father-fused mortals are potential finaliters; their destination is the Universal Father, and him they do attain, but within the purview of the present universe age, finaliters, as such, are not destiny attainers. They remain unfinished creatures — sixth-stage spirits — and hence nonactive in the evolutionary domains of prelight-and-life status.

When a mortal finaliter is Trinity embraced — becomes a Trinitized Son, such as a Mighty Messenger — then has that finaliter attained destiny, at least for the present universe age. Mighty Messengers and their fellows may not in the exact sense be seventh-stage spirits, but in addition to other things the Trinity embrace endows them with everything which a finaliter will sometime achieve as a seventh-stage spirit. After Spirit-fused or Son-fused mortals are trinitized, they pass through the Paradise experience with the Adjuster-fused ascenders, with whom they are then identical in all matters pertaining to super-universe administration. These Trinitized Sons of Selection or of Attainment at least for now are finished creatures, in contrast to the finaliters, who are at present unfinished creatures.

Thus, in the final analysis, it would be hardly proper to use the words "greater" or "lesser" in contrasting the destinies of the ascending orders of sonship. Every such son of God shares the fatherhood of God, and God loves each of his creature sons alike; he is no more a respecter of ascendant destinies than is he of the creatures who may attain such destinies. The Father loves *each* of his sons, and that affection is not less than true, holy, divine, unlimited, eternal, and unique — a love bestowed upon *this* son and upon *that* son, individually, personally, and exclusively. And such a love utterly eclipses all other facts. Sonship is the supreme relationship of the creature to the Creator.

As mortals you can now recognize your place in the family of divine sonship and begin to sense the obligation to avail yourselves of the advantages so freely provided in and by the Paradise plan for mortal survival, which plan has been so enhanced and illuminated by the life experience of a bestowal Son. Every facility and all power have been provided for insuring your ultimate attainment of the Paradise goal of divine perfection.

[Presented by a Mighty Messenger temporarily attached to the staff of Gabriel of Salvington.]

PAPER 41
PHYSICAL ASPECTS OF THE LOCAL UNIVERSE

THE CHARACTERISTIC SPACE phenomenon which sets off each local creation from all others is the presence of the Creative Spirit. All Nebadon is certainly pervaded by the space presence of the Divine Minister of Salvington, and such presence just as certainly terminates at the outer borders of our local universe. That which is pervaded by our local universe Mother Spirit is Nebadon; that which extends beyond her space presence is outside Nebadon, being the extra-Nebadon space regions of the super-universe of Orvonton, and other local universes.

The administrative organization of the grand universe discloses a clear-cut division between the governments of the central, super-, and local universes, and these divisions are paralleled in the dimensional separation of Havona, the seven super-universes, and the way that each local universe exists in its own four (or more) dimensional hyper-surface (M-brane) of the larger dimensional space-time of the super-universe.

1. THE NEBADON POWER CENTERS

A large number of Supreme Power Centers of the fourth order are permanently assigned to our local universe. These beings receive the incoming lines of power from the third-order centers of Uversa and relay the down-stepped and modified circuits to the power centers of our major and minor sectors, galaxies, constellations, and systems. These power centers actually exist in the higher dimensional space-time of the super-universe even though they are located in our four dimensional universe. They can take in energy from higher dimensions and reroute it into the four dimensions of our universe. They function to produce the living system of control and equalization which operates to maintain the balance and distribution of otherwise fluctuating and variable energies.

The local universe centers are stationed on Salvington, where they function at the exact energy center of that sphere. Architectural spheres, such as Salvington, Splandon, Ensa, Zion, Edentia, and Jerusem, are lighted, heated, and energized by methods which make them quite independent of the suns of space. These spheres were constructed — made to order — by the power centers and physical controllers and were designed to exert a powerful influence over energy distribution. Basing their activities on such focal points of energy control, the power centers, by their living presences, directionize and channelize the physical energies of space. And these energy circuits are basic to all physical-material and morontia-spiritual phenomena.

Ten Supreme Power Centers of the fifth order are assigned to each galaxies primary subdivisions, the constellations. These are always stationed on the constellation headquarters sphere. On Edentia there are also ten associated mechanical controllers and ten frandalanks who are in perfect and constant liaison with the near-by power centers.

2. THE SATANIA PHYSICAL CONTROLLERS

Satania is one of one hundred local systems which make up the administrative organization of the constellation of Norlatiadek, having as immediate neighbors the systems of Sandmatia, Assuntia, Porogia, Sortoria, Rantulia, and Glantonia. The Norlatiadek systems differ in many respects, but all are evolutionary and progressive, very much like Satania.

Except for the presence of the assigned power center, the supervision of the entire physical-energy system of Satania is centered on Jerusem. A Master Physical Controller, stationed on this headquarters sphere, works in co-ordination with the system power center, serving as liaison chief of the power inspectors headquartered on Jerusem and functioning throughout the local system.

The circuitizing and channelizing of energy is supervised by the five hundred thousand living and intelligent energy manipulators scattered throughout Satania. Through the action of such physical controllers the supervising power centers are in complete and perfect control of a majority of the basic energies of space. This group of living entities can mobilize, transform, transmute, manipulate, and transmit nearly all of the higher dimensional physical energies of organized space.

These intelligent creatures of power control and energy direction must adjust their technique on each sphere in accordance with the physical constitution and architecture of that planet. The power-energy supervision of the evolutionary inhabited worlds is the responsibility of the Master Physical Controllers, but these beings are not responsible for all energy misbehavior on Urantia. There are a number of reasons for such disturbances, some of which are beyond the domain and control of the physical custodians.

3. ORIGIN OF INHABITED WORLDS

The physical aspects of the individual worlds are largely determined by mode of origin, astronomical situation, and physical environment. Age, size, rate of revolution, and velocity through space are also determining factors. Both the gas-contraction and the solid-accretion worlds are characterized by mountains and, during their earlier life, when not too small, by water and air. The molten-split and collisional worlds are sometimes without extensive mountain ranges.

During the earlier ages of all these new worlds, earthquakes are frequent, and they are all characterized by great physical disturbances; especially is this true of the gas-contraction spheres. Planets having a dual origin like Urantia pass through a less violent and stormy youthful career.

Urantia is comparatively isolated on the outskirts of Satania, your solar system, with one exception, being the farthest removed from Jerusem, while Satania itself is next to the outermost system of Norlatiadek. You were truly among the least of all creation until Michael's bestowal elevated your planet to a position of honor and great universe interest. Sometimes the last is first, while truly the least becomes greatest.

[Presented by an Archangel in collaboration with the Chief of Nebadon Power Centers.]

[JFC Note: most of this chapter was deleted as obsolete science information from the 1930's, if interested see any modern book on astronomy or the Wikipedia article on the Universe.]

PAPER 42
ENERGY — MIND AND MATTER

THE FOUNDATION of the universe is material in the sense that energy is the basis of all existence, and pure energy is controlled by the Universal Father. Energy is the one thing which stands as an everlasting monument demonstrating and proving the existence and presence of the Universal Absolute. This vast stream of energy proceeding from the Paradise Presences has never lapsed, never failed; there has never been a break in the infinite upholding.

The manipulation of universe energy is ever in accordance with the personal will and the all-wise mandates of the Universal Father. This personal control of manifested power and circulating energy is modified by the co-ordinate acts and decisions of the Eternal Son, as well as by the united purposes of the Son and the Father executed by the Conjoint Actor. These divine beings act personally and as individuals; they also function in the persons and powers of an almost unlimited number of subordinates, each variously expressive of the eternal and divine purpose in the universe of universes. But these functional and provisional modifications or transmutations of divine power in no way lessen the truth of the statement that all force-energy is under the ultimate control of a personal God resident at the center of all things.

1. PARADISE FORCES AND ENERGIES

The foundation of the universe is material, but the essence of life is spirit. The Father of spirits is also the ancestor of universes; the eternal Father of the Original Son is also the eternity-source of the original pattern, the Isle of Paradise.

Matter — energy — for they are but diverse manifestations of the same cosmic reality, as a universe phenomenon is inherent in the Universal Father. "In him all things consist." Matter may appear to manifest inherent energy and to exhibit self-contained powers, but the lines of gravity involved in the energies concerned in all these physical phenomena are derived from, and are dependent on, Paradise. The ultimaton, the first measurable form of energy, has Paradise as its originator.

There is innate in matter and present in universal space a form of energy not known on Urantia. When this discovery is finally made, then will physicists feel that they have solved, almost at least, the mystery of matter. And so will they have approached one step nearer the Creator; so will they have mastered one more phase of the divine technique; but in no sense will they have found God, neither will they have established the existence of matter or the operation of natural laws apart from the cosmic technique of Paradise and the motivating purpose of the Universal Father.

Subsequent to even still greater progress and further discoveries, after Urantia has advanced immeasurably in comparison with present knowledge, though you should gain control of the energy revolutions of the electrical units of matter to the extent of modifying their physical manifestations — even after all such possible progress, forever will scientists be powerless to add to matter that which we call life.

The creation of energy and the bestowal of life are the prerogatives of the Universal Father and his associate Creator personalities. The river of energy and life is a continuous outpouring from the Deities, the universal and united stream of Paradise force going forth to all space. This divine energy pervades all creation. The force organizers initiate those changes and institute those modifications of space-force which eventuate in energy; the power directors transmute energy into matter; thus the material worlds are born. The Life Carriers initiate those processes in dead matter which we call life, material life. The Morontia Power Supervisors likewise perform throughout the transition realms between the material and the spiritual worlds. The higher spirit Creators inaugurate similar processes in divine forms of energy, and there ensue the higher spirit forms of intelligent life.

Energy proceeds from Paradise, fashioned after the divine order. Energy — pure energy — partakes of the nature of the divine organization; it is fashioned after the similitude of the three Gods embraced in one, as they function at the headquarters of the universe of universes. And all force is circuited in Paradise, comes from the Paradise Presences and returns thereto, and is in essence a manifestation of the uncaused Cause — the Universal Father; and without the Father would not anything exist that does exist.

Force derived from self-existent Deity is in itself ever existent. Force-energy is imperishable, indestructible; these manifestations of the Infinite may be subject to unlimited transmutation, endless transformation, and eternal metamorphosis; but in no sense or degree, not even to the slightest imaginable extent, could they or ever shall they suffer extinction. But energy, though springing from the Infinite, is not infinitely manifest; there are outer limits to the presently conceived master universe.

Energy is eternal but not infinite; it ever responds to the all-embracing grasp of Infinity. Forever force and energy go on; having gone out from Paradise, they must return thereto, even if age upon age be required for the completion of the ordained circuit. That which is of Paradise Deity origin can have only a Paradise destination or a Deity destiny.

And all this confirms our belief in a circular, somewhat limited, but orderly and far-flung universe of universes. If this were not true, then evidence of energy depletion at some point would sooner or later appear. All laws, organizations, administration, and the testimony of universe explorers — everything points to the existence of an infinite God but, as yet, a finite universe of universes, a circularity of endless existence, well-nigh limitless but, nevertheless, finite in contrast with infinity.

2. UNIVERSAL NONSPIRITUAL ENERGY SYSTEMS (PHYSICAL ENERGIES)

It is indeed difficult to find suitable words in the English language whereby to designate and wherewith to describe the various levels of force and energy — physical, mindal, or spiritual. These narratives cannot altogether follow your accepted definitions of force, energy, and power. There is such paucity of language that we must use these terms in multiple meanings. In this paper, for example, the word *energy* is used to denote all phases and forms of phenomenal motion, action, and potential, while *force* is applied to the pre-gravity, and *power* to the post-gravity, stages of energy.

I will, however, endeavor to lessen conceptual confusion by suggesting the advisability of adopting the following classification for cosmic force, emergent energy, and universe power — physical energy:

1. *Space potency.* This is the unquestioned free space presence of the Unqualified Absolute. The extension of this concept connotes the universe force-space potential inherent in the functional totality of the Unqualified Absolute, while the intension of this concept implies the totality of cosmic reality — universes — which emanated eternity-wise from the never-beginning, never-ending, never-moving, never-changing Isle of Paradise.

The phenomena indigenous to the nether side of Paradise probably embrace three zones of absolute force presence and performance: the fulcral zone of the Unqualified Absolute, the zone of the Isle of Paradise itself, and the intervening zone of certain unidentified equalizing and compensating agencies or functions. These triconcentric zones are the centrum of the Paradise cycle of cosmic reality.

Space potency is a pre-reality; it is the domain of the Unqualified Absolute and is responsive only to the personal grasp of the Universal Father, notwithstanding that it is seemingly modifiable by the presence of the Primary Master Force Organizers.

On Uversa, space potency is spoken of as ABSOLUTA.

2. *Primordial force.* This represents the first basic change in space potency and may be one of the nether Paradise functions of the Unqualified

Absolute. We know that the space presence going out from nether Paradise is modified in some manner from that which is incoming. But regardless of any such possible relationships, the openly recognized transmutation of space potency into primordial force is the primary differentiating function of the tension-presence of the living Paradise force organizers.

Passive and potential force becomes active and primordial in response to the resistance afforded by the space presence of the Primary Eventuated Master Force Organizers. Force is now emerging from the exclusive domain of the Unqualified Absolute into the realms of multiple response — response to certain primal motions initiated by the God of Action and thereupon to certain compensating motions emanating from the Universal Absolute. Primordial force is seemingly reactive to transcendental causation in proportion to absoluteness.

Primordial force is sometimes spoken of as *pure energy*; on Uversa we refer to it as SEGREGATA.

3. *Emergent energies*. The passive presence of the primary force organizers is sufficient to transform space potency into primordial force, and it is upon such an activated space field that these same force organizers begin their initial and active operations. Primordial force is destined to pass through two distinct phases of transmutation in the realms of energy manifestation before appearing as universe power. These two levels of emerging energy are:

a. *Puissant energy*. This is the powerful-directional, mass-movemented, mighty-tensioned, and forcible-reacting energy — gigantic energy systems set in motion by the activities of the primary force organizers. This primary or puissant energy is not at first definitely responsive to the Paradise-gravity pull though probably yielding an aggregate-mass or space-directional response to the collective group of absolute influences operative from the nether side of Paradise. When energy emerges to the level of initial response to the circular and absolute-gravity grasp of Paradise, the primary force organizers give way to the functioning of their secondary associates.

b. *Gravity energy*. The now-appearing gravity-responding energy carries the potential of universe power and becomes the active ancestor of all universe matter. This secondary or gravity energy is the product of the energy elaboration resulting from the pressure-presence and the tension-trends set up by the Associate Transcendental Master Force Organizers. In response to the work of these force manipulators, space-energy rapidly passes from the puissant to the gravity stage, thus becoming directly responsive to the circular grasp of Paradise (absolute) gravity while disclosing a certain potential for sensitivity to the linear-gravity pull inherent in the soon appearing material mass of the electronic and the post-electronic stages of energy and matter. Upon the appearance of gravity response, the Associate Master Force Organizers may retire from the energy cyclones of space provided the Universe Power Directors are assignable to that field of action.

We are quite uncertain regarding the exact causes of the early stages of force evolution, but we recognize the intelligent action of the Ultimate in both levels of emergent-energy manifestation. Puissant and gravity energies, when regarded collectively, are spoken of on Uversa as ULTIMATA.

4. *Universe power*. Space-force has been changed into space-energy and thence into the energy of gravity control. Thus has physical energy been ripened to that point where it can be directed into channels of power and made to serve the manifold purposes of the universe Creators. This work is carried on by the versatile directors, centers, and controllers of physical energy in the grand universe — the organized and inhabited creations. These Universe Power Directors assume the more or less complete control of twenty-one of the thirty phases of energy constituting the present energy system of the seven super-universes. This domain of power-energy-matter is the realm of the intelligent activities of the Sevenfold, functioning under the time-space over-control of the Supreme.

On Uversa we refer to the realm of universe power as GRAVITA.

5. *Havona energy*. In concept this narrative has been moving Paradise-ward as transmuting space-force has been followed, level by level, to the working level of the energy-power of the universes of time and space. Continuing Paradiseward, there is next encountered a pre-existent phase of energy which is characteristic of the central universe. Here the evolutionary cycle seems to turn back upon itself; energy-power now seems to begin to

swing back towards force, but force of a nature very unlike that of space potency and primordial force. Havona energy systems are not dual; they are triune. This is the existential energy domain of the Conjoint Actor, functioning in behalf of the Paradise Trinity.

On Uversa these energies of Havona are known as TRIATA.

6. *Transcendental energy*. This energy system operates on and from the upper level of Paradise and only in connection with the absonite peoples. On Uversa it is denominated TRANOSTA.

7. *Monota*. Energy is close of kin to divinity when it is Paradise energy. We incline to the belief that monota is the living, non-spirit energy of Paradise — an eternity counterpart of the living, spirit energy of the Original Son — hence the nonspiritual energy system of the Universal Father.

We cannot differentiate the *nature* of Paradise spirit and Paradise monota; they are apparently alike. They have different names, but you can hardly be told very much about a reality whose spiritual and whose nonspiritual manifestations are distinguishable only by *name*.

We know that finite creatures can attain the worship experience of the Universal Father through the ministry of God the Sevenfold and the Thought Adjusters, but we doubt that any sub-absolute personality, even power directors, can comprehend the energy infinity of the First Great Source and Center. One thing is certain: If the power directors are conversant with the technique of the metamorphosis of space-force, they do not reveal the secret to the rest of us. It is my opinion that they do not fully comprehend the function of the force organizers.

These power directors themselves are energy catalyzers; that is, they cause energy to segment, organize, or assemble in unit formation by their presence. And all this implies that there must be something inherent in energy which causes it thus to function in the presence of these power entities. The Nebadon Melchizedeks long since denominated the phenomenon of the transmutation of cosmic force into universe power as one of the seven "infinities of divinity." And that is as far as you will advance on this point during your local universe ascension.

Notwithstanding our inability fully to comprehend the origin, nature, and transmutations of cosmic force, we are fully conversant with all phases of emergent-energy behavior from the times of its direct and unmistakable response to the action of Paradise gravity — about the time of the beginning of the function of the super-universe power directors.

3. ENERGY AND MATTER TRANSMUTATIONS

The power centers and their associates are much concerned in the work of transmuting the ultimaton into the circuits and revolutions of the electron. These unique beings control and compound power by their skillful manipulation of the basic units of materialized energy, the ultimatums. They are masters of energy as it circulates in this primitive state. In liaison with the physical controllers they are able to effectively control and direct energy even after it has transmuted to the electrical level, the so-called electronic stage. But their range of action is enormously curtailed when electronically organized energy swings into the whirls of the atomic systems. Upon such materialization, these energies fall under the complete grasp of the drawing power of linear gravity.

Gravity acts positively on the power lanes and energy channels of the power centers and the physical controllers, but these beings have only a negative relation to gravity — the exercise of their antigravity endowments.

Throughout all organized space there are gravity-responding energy currents, power circuits, and ultimatonic activities, as well as organizing electronic energies. The blazing suns can transform matter into various forms of energy, but the dark worlds and all outer space can slow down electronic and ultimatonic activity to the point of converting these energies into the matter of the realms.

Throughout all of this never-ending metamorphosis of energy and matter we must reckon with the influence of gravity pressure and with the antigravity behavior of the ultimatonic energies. Temperature, energy currents, distance, and the presence of the living force organizers and the power directors also have a bearing on all transmutation phenomena of energy and matter. The relative integrity of matter is assured by the fact that energy can be absorbed or released only in those exact amounts which Urantia scientists have designated quanta. This wise provision in the material realms serves to maintain the universes as going concerns.

The quantity of energy taken in or given out when electronic or other positions are shifted is always a "quantum".

4. UNIVERSAL NONSPIRITUAL ENERGY SYSTEMS (MATERIAL MIND SYSTEMS)

The endless sweep of relative cosmic reality from the absoluteness of Paradise monota to the absoluteness of space potency, is suggestive of certain evolutions of relationship in the nonspiritual realities of the First Source and Center — those realities which are concealed in space potency, revealed in monota, and provisionally disclosed on intervening cosmic levels. This eternal cycle of energy, being circuited in the Father of universes, is absolute and, being absolute, is expansile in neither fact nor value; nevertheless the Primal Father is even now — as always — self-realizing of an ever-expanding arena of time-space, and of time-space-transcended, meanings, an arena of changing relationships wherein energy-matter is being progressively subjected to the over-control of living and divine spirit through the experiential striving of living and personal mind.

The universal nonspiritual energies are reassociated in the living systems of non-Creator minds on various levels, certain of which may be depicted as follows:

1. *Preadjutant-spirit minds*. This level of mind is non-experiencing and on the inhabited worlds is ministered by the Master Physical Controllers. This is mechanical mind, the non-teachable intellect of the most primitive forms of material life, but the non-teachable mind functions on many levels beside that of primitive planetary life.

2. *Adjutant-spirit minds*. This is the ministry of a local universe Mother Spirit functioning through her seven adjutant mind-spirits on the teachable (non-mechanical) level of material mind. On this level material mind is experiencing: as subhuman (animal) intellect in the first five adjutants; as

human (moral) intellect in the seven adjutants; as superhuman (midwayer) intellect in the last two adjutants.

3. *Evolving morontia minds* — the expanding consciousness of evolving personalities in the local universe ascending careers. This is the bestowal of the local universe Mother Spirit in liaison with the Creator Son. This mind level connotes the organization of the morontia type of life vehicle, a synthesis of the material and the spiritual which is effected by the Morontia Power Supervisors of a local universe. Morontia mind functions differentially in response to the 570 levels of morontia life, disclosing increasing associative capacity with the cosmic mind on the higher levels of attainment. This is the evolutionary course of mortal creatures, but mind of a nonmorontia order is also bestowed by a Universe Son and a Universe Spirit upon the nonmorontia children of the local creations.

The cosmic mind. This is the sevenfold diversified mind of time and space, one phase of which is ministered by each of the Seven Master Spirits to one of the seven super-universes. The cosmic mind encompasses all finite-mind levels and co-ordinates experientially with the evolutionary-deity levels of the Supreme Mind and transcendentally with the existential levels of absolute mind — the direct circuits of the Conjoint Actor.

On Paradise, mind is absolute; in Havona, absonite; in Orvonton, finite. Mind always connotes the presence-activity of living ministry plus varied energy systems, and this is true of all levels and of all kinds of mind. But beyond the cosmic mind it becomes increasingly difficult to portray the relationships of mind to nonspiritual energy. Havona mind is sub-absolute but super-evolutionary; being existential-experiential, it is nearer the absonite than any other concept revealed to you. Paradise mind is beyond human understanding; it is existential, non-spatial, and non-temporal. Nevertheless, all of these levels of mind are overshadowed by the universal presence of the Conjoint Actor — by the mind-gravity grasp of the God of mind on Paradise.

5. UNIVERSE MECHANISMS

In the evaluation and recognition of mind it should be remembered that the universe is neither mechanical nor magical; it is a creation of mind and a mechanism of law. But while in practical application the laws of nature operate in what seems to be the dual realms of the physical and the spiritual, in reality they are one. The First Source and Center is the primal cause of all materialization and at the same time the first and final Father of all spirits. The Paradise Father appears personally in the extra-Havona universes only as pure energy and pure spirit — as the Thought Adjusters and other similar fragmentations.

Mechanisms do not absolutely dominate the total creation; the universe of universes *in toto* is mind planned, mind made, and mind administered. But the divine mechanism of the universe of universes is altogether too perfect for the scientific methods of the finite mind of man to discern even a trace of the dominance of the infinite mind. For this creating, controlling, and upholding mind is neither material mind nor creature mind; it is spirit-mind functioning on and from creator levels of divine reality.

The ability to discern and discover mind in universe mechanisms depends entirely on the ability, scope, and capacity of the investigating mind engaged in such a task of observation. Time-space minds, organized out of the energies of time and space, are subject to the mechanisms of time and space.

Motion and universe gravitation are twin facets of the impersonal time-space mechanism of the universe of universes. The levels of gravity response for spirit, mind, and matter are quite independent of time, but only true spirit levels of reality are independent of space (non-spatial). The higher mind levels of the universe — the spirit-mind levels — may also be non-spatial, but the levels of material mind, such as human mind, are responsive to the interactions of universe gravitation, losing this response only in proportion to spirit identification. Spirit-reality levels are recognized by their spirit content, and spirituality in time and space is measured inversely to the linear-gravity response.

Linear-gravity response is a quantitative measure of non-spirit energy. All mass — organized energy — is subject to this grasp except as motion and mind act upon it. Linear gravity is the short-range cohesive force of the macrocosmos somewhat as the forces of intra-atomic cohesion are the short-range forces of the microcosmos. Physical materialized energy, organized as so-called matter, cannot traverse space without affecting linear-gravity response. Although such gravity response is directly proportional to mass, it is so modified by intervening space that the final result is no more than roughly approximated when expressed as inversely according to the square of the distance. Space eventually conquers linear gravitation because of the presence therein of the antigravity influences of numerous super-material forces which operate to neutralize gravity action and all responses thereto.

Extremely complex and highly automatic-appearing cosmic mechanisms always tend to conceal the presence of the originative or creative indwelling mind from any and all intelligences very far below the universe levels of the nature and capacity of the mechanism itself. Therefore is it inevitable that the higher universe mechanisms must appear to be mindless to the lower orders of creatures. The only possible exception to such a conclusion would be the implication of mindedness in the amazing phenomenon of an *apparently self-maintaining universe* — but that is a matter of philosophy rather than one of actual experience.

Since mind co-ordinates the universe, fixity of mechanisms is nonexistent. The phenomenon of progressive evolution associated with cosmic self-maintenance is universal. The evolutionary capacity of the universe is inexhaustible in the infinity of spontaneity. Progress towards harmonious unity, a growing experiential synthesis superimposed on an ever-increasing complexity of relationships, could be effected only by a purposive and dominant mind.

The higher the universe mind associated with any universe phenomenon, the more difficult it is for the lower types of mind to discover it. And since the mind of the universe mechanism is creative spirit-mind (even the mindedness of the Infinite), it can never be discovered or discerned by the lower-level minds of the universe, much less by the lowest mind of all, the human. The evolving animal mind, while naturally God-seeking, is not alone and of itself inherently God-knowing.

6. PATTERN AND FORM — MIND DOMINANCE

The evolution of mechanisms implies and indicates the concealed presence and dominance of creative mind. The ability of the mortal intellect to conceive, design, and create automatic mechanisms demonstrates the superior, creative, and purposive qualities of man's mind as the dominant influence on the planet. Mind always reaches out towards:

1. Creation of material mechanisms.
2. Discovery of hidden mysteries.
3. Exploration of remote situations.
4. Formulation of mental systems.
5. Attainment of wisdom goals.
6. Achievement of spirit levels.
7. The accomplishment of divine destinies — supreme, ultimate, and absolute.

Mind is always creative. The mind endowment of an individual animal, mortal, morontian, spirit ascender, or finality attainer is always competent to produce a suitable and serviceable body for the living creature identity. But the presence phenomenon of a personality or the pattern of an identity, as such, is not a manifestation of energy, either physical, mindal, or spiritual. The personality form is the *pattern* aspect of a living being; it connotes the *arrangement* of energies, and this, plus life and motion, is the *mechanism* of creature existence.

Even spirit beings have form, and these spirit forms (patterns) are real. Even the highest type of spirit personalities have forms — personality presences in every sense analogous to Urantia mortal bodies. Nearly all beings encountered in the seven super-universes are possessed of forms. But there are a few exceptions to this general rule: Thought Adjusters appear to be without form until after fusion with the surviving souls of their mortal associates. Solitary Messengers, Inspired Trinity Spirits, Personal Aids of the Infinite Spirit, Gravity Messengers, Transcendental Recorders, and certain others are also without discoverable form. But these are typical of the exceptional few; the great majority have bona fide personality forms, forms which are individually characteristic, and which are recognizable and personally distinguishable.

The liaison of the cosmic mind and the ministry of the adjutant mind-spirits evolve a suitable physical tabernacle for the evolving human being. Likewise does the morontia mind individualize the morontia form for all mortal survivors. As the mortal body is personal and characteristic for every human being, so will the morontia form be highly individual and adequately characteristic of the creative mind which dominates it. No two morontia forms are any more alike than any two human bodies. The Morontia Power Supervisors sponsor, and the attending seraphim provide, the undifferenti-ated morontia material wherewith the morontia life can begin to work. And after the morontia life it will be found that spirit forms are equally diverse, personal, and characteristic of their respective spirit-mind indwellers.

On a material world you think of a body as having a spirit, but we regard the spirit as having a body. The material eyes are truly the windows of the spirit-born soul. The spirit is the architect, the mind is the builder, the body is the material building.

Physical, spiritual, and mindal energies, as such and in their pure states, do not fully interact as actuals of the phenomenal universes. On Paradise the three energies are co-ordinate, in Havona co-ordinated, while in the universe levels of finite activities there must be encountered all ranges of material, mindal, and spiritual dominance. In non-personal situations of time and space, physical energy seems to predominate, but it also appears that the more nearly spirit-mind function approaches divinity of purpose and supremacy of action, the more nearly does the spirit phase become domi-nant; that on the ultimate level spirit-mind may become all but completely dominant. On the absolute level spirit certainly is dominant. And from there on out through the realms of time and space, wherever a divine spirit reality is present, whenever a real spirit-mind is functioning, there always tends to be produced a material or physical counterpart of that spirit reality.

The spirit is the creative reality; the physical counterpart is the time-space reflection of the spirit reality, the physical repercussion of the creative action of spirit-mind.

Mind universally dominates matter, even as it is in turn responsive to the ultimate over-control of spirit. And with mortal man, only that mind which freely submits itself to the spirit direction can hope to survive the mortal time-space existence as an immortal child of the eternal spirit world of the Supreme, the Ultimate, and the Absolute: the Infinite.

[Presented by a Mighty Messenger on duty in Nebadon and by the request of Gabriel.]

PAPER 43
THE CONSTELLATIONS

URANTIA IS COMMONLY REFERRED to as 606 of Satania in Norlatiadek of Nebadon, meaning the six-hundred-sixth inhabited world in the local system of Satania, situated in the constellation of Norlatiadek, one of the constellations of the Milky Way galaxy. Constellations are the primary divisions of a galaxy. Their rulers link the local systems of inhabited worlds to the galactic government, through the minor and major sectors, up to the central administration of the local universe on Salvington, and by reflectivity to the super-administration of the Ancients of Days on Uversa.

The government of your constellation is situated in a cluster of 771 architectural spheres, the centermost and largest of which is Edentia, the seat of the administration of the Constellation Fathers, the Most Highs of Norlatiadek. Edentia itself is approximately one hundred times as large as your world. The seventy major spheres surrounding Edentia are about ten times the size of Urantia, while the ten satellites which revolve around each of these seventy worlds are about the size of Urantia. These 771 architectural spheres are quite comparable in size to those at the capitols of other constellations.

Edentia time reckoning and distance measurement are those of Salvington, and like the spheres of the universe capital, the constellation headquarters worlds are fully supplied with all orders of celestial intelligences. In general, these personalities are not very different from those described in connection with the universe administration.

The supervisor seraphim, the third order of local universe angels, are assigned to the service of the constellations. They make their headquarters on the capital spheres and minister extensively to the encircling morontia-training worlds. In Norlatiadek the seventy major spheres, together with the seven hundred minor satellites, are inhabited by the univitatia, the permanent citizens of the constellation. All these architectural worlds are fully administered by the various groups of native life, for the greater part unrevealed but including the efficient spironga and the beautiful spornagia. Being the mid-point in the morontia-training regime, as you might suspect, the morontia life of the constellations is both typical and ideal.

1. THE CONSTELLATION HEADQUARTERS

Edentia abounds in fascinating highlands, extensive elevations of physical matter crowned with morontia life and overspread with spiritual glory, but there are no rugged mountain ranges such as appear on Urantia. There are tens of thousands of sparkling lakes and thousands upon thousands of interconnecting streams, but there are no great oceans nor torrential rivers. Only the highlands are devoid of these surface streams.

The water of Edentia and similar architectural spheres is no different from the water of the evolutionary planets. The water systems of such spheres are both surface and subterranean, and the moisture is in constant circulation. Edentia can be circumnavigated via these various water routes, though the chief channel of transportation is the atmosphere. Spirit beings would naturally travel above the surface of the sphere, while the morontia and material beings make use of material and semi-material means to negotiate atmospheric passage.

Edentia and its associated worlds have a true atmosphere, the usual three-gas mixture which is characteristic of such architectural creations, and which embodies the two elements of Urantian atmosphere plus that morontia gas suitable for the respiration of morontia creatures. But while this atmosphere is both material and morontial, there are no storms or hurricanes; neither is there summer nor winter. This absence of atmospheric disturbances and of seasonal variation makes it possible to embellish all outdoors on these especially created worlds.

The Edentia highlands are magnificent physical features, and their beauty is enhanced by the endless profusion of life which abounds throughout their length and breadth. Excepting a few rather isolated structures, these highlands contain no work of creature hands. Material and morontial ornamentations are limited to the dwelling areas. The lesser elevations are the sites of special residences and are beautifully embellished with both biologic and morontia art.

Situated on the summit of the seventh highland range are the resurrection halls of Edentia, wherein awaken the ascending mortals of the secondary modified order of ascension. These chambers of creature reassembly are under the supervision of the Melchizedeks. The first of the receiving spheres of Edentia (like the planet Melchizedek near Salvington) also has special resurrection halls, wherein the mortals of the modified orders of ascension are reassembled.

The Melchizedeks also maintain two special colleges on Edentia. One, the emergency school, is devoted to the study of problems growing out of the Satania rebellion. The other, the bestowal school, is dedicated to the mastery of the new problems arising out of the fact that Michael made his final bestowal on one of the worlds of Norlatiadek. This latter college was established almost four thousand years ago, immediately after the announcement by Michael that Urantia had been selected as the world for his final bestowal.

The sea of glass, the receiving area of Edentia, is near the administrative center and is encircled by the headquarters amphitheater. Surrounding this area are the governing centers for the seventy divisions of constellation affairs. One half of Edentia is divided into seventy triangular sections, whose boundaries converge at the headquarters buildings of their respective sectors. The remainder of this sphere is one vast natural park, the gardens of God.

During your periodic visits to Edentia, though the entire planet is open to your inspection, most of your time will be spent in that administrative triangle whose number corresponds to that of your current residential world. You will always be welcome as an observer in the legislative assemblies.

The morontia area assigned to ascending mortals resident on Edentia is located in the mid-zone of the thirty-fifth triangle adjoining the headquarters of the finaliters, situated in the thirty-sixth triangle. The general headquarters of the univitatia occupies an enormous area in the mid-region of the thirty-fourth triangle immediately adjoining the residential reservation of the morontia citizens. From these arrangements it may be seen that provision is made for the accommodation of at least seventy major divisions of celestial life, and also that each of these seventy triangular areas is correlated with some one of the seventy major spheres of morontia training.

The Edentia sea of glass is one enormous circular crystal about one hundred miles in circumference and about thirty miles in depth. This magnificent crystal serves as the receiving field for all transport seraphim and other beings arriving from points outside the sphere; such a sea of glass greatly facilitates the landing of transport seraphim.

A crystal field on this order is found on almost all architectural worlds; and it serves many purposes aside from its decorative value, being utilized for portraying super-universe reflectivity to assembled groups and as a factor in the energy-transformation technique for modifying the currents of space and for adapting other incoming physical-energy streams.

2. THE CONSTELLATION GOVERNMENT

The constellations are one of the autonomous units of a local universe, each constellation being administered according to its own legislative enactments. When the courts of Nebadon sit in judgment on universe affairs, all internal matters are adjudicated in accordance with the laws prevailing in the constellation concerned. These judicial decrees of Salvington, or any of the galactic or sector decrees, together with the legislative enactments of the constellations, are executed by the administrators of the local systems.

Constellations thus function as the lowest legislative or lawmaking units, while the local systems serve as the executive or enforcement units. The

Salvington government is the supreme judicial and co-ordinating authority and any disagreements between a constellation legislature and their galaxy can be passed up through the sectors to be ultimately heard in Salvington.

While the supreme judicial function rests with the central administration of a local universe, there are two subsidiary but major tribunals at the headquarters of each constellation, the Melchizedek council and the court of the Most High.

All judicial problems are first reviewed by the council of the Melchizedeks. Twelve of this order who have had certain requisite experience on the evolutionary planets and on the system headquarters worlds are empowered to review evidence, digest pleas, and formulate provisional verdicts, which are passed on to the court of the Most High, the reigning Constellation Father. The mortal division of this latter tribunal consists of seven judges, all of whom are ascendant mortals. The higher you ascend in the universe, the more certain you are to be judged by those of your own kind.

The constellation legislative body is divided into three groups. The legislative program of a constellation originates in the lower house of ascenders, a group presided over by a finaliter and consisting of one thousand representative mortals. Each system nominates ten members to sit in this deliberative assembly. On Edentia this body is not fully recruited at the present time.

The mid-chamber of legislators is composed of the seraphic hosts and their associates, other children of the local universe Mother Spirit. This group numbers one hundred and is nominated by the supervising personalities who preside over the various activities of such beings as they function within the constellation.

The advisory or highest body of constellation legislators consists of the house of peers — the house of the divine Sons. This corps is chosen by the Most High Fathers and numbers ten. Only Sons of special experience may serve in this upper house. This is the fact-finding and timesaving group which very effectively serves both of the lower divisions of the legislative assembly.

The combined council of legislators consists of three members from each of these separate branches of the constellation deliberative assembly and is presided over by the reigning junior Most High. This group sanctions the final form of all enactments and authorizes their promulgation by the broadcasters. The approval of this supreme commission renders legislative enactments the law of the realm; their acts are final. The legislative pronouncements of Edentia constitute the fundamental law of all Norlatiadek.

3. THE MOST HIGHS OF NORLATIADEK

The rulers of the constellations are of the Tertiary Vorondadek order of local universe sonship. When commissioned to active duty in the universe as constellation rulers or otherwise, these Sons are known as the *Most Highs* since they embody the highest administrative wisdom, coupled with the most farseeing and intelligent loyalty, of all the orders of the Local Universe Sons of God. Their personal integrity and their group loyalty have never been questioned; no disaffection of the Vorondadek Sons has ever occurred in Nebadon.

At least three Tertiary Vorondadek Sons are commissioned by Gabriel as the Most Highs of each of the Nebadon constellations. The presiding member of this trio is known as the *Constellation Father* and his two associates as the *senior Most High* and the *junior Most High*. A Constellation Father reigns for ten thousand standard years (about 50,000 Urantia years), having previously served as junior associate and as senior associate for equal periods.

The Psalmist knew that Edentia was ruled by three Constellation Fathers and accordingly spoke of their abode in the plural: "There is a river, the streams whereof shall make glad the city of God, the most holy place of the tabernacles of the Most Highs."

Down through the ages there has been great confusion on Urantia regarding the various universe rulers. Many later teachers confused their vague and indefinite tribal deities with the Most High Fathers. Still later, the Hebrews merged all of these celestial rulers into a composite Deity. One teacher understood that the Most Highs were not the Supreme Rulers, for he said, "He who dwells in the secret place of the Most High shall abide under the shadow of the Almighty." In the Urantia records it is very difficult at times to know exactly who is referred to by the term "Most High." But Daniel fully understood these matters. He said, "The Most High rules in the kingdom of men and gives it to whomsoever he will."

The Constellation Fathers are little occupied with the individuals of an inhabited planet, but they are closely associated with those legislative and lawmaking functions of the constellations which so greatly concern every mortal *race* and national *group* of the inhabited worlds.

Although the constellation regime stands between you and the universe administration, as individuals you would ordinarily be little concerned with the constellation government. Your great interest would normally center in the local system, Satania; but temporarily, Urantia is closely related to the constellation rulers because of certain system and planetary conditions growing out of the Lucifer rebellion.

The Edentia Most Highs seized certain phases of planetary authority on the rebellious worlds at the time of the Lucifer secession. They have continued to exercise this power, and the Ancients of Days long since confirmed this assumption of control over these wayward worlds. They will no doubt continue to exercise this assumed jurisdiction as long as Lucifer lives. Much of this authority would ordinarily, in a loyal system, be invested in the System Sovereign.

But there is still another way in which Urantia became peculiarly related to the Most Highs. When Michael, the Creator Son, was on his terminal bestowal mission, since the successor of Lucifer was not in full authority in the local system, all Urantia affairs which concerned the Michael bestowal were immediately supervised by the Most Highs of Norlatiadek.

4. MOUNT ASSEMBLY — THE FAITHFUL OF DAYS

The most holy mount of assembly is the dwelling place of the Faithful of Days, the representative of the Paradise Trinity who functions on Edentia.

This Faithful of Days is a Trinity Son of Paradise and has been present on Edentia as the personal representative of Immanuel since the creation of the headquarters world. Ever the Faithful of Days stands at the right hand of the Constellation Fathers to counsel them, but never does he proffer advice unless it is asked for. The high Sons of Paradise never participate in the conduct of the affairs of a local universe except upon the petition of the acting rulers of such domains. But all that a Union of Days is to a Creator Son, a Faithful of Days is to the Most Highs of a constellation.

The residence of the Edentia Faithful of Days is the constellation center of the Paradise system of extra-universe communication and intelligence. These Trinity Sons, with their staffs of Havona and Paradise personalities, in liaison with the supervising Recents of Days, are in direct and constant communication with their order throughout all the universes, even to Havona and Paradise.

The most holy mount is exquisitely beautiful and marvelously appointed, but the actual residence of the Paradise Son is modest in comparison with the central abode of the Most Highs and the surrounding seventy structures comprising the residential unit of the Vorondadek Sons. These appointments are exclusively residential; they are entirely separate from the extensive administrative headquarters buildings wherein the affairs of the constellation are transacted.

The residence of the Faithful of Days on Edentia is located to the north of these residences of the Most Highs and is known as the "mount of Paradise assembly." On this consecrated highland the ascending mortals periodically assemble to hear this Son of Paradise tell of the long and intriguing journey of progressing mortals through the one billion perfection worlds of Havona and on to the indescribable delights of Paradise. And it is at these special gatherings on Mount Assembly that the morontia mortals become more fully acquainted with the various groups of personalities of origin in the central universe.

The traitorous Lucifer, onetime sovereign of Satania, in announcing his claims to increased jurisdiction, sought to displace all superior orders of sonship in the governmental plan of the local universe. He purposed in his heart, saying: "I will exalt my throne above the Sons of God; I will sit upon the mount of assembly in the north; I will be like the Most High."

The System Sovereigns come periodically to the Edentia conclaves which deliberate on the welfare of the constellation. After the Satania rebellion the archrebels of Jerusem were wont to come up to these Edentia councils just as they had on former occasions. And there was found no way to stop this arrogant effrontery until after the bestowal of Michael on Urantia and his subsequent assumption of unlimited sovereignty throughout all Nebadon. Never, since that day, have these instigators of sin been permitted to sit in the Edentia councils of the loyal System Sovereigns.

That the teachers of olden times knew of these things is shown by the record: "And there was a day when the Sons of God came to present themselves before the Most Highs, and Satan came also and presented himself among them." And this is a statement of fact regardless of the connection in which it chances to appear.

Since the triumph of Christ, all Norlatiadek is being cleansed of sin and rebels. Sometime before Michael's death in the flesh the fallen Lucifer's associate, Satan, sought to attend such an Edentia conclave, but the solidification of sentiment against the archrebels had reached the point where the doors of sympathy were so well-nigh universally closed that there could be found no standing ground for the Satania adversaries. When there exists no open door for the reception of evil, there exists no opportunity for the entertainment of sin. The doors of the hearts of all Edentia closed against Satan; he was unanimously rejected by the assembled System Sovereigns, and it was at this time that the Son of Man "beheld Satan fall as lightning from heaven."

Since the Lucifer rebellion a new structure has been provided near the residence of the Faithful of Days. This temporary edifice is the headquarters of the Most High liaison, who functions in close touch with the Paradise Son as adviser to the constellation government in all matters respecting the policy and attitude of the order of Days toward sin and rebellion.

5. THE EDENTIA FATHERS SINCE THE LUCIFER REBELLION

The rotation of the Most Highs on Edentia was suspended at the time of the Lucifer rebellion. We now have the same rulers who were on duty at that time. We infer that no change in these rulers will be made until Lucifer and his associates are finally disposed of.

The present government of the constellation, however, has been expanded to include twelve Sons of the Tertiary Vorondadek order. These twelve are as follows:

1. The Constellation Father. The present Most High ruler of Norlatiadek is number 617,318 of the Vorondadek series of Nebadon. He saw service in many constellations throughout our local universe before taking up his Edentia responsibilities.
2. The senior Most High associate.
3. The junior Most High associate.
4. The Most High adviser, the personal representative of Michael since his attainment of the status of a Master Son.
5. The Most High executive, the personal representative of Gabriel stationed on Edentia ever since the Lucifer rebellion.
6. The Most High chief of planetary observers, the director of the Vorondadek observers stationed on the isolated worlds of Satania.
7. The Most High referee, the Vorondadek Son intrusted with the duty of adjusting all difficulties consequential to rebellion within the constellation.
8. The Most High emergency administrator, the Vorondadek Son charged with the task of adapting the emergency enactments of the Norlatiadek legislature to the rebellion-isolated worlds of Satania.
9. The Most High mediator, the Vorondadek Son assigned to harmonize the special bestowal adjustments on Urantia with the routine administration of the constellation. The presence of certain archangel activities and numerous other irregular ministrations on Urantia, together with the special activities of the Brilliant Evening Stars on Jerusem, necessitates the functioning of this Son.
10. The Most High judge-advocate, the head of the emergency tribunal devoted to the adjustment of the special problems of Norlatiadek growing out of the confusion consequent upon the Satania rebellion.

11. The Most High liaison, the Vorondadek Son attached to the Edentia rulers but commissioned as a special counselor with the Faithful of Days regarding the best course to pursue in the management of problems pertaining to rebellion and creature disloyalty.
12. The Most High director, the president of the emergency council of Edentia. All personalities assigned to Norlatiadek because of the Satania upheaval constitute the emergency council, and their presiding officer is a Vorondadek Son of extraordinary experience.

And this takes no account of the numerous Vorondadeks, envoys of Nebadon constellations, and others who are also resident on Edentia.

Ever since the Lucifer rebellion the Edentia Fathers have exercised a special care over Urantia and the other isolated worlds of Satania. Long ago the prophet recognized the controlling hand of the Constellation Fathers in the affairs of nations. "When the Most High divided to the nations their inheritance, when he separated the sons of Adam, he set the bounds of the people."

Every quarantined or isolated world has a Vorondadek Son acting as an observer. He does not participate in planetary administration except when ordered by the Constellation Father to intervene in the affairs of the nations. Actually it is this Most High observer who "rules in the kingdoms of men." Urantia is one of the isolated worlds of Norlatiadek, and a Vorondadek observer has been stationed on the planet ever since the Caligastia betrayal. When Machiventa Melchizedek ministered in semi-material form on Urantia, he paid respectful homage to the Most High observer then on duty, as it is written, "And Melchizedek, king of Salem, was the priest of the Most High." Melchizedek revealed the relations of this Most High observer to Abraham when he said, "And blessed be the Most High, who has delivered your enemies into your hand."

6. THE GARDENS OF GOD

The system capitals are particularly beautified with material and mineral constructions, while the universe headquarters is more reflective of spiritual glory, but the capitals of the constellations are the acme of morontia activities and living embellishments. On the constellation headquarters worlds living embellishment is more generally utilized, and it is this preponderance of life — botanic artistry — that causes these worlds to be called "the gardens of God."

About one half of Edentia is devoted to the exquisite gardens of the Most Highs, and these gardens are among the most entrancing morontia creations of the local universe. This explains why the extraordinarily beautiful places on the inhabited worlds of Norlatiadek are so often called "the garden of Eden."

Centrally located in this magnificent garden is the worship shrine of the Most Highs. The Psalmist must have known something about these things, for he wrote: "Who shall ascend the hill of the Most Highs? Who shall stand in this holy place? He who has clean hands and a pure heart, who has not lifted up his soul to vanity nor sworn deceitfully." At this shrine the Most Highs, on every tenth day of relaxation, lead all Edentia in the worshipful contemplation of God the Supreme.

The architectural worlds enjoy ten forms of life of the material order. On Urantia there is plant and animal life, but on such a world as Edentia there are ten divisions of the material orders of life. Were you to view these ten divisions of Edentia life, you would quickly classify the first three as vegetable and the last three as animal, but you would be utterly unable to comprehend the nature of the intervening four groups of prolific and fascinating forms of life.

Even the distinctively animal life is very different from that of the evolutionary worlds, so different that it is quite impossible to portray to mortal minds the unique character and affectionate nature of these nonspeaking creatures. There are thousands upon thousands of living creatures which your imagination could not possibly picture. The whole animal creation is of an entirely different order from the gross animal species of the evolutionary planets. But all this animal life is most intelligent and exquisitely serviceable, and all the various species are surprisingly gentle and touchingly companionable. There are no carnivorous creatures on such architectural worlds; there is nothing in all Edentia to make any living being afraid.

The vegetable life is also very different from that of Urantia, consisting of both material and morontia varieties. The material growths have a characteristic green coloration, but the morontia equivalents of vegetative life have a violet or orchid tinge of varying hue and reflection. Such morontia vegetation is purely an energy growth; when eaten there is no residual portion.

Being endowed with ten divisions of physical life, not to mention the morontia variations, these architectural worlds provide tremendous possibilities for the biologic beautification of the landscape and of the material and the morontia structures. The celestial artisans direct the native spornagia in this extensive work of botanic decoration and biologic embellishment. Whereas your artists must resort to inert paint and lifeless marble to portray their concepts, the celestial artisans and the univitatia more frequently utilize living materials to represent their ideas and to capture their ideals.

If you enjoy the flowers, shrubs, and trees of Urantia, then will you feast your eyes upon the botanical beauty and the floral grandeur of the supernal gardens of Edentia. But it is beyond my powers of description to undertake to convey to the mortal mind an adequate concept of these beauties of the heavenly worlds. Truly, eye has not seen such glories as await your arrival on these worlds of the mortal-ascension adventure.

7. THE UNIVITATIA

Univitatia are the permanent citizens of Edentia and its associated worlds, all seven hundred seventy worlds surrounding the constellation headquarters being under their supervision. These children of the Creator Son and the Creative Spirit are projected on a plane of existence in between the material and the spiritual, but they are not morontia creatures. The natives of each of the seventy major spheres of Edentia possess different visible forms, and the morontia mortals have their morontia forms attuned to correspond with the ascending scale of the univitatia each time they change residence from one Edentia sphere to another as they pass successively from world number one to world number seventy.

Spiritually, the univitatia are alike; intellectually, they vary as do mortals; in form, they much resemble the morontia state of existence, and they are created to function in seventy diverse orders of personality. Each of these orders of univitatia exhibits ten major variations of intellectual activity, and each of these varying intellectual types presides over the special training and cultural schools of progressive occupational or practical socialization on some one of the ten satellites which swing around each of the major Edentia worlds.

These seven hundred minor worlds are technical spheres of practical education in the working of the entire local universe and are open to all classes of intelligent beings. These training schools of special skill and technical knowledge are not conducted exclusively for ascending mortals, although morontia students constitute by far the largest group of all those who attend these courses of training. When you are received on any one of the seventy major worlds of social culture, you are immediately given clearance for each of the ten surrounding satellites.

In the various courtesy colonies, ascending morontia mortals predominate among the reversion directors, but the univitatia represent the largest group associated with the Nebadon corps of celestial artisans. In all Orvonton no extra-Havona beings excepting the Uversa abandonters can equal the univitatia in artistic skill, social adaptability, and co-ordinating cleverness.

These citizens of the constellation are not actually members of the artisan corps, but they freely work with all groups and contribute much to making the constellation worlds the chief spheres for the realization of the magnificent artistic possibilities of transition culture. They do not function beyond the confines of the constellation headquarters worlds.

8. THE EDENTIA TRAINING WORLDS

The physical endowment of Edentia and its surrounding spheres is well-nigh perfect; they could hardly equal the spiritual grandeur of the spheres of Salvington, but they far surpass the glories of the training worlds of Jerusem.

All these Edentia spheres are energized directly by the universal space currents, and their enormous power systems, both material and morontial, are expertly supervised and distributed by the constellation centers, assisted by a competent corps of Master Physical Controllers and Morontia Power Supervisors.

The time spent on the seventy training worlds of transition morontia culture associated with the Edentia age of mortal ascension, is the most settled period in an ascending mortal's career up to the status of a finaliter; this is really the typical morontia life. While you are rekeyed each time you pass from one major cultural world to another, you retain the same morontia body, and there are no periods of personality unconsciousness.

Your sojourn on Edentia and its associated spheres will be chiefly occupied with the mastery of group ethics, the secret of pleasant and profitable interrelationship between the various universe and super-universe orders of intelligent personalities.

On the mansion worlds you completed the unification of the evolving mortal personality; on the system capital you attained Jerusem citizenship and achieved the willingness to submit the self to the disciplines of group activities and co-ordinated undertakings; but now on the constellation training worlds you are to achieve the real socialization of your evolving morontia personality. This supernal cultural acquirement consists in learning how to:

1. Live happily and work effectively with ten diverse fellow morontians, while ten such groups are associated in companies of one hundred and then federated in corps of one thousand.

2. Abide joyfully and co-operate heartily with ten univitatia, who, though similar intellectually to morontia beings, are very different in every other way. And then must you function with this group of ten as it co-ordinates with ten other families, which are in turn confederated into a corps of one thousand univitatia.

3. Achieve simultaneous adjustment to both fellow morontians and these host univitatia. Acquire the ability voluntarily and effectively to co-operate with your own order of beings in close working association with a somewhat dissimilar group of intelligent creatures.

4. While thus socially functioning with beings like and unlike yourself, achieve intellectual harmony with, and make vocational adjustment to, both groups of associates.

5. While attaining satisfactory socialization of the personality on intellectual and vocational levels, further perfect the ability to live in intimate contact with similar and slightly dissimilar beings with ever-lessening irritability and ever-diminishing resentment. The reversion directors contribute much to this latter attainment through their group-play activities.

6. Adjust all of these various socialization techniques to the furtherance of the progressive co-ordination of the Paradise-ascension career; augment universe insight by enhancing the ability to grasp the eternal goal-meanings concealed within these seemingly insignificant time-space activities.

7. And then, climax all of these procedures of multi-socialization with the concurrent enhancement of spiritual insight as it pertains to the augmentation of all phases of personal endowment through group spiritual association and morontia co-ordination. Intellectually, socially, and spiritually two moral creatures do not merely double their personal potentials of universe achievement by partnership technique; they more nearly quadruple their attainment and accomplishment possibilities.

We have portrayed Edentia socialization as an association of a morontia mortal with a univitatia family group consisting of ten intellectually dissimilar individuals concomitant with a similar association with ten fellow morontians. But on the first seven major worlds only one ascending mortal lives with ten univitatia. On the second group of seven major worlds two mortals abide with each native group of ten, and so on up until, on the last group of seven major spheres, ten morontia beings are domiciled with ten univitatia. As you learn how better to socialize with the univitatia, you will practice such improved ethics in your relations with your fellow morontia progressors.

As ascending mortals you will enjoy your sojourn on the progress worlds of Edentia, but you will not experience that personal thrill of satisfaction which characterizes your initial contact with universe affairs on the system headquarters or your farewell touch with these realities on the final worlds of the universe capital.

9. CITIZENSHIP ON EDENTIA

After graduation from world number seventy, ascending mortals take up residence on Edentia. Ascenders now, for the first time, attend the "assemblies of Paradise" and hear the story of their far-flung career as it is depicted by the Faithful of Days, the first of the Supreme Trinity-origin Personalities they have met.

This entire sojourn on the constellation training worlds, culminating in Edentia citizenship, is a period of true and heavenly bliss for the morontia progressors. Throughout your sojourn on the system worlds you were evolving from a near-animal to a morontia creature; you were more material than spiritual. On the Salvington spheres you will be evolving from a morontia being to the status of a true spirit; you will be more spiritual than material. But on Edentia, ascenders are midway between their former and their future estates, midway in their passage from evolutionary animal to ascending spirit. During your whole stay on Edentia and its worlds you are "as the angels"; you are constantly progressing but all the while maintaining a general and a typical morontia status.

This constellation sojourn of an ascending mortal is the most uniform and stabilized epoch in the entire career of morontia progression. This experience constitutes the prespirit socialization training of the ascenders. It is analogous to the prefinaliter spiritual experience of Havona and to the preabsonite training on Paradise.

Ascending mortals on Edentia are chiefly occupied with the assignments on the seventy progressive univitatia worlds. They also serve in varied capacities on Edentia itself, mainly in conjunction with the constellation program concerned with group, racial, national, and planetary welfare. The Most Highs are not so much engaged in fostering individual advancement on the inhabited worlds; they rule in the kingdoms of men rather than in the hearts of individuals.

And on that day when you are prepared to leave Edentia for Zion, the capital of your local galaxy, you will pause and look back on one of the most beautiful and most refreshing of all your epochs of training this side of Paradise. But the glory of it all augments as you ascend inward and achieve increased capacity for enlarged appreciation of divine meanings and spiritual values.

[Sponsored by Malavatia Melchizedek.]

PAPER 44
THE CELESTIAL ARTISANS

AMONG THE COURTESY colonies of the various divisional and universe headquarters worlds, may be found the unique order of composite personalities denominated the celestial artisans. These beings are the master artists and artisans of the morontia and lower spirit realms. They are the spirits and semispirits who are engaged in morontia embellishment and in spiritual beautification. Such artisans are distributed throughout the grand universe — on the headquarters worlds of the super-universes, the local universes, the major and minor sectors of a local universe, the galaxies, constellations, and systems, as well as on all spheres settled in light and life; but one of their chief realms of activity is in the constellations and especially on the seven hundred seventy worlds surrounding each headquarters sphere.

Though their work may be almost incomprehensible to the material mind, it should be understood that the morontia and spirit worlds are not without their high arts and supernal cultures.

The celestial artisans are not created as such; they are a selected and recruited corps of beings composed of certain teacher personalities native to the central universe and their volunteer pupils drawn from the ascending mortals and numerous other celestial groups. The original teaching corps of these artisans was sometime assigned by the Infinite Spirit in collaboration with the Seven Master Spirits and consisted of seven thousand Havona instructors, one thousand to each of the seven divisions of artisans. With such a nucleus to start with, there has developed through the ages this brilliant body of skillful workers in spirit and morontia affairs.

Any morontia personality or spirit entity is eligible for admission to the corps of the celestial artisans; that is, any being below the rank of inherent divine sonship. Ascending sons of God from the evolutionary spheres may, after their arrival on the morontia worlds, apply for admission to the artisan corps and, if sufficiently gifted, may choose such a career for a longer or shorter period. But no one may enlist with the celestial artisans for less than one millennium, one thousand years of super-universe time.

All celestial artisans are registered on the super-universe headquarters but are directed by morontia supervisors on the local universe capitals. They are commissioned in the following seven major divisions of activity by the central corps of morontia supervisors functioning on the headquarters world of each local universe:

1. Celestial Musicians.
2. Heavenly Reproducers.
3. Divine Builders.
4. Thought Recorders.
5. Energy Manipulators.
6. Designers and Embellishers.
7. Harmony Workers.

The original teachers of these seven groups all hailed from the perfect worlds of Havona, and Havona contains the patterns, the pattern studies, for all phases and forms of spirit artistry. While it is a gigantic task to undertake to transfer these arts of Havona to the worlds of space, the celestial artisans have improved in technique and execution from age to age. As in all other phases of the ascending career those who are most advanced in any line of endeavor are required constantly to impart their superior knowledge and skill to their less favored fellows.

You will first begin to glimpse these transplanted arts of Havona on the mansion worlds, and their beauty and your appreciation of their beauty will heighten and brighten until you stand in the spirit halls of Salvington and behold the inspiring masterpieces of the supernal artists of the spirit realms.

All these activities of the morontia and spirit worlds are real. To spirit beings the spirit world is a reality. To us the material world is the more unreal. The higher forms of spirits freely pass through ordinary matter. High spirits are reactive to nothing material excepting certain of the basic energies. To material beings the spirit world is more or less unreal; to spirit beings the material world is almost entirely unreal, being merely a shadow of the substance of spirit realities.

I cannot, with exclusive spirit vision, perceive the building in which this narrative is being translated and recorded. A Divine Counselor from Uversa who chances to stand by my side perceives still less of these purely material creations. We discern how these material structures appear to you by viewing a spirit counterpart presented to our minds by one of our attending energy transformers. This material building is not exactly real to me, a spirit being, but it is, of course, very real and very serviceable to material mortals.

There are certain types of beings who are capable of discerning the reality of the creatures of both the spirit and the material worlds. Belonging to this class are the so-called fourth creatures of the Havona Servitals and the fourth creatures of the conciliators. The angels of time and space are endowed with the ability to discern both spirit and material beings as also are the ascending mortals subsequent to deliverance from the life in the flesh. After attainment of the higher spirit levels the ascenders are able to recognize material, morontia, and spirit realities.

There is also here with me a Mighty Messenger from Uversa, an ascendant Adjuster-fused, onetime mortal being, and he perceives you as you are, and at the same time he visualizes the Solitary Messenger, the supernaphim, and other celestial beings present. Never in your long ascendancy will you lose the power to recognize your associates of former existences. Always, as you ascend inward in the scale of life, will you retain the ability to recognize and fraternize with the fellow beings of your previous and lower levels of experience. Each new translation or resurrection will add one more group of spirit beings to your vision range without in the least depriving you of the ability to recognize your friends and fellows of former estates.

All this is made possible in the experience of ascending mortals by the action of the indwelling Thought Adjusters. Through their retention of the duplicates of your entire life's experiences, you are assured of never losing any true attribute you once had; and these Adjusters are going through with you, as a part of you, in reality, as *you*.

But I almost despair of being able to convey to the material mind the nature of the work of the celestial artisans. I am under the necessity of constantly perverting thought and distorting language in an effort to unfold to the mortal mind the reality of these morontia transactions and near-spirit phenomena. Your comprehension is incapable of grasping, and your language is inadequate for conveying, the meaning, value, and relationship of these semi-spirit activities. And I proceed with this effort to enlighten the human mind concerning these realities with the full understanding of the utter impossibility of my being very successful in such an undertaking.

I can do no more than attempt to sketch a crude parallelism between mortal material activities and the manifold functions of the celestial artisans. If Urantians were more advanced in art and other cultural accomplishments, then could I go that much farther in an effort to project the human mind from the things of matter to those of morontia. About all I can hope to accomplish is to make emphatic the fact of the reality of these transactions of the morontia and the spirit worlds.

1. THE CELESTIAL MUSICIANS

With the limited range of mortal hearing, you can hardly conceive of morontia melodies. There is even a material range of beautiful sound unrecognized by the human sense of hearing, not to mention the inconceivable scope of morontia and spirit harmony. Spirit melodies are not material sound waves but spirit pulsations received by the spirits of celestial personalities. There is a vastness of range and a soul of expression, as well as a grandeur of execution, associated with the melody of the spheres, that are wholly beyond human comprehension. I have seen millions of enraptured beings held in sublime ecstasy while the melody of the realm rolled in upon the spirit energy of the celestial circuits. These marvelous melodies can be broadcast to the uttermost parts of a universe.

The celestial musicians are occupied with the production of celestial harmony by the manipulation of the following spirit forces:

1. *Spiritual sound* — spirit current interruptions.

2. *Spiritual light* — the control and intensification of the light of the morontia and spiritual realms.

3. *Energy impingements* — melody produced by the skillful management of the morontia and spirit energies.

4. *Color symphonies* — melody of morontia color tones; this ranks among the highest accomplishments of the celestial musicians.

5. *Harmony of associated spirits* — the very arrangement and association of different orders of morontia and spirit beings produce majestic melodies.

6. *Melody of thought* — the thinking of spiritual thoughts can be so perfected as to burst forth in the melodies of Havona.

7. *The music of space* — by proper attunement the melodies of other spheres can be picked up on the universe broadcast circuits.

There are over one hundred thousand different modes of sound, color, and energy manipulation, techniques analogous to the human employment of musical instruments. Your ensembles of dancing undoubtedly represent a crude attempt of material creatures to approach the celestial harmony of being placement and personality arrangement. The other five forms of morontia melody are unrecognized by the sensory mechanism of material bodies.

Harmony, the music of the seven levels of melodious association, is the one universal code of spirit communication. Music, such as Urantia mortals understand, attains its highest expression in the schools of Jerusem, the system headquarters, where semi-material beings are taught the harmonies of sound. Mortals do not react to the other forms of morontia melody and celestial harmony.

Appreciation of music on Urantia is both physical and spiritual; and your human musicians have done much to elevate musical taste from the barbarous monotony of your early ancestors to the higher levels of sound appreciation. The majority of Urantia mortals react to music so largely with the material muscles and so slightly with the mind and spirit; but there has been a steady improvement in musical appreciation for more than thirty-five thousand years.

Tuneful syncopation represents a transition from the musical monotony of primitive man to the expressionful harmony and meaningful melodies of your later-day musicians. These earlier types of rhythm stimulate the reaction of the music-loving sense without entailing the exertion of the higher intellectual powers of harmony appreciation.

The best music of Urantia is just a fleeting echo of the magnificent strains heard by the celestial associates of your musicians, who left but snatches of these harmonies of morontia forces on record as the musical melodies of sound harmonics. Spirit-morontia music not infrequently employs all seven modes of expression and reproduction, so that the human mind is tremendously handicapped in any attempt to reduce these melodies of the higher spheres to mere notes of musical sound. Such an effort would be something like endeavoring to reproduce the strains of a great orchestra by means of a single musical instrument.

While you have assembled some beautiful melodies on Urantia, you have not progressed musically nearly so far as many of your neighboring planets in Satania. If Adam and Eve had only survived, then would you have had music in reality; but the gift of harmony, so large in their natures, has been so diluted by strains of unmusical tendencies that only once in a thousand mortal lives is there any great appreciation of harmonics. But be not discouraged; some day a real musician may appear on Urantia, and whole peoples will be enthralled by the magnificent strains of their melodies. One such human being could forever change the course of a whole nation, even the entire civilized world. It is literally true, "melody has power a whole world to transform." Forever, music will remain the universal language of men, angels, and spirits. Harmony is the speech of Havona.

2. THE HEAVENLY REPRODUCERS

Mortal man can hardly hope for more than a meager and distorted concept of the functions of the heavenly reproducers, which I must attempt to illustrate through the gross and limited symbolism of your material language. The spirit-morontia world has a thousand and one things of supreme value, things worthy of reproduction but unknown on Urantia, experiences that belong in the category of the activities which have hardly "entered into the mind of man," those realities which God has in waiting for those who survive the life in the flesh.

There are seven groups of the heavenly reproducers, and I will attempt to illustrate their work by the following classification:

1. *The singers* — harmonists who reiterate the specific harmonies of the past and interpret the melodies of the present. But all of this is effected on the morontia level.

2. *The color workers* — those artists of light and shade you might call sketchers and painters, artists who preserve passing scenes and transient episodes for future morontia enjoyment.

3. *The light picturizers* — the makers of the real semispirit-phenomena preservations of which motion pictures would be a very crude illustration.

4. *The historic pageanteers* — those who dramatically reproduce the crucial events of universe records and history.

5. *The prophetic artists* — those who project the meanings of history into the future.

6. *The life-story tellers* — those who perpetuate the meaning and signifi-

cance of life experience. The projection of present personal experiences into future attainment values.

7. *The administrative enactors* — those who depict the significance of governmental philosophy and administrative technique, the celestial dramatists of sovereignty.

Very often and effectively the heavenly reproducers collaborate with the reversion directors in combining memory recapitulation with certain forms of mind rest and personality diversion. Before the morontia conclaves and spirit assemblies these reproducers sometimes associate themselves in tremendous dramatic spectacles representative of the purpose of such gatherings. I recently witnessed such a stupendous presentation in which more than one million actors produced a succession of one thousand scenes.

The higher intellectual teachers and the transition ministers freely and effectively utilize these various groups of reproducers in their morontia educational activities. But not all of their efforts are devoted to transient illustration; much, very much, of their work is of a permanent nature and will forever remain as a legacy to all future time. So versatile are these artisans that, when they function en masse, they are able to re-enact an age, and in collaboration with the seraphic ministers they can actually portray the eternal values of the spirit world to the mortal seers of time.

3. THE DIVINE BUILDERS

There are cities "whose builder and maker is God." In spirit counterpart we have all that you mortals are familiar with and inexpressibly more. We have homes, spirit comforts, and morontia necessities. For every material satisfaction which humans are capable of enjoying, we have thousands of spiritual realities that serve to enrich and enlarge our existence. The divine builders function in seven groups:

1. *The home designers and builders* — those who construct and remodel the abodes assigned to individuals and working groups. These morontia and spirit domiciles are real. They would be invisible to your short-range vision,

but they are very real and beautiful to us. To a certain extent, all spirit beings may share with the builders certain details of the planning and creation of their morontia or spirit abodes. These homes are fitted up and embellished in accordance with the needs of the morontia or of the spirit creatures who are to inhabit them. There is abundant variety and ample opportunity for individual expression in all these constructions.

2. *The vocation builders* — those who function in designing and assembling the abodes of the regular and routine workers of the spirit and morontia realms. These builders are comparable to those who construct the Urantia workshops and other industrial plants. The transition worlds have a necessary economy of mutual ministry and specialized division of labor. We do not all do everything; there is diversity of function among morontia beings and evolving spirits, and these vocation builders not only build better workshops but also contribute to the vocational enhancement of the worker.

3. *The play builders.* Enormous edifices are utilized during the seasons of rest, what mortals would call recreation and, in a certain sense, play. Provision is made for a suitable setting for the reversion directors, the humorists of the morontia worlds, those transition spheres whereon takes place the training of ascendant beings but recently removed from the evolutionary planets. Even the higher spirits engage in a certain form of reminiscent humor during their periods of spiritual recharging.

4. *The worship builders* — the experienced architects of the spirit and the morontia temples. All the worlds of mortal ascent have temples of worship, and they are the most exquisite creations of the morontia realms and the spirit spheres.

5. *The education builders* — those who build the headquarters of morontia training and advanced spirit learning. Always is the way open to acquire more knowledge, to gain additional information respecting one's present and future work as well as universal cultural knowledge, information designed to make ascending mortals more intelligent and effective citizens of the morontia and spirit worlds.

6. *Morontia planners* — those who build for the co-ordinate association of all the personalities of all realms as they are at any one time present on any one sphere. These planners collaborate with the Morontia Power Supervisors to enrich the co-ordination of the progressive morontia life.

7. *The public builders* — the artisans who plan and construct the designated places of assembly other than those of worship. Great and magnificent are the places of common assembly.

While neither these structures nor their embellishment would be exactly real to the sensory comprehension of material mortals, they are very real to us. You would be unable to see these temples could you be there in the flesh; nevertheless, all of these super-material creations are actually there, and we clearly discern them and just as fully enjoy them.

4. THE THOUGHT RECORDERS

These artisans are devoted to the preservation and reproduction of the superior thought of the realms, and they function in seven groups:

1. *Thought preservers*. These are the artisans dedicated to the preservation of the higher thought of the realms. On the morontia worlds they truly treasure the gems of mentation. Before first coming to Urantia, I saw records and heard broadcasts of the ideation of some of the great minds of this planet. Thought recorders preserve such noble ideas in the tongue of Uversa.

Each super-universe has its own language, a tongue spoken by its personalities and prevailing throughout its sectors. This is known as the tongue of Uversa in our super-universe. Each local universe also has its own language. All of the higher orders of Nebadon are bilingual, speaking both the language of Nebadon and the tongue of Uversa. When two individuals from different local universes meet, they communicate in the tongue of Uversa; if, however, one of them hails from another super-universe, they must have recourse to a translator. In the central universe there is little need of a language; there exists perfect and well-nigh complete understanding; there, only the Gods are not fully comprehended. We are taught that a chance meeting on Paradise reveals more of mutual understanding than could be communicated by a mortal language in a thousand years. Even on Salvington we "know as we are known."

The ability to translate thought into language in the morontia and spirit spheres is beyond mortal comprehension. Our rate of reducing thought to a permanent record can be so speeded up by the expert recorders that the equivalent of over half a million words, or thought symbols, can be registered in one minute of Urantia time. These universe languages are far more replete than the speech of the evolving worlds. The concept symbols of Uversa embrace more than a billion characters, although the basic alphabet contains only seventy symbols. The language of Nebadon is not quite so elaborate, the basic symbols, or alphabet, being forty-eight in number.

2. *Concept recorders*. This second group of recorders are concerned with the preservation of concept pictures, idea patterns. This is a form of permanent recording unknown on the material realms, and by this method I could gain more knowledge in one hour of your time than you could gain in one hundred years of perusing ordinary written language.

3. *Ideograph recorders*. We have the equivalent of both your written and spoken word, but in preserving thought, we usually employ concept picturization and ideograph techniques. Those who preserve ideographs are able to improve one thousandfold upon the work of the concept recorders.

4. *Promoters of oratory*. This group of recorders are occupied with the task of preserving thought for reproduction by oratory. But in the language of Nebadon we could, in a half hour's address, cover the subject matter of the entire lifetime of a Urantia mortal. Your only hope of comprehending these transactions is to pause and consider the technique of your disordered and garbled dream life — how you can in a few seconds traverse years of experience in these fantasies of the night season.

The oratory of the spirit world is one of the rare treats which await you who have heard only the crude and stumbling orations of Urantia. There is harmony of music and euphony of expression in the orations of Salvington and Edentia which are inspiring beyond description. These burning concepts are like gems of beauty in diadems of glory.

5. *The broadcast directors*. The broadcasts of Paradise, the super-universes, and the local universes are under the general supervision of this group of thought conservers. They serve as censors and editors as well as co-ordinators of the broadcast material, making a super-universe adaptation of all Paradise broadcasts and adapting and translating the broadcasts of the Ancients of Days into the individual tongues of the local universes.

The local universe broadcasts must also be modified for reception by the systems and the individual planets. The transmittal of these space reports is carefully supervised, and there is always a back registry to insure the proper reception of every report on every world in a given circuit. These broadcast directors are technically expert in the utilization of the currents of space for all purposes of intelligence communication.

6. *The rhythm recorders*. Urantians would undoubtedly denominate these artisans poets, although their work is very different from, and almost infinitely transcends, your poetic productions. Rhythm is less exhausting to both morontia and spirit beings, and so an effort is frequently made to increase efficiency, as well as to augment pleasure, by executing numerous functions in rhythmic form. I only wish you might be privileged to hear some of the poetic broadcasts of the Edentia assemblies and to enjoy the richness of the color and tone of the constellation geniuses who are masters of this exquisite form of self-expression and social harmonization.

7. *The morontia recorders*. I am at a loss to know how to depict to the material mind the function of this important group of thought recorders assigned to the work of preserving the ensemble pictures of the various groupings of morontia affairs and spirit transactions; crudely illustrated, they are the group photographers of the transition worlds. They save for the future the vital scenes and associations of these progressive epochs, preserving them in the archives of the morontia halls of records.

5. THE ENERGY MANIPULATORS

These interesting and effective artisans are concerned with every kind of energy: physical, mindal, and spiritual.

1. *Physical-energy manipulators*. The physical-energy manipulators serve for long periods with the power directors and are experts in the manipulation and control of many phases of physical energy. They are conversant with the three basic currents and the thirty subsidiary energy segregations of the super-universes. These beings are of inestimable assistance to the Morontia Power Supervisors of the transition worlds. They are the persistent students of the cosmic projections of Paradise.

2. *Mind-energy manipulators*. These are the experts of intercommunication between morontia and other types of intelligent beings. This form of communication between mortals is practically nonexistent on Urantia. These are the specialists who promote the ability of the ascending morontia beings to communicate with one another, and their work embraces numerous unique adventures in intellect liaison which are far beyond my power to portray to the material mind. These artisans are the keen students of the mind circuits of the Infinite Spirit.

3. *Spiritual-energy manipulators*. The manipulators of spiritual energy are an intriguing group. Spiritual energy acts in accordance with established laws, just as does physical energy. That is, spirit force, when studied, yields dependable deductions and can be precisely dealt with, even as can the physical energies. There are just as certain and reliable laws in the spirit world as obtain in the material realms. During the last few millions of years many improved techniques for the intake of spiritual energy have been effected by these students of the fundamental laws of the Eternal Son governing spirit energy as applied to the morontia and other orders of celestial beings throughout the universes.

4. *The compound manipulators*. This is the adventurous group of well-trained beings who are dedicated to the functional association of the three original phases of divine energy manifested throughout the universes as physical, mindal, and spiritual energies. These are the keen personalities who are in reality seeking to discover the universe presence of God the Supreme, for in this Deity personality there must occur the experiential

unification of all grand universe divinity. And to a certain extent, these artisans have in recent times met with some success.

5. *The transport advisers*. This corps of technical advisers to the transport seraphim are most proficient in collaborating with the star students in working out routings and in otherwise assisting the chiefs of transport on the worlds of space. They are the traffic supervisors of the spheres and are present on all inhabited planets. Urantia is served by a corps of seventy transport advisers.

6. *The experts of communication*. Urantia, likewise, is served by twelve technicians of interplanetary and inter-universe communication. These long-experienced beings are expert in the knowledge of the laws of transmittal and interference as applied to the communications of the realms. This corps is concerned with all forms of space messages except those of Gravity and Solitary Messengers. On Urantia much of their work must be accomplished over the archangels' circuit.

7. *The teachers of rest*. Divine rest is associated with the technique of spiritual-energy intake. Morontia and spirit energy must be replenished just as certainly as physical energy, but not for the same reasons. I am, perforce, compelled to employ crude illustrations in my attempts to enlighten you; nevertheless, we of the spirit world must stop our regular activities periodically and betake ourselves to suitable places of rendezvous where we enter the divine rest and thus recuperate our depleting energies.

You will receive your first lessons in these matters when you reach the mansion worlds after you have become morontia beings and have begun to experience the technique of spirit affairs. You know of the innermost circle of Havona and that, after the pilgrims of space have traversed the preceding circles, they must be inducted into the long and revivifying rest of Paradise. This is not only a technical requirement of transit from the career of time to the service of eternity, but it is also a necessity, a form of rest required to replenish the energy losses incident to the final steps of the ascendant experience and to store reserves of spirit power for the next stage of the endless career.

These energy manipulators also function in hundreds of other ways too numerous to catalogue, such as counseling with the seraphim, cherubim, and sanobim regarding the most efficient modes of energy intake and as to the maintenance of the most helpful balances of divergent forces between active cherubim and passive sanobim. In many other ways do these experts lend assistance to morontia and spirit creatures in their efforts to understand the divine rest, which is so essential to the effective utilization of the basic energies of space.

6. THE DESIGNERS AND EMBELLISHERS

How I wish I knew how to portray the exquisite work of these unique artisans! Every attempt on my part to explain the work of spirit embellishment would only recall to material minds your own crude but worthy efforts to do these things on your world of mind and matter.

This corps, while embracing over one thousand subdivisions of activity, is grouped under the following seven major heads:

1. *The craftworkers of color*. These are they who make the ten thousand color tones of spirit reflection peal forth their exquisite messages of harmonious beauty. Aside from color perception there is nothing in human experience to which these activities may be compared.

2. *The sound designers*. Spirit waves of diverse identity and morontia appreciation are depicted by these designers of what you would call sound. These impulses are in reality the superb reflections of the naked and glorious spirit-souls of the celestial hosts.

3. *The emotion designers*. These enhancers and conservators of feeling are those who preserve the sentiments of morontia and the emotions of divinity for the study and edification of the children of time and for the inspiration and beautification of morontia progressors and advancing spirits.

4. *The artists of odor*. This comparison of supernal spirit activities to the physical recognition of chemical odors is, indeed, unfortunate, but Urantia mortals could hardly recognize this ministry by any other name. These arti-

sans create their varied symphonies for the edification and delight of the advancing children of light. You have nothing on earth to which this type of spiritual grandeur can be even remotely compared.

5. *The presence embellishers.* These artisans are not occupied with the arts of self-adornment or the technique of creature beautification. They are devoted to the production of multitudinous and joyous reactions in individual morontia and spirit creatures by dramatizing the significance of relationship through the positional values assigned to different morontia and spirit orders in the composite ensembles of these diversified beings. These artists arrange super-material beings as you would living musical notes, odors, sights, and then blend them into the anthems of glory.

6. *The taste designers.* And how can you be told of these artists! Faintly I might suggest that they are improvers of morontia taste, and they also endeavor to increase the appreciation of beauty through the sharpening of the evolving spirit senses.

7. *The morontia synthesizers.* These are the master craftsmen who, when all others have made their respective contributions, then add the culminating and finishing touches to the morontia ensemble, thus achieving an inspiring portrayal of the divinely beautiful, an enduring inspiration to spirit beings and their morontia associates. But you must await your deliverance from the animal body before you can begin to conceive of the artistic glories and aesthetic beauties of the morontia and spirit worlds.

7. THE HARMONY WORKERS

These artists are not concerned with music, painting, or anything similar, as you might be led to surmise. They are occupied with the manipulation and organization of specialized forces and energies which are present in the spirit world, but which are not recognized by mortals.

Beauty, rhythm, and harmony are intellectually associated and spiritually akin. Truth, fact, and relationship are intellectually inseparable and associated with the philosophic concepts of beauty. Goodness, righteousness, and justice are philosophically interrelated and spiritually bound up together with living truth and divine beauty.

Cosmic concepts of true philosophy, the portrayal of celestial artistry, or the mortal attempt to depict the human recognition of divine beauty can never be truly satisfying if such attempted creature progression is ununified. These expressions of the divine urge within the evolving creature may be intellectually true, emotionally beautiful, and spiritually good; but the real soul of expression is absent unless these realities of truth, meanings of beauty, and values of goodness are unified in the life experience of the artisan, the scientist, or the philosopher.

These divine qualities are perfectly and absolutely unified in God. And every God-knowing man or angel possesses the potential of unlimited self-expression on ever-progressive levels of unified self-realization by the technique of the never-ending achievement of Godlikeness — the experiential blending in the evolutionary experience of eternal truth, universal beauty, and divine goodness.

8. MORTAL ASPIRATIONS AND MORONTIA ACHIEVEMENTS

Although celestial artisans do not personally work on material planets, such as Urantia, they do come, from time to time, from the headquarters of the system to proffer help to the naturally gifted individuals of the mortal races. When thus assigned, these artisans temporarily work under the supervision of the planetary angels of progress. The seraphic hosts co-operate with these artisans in attempting to assist those mortal artists who possess inherent endowments, and who also possess Adjusters of special and previous experience.

There are three possible sources of special human ability: At the bottom *always* there exists the natural or inherent aptitude. Special ability is never an arbitrary gift of the Gods; there is always an ancestral foundation for every outstanding talent. In addition to this natural ability, or rather supplemental thereto, there may be contributed the leadings of the Thought Adjuster in those individuals whose indwelling Adjusters may have had actual and bona fide experiences along such lines on other worlds and in other mortal creatures. In those cases where both the human mind and the indwelling Adjuster are unusually skillful, the spirit artisans may be delegated to act as harmonizers of these talents and otherwise to assist and inspire these mortals to seek for ever-perfecting ideals and to attempt their enhanced portrayal for the edification of the realm.

There is no caste in the ranks of spirit artisans. No matter how lowly your origin, if you have ability and the gift of expression, you will gain adequate recognition and receive due appreciation as you ascend upward in the scale of morontia experience and spiritual attainment. There can be no handicap of human heredity or deprivation of mortal environment which the morontia career will not fully compensate and wholly remove. And all such satisfactions of artistic achievement and expressionful self-realization will be effected by your own personal efforts in progressive advancement. At last the aspirations of evolutionary mediocrity may be realized. While the Gods do not arbitrarily bestow talents and ability upon the children of time, they do provide for the attainment of the satisfaction of all their noble longings and for the gratification of all human hunger for supernal self-expression.

But every human being should remember: Many ambitions to excel which tantalize mortals in the flesh will not persist with these same mortals in the morontia and spirit careers. The ascending morontians learn to socialize their former purely selfish longings and egoistic ambitions. Nevertheless, those things which you so earnestly longed to do on earth and which circumstances so persistently denied you, if, after acquiring true mota insight in the morontia career, you still desire to do, then will you most certainly be granted every opportunity fully to satisfy your long-cherished desires.

Before ascending mortals leave the local universe to embark upon their spirit careers, they will be satiated respecting every intellectual, artistic, and social longing or true ambition which ever characterized their mortal or morontia planes of existence. This is the achievement of equality of the satisfaction of self-expression and self-realization but not the attainment of identical experiential status nor the complete obliteration of characteristic individuality in skill, technique, and expression. But the new spirit differential of personal experiential attainment will not become thus leveled off and equalized until after you have finished the last circle of the Havona career. And then will the Paradise residents be confronted with the necessity of adjusting to that absonite differential of personal experience which can be leveled off only by the group attainment of the ultimate of creature status — the seventh-stage-spirit destiny of the mortal finaliters.

And this is the story of the celestial artisans, that cosmopolitan body of exquisite workers who do so much to glorify the architectural spheres with the artistic portrayals of the divine beauty of the Paradise Creators.

[Indited by an Archangel of Nebadon.]

PAPER 45
THE LOCAL SYSTEM ADMINISTRATION

THE ADMINISTRATIVE CENTER of Satania consists of a cluster of architectural spheres, fifty-seven in number — Jerusem itself, the seven major satellites, and the forty-nine sub-satellites. Jerusem, the system capital, is almost one hundred times the size of Urantia, although its gravity is a trifle less. Jerusem's major satellites are the seven transition worlds, each of which is about ten times as large as Urantia, while the seven sub-satellites of these transition spheres are just about the size of Urantia.

The seven mansion worlds are the seven sub-satellites of transition world number one.

This entire system of fifty-seven architectural worlds is independently lighted, heated, watered, and energized by the co-ordination of the Satania Power Center and the Master Physical Controllers in accordance with the established technique of the physical organization and arrangement of these specially created spheres. They are also physically cared for and otherwise maintained by the native spornagia.

1. TRANSITIONAL CULTURE WORLDS

The seven major worlds swinging around Jerusem are generally known as the transitional culture spheres. Their rulers are designated from time to time by the Jerusem supreme executive council. These spheres are numbered and named as follows:

Number 1. The Finaliter World. This is the headquarters of the finaliter corps of the local system and is surrounded by the receiving worlds, the seven mansion worlds, dedicated so fully to the scheme of mortal ascension. The finaliter world is accessible to the inhabitants of all seven mansion worlds. Transport seraphim carry ascending personalities back and forth on these pilgrimages, which are designed to cultivate their faith in the ultimate destiny of transition mortals. Although the finaliters and their structures are not ordinarily perceptible to morontia vision, you will be more than thrilled, from time to time, when the energy transformers and the Morontia Power Supervisors enable you momentarily to glimpse these high spirit personalities who have actually completed the Paradise ascension, and who have returned to the very worlds where you are beginning this long journey, as the pledge of assurance that you may and can complete the stupendous undertaking. All mansion world sojourners go to the finaliter sphere at least once a year for these assemblies of finaliter visualization.

Number 2. The Morontia World. This planet is the headquarters of the supervisors of morontia life and is surrounded by the seven spheres whereon the morontia chiefs train their associates and helpers, both morontia beings and ascending mortals.

In passing through the seven mansion worlds, you will also progress through these cultural and social spheres of increasing morontia contact. When you advance from the first to the second mansion world, you will become eligible for a visitor's permit to transitional headquarters number two, the morontia world, and so on. And when present on any one of these six cultural spheres, you may, on invitation, become a visitor and observer on any of the seven surrounding worlds of associated group activities.

Number 3. The Angelic World. This is the headquarters of all the seraphic hosts engaged in system activities and is surrounded by the seven worlds of angelic training and instruction. These are the seraphic social spheres.

Number 4. The Super-angel World. This sphere is the Satania home of the Brilliant Evening Stars and a vast concourse of co-ordinate and near-co-ordinate beings. The seven satellites of this world are assigned to the seven major groups of these unnamed celestial beings.

Number 5. The World of the Sons. This planet is the headquarters of the divine Sons of all orders, including the creature-trinitized sons. The surrounding seven worlds are devoted to certain individual groupings of these divinely related sons.

Number 6. The World of the Spirit. This sphere serves as the system rendezvous of the high personalities of the Infinite Spirit. Its seven surrounding satellites are assigned to individual groups of these diverse orders. But on transition world number six there is no representation of the Spirit, neither is such a presence to be observed on the system capitals; the Divine Minister of Salvington is *everywhere* in Nebadon.

Number 7. The World of the Father. This is the silent sphere of the system. No group of beings is domiciled on it. The great temple of light occupies a central place, but no one can be discerned therein. All beings of all the system worlds are welcomed as worshipers.

The seven satellites surrounding the Father's world are variously utilized in the different systems. In Satania they are now used as the detention spheres for the interned groups of the Lucifer rebellion. The constellation capital, Edentia, has no analogous prison worlds; the few seraphim and cherubim who went over to the rebels in the Satania rebellion have been long since confined on these isolation worlds of Jerusem.

As a sojourner on the seventh mansion world, you have access to the seventh transition world, the sphere of the Universal Father, and are also permitted to visit the Satania prison worlds surrounding this planet, whereon are now confined Lucifer and the majority of those personalities who followed him in rebellion against Michael. And this sad spectacle has been observable during these recent ages and will continue to serve as a solemn warning to all Nebadon until the Ancients of Days shall adjudicate the sin of Lucifer and his fallen associates who rejected the salvation proffered by Michael, their universe Father.

2. THE SYSTEM SOVEREIGN

The chief executive of a local system of inhabited worlds is a primary Lanonandek Son, the System Sovereign. In our local universe these sovereigns are intrusted with large executive responsibilities, unusual personal prerogatives. Not all universes, even in Orvonton, are so organized as to permit the System Sovereigns to exercise such unusually wide powers of personal discretion in the direction of system affairs. But in all the history of Nebadon these untrammeled executives have exhibited disloyalty only three times. The Lucifer rebellion in the system of Satania was the last and the most widespread of all.

In Satania, even after this disastrous upheaval, absolutely no changes have been made in the technique of system administration. The present System Sovereign possesses all the power and exercises all the authority that were invested in his unworthy predecessor except for certain matters now under the supervision of the Constellation Fathers which the Ancients of Days have not yet fully restored to Lanaforge, the successor of Lucifer.

The present head of Satania is a gracious and brilliant ruler, and he is a rebellion-tested sovereign. When serving as an assistant System Sovereign, Lanaforge was faithful to Michael in an earlier upheaval in the universe of Nebadon. This mighty and brilliant Lord of Satania is a tried and tested administrator. At the time of the second system rebellion in Nebadon, when the System Sovereign stumbled and fell into darkness, Lanaforge, the first assistant to the erring chief, seized the reins of government and so conducted the affairs of the system that comparatively few personalities were lost either on the headquarters worlds or on the inhabited planets of that unfortunate system. Lanaforge bears the distinction of being the only primary Lanonandek Son in all Nebadon who thus functioned loyally in the service of Michael and in the very presence of the default of his brother of superior authority and antecedent rank. Lanaforge will probably not be removed from Jerusem until all the results of the former folly have been overcome and the products of rebellion removed from Satania.

While all the affairs of the isolated worlds of Satania have not been returned to his jurisdiction, Lanaforge discloses great interest in their welfare, and he is a frequent visitor on Urantia. As in other and normal systems, the Sovereign presides over the system council of world rulers, the Planetary Princes and the resident governors general of the isolated worlds. This planetary council assembles from time to time on the headquarters of the system — "When the Sons of God come together."

Once a week, every ten days on Jerusem, the Sovereign holds a conclave with some one group of the various orders of personalities domiciled on the headquarters world. These are the charmingly informal hours of Jerusem, and they are never-to-be-forgotten occasions. On Jerusem there exists the utmost fraternity between all the various orders of beings and between each of these groups and the System Sovereign.

These unique assemblages occur on the sea of glass, the great gathering field of the system capital. They are purely social and spiritual occasions; nothing pertaining to the planetary administration or even to the ascendant plan is ever discussed. Ascending mortals come together at these times merely to enjoy themselves and to meet their fellow Jerusemites. Those groups which are not being entertained by the Sovereign at these weekly relaxations meet at their own headquarters.

3. THE SYSTEM GOVERNMENT

The chief executive of a local system, the System Sovereign, is always supported by two or three Lanonandek Sons, who function as first and second assistants. But at the present time the system of Satania is administered by a staff of seven Lanonandeks:

1. *The System Sovereign* — Lanaforge, number 2,709 of the primary order and successor to the apostate Lucifer.

2. *The first assistant Sovereign* — Mansurotia, number 17,841 of the tertiary Lanonandeks. He was dispatched to Satania along with Lanaforge.

3. *The second assistant Sovereign* — Sadib, number 271,402 of the tertiary order. Sadib also came to Satania with Lanaforge.

4. *The custodian of the system* — Holdant, number 19 of the tertiary corps, the holder and controller of all interned spirits above the order of mortal existence. Holdant likewise came to Satania with Lanaforge.

5. *The system recorder* — Vilton, secretary of the Lanonandek ministry of Satania, number 374 of the third order. Vilton was a member of the original Lanaforge group.

6. *The bestowal director* — Fortant, number 319,847 of the reserves of the secondary Lanonandeks and temporary director of all universe activities transplanted to Jerusem since Michael's bestowal on Urantia. Fortant has been attached to the staff of Lanaforge for two thousand years of Urantia time.

7. *The high counselor* — Hanavard, number 67 of the primary Lanonandek Sons and a member of the high corps of universe counselors and co-ordinators. He functions as acting chairman of the executive council of Satania. Hanavard is the twelfth of this order so to serve on Jerusem since the Lucifer rebellion.

This executive group of seven Lanonandeks constitutes the expanded emergency administration made necessary by the exigencies of the Lucifer rebellion. There are only minor courts on Jerusem since the system is the unit of administration, not adjudication, but the Lanonandek administration is supported by the Jerusem executive council, the supreme advisory body of Satania. This council consists of twelve members:

1. Hanavard, the Lanonandek chairman.
2. Lanaforge, the System Sovereign.
3. Mansurotia, the first assistant Sovereign.
4. The chief of Satania Melchizedeks.
5. The acting director of the Satania Life Carriers.
6. The chief of the Satania finaliters.

7. The original Adam of Satania, the supervising head of the Material Sons.
8. The director of the Satania seraphic hosts.
9. The chief of the Satania physical controllers.
10. The director of the system Morontia Power Supervisors.
11. The acting director of system midway creatures.
12. The acting head of the corps of ascending mortals.

This council periodically chooses three members to represent the local system on the supreme council at galaxy headquarters, but this representation is suspended by rebellion. Satania now has an observer at the headquarters of the galaxy, but since the bestowal of Michael the system has resumed the election of ten members to the Edentia legislature.

4. THE FOUR AND TWENTY COUNSELORS

At the center of the seven angelic residential circles on Jerusem is located the headquarters of the Urantia advisory council, the four and twenty counselors. John the Revelator called them the four and twenty elders: "And round about the throne were four and twenty seats, and upon the seats I saw four and twenty elders sitting, clothed in white raiment." The throne in the center of this group is the judgment seat of the presiding archangel, the throne of the resurrection roll call of mercy and justice for all Satania. This judgment seat has always been on Jerusem, but the twenty-four surrounding seats were placed in position no more than two thousand years ago, soon after Christ Michael was elevated to the full sovereignty of Nebadon. These four and twenty counselors are his personal agents on Jerusem, and they have authority to represent the Master Son in all matters concerning the roll calls of Satania and in many other phases of the scheme of mortal ascension on the isolated worlds of the system. They are the designated agents for executing the special requests of Gabriel and the unusual mandates of Michael.

These twenty-four counselors have been recruited from various groups of Urantians, and the last of these were assembled at the time of the resurrection roll call of Michael, two thousand years ago. This Urantia advisory council is made up of the following members:

1. *Onagar*, the master mind of the pre-Planetary Prince age, who directed his fellows in the worship of "The Breath Giver."

2. *Mansant*, the great teacher of the post-Planetary Prince age on Urantia, who pointed his fellows to the veneration of "The Great Light."

3. *Onamonalonton*, a leader of the Native Americans and the one who directed them from the worship of many gods to the veneration of "The Great Spirit."

4. *Orlandof*, a prince of the "blue" men and their leader in the recognition of the divinity of "The Supreme Chief."

5. *Porshunta*, the oracle of the "orange" men and the leader of this people in the worship of "The Great Teacher."

6. *Singlangton*, the first of the "yellow" men to teach and lead his people in the worship of "One Truth" instead of many. Thousands of years ago they knew of the one God.

7. *Fantad*, the deliverer of the "green" men from darkness and their leader in the worship of "The One Source of Life."

8. *Orvonon*, the enlightener of the "indigo" people and their leader in the one-time service of "The God of Gods."

9. *Adam*, the discredited but rehabilitated planetary father of Urantia, a Material Son of God who was relegated to the likeness of mortal flesh, but who survived and was subsequently elevated to this position by the decree of Michael.

10. *Eve*, the mother of the "violet" people of Urantia, who suffered the

penalty of default with her mate and was also rehabilitated with him and assigned to serve with this group of mortal survivors.

11. *Enoch*, the first of the mortals of Urantia to fuse with the Thought Adjuster during the mortal life in the flesh.

12. *Moses*, the emancipator of a remnant of the "violet" people and the instigator of the revival of the worship of the Universal Father under the name of "The God of Israel."

13. *Elijah*, a translated soul of brilliant spiritual achievement during the post-Material Son age.

14. *Machiventa Melchizedek*, the only Son of this order to bestow himself upon Urantia. While still numbered as a Melchizedek, he has become "forever a minister of the Most Highs," eternally assuming the assignment of service as a mortal ascender, having sojourned on Urantia in the likeness of mortal flesh at Salem in the days of Abraham. This Melchizedek has latterly been proclaimed vicegerent Planetary Prince of Urantia with headquarters on Jerusem and authority to act in behalf of Michael, who is actually the Planetary Prince of the world whereon he experienced his terminal bestowal in human form. Notwithstanding this, Urantia is still supervised by successive resident governors general, members of the four and twenty counselors.

15. *John the Baptist*, the forerunner of Michael's mission on Urantia and, in the flesh, distant cousin of the Son of Man.

16. *1-2-3 the First*, the leader of the loyal midway creatures in the service of Gabriel at the time of the Caligastia betrayal, elevated to this position by Michael soon after his entrance upon unconditioned sovereignty.

These selected personalities are exempt from the ascension regime for the time being, on Gabriel's request, and we have no idea how long they may serve in this capacity.

Seats numbers 17, 18, 19, and 20 are not permanently occupied. They are temporarily filled by the unanimous consent of the sixteen permanent members, being kept open for later assignment to ascending mortals from the present post-bestowal Son age on Urantia.

Numbers 21, 22, 23, and 24 are likewise temporarily filled while being held in reserve for the great teachers of other and subsequent ages which undoubtedly will follow the present age. Eras of the Magisterial Sons and Teacher Sons and the ages of light and life are to be anticipated on Urantia, regardless of unexpected visitations of divine Sons which may or may not occur.

5. THE MATERIAL SONS

The great divisions of celestial life have their headquarters and immense preserves on Jerusem, including the various orders of divine Sons, high spirits, super-angels, angels, and midway creatures. The central abode of this wonderful sector is the chief temple of the Material Sons.

The domain of the Adams is the center of attraction to all new arrivals on Jerusem. It is an enormous area consisting of one thousand centers, although each family of Material Sons and Daughters lives on an estate of its own up to the time of the departure of its members for service on the evolutionary worlds of space or until their embarkation upon the Paradise-ascension career.

These Material Sons are the highest type of sex-reproducing beings to be found on the training spheres of the evolving universes. And they are really material; even the Planetary Adams and Eves are plainly visible to the mortal races of the inhabited worlds. These Material Sons are the last and physical link in the chain of personalities extending from divinity and perfection above down to humanity and material existence below. These Sons provide the inhabited worlds with a mutually contactable intermediary between the invisible Planetary Prince and the material creatures of the realms.

At the last millennial registration on Salvington there were of record in Norlatiadek 161,432,840 Material Sons and Daughters of citizenship status on the local system capitals. The number of Material Sons varies in the different systems, and their number is being constantly increased by natural reproduction. In the exercise of their reproductive functions they are not guided wholly by the personal desires of the contacting personalities but also by the higher governing bodies and advisory councils.

These Material Sons and Daughters are the permanent inhabitants of Jerusem and its associated worlds. They occupy vast estates on Jerusem and participate liberally in the local management of the capital sphere, administering practically all routine affairs with the assistance of the midwayers and the ascenders.

On Jerusem these reproducing Sons are permitted to experiment with the ideals of self-government after the manner of the Melchizedeks, and they are achieving a very high type of society. The higher orders of sonship reserve the veto functions of the realm, but in nearly every respect the Jerusem Adamites govern themselves by universal suffrage and representative government. Some time they hope to be granted virtually complete autonomy.

The character of the service of the Material Sons is largely determined by their ages. While they are not eligible for admission to the Melchizedek University of Salvington — being material and ordinarily limited to certain planets — nevertheless, the Melchizedeks maintain strong faculties of teachers on the headquarters of each system for the instruction of the younger generations of Material Sons. The educational and spiritual training systems provided for the development of the younger Material Sons and Daughters are the acme of perfection in scope, technique, and practicability.

6. ADAMIC TRAINING OF ASCENDERS

The Material Sons and Daughters, together with their children, present an engaging spectacle which never fails to arouse the curiosity and intrigue the attention of all ascending mortals. They are so similar to your own material sex races that you both find much of common interest to engage your thoughts and occupy your seasons of fraternal contact.

Mortal survivors spend much of their leisure on the system capital observing and studying the life habits and conduct of these superior semi-physical sex creatures, for these citizens of Jerusem are the immediate sponsors and mentors of the mortal survivors from the time they attain citizenship on the headquarters world until they take leave for Edentia.

On the seven mansion worlds ascending mortals are afforded ample opportunities for compensating any and all experiential deprivations suffered on their worlds of origin, whether due to inheritance, environment, or unfortunate premature termination of the career in the flesh. This is in every sense true except in the mortal sex life and its attendant adjustments. Thousands of mortals reach the mansion worlds without having benefited particularly from the disciplines derived from fairly average sex relations on their native spheres. The mansion world experience can provide little opportunity for compensating these very personal deprivations. Sex experience in a physical sense is past for these ascenders, but in close association with the Material Sons and Daughters, both individually and as members of their families, these sex-deficient mortals are enabled to compensate the social, intellectual, emotional, and spiritual aspects of their deficiency. Thus are all those humans whom circumstances or bad judgment deprived of the benefits of advantageous sex association on the evolutionary worlds, here on the system capitals afforded full opportunity to acquire these essential mortal experiences in close and loving association with the supernal Adamic sex creatures of permanent residence on the system capitals.

However, while actual sex activity is now past for those in a morontia body, the reversion directors and play coordinators have such "virtual reality" techniques available that these urges can still be experienced, fulfilled, and worked through if so desired. The ultimate goal is to transmute and uplift the sex urge into higher creative activities. [1]

No surviving mortal, midwayer, or seraphim may ascend to Paradise, attain the Father, and be mustered into the Corps of the Finality without having passed through that sublime experience of achieving parental relationship to an evolving child of the worlds or some other experience analogous and equivalent thereto. The relationship of child and parent is

---

1. *JFC Note: Also see Paper 50 section 3, the volunteer assistants of a Planetary Prince do become physical again, can have sex and reproduce, so this urge can still be utilized in a useful way. One can always volunteer for this service.*

fundamental to the essential concept of the Universal Father and his universe children. Therefore does such an experience become indispensable to the experiential training of all ascenders.

The ascending midway creatures and the evolutionary seraphim must pass through this parenthood experience in association with the Material Sons and Daughters of the system headquarters. Thus do such non-reproducing ascenders obtain the experience of parenthood by assisting the Jerusem Adams and Eves in rearing and training their progeny.

All mortal survivors who have not experienced parenthood on the evolutionary worlds must also obtain this necessary training while sojourning in the homes of the Jerusem Material Sons and as parental associates of these superb fathers and mothers. This is true except in so far as such mortals have been able to compensate their deficiencies on the system nursery located on the first transitional-culture world of Jerusem.

This probation nursery of Satania is maintained by certain morontia personalities on the finaliters' world, one half of the planet being devoted to this work of child rearing. Here are received and reassembled certain children of surviving mortals, such as those offspring who perished on the evolutionary worlds before acquiring spiritual status as individuals. The ascension of either of its natural parents insures that such a mortal child of the realms will be accorded repersonalization on the system finaliter planet and there be permitted to demonstrate by subsequent freewill choice whether or not it elects to follow the parental path of mortal ascension. Children here appear as on the nativity world except for the absence of sex differentiation. There is no reproduction of mortal kind after the life experience on the inhabited worlds.

Mansion world students who have one or more children in the probationary nursery on the finaliters' world, and who are deficient in essential parental experience, may apply for a Melchizedek permit which will effect their temporary transfer from ascension duties on the mansion worlds to the finaliter world, where they are granted opportunity to function as associate parents to their own and other children. This service of parental ministry may be later accredited on Jerusem as the fulfillment of one half of the training which such ascenders are required to undergo in the families of the Material Sons and Daughters.

The probation nursery itself is supervised by one thousand couples of Material Sons and Daughters, volunteers from the Jerusem colony of their order. They are immediately assisted by about an equal number of volunteer midsonite parental groups who stop off here to render this service on their way from the midsonite world of Satania to the unrevealed destiny on their special worlds of reservation among the finaliter spheres of Salvington.

7. THE MELCHIZEDEK SCHOOLS

The Melchizedeks are the directors of that large corps of instructors — partially spiritualized will creatures and others — who function so acceptably on Jerusem and its associated worlds but especially on the seven mansion worlds. These are the detention planets, where those mortals who fail to achieve fusion with their indwelling Adjusters during the life in the flesh are rehabilitated in transient form to receive further help and to enjoy extended opportunity for continuing their strivings for spiritual attainment, those very efforts which were prematurely interrupted by death. Or if, for any other reason of hereditary handicap, unfavorable environment, or conspiracy of circumstances, this soul attainment was not completed, no matter what the reason, all who are true of purpose and worthy in spirit find themselves, as themselves, present on the continuing planets, where they must learn to master the essentials of the eternal career, to possess themselves of traits which they could not, or did not, acquire during the lifetime in the flesh.

The Brilliant Evening Stars (and their unnamed co-ordinates) frequently serve as teachers in the various educational enterprises of the universe, including those sponsored by the Melchizedeks. Also do the Trinity Teacher Sons collaborate, and they impart the touches of Paradise perfection to these progressive training schools. But all these activities are not exclusively devoted to the advancement of ascending mortals; many are equally occupied with the progressive training of the native spirit personalities of Nebadon.

The Melchizedek Sons conduct upward of thirty different educational centers on Jerusem. These training schools begin with the college of self-evaluation and end with the schools of Jerusem citizenship, wherein the

Material Sons and Daughters join with the Melchizedeks and others in their supreme effort to qualify the mortal survivors for the assumption of the high responsibilities of representative government. The entire universe is organized and administered on the *representative* plan. Representative government is the divine ideal of self-government among non-perfect beings.

Every one hundred years of universe time each system selects its ten representatives to sit in the constellation legislature. They are chosen by the Jerusem council of one thousand, an elective body charged with the duty of representing the system groups in all such delegated or appointive matters. All representatives or other delegates are selected by the council of one thousand electors, and they must be graduates of the highest school of the Melchizedek College of Administration, as also are all of those who constitute this group of one thousand electors. This school is fostered by the Melchizedeks, latterly assisted by the finaliters.

There are many elective bodies on Jerusem, and they are voted into authority from time to time by three orders of citizenship — the Material Sons and Daughters, the seraphim and their associates, including midway creatures, and the ascending mortals. To receive nomination for representative honor a candidate must have gained requisite recognition from the Melchizedek schools of administration.

Suffrage is universal on Jerusem among these three groups of citizenship, but the vote is differentially cast in accordance with the recognized and duly registered personal possession of mota — morontia wisdom. The vote cast at a Jerusem election by any one personality has a value ranging from one up to one thousand. Jerusem citizens are thus classified in accordance with their mota achievement.

From time to time Jerusem citizens present themselves to the Melchizedek examiners, who certify to their attainment of morontia wisdom. Then they go before the examining corps of the Brilliant Evening Stars or their designates, who ascertain the degree of spirit insight. Next they appear in the presence of the four and twenty counselors and their associates, who pass upon their status of experiential attainment of socialization. These three factors are then carried to the citizenship registrars of representative government, who quickly compute the mota status and assign suffrage qualifications in accordance therewith.

Under the supervision of the Melchizedeks the ascending mortals, especially those who are tardy in their personality unification on the new morontia levels, are taken in hand by the Material Sons and are given intensive training designed to rectify such deficiencies. No ascending mortal leaves the system headquarters for the more extensive and varied socialization career of the constellation until these Material Sons certify to the achievement of mota personality — an individuality combining the completed mortal existence in experiential association with the budding morontia career, both being duly blended by the spiritual over-control of the Thought Adjuster.

[Presented by a Melchizedek of temporary assignment on Urantia.]

PAPER 46
THE LOCAL SYSTEM HEADQUARTERS

JERUSALEM, the headquarters of Satania, is an average capital of a local system, and aside from numerous irregularities occasioned by the Lucifer rebellion and the bestowal of Michael on Urantia, it is typical of similar spheres. Your local system has passed through some stormy experiences, but it is at present being administered most efficiently, and as the ages pass, the results of disharmony are being slowly but surely eradicated. Order and good will are being restored, and the conditions on Jerusem are more and more approaching the heavenly status of your traditions, for the system headquarters is truly the heaven visualized by the majority of religious believers.

1. PHYSICAL ASPECTS OF JERUSEM

Jerusem is divided into one thousand latitudinal sectors and ten thousand longitudinal zones. The sphere has seven major capitals and seventy minor administrative centers. The seven sectional capitals are concerned with diverse activities, and the System Sovereign is present in each at least once a year.

The standard mile of Jerusem is equivalent to about seven Urantia miles. The standard weight, the "gradant," is built up through the decimal system from the mature ultimaton and represents almost exactly ten ounces of your weight. The Satania day equals three days of Urantia time, less one hour, four minutes, and fifteen seconds, that being the time of the axial revolution of Jerusem. The system year consists of one hundred Jerusem days. The time of the system is broadcast by the master chronoldeks.

The energy of Jerusem is superbly controlled and circulates about the sphere in the zone channels, which are directly fed from the energy charges of space and expertly administered by the Master Physical Controllers. The natural resistance to the passage of these energies through the physical channels of conduction yields the heat required for the production of the equable temperature of Jerusem. The full-light temperature is maintained at about 70 degrees Fahrenheit, while during the period of light recession it falls to a little lower than 50 degrees.

The lighting system of Jerusem should not be so difficult for you to comprehend. There are no days and nights, no seasons of heat and cold. The power transformers maintain one hundred thousand centers from which rarefied energies are projected upward through the planetary atmosphere, undergoing certain changes, until they reach the electric air-ceiling of the sphere; and then these energies are reflected back and down as a gentle, sifting, and even light of about the intensity of Urantia sunlight when the sun is shining overhead at ten o'clock in the morning.

Under such conditions of lighting, the light rays do not seem to come from one place; they just sift out of the sky, emanating equally from all space directions. This light is very similar to natural sunlight except that it contains very much less heat. Thus it will be recognized that such headquarters worlds are not luminous in space; if Jerusem were very near Urantia, it would not be visible.

The gases which reflect this light-energy from the Jerusem upper ionosphere back to the ground are very similar to those in the Urantia upper air belts which are concerned with the auroral phenomena of your so-called northern lights, although these are produced by different causes. On Urantia it is this same gas shield which prevents the escape of the terrestrial broadcast waves, reflecting them earthward when they strike this gas belt in their direct outward flight. In this way broadcasts are held near the surface as they journey through the air around your world.

This lighting of the sphere is uniformly maintained for seventy-five per cent of the Jerusem day, and then there is a gradual recession until, at the time of minimum illumination, the light is about that of your full moon on a clear night. This is the quiet hour for all Jerusem. Only the broadcast-receiving stations are in operation during this period of rest and rehabilitation.

The seven transitional study worlds and their forty-nine satellites are heated, lighted, energized, and watered by the Jerusem technique.

2. PHYSICAL FEATURES OF JERUSEM

On Jerusem you will miss the rugged mountain ranges of Urantia and other evolved worlds since there are neither earthquakes nor rainfalls, but you will enjoy the beauteous highlands and other unique variations of topography and landscape. Enormous areas of Jerusem are preserved in a "natural state," and the grandeur of such districts is quite beyond the powers of human imagination.

There are thousands upon thousands of small lakes but no raging rivers nor expansive oceans. There is no rainfall, neither storms nor blizzards, on any of the architectural worlds, but there is the daily precipitation of the condensation of moisture during the time of lowest temperature attending the light recession. (The dew point is higher on a three-gas world than on a two-gas planet like Urantia.) The physical plant life and the morontia world of living things both require moisture, but this is largely supplied by the subsoil system of circulation which extends all over the sphere, even up to the very tops of the highlands. This water system is not entirely subsurface, for there are many canals interconnecting the sparkling lakes of Jerusem.

The atmosphere of Jerusem is a three-gas mixture. This air is very similar to that of Urantia with the addition of a gas adapted to the respiration of the morontia order of life. This third gas in no way unfits the air for the respiration of animals or plants of the material orders.

The transportation system is allied with the circulatory streams of energy movement, these main energy currents being located at ten-mile intervals. By adjustment of physical mechanisms the material beings of the planet can proceed at a pace varying from two to five hundred miles per hour. The transport birds fly at about one hundred miles an hour. The air mechanisms of the Material Sons travel around five hundred miles per hour. Material and early morontia beings must utilize these mechanical means of transport, but spirit personalities proceed by liaison with the superior forces and spirit sources of energy.

Jerusem and its associated worlds are endowed with the ten standard divisions of physical life characteristic of the architectural spheres of Nebadon. And since there is no organic evolution on Jerusem, there are no conflicting forms of life, no struggle for existence, no survival of the fittest. Rather is there a creative adaptation which foreshadows the beauty, the harmony, and the perfection of the eternal worlds of the central and divine universe. And in all this creative perfection there is the most amazing inter-mingling of physical and of morontia life, artistically contrasted by the celestial artisans and their fellows.

Jerusem is indeed a foretaste of paradisiacal glory and grandeur. But you can never hope to gain an adequate idea of these glorious architectural worlds by any attempted description. There is so little that can be compared with aught on your world, and even then the things of Jerusem so transcend the things of Urantia that the comparison is almost grotesque. Until you actually arrive on Jerusem, you can hardly entertain anything like a true concept of the heavenly worlds, but that is not so long a time in the future when your coming experience on the system capital is compared with your sometime arrival on the more remote training spheres of the universe, the super-universe, and of Havona.

The manufacturing or laboratory sector of Jerusem is an extensive domain, one which Urantians would hardly recognize since it has no smoking chimneys; nevertheless, there is an intricate material economy associated with these special worlds, and there is a perfection of mechanical technique and physical achievement which would astonish and even awe your most experienced chemists and inventors. Pause to consider that this first world of detention in the Paradise journey is far more material than spiritual. Throughout your stay on Jerusem and its transition worlds you are far nearer your earth life of material things than your later life of advancing spirit existence.

Mount Seraph is the highest elevation on Jerusem, almost fifteen thousand feet, and is the point of departure for all transport seraphim. Numerous mechanical developments are used in providing initial energy for escaping the planetary gravity and overcoming the air resistance. A seraphic transport departs every three seconds of Urantia time throughout the light period and, sometimes, far into the recession. The transporters take off at about twenty-five standard miles per second of Urantia time and do not attain standard velocity until they are over two thousand miles away from Jerusem.

Transports arrive on the crystal field, the so-called sea of glass. Around this area are the receiving stations for the various orders of beings who traverse space by seraphic transport. Near the polar crystal receiving station for student visitors you may ascend the pearly observatory and view the immense relief map of the entire headquarters planet.

3. THE JERUSEM BROADCASTS

The super-universe and Paradise-Havona broadcasts are received on Jerusem in liaison with Salvington, Splandon, Ensa, Zion, and Edentia and by a technique involving the polar crystal, the sea of glass. In addition to provisions for the reception of these extra-Nebadon communications, there are three distinct groups of receiving stations. These separate but tricircular groups of stations are adjusted to the reception of broadcasts from the local worlds, from the constellation headquarters, and from the capital of the local galaxy. All these broadcasts are automatically displayed so as to be discernible by all types of beings present in the central broadcast amphitheater; of all preoccupations for an ascendant mortal on Jerusem, none is more engaging and engrossing than that of listening in on the never-ending stream of universe space reports.

This Jerusem broadcast-receiving station is encircled by an enormous amphitheater, constructed of scintillating materials largely unknown on Urantia and seating over five billion beings — material and morontia — besides accommodating innumerable spirit personalities. It is the favorite diversion for all Jerusem to spend their leisure at the broadcast station, there to learn of the welfare and state of the universe. And this is the only planetary activity which is not slowed down during the recession of light.

At this broadcast-receiving amphitheater the Salvington messages are coming in continuously. Near by, the Edentia word of the Most High Constellation Fathers is received at least once a day. Periodically the regular and special broadcasts of Uversa are relayed through Salvington, and when Paradise messages are in reception, the entire population is assembled around the sea of glass, and the Uversa friends add the reflectivity phenomena to the technique of the Paradise broadcast so that everything heard becomes visible. And it is in this manner that continual foretastes of advancing beauty and grandeur are afforded the mortal survivors as they journey inward on the eternal adventure.

The Jerusem sending station is located at the opposite pole of the sphere. All broadcasts to the individual worlds are relayed from the system capitals except the Michael messages, which sometimes go direct to their destinations over the archangels' circuit.

4. RESIDENTIAL AND ADMINISTRATIVE AREAS

Considerable portions of Jerusem are assigned as residential areas, while other portions of the system capital are given over to the necessary administrative functions involving the supervision of the affairs of 619 inhabited spheres, 56 transitional-culture worlds, and the system capital itself. On Jerusem and in Nebadon these arrangements are designed as follows:

1. *The circles* — the nonnative residential areas.
2. *The squares* — the system executive-administrative areas.

3. *The rectangles* — the rendezvous of the lower native life.
4. *The triangles* — the local or Jerusem administrative areas.

This arrangement of the system activities into circles, squares, rectangles, and triangles is common to all the system capitals of Nebadon. In another universe an entirely different arrangement might prevail. These are matters determined by the diverse plans of the Creator Sons.

Our narrative of these residential and administrative areas takes no account of the vast and beautiful estates of the Material Sons of God, the permanent citizens of Jerusem, neither do we mention numerous other fascinating orders of spirit and near-spirit creatures. For example: Jerusem enjoys the efficient services of the spironga of design for system function. These beings are devoted to spiritual ministry in behalf of the super-material residents and visitors. They are a wonderful group of intelligent and beautiful beings who are the transition servants of the higher morontia creatures and of the morontia helpers who labor for the upkeep and embellishment of all morontia creations. They are on Jerusem what the midway creatures are on Urantia, midway helpers functioning between the material and the spiritual.

The system capitals are unique in that they are the only worlds which exhibit well-nigh perfectly all three phases of universe existence: the material, the morontial, and the spiritual. Whether you are a material, morontia, or spirit personality, you will feel at home on Jerusem; so also do the combined beings, such as the midway creatures and the Material Sons.

Jerusem has great buildings of both material and morontia types, while the embellishment of the purely spiritual zones is no less exquisite and replete. If I only had words to tell you of the morontia counterparts of the marvelous physical equipment of Jerusem! If I could only go on to portray the sublime grandeur and exquisite perfection of the spiritual appointments of this headquarters world! Your most imaginative concept of perfection of beauty and repleteness of appointment would hardly approach these grandeurs. And Jerusem is but the first step on the way to the supernal perfection of Paradise beauty.

5. THE JERUSEM CIRCLES

The residential reservations assigned to the major groups of universe life are designated the Jerusem circles. Those circle groups which find mention in these narratives are the following:

1. The circles of the Sons of God.
2. The circles of the angels and higher spirits.
3. The circles of the Universe Aids, including the creature-trinitized sons not assigned to the Trinity Teacher Sons.
4. The circles of the Master Physical Controllers.
5. The circles of the assigned ascending mortals, including the midway creatures.
6. The circles of the courtesy colonies.
7. The circles of the Corps of the Finality.

Each of these residential groupings consists of seven concentric and successively elevated circles. They are all constructed along the same lines but are of different sizes and are fashioned of differing materials. They are all surrounded by far-reaching enclosures, which mount up to form extensive promenades entirely encompassing every group of seven concentric circles.

1. *Circles of the Sons of God.* Though the Sons of God possess a social planet of their own, one of the transitional-culture worlds, they also occupy these extensive domains on Jerusem. On their transitional-culture world the ascending mortals freely mingle with all orders of divine sonship. There you will personally know and love these Sons, but their social life is largely confined to this special world and its satellites. In the Jerusem circles, however, these various groups of sonship may be observed at work. And since morontia vision is of enormous range, you can walk about on the Sons' promenades and overlook the intriguing activities of their numerous orders.

These seven circles of the Sons are concentric and successively elevated so that each of the outer and larger circles overlooks the inner and smaller ones, each being surrounded by a public promenade wall. These walls are constructed of crystal gems of gleaming brightness and are so elevated as to overlook all of their respective residential circles. The many gates — from fifty to one hundred and fifty thousand — which penetrate each of these walls consist of single pearly crystals.

The first circle of the domain of the Sons is occupied by the Magisterial Sons and their personal staffs. Here center all of the plans and immediate activities of the bestowal and adjudicational services of these juridical Sons. It is also through this center that the Avonals of the system maintain contact with the universe.

The second circle is occupied by the Trinity Teacher Sons. In this sacred domain the Daynals and their associates carry forward the training of the newly arrived primary Teacher Sons. And in all of this work they are ably assisted by a division of certain co-ordinates of the Brilliant Evening Stars. The creature-trinitized sons occupy a sector of the Daynal circle. The Trinity Teacher Sons come the nearest to being the personal representatives of the Universal Father in a local system; they are at least Trinity-origin beings. This second circle is a domain of extraordinary interest to all the peoples of Jerusem.

The third circle is devoted to the Melchizedeks. Here the system chiefs reside and supervise the almost endless activities of these versatile Sons. From the first of the mansion worlds on through all the Jerusem career of ascending mortals, the Melchizedeks are foster fathers and ever-present advisers. It would not be amiss to say that they are the dominant influence on Jerusem aside from the ever-present activities of the Material Sons and Daughters.

The fourth circle is the home of the Vorondadeks and all other orders of the visiting and observer Sons who are not otherwise provided for. The Most High Constellation Fathers take up their abode in this circle when on visits of inspection to the local system. Perfectors of Wisdom, Divine Counselors, and Universal Censors all reside in this circle when on duty in the system.

The fifth circle is the abode of the Lanonandeks, the sonship order of the System Sovereigns and the Planetary Princes. The three groups mingle as one when at home in this domain. The system reserves are held in this circle, while the System Sovereign has a temple situated at the center of the governing group of structures on administration hill.

The sixth circle is the tarrying place of the system Life Carriers. All orders of these Sons are here assembled, and from here they go forth on their world assignments.

The seventh circle is the rendezvous of the ascending sons, those assigned mortals who may be temporarily functioning on the system headquarters, together with their seraphic consorts. All ex-mortals above the status of Jerusem citizens and below that of finaliters are reckoned as belonging to the group having its headquarters in this circle.

These circular reservations of the Sons occupy an enormous area, and until two thousand years ago there existed a great open space at its center. This central region is now occupied by the Michael memorial, completed some five hundred years ago. Four hundred and ninety-five years ago, when this temple was dedicated, Michael was present in person, and all Jerusem heard the touching story of the Master Son's bestowal on Urantia, the least of Satania. The Michael memorial is now the center of all activities embraced in the modified management of the system occasioned by Michael's bestowal, including most of the more recently transplanted Salvington activities. The memorial staff consists of over one million personalities.

2. *The circles of the angels*. Like the residential area of the Sons, these circles of the angels consist of seven concentric and successively elevated circles, each overlooking the inner areas.

The first circle of the angels is occupied by the Higher Personalities of the Infinite Spirit who may be stationed on the headquarters world — Solitary Messengers and their associates. The second circle is dedicated to the messenger hosts, Technical Advisers, companions, inspectors, and recorders as they may chance to function on Jerusem from time to time. The third circle is held by the ministering spirits of the higher orders and groupings.

The fourth circle is held by the administrator seraphim, and the seraphim serving in a local system like Satania are an "innumerable host of angels." The fifth circle is occupied by the planetary seraphim, while the sixth is the home of the transition ministers. The seventh circle is the tarrying sphere of certain unrevealed orders of seraphim. The recorders of all these groups of angels do not sojourn with their fellows, being domiciled in the Jerusem temple of records. All records are preserved in triplicate in this threefold hall of archives. On a system headquarters, records are always preserved in material, in morontia, and in spirit form.

These seven circles are surrounded by the exhibit panorama of Jerusem, five thousand standard miles in circumference, which is devoted to the presentation of the advancing status of the peopled worlds of Satania and is constantly revised so as to truly represent up-to-date conditions on the individual planets. I doubt not that this vast promenade overlooking the circles of the angels will be the first sight of Jerusem to claim your attention when you are permitted extended leisure on your earlier visits.

These exhibits are in charge of the native life of Jerusem, but they are assisted by the ascenders from the various Satania worlds who are tarrying on Jerusem en route to Edentia. The portrayal of planetary conditions and world progress is effected by many methods, some known to you, but mostly by techniques unknown on Urantia. These exhibits occupy the outer edge of this vast wall. The remainder of the promenade is almost entirely open, being highly and magnificently embellished.

3. *The circles of the Universe Aids* have the headquarters of the Evening Stars situated in the enormous central space. Here is located the system headquarters of Galantia, the associate head of this powerful group of superangels, being the first commissioned of all the ascendant Evening Stars. This is one of the most magnificent of all the administrative sectors of Jerusem, even though it is among the more recent constructions. This center is fifty miles in diameter. The Galantia headquarters is a monolithic cast crystal, wholly transparent. These material-morontia crystals are greatly appreciated by both morontia and material beings. The created Evening Stars exert their influence all over Jerusem, being possessed of such extra-personality attributes. The entire world has been rendered spiritually fragrant since so many of their activities were transferred here from Salvington.

4. *The circles of the Master Physical Controllers.* The various orders of the Master Physical Controllers are concentrically arranged around the vast temple of power, wherein presides the power chief of the system in association with the chief of the Morontia Power Supervisors. This temple of power is one of two sectors on Jerusem where ascending mortals and midway creatures are not permitted. The other one is the dematerializing sector in the

area of the Material Sons, a series of laboratories wherein the transport seraphim transform material beings into a state quite like that of the morontia order of existence.

5. *The circles of the ascending mortals*. The central area of the circles of the ascending mortals is occupied by a group of 619 planetary memorials representative of the inhabited worlds of the system, and these structures periodically undergo extensive changes. It is the privilege of the mortals from each world to agree, from time to time, upon certain of the alterations or additions to their planetary memorials. Many changes are even now being made in the Urantia structures. The center of these 619 temples is occupied by a working model of Edentia and its many worlds of ascendant culture. This model is forty miles in diameter and is an actual reproduction of the Edentia system, true to the original in every detail.

Ascenders enjoy their Jerusem services and take pleasure in observing the techniques of other groups. Everything done in these various circles is open to the full observation of all Jerusem.

The activities of such a world are of three distinct varieties: work, progress, and play. Stated otherwise, they are: service, study, and relaxation. The composite activities consist of social intercourse, group entertainment, and divine worship. There is great educational value in mingling with diverse groups of personalities, orders very different from one's own fellows.

6. *The circles of the courtesy colonies*. The seven circles of the courtesy colonies are graced by three enormous structures: the vast astronomic observatory of Jerusem, the gigantic art gallery of Satania, and the immense assembly hall of the reversion directors, the theater of morontia activities devoted to rest and recreation.

The celestial artisans direct the spornagia and provide the host of creative decorations and monumental memorials which abound in every place of public assembly. The studios of these artisans are among the largest and most beautiful of all the matchless structures of this wonderful world. The other courtesy colonies maintain extensive and beautiful headquarters. Many of these buildings are constructed wholly of crystal gems. All the architectural worlds abound in crystals and the so-called precious metals.

7. *The circles of the finaliters* have a unique structure at the center. And this same vacant temple is found on every system headquarters world throughout Nebadon. This edifice on Jerusem is sealed with the insignia of Michael, and it bears this inscription: "Undedicated to the seventh stage of spirit — to the eternal assignment." Gabriel placed the seal on this temple of mystery, and none but Michael can or may break the seal of sovereignty affixed by the Bright and Morning Star. Some day you shall look upon this silent temple, even though you may not penetrate its mystery.

Other Jerusem circles: In addition to these residential circles there are on Jerusem numerous additional designated abodes.

6. THE EXECUTIVE-ADMINISTRATIVE SQUARES

The executive-administrative divisions of the system are located in the immense departmental squares, one thousand in number. Each administrative unit is divided into one hundred subdivisions of ten subgroups each. These one thousand squares are clustered in ten grand divisions, thus constituting the following ten administrative departments:

1. Physical maintenance and material improvement, the domains of physical power and energy.
2. Arbitration, ethics, and administrative adjudication.
3. Planetary and local affairs.
4. Constellation and universe affairs.
5. Education and other Melchizedek activities.
6. Planetary and system physical progress, the scientific domains of Satania activities.
7. Morontia affairs.
8. Pure spirit activities and ethics.
9. Ascendant ministry.
10. Grand universe philosophy.

These structures are transparent; hence all system activities can be viewed even by student visitors.

7. THE RECTANGLES — THE SPORNAGIA

The one thousand *rectangles* of Jerusem are occupied by the lower native life of the headquarters planet, and at their center is situated the vast circular headquarters of the spornagia.

On Jerusem you will be amazed by the agricultural achievements of the wonderful spornagia. There the land is cultivated largely for aesthetic and ornamental effects. The spornagia are the landscape gardeners of the headquarters worlds, and they are both original and artistic in their treatment of the open spaces of Jerusem. They utilize both animals and numerous mechanical contrivances in the culture of the soil. They are intelligently expert in the employment of the power agencies of their realms as well as in the utilization of numerous orders of their lesser brethren of the lower animal creations, many of which are provided them on these special worlds. This order of animal life is now largely directed by the ascending midway creatures from the evolutionary spheres.

Spornagia are not Adjuster indwelt. They do not possess survival souls, but they do enjoy long lives, sometimes to the extent of forty to fifty thousand standard years. Their number is legion, and they afford physical ministry to all orders of universe personalities requiring material service.

Although spornagia neither possess nor evolve survival souls, though they do not have personality, nevertheless, they do evolve an individuality which can experience reincarnation. When, with the passing of time, the physical bodies of these unique creatures deteriorate from usage and age, their creators, in collaboration with the Life Carriers, fabricate new bodies in which the old spornagia re-establish their residences.

Spornagia are the only creatures in all the universe of Nebadon who experience this or any other sort of reincarnation. They are only reactive to the first five of the adjutant mind-spirits; they are not responsive to the spirits of worship and wisdom. But the five-adjutant mind equivalates to a totality or sixth reality level, and it is this factor which persists as an experiential identity.

I am quite without comparisons in undertaking to describe these useful and unusual creatures as there are no animals on the evolutionary worlds comparable to them. They are not evolutionary beings, having been projected by the Life Carriers in their present form and status. They are bisexual and procreate as they are required to meet the needs of a growing population.

Perhaps I can best suggest to Urantia minds something of the nature of these beautiful and serviceable creatures by saying that they embrace the combined traits of a faithful horse and an affectionate dog and manifest an intelligence exceeding that of the highest type of chimpanzee. And they are very beautiful, as judged by the physical standards of Urantia. They are most appreciative of the attentions shown them by the material and semi-material sojourners on these architectural worlds. They have a vision which permits them to recognize — in addition to material beings — the morontia creations, the lower angelic orders, midway creatures, and some of the lower orders of spirit personalities. They do not comprehend worship of the Infinite, nor do they grasp the import of the Eternal, but they do, through affection for their masters, join in the outward spiritual devotions of their realms.

There are those who believe that, in a future universe age, these faithful spornagia will escape from their animal level of existence and attain a worthy evolutionary destiny of progressive intellectual growth and even spiritual achievement.

8. THE JERUSEM TRIANGLES

The purely local and routine affairs of Jerusem are directed from the one hundred *triangles*. These units are clustered around the ten marvelous structures domiciling the local administration of Jerusem. The triangles are surrounded by the panoramic depiction of the system headquarters history. At present there is an erasure of over two standard miles in this circular story. This sector will be restored upon the readmission of Satania into the constellation family. Every provision for this event has been made by the decrees of Michael, but the tribunal of the Ancients of Days has not yet finished the adjudication of the affairs of the Lucifer rebellion. Satania may not come back into the full fellowship of Norlatiadek so long as it harbors archrebels, high created beings who have fallen from light into darkness.

When Satania can return to the constellation fold, then will come up for consideration the readmission of the isolated worlds into the system family of inhabited planets, accompanied by their restoration to the spiritual communion of the realms. But even if Urantia were restored to the system circuits, you would still be embarrassed by the fact that your whole system rests under a Norlatiadek quarantine partially segregating it from all other systems.

But ere long, the adjudication of Lucifer and his associates will restore the Satania system to the Norlatiadek constellation, and subsequently, Urantia and the other isolated spheres will be restored to the Satania circuits, and again will such worlds enjoy the privileges of interplanetary communication and intersystem communion.

There will come an end for rebels and rebellion. The Supreme Rulers are merciful and patient, but the law of deliberately nourished evil is universally and unerringly executed. "The wages of sin is death" — eternal obliteration.

[Presented by an Archangel of Nebadon.]

PAPER 47
THE SEVEN MANSION WORLDS

THE CREATOR SON, when on Urantia, spoke of the "many mansions in the Father's universe." In a certain sense, all fifty-six of the encircling worlds of Jerusem are devoted to the transitional culture of ascending mortals, but the seven satellites of world number one are more specifically known as the mansion worlds.

Transition world number one itself is quite exclusively devoted to ascendant activities, being the headquarters of the finaliter corps assigned to Satania. This world now serves as the headquarters for more than one hundred thousand companies of finaliters, and there are one thousand glorified beings in each of these groups.

When a system is settled in light and life, and as the mansion worlds one by one cease to serve as mortal-training stations, they are taken over by the increasing finaliter population which accumulates in these older and more highly perfected systems.

The seven mansion worlds are in charge of the morontia supervisors and the Melchizedeks. There is an acting governor on each world who is directly responsible to the Jerusem rulers. The Uversa conciliators maintain headquarters on each of the mansion worlds, while adjoining is the local rendezvous of the Technical Advisers. The reversion directors and celestial artisans maintain group headquarters on each of these worlds. The spironga function from mansion world number two onward, while all seven, in common with the other transitional-culture planets and the headquarters world, are abundantly provided with spornagia of standard creation.

1. THE FINALITERS' WORLD

Although only finaliters and certain groups of salvaged children and their caretakers are resident on transitional world number one, provision is made for the entertainment of all classes of spirit beings, transition mortals, and student visitors. The spornagia, who function on all of these worlds, are hospitable hosts to all beings whom they can recognize. They have a vague feeling concerning the finaliters but cannot visualize them. They must regard them much as you do the angels in your present physical state.

Though the finaliter world is a sphere of exquisite physical beauty and extraordinary morontia embellishment, the great spirit abode located at the center of activities, the temple of the finaliters, is not visible to the unaided material or early morontia vision. But the energy transformers are able to visualize many of these realities to ascending mortals, and from time to time they do thus function, as on the occasions of the class assemblies of the mansion world students on this cultural sphere.

All through the mansion world experience you are in a way spiritually aware of the presence of your glorified brethren of Paradise attainment, but it is very refreshing, now and then, actually to perceive them as they function in their headquarters abodes. You will not spontaneously visualize finaliters until you acquire true spirit vision.

On the first mansion world all survivors must pass the requirements of the parental commission from their native planets. The present Urantia commission consists of twelve parental couples, recently arrived, who have had mortal experience in rearing three or more children to the pubescent age. Service on this commission is rotational and is for only ten years as a rule. All who fail to satisfy these commissioners as to their parental experience must further qualify by service in the homes of the Material Sons on Jerusem or in part in the probationary nursery on the finaliters' world.

But irrespective of parental experience, mansion world parents who have growing children in the probation nursery are given every opportunity to collaborate with the morontia custodians of such children regarding their instruction and training. These parents are permitted to journey there for visits as often as four times a year. And it is one of the most touchingly beautiful scenes of all the ascending career to observe the mansion world parents embrace their material offspring on the occasions of their periodic pilgrimages to the finaliter world. While one or both parents may leave a mansion world ahead of the child, they are quite often contemporary for a season.

No ascending mortal can escape the experience of rearing children — their own or others — either on the material worlds or subsequently on the finaliter world or on Jerusem. Fathers must pass through this essential experience just as certainly as mothers. It is an unfortunate and mistaken notion of modern peoples on Urantia that child culture is largely the task of mothers. Children need fathers as well as mothers, and fathers need this parental experience as much as do mothers.

2. THE PROBATIONARY NURSERY

The infant-receiving schools of Satania are situated on the finaliter world, the first of the Jerusem transition-culture spheres. These infant-receiving schools are enterprises devoted to the nurture and training of the children of time, including those who have died on the evolutionary worlds of space before the acquirement of individual status on the universe records. In the event of the survival of either or both of such a child's parents, the guardian of destiny deputizes her associated cherubim as the custodian of the child's potential identity, charging the cherubim with the responsibility of delivering this undeveloped soul into the hands of the Mansion World Teachers in the probationary nurseries of the morontia worlds.

It is these same deserted cherubim who, as Mansion World Teachers, under the supervision of the Melchizedeks, maintain such extensive educational facilities for the training of the probationary wards of the finaliters. These wards of the finaliters, these infants of ascending mortals, are always personalized as of their exact physical status at the time of death except for reproductive potential. This awakening occurs at the exact time of the parental arrival on the first mansion world. And then are these children given every opportunity, as they are, to choose the heavenly way just as they would have made such a choice on the worlds where death so untimely terminated their careers.

On the nursery world, probationary creatures are grouped according to whether or not they have Adjusters, for the Adjusters come to indwell these material children just as on the worlds of time. Children of pre-Adjuster ages are cared for in families of five, ranging in ages from one year and under up to approximately five years, or that age when the Adjuster arrives.

All children on the evolving worlds who have Thought Adjusters, but who before death had not made a choice concerning the Paradise career, are also repersonalized on the finaliter world of the system, where they likewise grow up in the families of the Material Sons and their associates as do those little ones who arrived without Adjusters, but who will subsequently receive the Mystery Monitors after attaining the requisite age of moral choice.

The Adjuster-indwelt children and youths on the finaliter world are also reared in families of five, ranging in ages from six to fourteen; approximately, these families consist of children whose ages are six, eight, ten, twelve, and fourteen. Any time after sixteen, if final choice has been made, they translate to the first mansion world and begin their Paradise ascent. Some make a choice before this age and go on to the ascension spheres, but very few children under sixteen years of age, as reckoned by Urantia standards, will be found on the mansion worlds.

The guardian seraphim attend these youths in the probationary nursery on the finaliter world just as they spiritually minister to mortals on the evolutionary planets, while the faithful spornagia minister to their physical necessities. And so do these children grow up on the transition world until such time as they make their final choice.

When material life has run its course, if no choice has been made for the ascendant life, or if these children of time definitely decide against the Havona adventure, death automatically terminates their probationary careers. There is no adjudication of such cases; there is no resurrection from such a second death. They simply become as though they had not been.

But if they choose the Paradise path of perfection, they are immediately made ready for translation to the first mansion world, where many of them arrive in time to join their parents in the Havona ascent. After passing through Havona and attaining the Deities, these salvaged souls of mortal origin constitute the permanent ascendant citizenship of Paradise. These children who have been deprived of the valuable and essential evolutionary experience on the worlds of mortal nativity are not mustered into the Corps of the Finality.

3. THE FIRST MANSION WORLD

On the mansion worlds the resurrected mortal survivors resume their lives just where they left off when overtaken by death. When you go from Urantia to the first mansion world, you will notice considerable change, but if you had come from a more normal and progressive sphere of time, you would hardly notice the difference except for the fact that you were in possession of a different body; the tabernacle of flesh and blood has been left behind on the world of nativity.

The very center of all activities on the first mansion world is the resurrection hall, the enormous temple of personality assembly. This gigantic structure consists of the central rendezvous of the seraphic destiny guardians, the Thought Adjusters, and the archangels of the resurrection. The Life Carriers also function with these celestial beings in the resurrection of the dead.

The mortal-mind transcripts and the active creature-memory patterns as transformed from the material levels to the spiritual are the individual possession of the detached Thought Adjusters; these spiritized factors of mind, memory, and creature personality are forever a part of such Adjusters. The creature mind-matrix and the passive potentials of identity are present in the morontia soul intrusted to the keeping of the seraphic destiny guardians. And it is the reuniting of the morontia-soul trust of the seraphim and the spirit-mind trust of the Adjuster that reassembles creature personality and constitutes resurrection of a sleeping survivor.

If a transitory personality of mortal origin should never be thus reassembled, the spirit elements of the non-surviving mortal creature would forever continue as an integral part of the individual experiential endowment of the onetime indwelling Adjuster.

From the Temple of New Life there extend seven radial wings. There are one hundred thousand personal resurrection chambers in each of these seven wings terminating in the circular class assembly halls, which serve as the awakening chambers for as many as one million individuals. These halls are surrounded by the personality assembly chambers. Regardless of the technique which may be employed on the individual worlds of time in connection with special or dispensational resurrections, the real and conscious reassembly of actual and complete personality takes place in the resurrection halls of mansonia number one. Throughout all eternity you will recall the profound memory impressions of your first witnessing of these resurrection mornings.

From the resurrection halls you proceed to the Melchizedek sector, where you are assigned permanent residence. Then you enter upon ten days of personal liberty. You are free to explore the immediate vicinity of your new home and to familiarize yourself with the program which lies immediately ahead. You also have time to gratify your desire to consult the registry and call upon your loved ones and other earth friends who may have preceded you to these worlds. At the end of your ten-day period of leisure you begin the second step in the Paradise journey, for the mansion worlds are actual training spheres, not merely detention planets.

On mansion world number one (or another in case of advanced status) you will resume your intellectual training and spiritual development at the exact level whereon they were interrupted by death. Between the time of planetary death or translation and resurrection on the mansion world, mortal man gains absolutely nothing aside from experiencing the fact of survival. You begin over there right where you leave off down here.

Almost the entire experience of mansion world number one pertains to deficiency ministry. Survivors arriving on this first of the detention spheres present so many and such varied defects of creature character and deficiencies of mortal experience that the major activities of the realm are occupied with the correction and cure of these manifold legacies of the life in the flesh on the material evolutionary worlds of time and space.

The sojourn on mansion world number one is designed to develop mortal survivors at least up to the status of the post-Adamic dispensation on the normal evolutionary worlds. Spiritually, of course, the mansion world students are far in advance of such a state of mere human development.

If you are not to be detained on mansion world number one, at the end of ten days you will enter the translation sleep and proceed to world number two, and every ten days thereafter you will thus advance until you arrive on the world of your assignment.

The center of the seven major circles of the first mansion world administration is occupied by the temple of the Morontia Companions, the personal guides assigned to ascending mortals. These companions are the offspring of the local universe Mother Spirit, and there are several million of them on the morontia worlds of Satania. Aside from those assigned as group companions, you will have much to do with the interpreters and translators, the building custodians, and the excursion supervisors. And all of these companions are most co-operative with those who have to do with developing your personality factors of mind and spirit within the morontia body.

As you start out on the first mansion world, one Morontia Companion is assigned to each company of one thousand ascending mortals, but you will encounter larger numbers as you progress through the seven mansion spheres. These beautiful and versatile beings are companionable associates and charming guides. They are free to accompany individuals or selected groups to any of the transition-culture spheres, including their satellite worlds. They are the excursion guides and leisure associates of all ascending mortals. They often accompany survivor groups on periodic visits to Jerusem, and on any day you are there, you can go to the registry sector of the system capital and meet ascending mortals from all seven of the mansion worlds since they freely journey back and forth between their residential abodes and the system headquarters.

4. THE SECOND MANSION WORLD

It is on this sphere that you are more fully inducted into the mansonia life. The groupings of the morontia life begin to take form; working groups and social organizations start to function, communities take on formal proportions, and the advancing mortals inaugurate new social orders and governmental arrangements.

Spirit-fused survivors occupy the mansion worlds in common with the Adjuster-fused ascending mortals. While the various orders of celestial life differ, they are all friendly and fraternal. In all the worlds of ascension you will find nothing comparable to human intolerance and the discriminations of inconsiderate caste systems.

As you ascend the mansion worlds one by one, they become more crowded with the morontia activities of advancing survivors. As you go forward, you will recognize more and more of the Jerusem features added to the mansion worlds. The sea of glass makes its appearance on the second mansonia.

A newly developed and suitably adjusted morontia body is acquired at the time of each advance from one mansion world to another. You go to sleep with the seraphic transport and awake with the new but undeveloped body in the resurrection halls, much as when you first arrived on mansion world number one except that the Thought Adjuster does not leave you during these transit sleeps between the mansion worlds. Your personality remains intact after you once pass from the evolutionary worlds to the initial mansion world.

Your Adjuster memory remains fully intact as you ascend the morontia life. Those mental associations that were purely animalistic and wholly material naturally perished with the physical brain, but everything in your mental life which was worth while, and which had survival value, was counter-parted by the Adjuster and is retained as a part of personal memory all the way through the ascendant career. You will be conscious of all your worth-while experiences as you advance from one mansion world to another and from one section of the universe to another — even to Paradise.

Though you have morontia bodies, you continue, through all seven of these worlds, to eat, drink, and rest. You partake of the morontia order of food, a kingdom of living energy unknown on the material worlds. Both food and water are fully utilized in the morontia body; there is no residual waste. Pause to consider: Mansonia number one is a very material sphere, presenting the early beginnings of the morontia regime. You are still a near human and not far removed from the limited viewpoints of mortal life, but each world discloses definite progress. From sphere to sphere you grow less material, more intellectual, and slightly more spiritual. The spiritual progress is greatest on the last three of these seven progressive worlds.

Biological deficiencies were largely made up on the first mansion world. There defects in planetary experiences pertaining to sex life, family association, and parental function were either corrected or were projected for future rectification among the Material Son families on Jerusem.

Mansonia number two more specifically provides for the removal of all phases of intellectual conflict and for the cure of all varieties of mental disharmony. The effort to master the significance of morontia mota, begun on the first mansion world, is here more earnestly continued. The development on mansonia number two compares with the intellectual status of the post-Magisterial Son culture of the ideal evolutionary worlds.

5. THE THIRD MANSION WORLD

Mansonia the third is the headquarters of the Mansion World Teachers. Though they function on all seven of the mansion spheres, they maintain their group headquarters at the center of the school circles of world number three. There are millions of these instructors on the mansion and higher morontia worlds. These advanced and glorified cherubim serve as morontia teachers all the way up from the mansion worlds to the last sphere of local universe ascendant training. They will be among the last to bid you an affectionate adieu when the farewell time draws near, the time when you bid good-bye — at least for a few ages — to the universe of your origin, when you enseraphim for transit to the receiving worlds of the super-universe.

When sojourning on the first mansion world, you have permission to visit the first of the transition worlds, the headquarters of the finaliters and the system probationary nursery for the nurture of undeveloped evolutionary children. When you arrive on mansonia number two, you receive permission periodically to visit transition world number two, where are located the morontia supervisor headquarters for all Satania and the training schools for the various morontia orders. When you reach mansion world number three, you are immediately granted a permit to visit the third transition sphere, the headquarters of the angelic orders and the home of their various system training schools. Visits to Jerusem from this world are increasingly profitable and are of ever-heightening interest to the advancing mortals.

Mansonia the third is a world of great personal and social achievement for all who have not made the equivalent of these circles of culture prior to release from the flesh on the mortal nativity worlds. On this sphere more positive educational work is begun. The training of the first two mansion worlds is mostly of a deficiency nature — negative — in that it has to do with supplementing the experience of the life in the flesh. On this third mansion world the survivors really begin their progressive morontia culture. The chief purpose of this training is to enhance the understanding of the correlation of morontia mota and mortal logic, the co-ordination of morontia mota and human philosophy. Surviving mortals now gain practical insight into true metaphysics. This is the real introduction to the intelligent comprehension of cosmic meanings and universe interrelationships. The culture of the third mansion world partakes of the nature of the post-bestowal Son age of a normal inhabited planet.

6. THE FOURTH MANSION WORLD

When you arrive on the fourth mansion world, you have well entered upon the morontia career; you have progressed a long way from the initial material existence. Now are you given permission to make visits to transition world number four, there to become familiar with the headquarters and training schools of the super-angels, including the Brilliant Evening Stars. Through the good offices of these super-angels of the fourth transition world the morontia visitors are enabled to draw very close to the various orders of the Sons of God during the periodic visits to Jerusem, for new sectors of the system capital are gradually opening up to the advancing mortals as they make these repeated visits to the headquarters world. New grandeurs are progressively unfolding to the expanding minds of these ascenders.

On the fourth mansonia the individual ascender more fittingly finds his place in the group working and class functions of the morontia life. Ascenders here develop increased appreciation of the broadcasts and other phases of local universe culture and progress.

It is during the period of training on world number four that the ascending mortals are really first introduced to the demands and delights of the true social life of morontia creatures. And it is indeed a new experience for evolutionary creatures to participate in social activities which are predicated neither on personal aggrandizement nor on self-seeking conquest. A new social order is being introduced, one based on the understanding sympathy of mutual appreciation, the unselfish love of mutual service, and the overmastering motivation of the realization of a common and supreme destiny — the Paradise goal of worshipful and divine perfection. Ascenders are all becoming self-conscious of God-knowing, God-revealing, God-seeking, and God-finding.

The intellectual and social culture of this fourth mansion world is comparable to the mental and social life of the post-Teacher Son age on the planets of normal evolution. The spiritual status is much in advance of such a mortal dispensation.

7. THE FIFTH MANSION WORLD

Transport to the fifth mansion world represents a tremendous forward step in the life of a morontia progressor. The experience on this world is a real foretaste of Jerusem life. Here you begin to realize the high destiny of the loyal evolutionary worlds since they may normally progress to this stage during their natural planetary development. The culture of this mansion world corresponds in general to that of the early era of light and life on the planets of normal evolutionary progress. And from this you can understand why it is so arranged that the highly cultured and progressive types of beings who sometimes inhabit these advanced evolutionary worlds are exempt from passing through one or more, or even all, of the mansion spheres.

Having mastered the local universe language before leaving the fourth mansion world, you now devote more time to the perfection of the tongue of Uversa to the end that you may be proficient in both languages before arriving on Jerusem with residential status. All ascending mortals are bilingual from the system headquarters up to Havona. And then it is only necessary to enlarge the super-universe vocabulary, still additional enlargement being required for residence on Paradise.

Upon arrival on mansonia number five the pilgrim is given permission to visit the transition world of corresponding number, the Sons' headquarters. Here the ascendant mortal becomes personally familiar with the various groups of divine sonship. He has heard of these superb beings and has already met them on Jerusem, but now he comes really to know them.

On the fifth mansonia you begin to learn of the constellation study worlds. Here you meet the first of the instructors who begin to prepare you for the subsequent constellation sojourn. More of this preparation continues on worlds six and seven, while the finishing touches are supplied in the sector of the ascending mortals on Jerusem.

A real birth of cosmic consciousness takes place on mansonia number five. You are becoming universe minded. This is indeed a time of expanding horizons. It is beginning to dawn upon the enlarging minds of the ascending mortals that some stupendous and magnificent, some supernal and divine, destiny awaits all who complete the progressive Paradise ascension, which has been so laboriously but so joyfully and auspiciously begun. At about this point the average mortal ascender begins to manifest bona fide experiential enthusiasm for the Havona ascent. Study is becoming voluntary, unselfish service natural, and worship spontaneous. A real morontia character is budding; a real morontia creature is evolving.

8. THE SIXTH MANSION WORLD

Sojourners on this sphere are permitted to visit transition world number six, where they learn more about the high spirits of the super-universe, although they are not able to visualize many of these celestial beings. Here they also receive their first lessons in the prospective spirit career which so immediately follows graduation from the morontia training of the local universe.

The assistant System Sovereign makes frequent visits to this world, and the initial instruction is here begun in the techniques of galaxy and universe administration. The first lessons embracing the affairs of a whole universe are now imparted.

This is a brilliant age for ascending mortals and usually witnesses the perfect fusion of the human mind and the divine Adjuster. In potential, this fusion may have occurred previously, but the actual working identity many times is not achieved until the time of the sojourn on the fifth mansion world or even the sixth.

The union of the evolving immortal soul with the eternal and divine Adjuster is signalized by the seraphic summoning of the supervising super-angel for resurrected survivors and of the archangel of record for those going to judgment on the third day; and then, in the presence of such a survivor's morontia associates, these messengers of confirmation speak: "This is a beloved son in whom I am well pleased." This simple ceremony marks the entrance of an ascending mortal upon the eternal career of Paradise service.

Immediately upon the confirmation of Adjuster fusion the new morontia being is introduced to his fellows for the first time by his new name and is granted the forty days of spiritual retirement from all routine activities wherein to commune with himself and to choose some one of the optional routes to Havona and to select from the differential techniques of Paradise attainment.

[JFC: for an alternate description of this kind of spiritual vocation selection see "A Treatise on Cosmic Fire", by Alice A. Bailey, Section Three, Division B "The Nature of the Seven Cosmic Paths" pages 1241-1266.]

But still are these brilliant beings more or less material; they are far from being true spirits; they are more like super-mortals, spiritually speaking, still a little lower than the angels. But they are truly becoming marvelous creatures.

During the sojourn on world number six the mansion world students achieve a status which is comparable with the exalted development charac-terizing those evolutionary worlds which have normally progressed beyond the initial stage of light and life. The organization of society on this mansonia is of a high order. The shadow of the mortal nature grows less and less as these worlds are ascended one by one. You are becoming more and more adorable as you leave behind the coarse vestiges of planetary animal origin. "Coming up through great tribulation" serves to make glorified mortals very kind and understanding, very sympathetic and tolerant.

9. THE SEVENTH MANSION WORLD

The experience on this sphere is the crowning achievement of the immediate post-mortal career. During your sojourn here you will receive the instruction of many teachers, all of whom will co-operate in the task of preparing you for residence on Jerusem. Any discernible differences between those mortals hailing from the isolated and retarded worlds and those survivors from the more advanced and enlightened spheres are virtually obliterated during the sojourn on the seventh mansion world. Here you will be purged of all the remnants of unfortunate heredity, unwholesome environment, and unspiritual planetary tendencies. The last remnants of the "mark of the beast" are here eradicated.

While sojourning on mansonia number seven, permission is granted to visit transition world number seven, the world of the Universal Father. Here you begin a new and more spiritual worship of the unseen Father, a habit you will increasingly pursue all the way up through your long ascending career. You find the Father's temple on this world of transitional culture, but you do not see the Father.

Now begins the formation of classes for graduation to Jerusem. You have gone from world to world as individuals, but now you prepare to depart for Jerusem in groups, although, within certain limits, an ascender may elect to tarry on the seventh mansion world for the purpose of enabling a tardy member of his earthly or mansonia working group to catch up with him.

The personnel of the seventh mansonia assemble on the sea of glass to witness your departure for Jerusem with residential status. Hundreds or thousands of times you may have visited Jerusem, but always as a guest; never before have you proceeded toward the system capital in the company of a group of your fellows who were bidding an eternal farewell to the whole mansonia career as ascending mortals. You will soon be welcomed on the receiving field of the headquarters world as Jerusem citizens.

You will greatly enjoy your progress through the seven dematerializing worlds; they are really demortalizing spheres. You are mostly human on the first mansion world, just a mortal being minus a material body, a human mind housed in a morontia form — a material body of the morontia world but not a mortal house of flesh and blood. You really pass from the mortal state to the immortal status at the time of Adjuster fusion, and by the time you have finished the Jerusem career, you will be full-fledged morontians.

10. JERUSEM CITIZENSHIP

The reception of a new class of mansion world graduates is the signal for all Jerusem to assemble as a committee of welcome. Even the spornagia enjoy the arrival of these triumphant ascenders of evolutionary origin, those who have run the planetary race and finished the mansion world progression. Only the physical controllers and Morontia Power Supervisors are absent from these occasions of rejoicing.

John the Revelator saw a vision of the arrival of a class of advancing mortals from the seventh mansion world to their first heaven, the glories of Jerusem. He recorded: "And I saw as it were a sea of glass mingled with fire; and those who had gained the victory over the beast that was originally in them and over the image that persisted through the mansion worlds and finally over the last mark and trace, standing on the sea of glass, having the harps of God, and singing the song of deliverance from mortal fear and death." (Perfected space communication is to be had on all these worlds; and your anywhere reception of such communications is made possible by carrying the "harp of God," a morontia contrivance compensating for the inability to directly adjust the immature morontia sensory mechanism to the reception of space communications.)

Paul also had a view of the ascendant-citizen corps of perfecting mortals on Jerusem, for he wrote: "But you have come to Mount Zion and to the city of the living God, the heavenly Jerusalem, and to an innumerable company of angels, to the grand assembly of Michael, and to the spirits of just men being made perfect."

After mortals have attained residence on the system headquarters, no more literal resurrections will be experienced. The morontia form granted you on departure from the mansion world career is such as will see you through to the end of the local universe experience. Changes will be made from time to time, but you will retain this same form until you bid it farewell when you emerge as first-stage spirits preparatory for transit to the super-universe worlds of ascending culture and spirit training.

Seven times do those mortals who pass through the entire mansonia career experience the adjustment sleep and the resurrection awakening. But the last resurrection hall, the final awakening chamber, was left behind on the seventh mansion world. No more will a form-change necessitate the lapse of consciousness or a break in the continuity of personal memory.

The mortal personality initiated on the evolutionary worlds and taberna-cled in the flesh — indwelt by the Mystery Monitors and invested by the Spirit of Truth — is not fully mobilized, realized, and unified until that day when such a Jerusem citizen is given clearance for Edentia and proclaimed a true member of the morontia corps of Nebadon — an immortal survivor of Adjuster association, a Paradise ascender, a personality of morontia status, and a true child of the Most Highs.

Mortal death is a technique of escape from the material life in the flesh; and the mansonia experience of progressive life through seven worlds of corrective training and cultural education represents the introduction of mortal survivors to the morontia career, the transition life which intervenes between the evolutionary material existence and the higher spirit attainment of the ascenders of time who are destined to achieve the portals of eternity.

[Sponsored by a Brilliant Evening Star.]

PAPER 48
THE MORONTIA LIFE

THE GODS CANNOT — at least they do not — transform a creature of gross animal nature into a perfected spirit by some mysterious act of creative magic. When the Creators desire to produce perfect beings, they do so by direct and original creation, but they never undertake to convert animal-origin and material creatures into beings of perfection in a single step.

The morontia life, extending as it does over the various stages of the local universe career, is the only possible approach whereby material mortals could attain the threshold of the spirit world. What magic could death, the natural dissolution of the material body, hold that such a simple step should instantly transform the mortal and material mind into an immortal and perfected spirit? Such beliefs are but ignorant superstitions and pleasing fables.

Always this morontia transition intervenes between the mortal estate and the subsequent spirit status of surviving human beings. This intermediate state of universe progress differs markedly in the various local creations, but in intent and purpose they are all quite similar. The arrangement of the mansion and higher morontia worlds in Nebadon is fairly typical of the morontia transition regimes in this part of Orvonton.

1. MORONTIA MATERIALS

The morontia realms are the local universe liaison spheres between the material and spiritual levels of creature existence. This morontia life has been known on Urantia since the early days of the Planetary Prince. From time to time this transition state has been taught to mortals, and the concept, in distorted form, has found a place in present-day religions.

The morontia spheres are the transition phases of mortal ascension through the progression worlds of the local universe. Only the seven worlds surrounding the finaliters' sphere of the local systems are called mansion worlds, but all fifty-six of the system transition abodes, in common with the higher spheres around the constellations, galaxies, minor and major sector capitals, and the universe headquarters, are called morontia worlds. These creations partake of the physical beauty and the morontia grandeur of the local universe headquarters spheres.

All of these worlds are architectural spheres, and they have just double the number of elements of the evolved planets. Such made-to-order worlds not only abound in the heavy metals and crystals, having one hundred physical elements, but likewise have exactly one hundred forms of a unique energy organization called *morontia material*. The Master Physical Controllers and the Morontia Power Supervisors are able so to modify the revolutions of the primary units of matter and at the same time so to transform these associations of energy as to create this new substance.

The early morontia life in the local systems is very much like that of your present material world, becoming less physical and more truly morontial on the constellation study worlds. And as you advance to the galaxy, minor and major sector capitals, and to the Salvington spheres, you increasingly attain spiritual levels.

The Morontia Power Supervisors are able to effect a union of material and of spiritual energies, thereby organizing a morontia form of materialization which is receptive to the superimposition of a controlling spirit. When you traverse the morontia life of Nebadon, these same patient and skillful Morontia Power Supervisors will successively provide you with 570 morontia bodies, each one a phase of your progressive transformation. From the time of leaving the material worlds until you are constituted a first-stage spirit on Salvington, you will undergo just 570 separate and ascending morontia changes. Eight of these occur in the system, seventy-one in the constellation, and 491 during the sojourn on the spheres of the galaxy, minor and major sectors, and on Salvington.

In the days of the mortal flesh the divine spirit indwells you, almost as a thing apart — in reality an invasion of man by the bestowed spirit of the Universal Father. But in the morontia life the spirit will become a real part of your personality, and as you successively pass through the 570 progressive transformations, you ascend from the material to the spiritual estate of creature life.

Paul learned of the existence of the morontia worlds and of the reality of morontia materials, for he wrote, "They have in heaven a better and more enduring substance." And these morontia materials are real, literal, even as in "the city which has foundations, whose builder and maker is God." And each of these marvelous spheres is "a better country, that is, a heavenly one."

2. MORONTIA POWER SUPERVISORS

These unique beings are exclusively concerned with the supervision of those activities which represent a working combination of spiritual and physical or semi-material energies. They are exclusively devoted to the ministry of morontia progression. Not that they so much minister to mortals during the transition experience, but they rather make possible the transition environment for the progressing morontia creatures. They are the channels of morontia power which sustain and energize the morontia phases of the transition worlds.

Morontia Power Supervisors are the offspring of a local universe Mother Spirit. They are fairly standard in design though differing slightly in nature in the various local creations. They are created for their specific function and require no training before entering upon their responsibilities.

The creation of the first Morontia Power Supervisors is simultaneous with the arrival of the first mortal survivor on the shores of some one of the first mansion worlds in a local universe. They are created in groups of one thousand, classified as follows:

1. Circuit Regulators 400
2. System Co-ordinators 200
3. Planetary Custodians 100
4. Combined Controllers . . . 100
5. Liaison Stabilizers 100
6. Selective Assorters 50
7. Associate Registrars 50

The power supervisors always serve in their native universe. They are directed exclusively by the joint spirit activity of the Universe Son and the Universe Spirit but are otherwise a wholly self-governing group. They maintain headquarters on each of the first mansion worlds of the local systems, where they work in close association with both the physical controllers and the seraphim but function in a world of their own as regards energy manifestation and spirit application.

They also sometimes work in connection with super-material phenomena on the evolutionary worlds as ministers of temporary assignment. But they rarely serve on the inhabited planets; neither do they work on the higher training worlds of the super-universe, being chiefly devoted to the transition regime of morontia progression in a local universe.

1. *Circuit Regulators*. These are the unique beings who co-ordinate physical and spiritual energy and regulate its flow into the segregated channels of the morontia spheres, and these circuits are exclusively planetary, limited to a single world. The morontia circuits are distinct from, and supplementary to, both physical and spiritual circuits on the transition worlds, and it requires millions of these regulators to energize even a system of mansion worlds like that of Satania.

Circuit regulators initiate those changes in material energies which render them subject to the control and regulation of their associates. These beings are morontia power generators as well as circuit regulators. These living morontia dynamos seem to transform the everywhere energies of space into those materials which the morontia supervisors weave into the bodies and life activities of the ascending mortals.

2. *System Co-ordinators.* Since each morontia world has a separate order of morontia energy, it is exceedingly difficult for humans to visualize these spheres. But on each successive transition sphere, mortals will find the plant life and everything else pertaining to the morontia existence progressively modified to correspond with the advancing spiritization of the ascending survivor. And since the energy system of each world is thus individualized, these co-ordinators operate to harmonize and blend such differing power systems into a working unit for the associated spheres of any particular group.

Ascending mortals gradually progress from the physical to the spiritual as they advance from one morontia world to another; hence the necessity for providing an ascending scale of morontia spheres and an ascending scale of morontia forms.

When mansion world ascenders pass from one sphere to another, they are delivered by the transport seraphim to the receivers of the system co-ordinators on the advanced world. Here in those unique temples at the center of the seventy radiating wings wherein are the chambers of transition similar to the resurrection halls on the initial world of reception for earth-origin mortals, the necessary changes in creature form are skillfully effected by the system co-ordinators. These early morontia-form changes require about seven days of standard time for their accomplishment.

3. *Planetary Custodians.* Each morontia world, from the mansion spheres up to the universe headquarters, is in the custody — as regards morontia affairs — of seventy guardians. They constitute the local planetary council of supreme morontia authority. This council grants material for morontia forms to all ascending creatures who land on the spheres and authorizes those changes in creature form which make it possible for an ascender to proceed to the succeeding sphere. After the mansion worlds have been traversed, you will translate from one phase of morontia life to another without having to surrender consciousness. Unconsciousness attends only the earlier metamorphoses and the later transitions from one universe to another and from Havona to Paradise.

4. *Combined Controllers*. One of these highly mechanical beings is always stationed at the center of each administrative unit of a morontia world. A combined controller is sensitive to, and functional with, physical, spiritual, and morontial energies; and with this being there are always associated two system co-ordinators, four circuit regulators, one planetary custodian, one liaison stabilizer, and either an associate registrar or a selective assorter.

5. *Liaison Stabilizers*. These are the regulators of the morontia energy in association with the physical and spirit forces of the realm. They make possible the conversion of morontia energy into morontia material. The whole morontia organization of existence is dependent on the stabilizers. They slow down the energy revolutions to that point where physicalization can occur. But I have no terms with which I can compare or illustrate the ministry of such beings. It is quite beyond human imagination.

6. *Selective Assorters*. As you progress from one class or phase of a morontia world to another, you must be re-keyed or advance-tuned, and it is the task of the selective assorters to keep you in progressive synchrony with the morontia life.

While the basic morontia forms of life and matter are identical from the first mansion world to the last universe transition sphere, there is a functional progression which gradually extends from the material to the spiritual. Your adaptation to this basically uniform but successively advancing and spiritizing creation is effected by this selective re-keying. Such an adjustment in the mechanism of personality is tantamount to a new creation, notwithstanding that you retain the same morontia form.

You may repeatedly subject yourself to the test of these examiners, and as soon as you register adequate spiritual achievement, they will gladly certify you for advanced standing. These progressive changes result in altered reactions to the morontia environment, such as modifications in food requirements and numerous other personal practices.

The selective assorters are also of great service in the grouping of morontia personalities for purposes of study, teaching, and other projects.

They naturally indicate those who will best function in temporary association.

7. *Associate Registrars*. The morontia world has its own recorders, who serve in association with the spirit recorders in the supervision and custody of the records and other data indigenous to the morontia creations. The morontia records are available to all orders of personalities.

All morontia transition realms are accessible alike to material and spirit beings. As morontia progressors you will remain in full contact with the material world and with material personalities, while you will increasingly discern and fraternize with spirit beings; and by the time of departure from the morontia regime, you will have seen all orders of spirits with the exception of a few of the higher types, such as Solitary Messengers.

3. MORONTIA COMPANIONS

These hosts of the mansion and morontia worlds are the offspring of a local universe Mother Spirit. They are created from age to age in groups of one hundred thousand.

Morontia Companions are trained for service by the Melchizedeks on a special planet near Salvington; they do not pass through the central Melchizedek schools. In service they range from the lowest mansion worlds of the systems to the highest study spheres of Salvington, but they are seldom encountered on the inhabited worlds. They serve under the general supervision of the Sons of God and under the immediate direction of the Melchizedeks.

The Morontia Companions maintain headquarters on each of the first mansion worlds on all of the local systems. They are almost wholly a self-governing order and are, in general, an intelligent and loyal group of beings; but every now and then, in connection with certain unfortunate celestial upheavals, they have been known to go astray. Thousands of these useful creatures were lost during the times of the Lucifer rebellion in Satania. Your local system now has its full quota of these beings, the loss of the Lucifer rebellion having only recently been made up.

There are two distinct types of Morontia Companions; one type is aggressive, the other retiring, but otherwise they are equal in status. They are not sex creatures, but they manifest a touchingly beautiful affection for one another. And while they are hardly companionate in the material (human) sense, they are very close of kin to the human races in the order of creature existence. The midway creatures of the worlds are your nearest of kin; then come the morontia cherubim, and after them the Morontia Companions.

These companions are touchingly affectionate and charmingly social beings. They possess distinct personalities, and when you meet them on the mansion worlds, after learning to recognize them as a class, you will soon discern their individuality. Mortals all resemble one another; at the same time each of you possesses a distinct and recognizable personality.

Something of an idea of the nature of the work of these Morontia Companions may be derived from the following classification of their activities in a local system:

1. *Pilgrim Guardians* are not assigned to specific duties in their association with the morontia progressors. These companions are responsible for the whole of the morontia career and are therefore the co-ordinators of the work of all other morontia and transition ministers.

2. *Pilgrim Receivers and Free Associators*. These are the social companions of the new arrivals on the mansion worlds. One of them will certainly be on hand to welcome you when you awaken on the initial mansion world from the first transit sleep of time, when you experience the resurrection from the death of the flesh into the morontia life. And from the time you are thus formally welcomed on awakening to that day when you leave the local universe as a first-stage spirit, these Morontia Companions are ever with you.

Companions are not assigned permanently to individuals. An ascending mortal on one of the mansion or higher worlds might have a different companion on each of several successive occasions and again might go for long periods without one. It would all depend on the requirements and also on the supply of companions available.

3. *Hosts to Celestial Visitors*. These gracious creatures are dedicated to the entertainment of the superhuman groups of student visitors and other celestials who may chance to sojourn on the transition worlds. You will have ample opportunity to visit within any realm you have experientially attained. Student visitors are allowed on all inhabited planets, even those in isolation.

4. *Co-ordinators and Liaison Directors*. These companions are dedicated to the facilitation of morontia intercourse and to the prevention of confusion. They are the instructors of social conduct and morontia progress, sponsoring classes and other group activities among the ascending mortals. They maintain extensive areas wherein they assemble their pupils and from time to time make requisition on the celestial artisans and the reversion directors for the embellishment of their programs. As you progress, you will come in intimate contact with these companions, and you will grow exceedingly fond of both groups. It is a matter of chance as to whether you will be associated with an aggressive or a retiring type of companion.

5. *Interpreters and Translators*. During the early mansonia career you will have frequent recourse to the interpreters and the translators. They know and speak all the tongues of a local universe; they are the linguists of the realms.

You will not acquire new languages automatically; you will learn a language over there much as you do down here, and these brilliant beings will be your language teachers. The first study on the mansion worlds will be the tongue of Satania and then the language of Nebadon. And while you are mastering these new tongues, the Morontia Companions will be your efficient interpreters and patient translators. You will never encounter a visitor on any of these worlds but that some one of the Morontia Companions will be able to officiate as interpreter.

6. *Excursion and Reversion Supervisors*. These companions will accompany you on the longer trips to the headquarters sphere and to the surrounding worlds of transition culture. They plan, conduct, and supervise all such individual and group tours about the system worlds of training and culture.

7. *Area and Building Custodians*. Even the material and morontia structures increase in perfection and grandeur as you advance in the mansonia career. As individuals and as groups you are permitted to make certain changes in the abodes assigned as headquarters for your sojourn on the different mansion worlds. Many of the activities of these spheres take place in the open enclosures of the variously designated circles, squares, and triangles. The majority of the mansion world structures are roofless, being enclosures of magnificent construction and exquisite embellishment. The climatic and other physical conditions prevailing on the architectural worlds make roofs wholly unnecessary.

These custodians of the transition phases of ascendant life are supreme in the management of morontia affairs. They were created for this work, and pending the factualization of the Supreme Being, always will they remain Morontia Companions; never do they perform other duties.

As systems and universes are settled in light and life, the mansion worlds increasingly cease to function as transition spheres of morontia training. More and more the finaliters institute their new training regime, which appears to be designed to translate the cosmic consciousness from the present level of the grand universe to that of the future outer universes. The Morontia Companions are destined to function increasingly in association with the finaliters and in numerous other realms not at present revealed on Urantia.

You can forecast that these beings are probably going to contribute much to your enjoyment of the mansion worlds, whether your sojourn is to be long or short. And you will continue to enjoy them all the way up to Salvington. They are not, technically, essential to any part of your survival experience. You could reach Salvington without them, but you would greatly miss them. They are the personality luxury of your ascending career in the local universe.

4. THE REVERSION DIRECTORS

Joyful mirth and the smile-equivalent are as universal as music. There is a morontial and a spiritual equivalent of mirth and laughter. The ascendant life is about equally divided between work and play — freedom from assignment.

Celestial relaxation and superhuman humor are quite different from their human analogues, but we all actually indulge in a form of both; and they really accomplish for us, in our state, just about what ideal humor is able to do for you on Urantia. The Morontia Companions are skillful play sponsors, and they are most ably supported by the reversion directors.

You would probably best understand the work of the reversion directors if they were likened to the higher types of humorists on Urantia, though that would be an exceedingly crude and somewhat unfortunate way in which to try to convey an idea of the function of these directors of change and relaxation, these ministers of the exalted humor of the morontia and spirit realms.

In discussing spirit humor, first let me tell you what it is *not*. Spirit jest is never tinged with the accentuation of the misfortunes of the weak and erring. Neither is it ever blasphemous of the righteousness and glory of divinity. Our humor embraces three general levels of appreciation:

1. *Reminiscent jests*. Quips growing out of the memories of past episodes in one's experience of combat, struggle, and sometimes fearfulness, and ofttimes foolish and childish anxiety. To us, this phase of humor derives from the deep-seated and abiding ability to draw upon the past for memory material with which pleasantly to flavor and otherwise lighten the heavy loads of the present.

2. *Current humor*. The senselessness of much that so often causes us serious concern, the joy at discovering the unimportance of much of our serious personal anxiety. We are most appreciative of this phase of humor when we are best able to discount the anxieties of the present in favor of the certainties of the future.

3. *Prophetic joy*. It will perhaps be difficult for mortals to envisage this phase of humor, but we do get a peculiar satisfaction out of the assurance "that all things work together for good" — for spirits and morontians as well as for mortals. This aspect of celestial humor grows out of our faith in the

loving over-care of our superiors and in the divine stability of our Supreme Directors.

But the reversion directors of the realms are not concerned exclusively with depicting the high humor of the various orders of intelligent beings; they are also occupied with the leadership of diversion, spiritual recreation and morontia entertainment. And in this connection they have the hearty co-operation of the celestial artisans.

The reversion directors themselves are not a created group; they are a recruited corps embracing beings ranging from the Havona natives down through the messenger hosts of space and the ministering spirits of time to the morontia progressors from the evolutionary worlds. All are volunteers, giving themselves to the work of assisting their fellows in the achievement of thought change and mind rest, for such attitudes are most helpful in recuperating depleted energies.

When partially exhausted by the efforts of attainment, and while awaiting the reception of new energy charges, there is agreeable pleasure in living over again the enactments of other days and ages. *The early experiences of the race or the order are restful to reminisce.* And that is exactly why these artists are called reversion directors — they assist in reverting the memory to a former state of development or to a less experienced status of being.

All beings enjoy this sort of reversion except those who are inherent Creators, hence automatic self-rejuvenators, and certain highly specialized types of creatures, such as the power centers and the physical controllers, who are always and eternally thoroughly businesslike in all their reactions. These periodic releases from the tension of functional duty are a regular part of life on all worlds throughout the universe of universes but not on the Isle of Paradise. Beings indigenous to the central abode are incapable of depletion and are not, therefore, subject to re-energizing. And with such beings of eternal Paradise perfection there can be no such reversion to evolutionary experiences.

Most of us have come up through lower stages of existence or through progressive levels of our orders, and it is refreshing and in a measure amusing to look back upon certain episodes of our early experience. There is a restfulness in the contemplation of that which is old to one's order, and which lingers as a memory possession of the mind. The future signifies struggle and advancement; it bespeaks work, effort, and achievement; but the past savors of things already mastered and achieved; contemplation of the past permits of relaxation and such a carefree review as to provoke spirit mirth and a morontia state of mind verging on merriment.

Even mortal humor becomes most hearty when it depicts episodes affecting those just a little beneath one's present developmental state, or when it portrays one's supposed superiors falling victim to the experiences which are commonly associated with supposed inferiors. You of Urantia have allowed much that is at once vulgar and unkind to become confused with your humor, but on the whole, you are to be congratulated on a comparatively keen sense of humor. Some of you have a rich vein of it and are greatly helped in your earthly careers thereby. Apparently you received much in the way of humor from your Adamic inheritance, much more than was secured of either music or art.

All Satania, during times of play, those times when its inhabitants refreshingly resurrect the memories of a lower stage of existence, is edified by the pleasant humor of a corps of reversion directors from Urantia. The sense of celestial humor we have with us always, even when engaged in the most difficult of assignments. It helps to avoid an overdevelopment of the notion of one's self-importance. But we do not give rein to it freely, as you might say, "have fun," except when we are in recess from the serious assignments of our respective orders.

When we are tempted to magnify our self-importance, if we stop to contemplate the infinity of the greatness and grandeur of our Makers, our own self-glorification becomes sublimely ridiculous, even verging on the humorous. One of the functions of humor is to help all of us take ourselves less seriously. *Humor is the divine antidote for exaltation of ego.*

The need for the relaxation and diversion of humor is greatest in those orders of ascendant beings who are subjected to sustained stress in their upward struggles. The two extremes of life have little need for humorous diversions. Primitive men have no capacity therefor, and beings of Paradise perfection have no need thereof. The hosts of Havona are naturally a joyous and exhilarating assemblage of supremely happy personalities. On Paradise the quality of worship obviates the necessity for reversion activities. But among those who start their careers far below the goal of Paradise perfection, there is a large place for the ministry of the reversion directors.

The higher the mortal species, the greater the stress and the greater the capacity for humor as well as the necessity for it. In the spirit world the opposite is true: The higher we ascend, the less the need for the diversions of reversion experiences. But proceeding down the scale of spirit life from Paradise to the seraphic hosts, there is an increasing need for the mission of mirth and the ministry of merriment. Those beings who most need the refreshment of periodic reversion to the intellectual status of previous experiences are the higher types of the human species, the morontians, angels, and the Material Sons, together with all similar types of personality.

Humor should function as an automatic safety valve to prevent the building up of excessive pressures due to the monotony of sustained and serious self-contemplation in association with the intense struggle for developmental progress and noble achievement. Humor also functions to lessen the shock of the unexpected impact of fact or of truth, rigid unyielding fact and flexible ever-living truth. The mortal personality, never sure as to which will next be encountered, through humor swiftly grasps — sees the point and achieves insight — the unexpected nature of the situation be it fact or be it truth.

While the humor of Urantia is exceedingly crude and most inartistic, it does serve a valuable purpose both as a health insurance and as a liberator of emotional pressure, thus preventing injurious nervous tension and over-serious self-contemplation. Humor and play — relaxation — are never reactions of progressive exertion; always are they the echoes of a backward glance, a reminiscence of the past. Even on Urantia and as you now are, you always find it rejuvenating when for a short time you can suspend the exertions of the newer and higher intellectual efforts and revert to the more simple engagements of your ancestors.

The principles of Urantian play life are philosophically sound and continue to apply on up through your ascending life, through the circuits of Havona to the eternal shores of Paradise. As ascendant beings you are in possession of personal memories of all former and lower existences, and without such identity memories of the past there would be no basis for the humor of the present, either mortal laughter or morontia mirth. It is this recalling of past experiences that provides the basis for present diversion and amusement. And so you will enjoy the celestial equivalents of your earthly humor all the way up through your long morontia, and then increasingly spiritual, careers. And that part of God (the Adjuster) which becomes an eternal part of the personality of an ascendant mortal contributes the overtones of divinity to the joyous expressions, even spiritual laughter, of the ascending creatures of time and space.

5. THE MANSION WORLD TEACHERS

The Mansion World Teachers are a corps of deserted but glorified cherubim and sanobim. When a pilgrim of time advances from a trial world of space to the mansion and associated worlds of morontia training, he is accompanied by his personal or group seraphim, the guardian of destiny. In the worlds of mortal existence the seraphim is ably assisted by cherubim and sanobim; but when her mortal ward is delivered from the bonds of the flesh and starts out on the ascendant career, when the post-material or morontia life begins, the attending seraphim has no further need of the ministrations of her former lieutenants, the cherubim and sanobim.

These deserted assistants of the ministering seraphim are often summoned to universe headquarters, where they pass into the intimate embrace of the Universe Mother Spirit and then go forth to the system training spheres as Mansion World Teachers. These teachers often visit the material worlds and function from the lowest mansion worlds on up to the highest of the educational spheres connected with the universe headquarters. Upon their own motion they may return to their former associative work with the ministering seraphim.

There are billions upon billions of these teachers in Satania, and their numbers constantly increase because, in the majority of instances, when a seraphim proceeds inward with an Adjuster-fused mortal, both a cherubim and a sanobim are left behind.

Mansion World Teachers, like most of the other instructors, are commissioned by the Melchizedeks. They are generally supervised by the Morontia Companions, but as individuals and as teachers they are supervised by the acting heads of the schools or spheres wherein they may be functioning as instructors.

These advanced cherubim usually work in pairs as they did when attached to the seraphim. They are by nature very near the morontia type of existence, and they are inherently sympathetic teachers of the ascending mortals and most efficiently conduct the program of the mansion world and morontia educational system.

In the schools of the morontia life these teachers engage in individual, group, class, and mass teaching. On the mansion worlds such schools are organized in three general groups of one hundred divisions each: the schools of thinking, the schools of feeling, and the schools of doing. When you reach the constellation, there are added the schools of ethics, the schools of administration, and the schools of social adjustment. On the galaxy headquarters worlds you will enter the schools of philosophy, divinity, and pure spirituality.

Those things which you might have learned on earth, but which you failed to learn, must be acquired under the tutelage of these faithful and patient teachers. There are no royal roads, short cuts, or easy paths to Paradise. Irrespective of the individual variations of the route, you master the lessons of one sphere before you proceed to another; at least this is true after you once leave the world of your nativity.

One of the purposes of the morontia career is to effect the permanent eradication from the mortal survivors of such animal vestigial traits as procrastination, equivocation, insincerity, problem avoidance, unfairness, and ease seeking. The mansonia life early teaches the young morontia pupils that postponement is in no sense avoidance. After the life in the flesh, time is no longer available as a technique of dodging situations or of circumventing disagreeable obligations.

Beginning service on the lowest of the tarrying spheres, the Mansion World Teachers advance, with experience, through the educational spheres of the system and the constellation up to the training worlds of Salvington. They are subjected to no special discipline either before or after their embrace by the Universe Mother Spirit. They have already been trained for their work while serving as seraphic associates on the worlds native to their pupils of mansion world sojourn. They have had actual experience with these advancing mortals on the inhabited worlds. They are practical and sympathetic teachers, wise and understanding instructors, able and efficient guides. They are entirely familiar with the ascendant plans and thoroughly experienced in the initial phases of the progression career.

Many of the older of these teachers, those who have long served on the worlds of the Salvington circuit, are re-embraced by the Universe Mother Spirit, and from this second embrace these cherubim and sanobim emerge with the status of seraphim.

6. MORONTIA WORLD SERAPHIM — TRANSITION MINISTERS

While all orders of angels, from the planetary helpers to the supreme seraphim, minister on the morontia worlds, the transition ministers are more exclusively assigned to these activities. These angels are of the sixth order of seraphic servers, and their ministry is devoted to facilitating the transit of material and mortal creatures from the temporal life in the flesh on into the early stages of morontia existence on the seven mansion worlds.

You should understand that the morontia life of an ascending mortal is really initiated on the inhabited worlds at the conception of the soul, at that moment when the creature mind of moral status is indwelt by the spirit Adjuster. And from that moment on, the mortal soul has potential capacity for super-mortal function, even for recognition on the higher levels of the morontia spheres of the local universe.

You will not, however, be conscious of the ministry of the transition seraphim until you attain the mansion worlds, where they labor untiringly for the advancement of their mortal pupils, being assigned for service in the following seven divisions:

1. *Seraphic Evangels.* The moment you consciousize on the mansion worlds, you are classified as evolving spirits in the records of the system.

True, you are not yet spirits in reality, but you are no longer mortal or material beings; you have embarked upon the prespirit career and have been duly admitted to the morontia life.

On the mansion worlds the seraphic evangels will help you to choose wisely among the optional routes to Edentia, Salvington, Uversa, and Havona. If there are a number of equally advisable routes, these will be put before you, and you will be permitted to select the one that most appeals to you. These seraphim then make recommendations to the four and twenty advisers on Jerusem concerning that course which would be most advantageous for each ascending soul.

You are not given unrestricted choice as to your future course; but you may choose within the limits of that which the transition ministers and their superiors wisely determine to be most suitable for your future spirit attainment. The spirit world is governed on the principle of respecting your freewill choice provided the course you may choose is not detrimental to you or injurious to your fellows.

These seraphic evangels are dedicated to the proclamation of the gospel of eternal progression, the triumph of perfection attainment. On the mansion worlds they proclaim the great law of the conservation and dominance of goodness: No act of good is ever wholly lost; it may be long thwarted but never wholly annulled, and it is eternally potent in proportion to the divinity of its motivation.

Even on Urantia they counsel the human teachers of truth and righteousness to adhere to the preaching of "the goodness of God, which leads to repentance," to proclaim "the love of God, which casts out all fear." Even so have these truths been declared on your world:

The Gods are my caretakers; I shall not stray;

Side by side they lead me in the beautiful paths and glorious refreshing of life everlasting.

I shall not, in this Divine Presence, want for food nor thirst for water.

Though I go down into the valley of uncertainty or ascend up into the worlds of doubt,

Though I move in loneliness or with the fellows of my kind,

Though I triumph in the choirs of light or falter in the solitary places of the spheres,
Your good spirit shall minister to me, and your glorious angel will comfort me.
Though I descend into the depths of darkness and death itself,
I shall not doubt you nor fear you,
For I know that in the fullness of time and the glory of your name
You will raise me up to sit with you on the battlements on high.

That is the story whispered in the night season to the shepherd boy. He could not retain it word for word, but to the best of his memory he gave it much as it is recorded today.

These seraphim are also the evangels of the gospel of perfection attainment for the whole system as well as for the individual ascender. Even now in the young system of Satania their teachings and plans encompass provisions for the future ages when the mansion worlds will no longer serve the mortal ascenders as steppingstones to the spheres on high.

2. *Racial Interpreters*. All races of mortal beings are not alike. True, there is a planetary pattern running through the physical, mental, and spiritual natures and tendencies of the various races of a given galaxy, constellation, and system ; but there are also distinct racial types, and very definite social tendencies characterize the offspring of these different basic types of human beings. On the worlds of time the seraphic racial interpreters further the efforts of the race commissioners to harmonize the varied viewpoints of the races, and they continue to function on the mansion worlds, where these same differences tend to persist in a measure. These brilliant beings are the skillful sociologists and the wise ethnic advisers of the first heaven.

You should consider the statement about "heaven" and the "heaven of heavens." The heaven conceived by most of your prophets was the first of the mansion worlds of the local system. When the apostle spoke of being "caught up to the third heaven," he referred to that experience in which his Adjuster was detached during sleep and in this unusual state made a projection to the third of the seven mansion worlds. Some of your wise men saw the vision of the greater heaven, "the heaven of heavens," of which the sevenfold mansion world experience was but the first; the second being Jerusem; the third, Edentia and its satellites; the fourth, Zion and the surrounding educational spheres; the fifth, Ensa; the sixth, Splandon; and the seventh, Salvington.

3. *Mind Planners.* These seraphim are devoted to the effective grouping of morontia beings and to organizing their teamwork on the mansion worlds. They are the psychologists of the first heaven. The majority of this particular division of seraphic ministers have had previous experience as guardian angels to the children of time, but their wards, for some reason, failed to personalize on the mansion worlds or else survived by the technique of Spirit fusion.

It is the task of the mind planners to study the nature, experience, and status of the Adjuster souls in transit through the mansion worlds and to facilitate their grouping for assignment and advancement. But these mind planners do not scheme, manipulate, or otherwise take advantage of the ignorance or other limitations of mansion world students. They are wholly fair and eminently just. They respect your newborn morontia will; they regard you as independent volitional beings, and they seek to encourage your speedy development and advancement. Here you are face to face with true friends and understanding counselors, angels who are really able to help you "to see yourself as others see you" and "to know yourself as angels know you."

Even on Urantia, these seraphim teach the everlasting truth: If your own mind does not serve you well, you can exchange it for the mind of Jesus of Nazareth, who always serves you well.

4. *Morontia Counselors.* These ministers receive their name because they are assigned to teach, direct, and counsel the surviving mortals from the worlds of human origin, souls in transit to the higher schools of the system headquarters. They are the teachers of those who seek insight into the experiential unity of divergent life levels, those who are attempting the integration of meanings and the unification of values. This is the function of philosophy in mortal life, of mota on the morontia spheres.

Mota is more than a superior philosophy; it is to philosophy as two eyes are to one; it has a stereoscopic effect on meanings and values. Material man sees the universe, as it were, with but one eye — flat. Mansion world students achieve cosmic perspective — depth — by superimposing the perceptions of the morontia life upon the perceptions of the physical life. And they are enabled to bring these material and morontial viewpoints into true focus largely through the untiring ministry of their seraphic counselors, who so patiently teach the mansion world students and the morontia progressors. Many of the teaching counselors of the supreme order of seraphim began their careers as advisers of the newly liberated souls of the mortals of time.

5. *Technicians*. These are the seraphim who help new ascenders adjust themselves to the new and comparatively strange environment of the morontia spheres. Life on the transition worlds entails real contact with the energies and materials of both the physical and morontia levels and to a certain extent with spiritual realities. Ascenders must acclimatize to every new morontia level, and in all of this they are greatly helped by the seraphic technicians. These seraphim act as liaisons with the Morontia Power Supervisors and with the Master Physical Controllers and function extensively as instructors of the ascending pilgrims concerning the nature of those energies which are utilized on the transition spheres. They serve as emergency space traversers and perform numerous other regular and special duties.

6. *Recorder-Teachers*. These seraphim are the recorders of the borderland transactions of the spiritual and the physical, of the relationships of men and angels, of the morontia transactions of the lower universe realms. They also serve as instructors regarding the efficient and effective techniques of fact recording. There is an artistry in the intelligent assembly and co-ordination of related data, and this art is heightened in collaboration with the celestial artisans, and even the ascending mortals become thus affiliated with the recording seraphim.

The recorders of all the seraphic orders devote a certain amount of time to the education and training of the morontia progressors. These angelic custodians of the facts of time are the ideal instructors of all fact seekers. Before leaving Jerusem, you will become quite familiar with the history of

Satania and its 619 inhabited worlds, and much of this story will be imparted by the seraphic recorders.

These angels are all in the chain of recorders extending from the lowest to the highest custodians of the facts of time and the truths of eternity. Some day they will teach you to seek truth as well as fact, to expand your soul as well as your mind. Even now you should learn to water the garden of your heart as well as to seek for the dry sands of knowledge. Forms are valueless when lessons are learned. No chick may be had without the shell, and no shell is of any worth after the chick is hatched. But sometimes error is so great that its rectification by revelation would be fatal to those slowly emerging truths which are essential to its experiential overthrow. When children have their ideals, do not dislodge them; let them grow. And while you are learning to think as men, you should also be learning to pray as children.

Law is life itself and not the rules of its conduct. Evil is a transgression of law, not a violation of the rules of conduct pertaining to life, which *is* the law. Falsehood is not a matter of narration technique but something premeditated as a perversion of truth. The creation of new pictures out of old facts, the restatement of parental life in the lives of offspring — these are the artistic triumphs of truth. The shadow of a hair's turning, premeditated for an untrue purpose, the slightest twisting or perversion of that which is principle — these constitute falseness. But the fetish of factualized truth, fossilized truth, the iron band of so-called unchanging truth, holds one blindly in a closed circle of cold fact. One can be technically right as to fact and everlastingly wrong in the truth.

7. *Ministering Reserves.* A large corps of all orders of the transition seraphim is held on the first mansion world. Next to the destiny guardians, these transition ministers draw the nearest to humans of all orders of seraphim, and many of your leisure moments will be spent with them. Angels take delight in service and, when unassigned, often minister as volunteers. The soul of many an ascending mortal has for the first time been kindled by the divine fire of the will-to-service through personal friendship with the volunteer servers of the seraphic reserves.

From them you will learn to let pressure develop stability and certainty; to be faithful and earnest and, withal, cheerful; to accept challenges without complaint and to face difficulties and uncertainties without fear. They will ask: If you fail, will you rise indomitably to try anew? If you succeed, will you maintain a well-balanced poise — a stabilized and spiritualized attitude — throughout every effort in the long struggle to break the fetters of material inertia, to attain the freedom of spirit existence?

Even as mortals, so have these angels been father to many disappointments, and they will point out that sometimes your most disappointing disappointments have become your greatest blessings. Sometimes the planting of a seed necessitates its death, the death of your fondest hopes, before it can be reborn to bear the fruits of new life and new opportunity. And from them you will learn to suffer less through sorrow and disappointment, first, by making fewer personal plans concerning other personalities, and then, by accepting your lot when you have faithfully performed your duty.

You will learn that you increase your burdens and decrease the likelihood of success by taking yourself too seriously. Nothing can take precedence over the work of your status sphere — this world or the next. Very important is the work of preparation for the next higher sphere, but nothing equals the importance of the work of the world in which you are actually living. But though the *work* is important, the *self* is not. When you feel important, you lose energy to the wear and tear of ego dignity so that there is little energy left to do the work. Self-importance, not work-importance, exhausts immature creatures; it is the self element that exhausts, not the effort to achieve. You can do important work if you do not become self-important; you can do several things as easily as one if you leave yourself out. Variety is restful; monotony is what wears and exhausts. Day after day is alike — just life or the alternative of death.

7. MORONTIA MOTA

The lower planes of morontia mota join directly with the higher levels of human philosophy. On the first mansion world it is the practice to teach the less advanced students by the parallel technique; that is, in one column are presented the more simple concepts of mota meanings, and in the opposite column citation is made of analogous statements of mortal philosophy.

Not long since, while executing an assignment on the first mansion world of Satania, I had occasion to observe this method of teaching; and though I may not undertake to present the mota content of the lesson, I am permitted to record the twenty-eight statements of human philosophy which this morontia instructor was utilizing as illustrative material designed to assist these new mansion world sojourners in their early efforts to grasp the significance and meaning of mota. These illustrations of human philosophy were:

- 1. A display of specialized skill does not signify possession of spiritual capacity. Cleverness is not a substitute for true character.
- 2. Few persons live up to the faith which they really have. Unreasoned fear is a master intellectual fraud practiced upon the evolving mortal soul.
- 3. Inherent capacities cannot be exceeded; a pint can never hold a quart. The spirit concept cannot be mechanically forced into the material memory mold.
- 4. Few mortals ever dare to draw anything like the sum of personality credits established by the combined ministries of nature and grace. The majority of impoverished souls are truly rich, but they refuse to believe it.
- 5. Difficulties may challenge mediocrity and defeat the fearful, but they only stimulate the true children of the Most Highs.
- 6. To enjoy privilege without abuse, to have liberty without license, to possess power and steadfastly refuse to use it for self-aggrandizement — these are the marks of high civilization.
- 7. Blind and unforeseen accidents do not occur in the cosmos. Neither do the celestial beings assist the lower being who refuses to act upon his light of truth.
- 8. Effort does not always produce joy, but there is no happiness without intelligent effort.
- 9. Action achieves strength; moderation eventuates in charm.
- 10. Righteousness strikes the harmony chords of truth, and the melody vibrates throughout the cosmos, even to the recognition of the Infinite.

- 11. The weak indulge in resolutions, but the strong act. Life is but a day's work — do it well. The act is ours; the consequences God's.
- 12. The greatest affliction of the cosmos is never to have been afflicted. Mortals only learn wisdom by experiencing tribulation.
- 13. Stars are best discerned from the lonely isolation of experiential depths, not from the illuminated and ecstatic mountain tops.
- 14. Whet the appetites of your associates for truth; give advice only when it is asked for.
- 15. Affectation is the ridiculous effort of the ignorant to appear wise, the attempt of the barren soul to appear rich.
- 16. You cannot perceive spiritual truth until you feelingly experience it, and many truths are not really felt except in adversity.
- 17. Ambition is dangerous until it is fully socialized. You have not truly acquired any virtue until your acts make you worthy of it.
- 18. Impatience is a spirit poison; anger is like a stone hurled into a hornet's nest.
- 19. Anxiety must be abandoned. The disappointments hardest to bear are those which never come.
- 20. Only a poet can discern poetry in the commonplace prose of routine existence.
- 21. The high mission of any art is, by its illusions, to foreshadow a higher universe reality, to crystallize the emotions of time into the thought of eternity.
- 22. The evolving soul is not made divine by what it does, but by what it strives to do.
- 23. Death added nothing to the intellectual possession or to the spiritual endowment, but it did add to the experiential status the consciousness of *survival*.
- 24. The destiny of eternity is determined moment by moment by the achievements of the day by day living. The acts of today are the destiny of tomorrow.

- 25. Greatness lies not so much in possessing strength as in making a wise and divine use of such strength.
- 26. Knowledge is possessed only by sharing; it is safeguarded by wisdom and socialized by love.
- 27. Progress demands development of individuality; mediocrity seeks perpetuation in standardization.
- 28. The argumentative defense of any proposition is inversely proportional to the truth contained.

Such is the work of the beginners on the first mansion world while the more advanced pupils on the later worlds are mastering the higher levels of cosmic insight and morontia mota.

[JFC comment: I believe that there are many books and teachings available that present introductions or even significant aspects of morontia mota. Two that I particularly like and have studied are "A Course in Miracles"(ACIM) published by the Foundation for Inner Peace, and the Agni Yoga Society series of books beginning with "Leaves of Morya's Garden". In particular ACIM is in a way the polar opposite of the Urantia2025 (UB). To me ACIM and UB are like the left and right eyes which, because of their different view-points, can create spiritual "depth" perception.]

8. THE MORONTIA PROGRESSORS

From the time of graduation from the mansion worlds to the attainment of spirit status in the super-universe career, ascending mortals are denominated morontia progressors. Your passage through this wonderful borderland life will be an unforgettable experience, a charming memory. It is the evolutionary portal to spirit life and the eventual attainment of creature perfection by which ascenders achieve the goal of time — the finding of God on Paradise.

There is a definite and divine purpose in all this morontia and subsequent spirit scheme of mortal progression, this elaborate universe training school for ascending creatures. It is the design of the Creators to afford the creatures of time a graduated opportunity to master the details of the operation and administration of the grand universe, and this long course of training is best carried forward by having the surviving mortal climb up gradually and by actual participation in every step of the ascent.

The mortal-survival plan has a practical and serviceable objective; you are not the recipients of all this divine labor and painstaking training only that you may survive just to enjoy endless bliss and eternal ease. There is a goal of transcendent service concealed beyond the horizon of the present universe age. If the Gods designed merely to take you on one long and eternal joy excursion, they certainly would not so largely turn the whole universe into one vast and intricate practical training school, requisition a substantial part of the celestial creation as teachers and instructors, and then spend ages upon ages piloting you, one by one, through this gigantic universe school of experiential training. The furtherance of the scheme of mortal progression seems to be one of the chief businesses of the present organized universe, and the majority of innumerable orders of created intelligences are either directly or indirectly engaged in advancing some phase of this progressive perfection plan.

In traversing the ascending scale of living existence from mortal man to the Deity embrace, you actually live the very life of every possible phase and stage of perfected creature existence within the limits of the present universe age. From mortal man to Paradise finaliter embraces all that now can be — encompasses everything presently possible to the living orders of intelligent, perfected finite creature beings. If the future destiny of the Paradise finaliters is service in new universes now in the making, it is assured that in this new and future creation there will be no created orders of experiential beings whose lives will be wholly different from those which mortal finaliters have lived on some world as a part of their ascending training, as one of the stages of their agelong progress from animal to angel and from angel to spirit and from spirit to God.

[Presented by an Archangel of Nebadon.]

PAPER 49
THE INHABITED WORLDS

ALL MORTAL-INHABITED worlds are evolutionary in origin and nature. These spheres are the spawning ground, the evolutionary cradle, of the mortal races of time and space. Each unit of the ascendant life is a veritable training school for the stage of existence just ahead, and this is true of every stage of man's progressive Paradise ascent; just as true of the initial mortal experience on an evolutionary planet as of the final universe headquarters school of the Melchizedeks, a school which is not attended by ascending mortals until just before their translation to the regime of the super-universe and the attainment of first-stage spirit existence.

All inhabited worlds are basically grouped for celestial administration into the local systems, and each of these local systems is limited to about one thousand evolutionary worlds. This limitation is by the decree of the Ancients of Days, and it pertains to actual evolutionary planets whereon mortals of survival status are living. Neither worlds finally settled in light and life nor planets in the prehuman stage of life development are reckoned in this group.

Satania itself is an unfinished system containing only 619 inhabited worlds. Such planets are numbered serially in accordance with their registration as inhabited worlds, as worlds inhabited by will creatures. Thus was Urantia given the number *606 of Satania*, meaning the 606th world in this local system on which the long evolutionary life process culminated in the appearance of human beings. There are thirty-six uninhabited planets nearing the life-endowment stage, and several are now being made ready for the Life Carriers. There are nearly two hundred spheres which are evolving so as to be ready for life implantation within the next few million years.

Not all planets are suited to harbor mortal life. Small ones having a high rate of axial revolution are wholly unsuited for life habitats. In several of the physical systems of Satania the planets revolving around the central sun are too large for habitation, their great mass occasioning oppressive gravity. Many of these enormous spheres have satellites, sometimes a half dozen or more, and these moons are often in size very near that of Urantia, so that they are almost ideal for habitation.

The oldest inhabited world of Satania, world number one, is Anova, one of the forty-four satellites revolving around an enormous dark planet but exposed to the differential light of three neighboring suns. Anova is in an advanced stage of progressive civilization.

1. THE PLANETARY LIFE

The universes of time and space are gradual in development; the progression of life — terrestrial or celestial — is neither arbitrary nor magical. Cosmic evolution may not always be understandable (predictable), but it is strictly non-accidental.

The biologic unit of material life is the protoplasmic cell, the communal association of chemical, electrical, and other basic energies. The chemical formulas differ in each system, and the technique of living cell reproduction is slightly different in each local universe, but the Life Carriers are always the living catalyzers who initiate the primordial reactions of material life; they are the instigators of the energy circuits of living matter.

All the worlds of a local system disclose unmistakable physical kinship; nevertheless, each planet has its own scale of life, no two worlds being exactly alike in plant and animal endowment. These planetary variations in the system life types result from the decisions of the Life Carriers. But these beings are neither capricious nor whimsical; the universes are conducted in accordance with law and order. The laws of Nebadon are the divine mandates of Salvington, and the evolutionary order of life in Satania is in consonance with the evolutionary pattern of Nebadon.

Evolution is the rule of human development, but the process itself varies greatly on different worlds. Life is sometimes initiated in one center, sometimes in three, as it was on Urantia. On the atmospheric worlds it usually has a marine origin, but not always; much depends on the physical status of a planet. The Life Carriers have great latitude in their function of life initiation.

In the development of planetary life the vegetable form always precedes the animal and is quite fully developed before the animal patterns differentiate. All animal types are developed from the basic patterns of the preceding vegetable kingdom of living things; they are not separately organized.

The early stages of life evolution are not altogether in conformity with your present-day views. *Mortal man is not an evolutionary accident.* There is a precise system, a universal law, which determines the unfolding of the planetary life plan on the spheres of space. Time and the production of large numbers of a species are not the controlling influences.

The process of planetary evolution is orderly and controlled. The development of higher organisms from lower groupings of life is not accidental. Sometimes evolutionary progress is temporarily delayed by the destruction of certain favorable lines of life plasm carried in a selected species. It often requires ages upon ages to recoup the damage occasioned by the loss of a single superior strain of human heredity. These selected and superior strains of living protoplasm should be jealously and intelligently guarded when once they make their appearance. And on most of the inhabited worlds these superior potentials of life are valued much more highly than on Urantia.

2. PLANETARY PHYSICAL TYPES

There is a standard and basic pattern of vegetable and animal life in each system. But the Life Carriers are oftentimes confronted with the necessity of modifying these basic patterns to conform to the varying physical conditions which confront them on numerous worlds of space. They foster a generalized system type of mortal creature, but there are seven distinct physical types as well as thousands upon thousands of minor variants of these seven outstanding differentiations:

1. Atmospheric types.
2. Elemental types.
3. Gravity types.
4. Temperature types.
5. Electric types.
6. Energizing types.
7. Unnamed types.

The Satania system contains all of these types and numerous intermediate groups, although some are very sparingly represented.

1. *The atmospheric types.* The physical differences of the worlds of mortal habitation are chiefly determined by the nature of the atmosphere; other influences which contribute to the planetary differentiation of life are relatively minor.

The present atmospheric status of Urantia is almost ideal for the support of the breathing type of man, but the human type can be so modified that it can live on both the super-atmospheric and the sub-atmospheric planets. Such modifications also extend to the animal life, which differs greatly on the various inhabited spheres. There is a very great modification of animal orders on both the sub- and the super-atmospheric worlds.

Of the atmospheric types in Satania, about two and one-half per cent are sub-breathers, about five per cent super-breathers, and over ninety-one per cent are mid-breathers, altogether accounting for ninety-eight and one-half per cent of the Satania worlds.

Beings such as the Urantia races are classified as mid-breathers; you represent the average or typical breathing order of mortal existence.

If mortals should inhabit a planet devoid of air they would belong to the separate order of non-breathers. This type represents a radical or extreme adjustment to the planetary environment and is separately considered. Nonbreathers account for the remaining one and one-half per cent of Satania worlds.

2. *The elemental types.* These differentiations have to do with the relation of mortals to water, air, and land, and there are four distinct species of intelligent life as they are related to these habitats. The Urantia races are of the land order.

It is quite impossible for you to envisage the environment which prevails during the early ages of some worlds. These unusual conditions make it necessary for the evolving animal life to remain in its marine nursery habitat for longer periods than on those planets which very early provide a hospitable land-and-atmosphere environment. Conversely, on some worlds of the super-breathers, when the planet is not too large, it is sometimes expedient to provide for a mortal type which can readily negotiate atmospheric passage. These air navigators sometimes intervene between the water and land groups, and they always live in a measure upon the ground, eventually evolving into land dwellers. But on some worlds, for ages they continue to fly even after they have become land-type beings.

It is both amazing and amusing to observe the early civilization of a primitive race of human beings taking shape, in one case, in the air and treetops and, in another, midst the shallow waters of sheltered tropic basins, as well as on the bottom, sides, and shores of these marine gardens of the dawn races of such extraordinary spheres. Even on Urantia there was a long age during which primitive man preserved himself and advanced his primitive civilization by living for the most part in the treetops as did his earlier arboreal ancestors. And on Urantia you still have a group of diminutive mammals (the bat family) that are air navigators, and your seals and whales, of marine habitat, are also of the mammalian order.

In Satania, of the elemental types, seven per cent are water, ten per cent air, seventy per cent land, and thirteen per cent combined land-and-air types. But these modifications of early intelligent creatures are neither human fishes nor human birds. They are of the human and prehuman types, neither super-fishes nor glorified birds but distinctly mortal.

3. *The gravity types.* By modification of creative design, intelligent beings are so constructed that they can freely function on spheres both smaller and larger than Urantia, thus being, in measure, accommodated to the gravity of those planets which are not of ideal size and density.

The various planetary types of mortals vary in height, the average in Nebadon being a trifle under seven feet. Some of the larger worlds are peopled with beings who are only about two and one-half feet in height. Mortal stature ranges from here on up through the average heights on the average-sized planets to around ten feet on the smaller inhabited spheres. In Satania there is only one race under four feet in height. Twenty per cent of the Satania inhabited worlds are peopled with mortals of the modified gravity types occupying the larger and the smaller planets.

4. *The temperature types.* It is possible to create living beings who can withstand temperatures both much higher and much lower than the life range of the Urantia races. There are five distinct orders of beings as they are classified with reference to heat-regulating mechanisms. In this scale the Urantia races are number three. Thirty per cent of Satania worlds are peopled with races of modified temperature types. Twelve per cent belong to the higher temperature ranges, eighteen per cent to the lower, as compared with Urantians, who function in the mid-temperature group.

5. *The electric types.* The electric, magnetic, and electronic behavior of the worlds varies greatly. There are ten designs of mortal life variously fashioned to withstand the differential energy of the spheres. These ten varieties also react in slightly different ways to the rays of ordinary sunlight. But these slight physical variations in no way affect the intellectual or the spiritual life.

Of the electric groupings of mortal life, almost twenty-three per cent belong to class number four, the Urantia type of existence.

6. *The energizing types.* Not all worlds are alike in the manner of taking in energy. Not all inhabited worlds have an atmospheric ocean suited to respiratory exchange of gases, such as is present on Urantia. During the earlier and the later stages of many planets, beings of your present order could not exist; and when the respiratory factors of a planet are very high or very low, but when all other prerequisites to intelligent life are adequate, the Life Carriers often establish on such worlds a modified form of mortal existence, beings who are competent to effect their life-process exchanges

directly by means of light-energy and the firsthand power transmutations of the Master Physical Controllers.

There are six differing types of animal and mortal nutrition: The sub-breathers employ the first type of nutrition, the marine dwellers the second, the mid-breathers the third, as on Urantia. The super-breathers employ the fourth type of energy intake, while the nonbreathers utilize the fifth order of nutrition and energy. The sixth technique of energizing is limited to the midway creatures.

7. *The unnamed types.* There are numerous additional physical variations in planetary life, but all of these differences are wholly matters of anatomical modification, physiologic differentiation, and electrochemical adjustment. Such distinctions do not concern the intellectual or the spiritual life.

3. WORLDS OF THE NONBREATHERS

The majority of inhabited planets are peopled with the breathing type of intelligent beings. But there are also orders of mortals who are able to live on worlds with little or no air. Of the Orvonton inhabited worlds this type amounts to less than seven per cent. In Nebadon this percentage is less than three. In all Satania there are only nine such worlds.

There are so very few of the non-breather type of inhabited worlds in Satania because this more recently organized section of Norlatiadek still abounds in meteoric space bodies; and worlds without a protective friction atmosphere are subject to incessant bombardment by these wanderers. Even some of the comets consist of meteor swarms, but as a rule they are disrupted smaller bodies of matter.

Millions upon millions of meteorites enter the atmosphere of Urantia daily, coming in at the rate of almost two hundred miles a second. On the non-breathing worlds the advanced races must do much to protect themselves from meteor damage by making electrical installations which operate to consume or shunt the meteors. Great danger confronts them when they venture beyond these protected zones. These worlds are also subject to disastrous electrical storms of a nature unknown on Urantia. During such times of tremendous energy fluctuation the inhabitants must take refuge in their special structures of protective insulation.

Life on the worlds of the nonbreathers is radically different from what it is on Urantia. The nonbreathers do not eat food or drink water as do the Urantia races. The reactions of the nervous system, the heat-regulating mechanism, and the metabolism of these specialized peoples are radically different from such functions of Urantia mortals. Almost every act of living, aside from reproduction, differs, and even the methods of procreation are somewhat different.

On the non-breathing worlds the animal species are radically unlike those found on the atmospheric planets. The non-breathing plan of life varies from the technique of existence on an atmospheric world; even in survival their peoples differ, being candidates for Spirit fusion. Nevertheless, these beings enjoy life and carry forward the activities of the realm with the same relative trials and joys that are experienced by the mortals living on atmospheric worlds. In mind and character the nonbreathers do not differ from other mortal types.

You would be more than interested in the planetary conduct of this type of mortal because such a race of beings inhabits a sphere in close proximity to Urantia.

4. EVOLUTIONARY WILL CREATURES

There are great differences between the mortals of the different worlds, even among those belonging to the same intellectual and physical types, but all mortals of will dignity are erect animals, bipeds.

The average special physical-sense endowment of human beings is twelve, though the special senses of the three-brained mortals are extended slightly beyond those of the one- and two-brained types; they can see and hear considerably more than the Urantia races.

Young are usually born singly, multiple births being the exception, and the family life is fairly uniform on all types of planets. Sex equality prevails on all advanced worlds; male and female are equal in mind endowment and spiritual status. We do not regard a planet as having emerged from barbarism so long as one sex seeks to tyrannize over the other. This feature of creature experience is always greatly improved after the arrival of a Material Son and Daughter.

Seasons and temperature variations occur on all sunlighted and sun-heated planets. Agriculture is universal on all atmospheric worlds; tilling the soil is the one pursuit that is common to the advancing races of all such planets.

Mortals all have the same general struggles with microscopic foes in their early days, such as you now experience on Urantia, though perhaps not so extensive. The length of life varies on the different planets from twenty-five years on the primitive worlds to near five hundred on the more advanced and older spheres.

Human beings are all gregarious, both tribal and racial. These group segregations are inherent in their origin and constitution. Such tendencies can be modified only by advancing civilization and by gradual spiritualization. The social, economic, and governmental problems of the inhabited worlds vary in accordance with the age of the planets and the degree to which they have been influenced by the successive sojourns of the divine Sons.

Mind is the bestowal of the Infinite Spirit and functions quite the same in diverse environments. The mind of mortals is akin, regardless of certain structural and chemical differences which characterize the physical natures of the will creatures of the local systems. Regardless of personal or physical planetary differences, the mental life of all these various orders of mortals is very similar, and their immediate careers after death are very much alike.

But mortal mind without immortal spirit cannot survive. The mind of man is mortal; only the bestowed spirit is immortal. Survival is dependent on spiritualization by the ministry of the Adjuster — on the birth and evolution of the immortal soul; at least, there must not have developed an antagonism towards the Adjuster's mission of effecting the spiritual transformation of the material mind.

5. THE PLANETARY SERIES OF MORTALS

It will be somewhat difficult to make an adequate portrayal of the planetary series of mortals because you know so little about them, and because there are so many variations. Mortal creatures may, however, be studied from numerous viewpoints, among which are the following:

- 1. Adjustment to planetary environment.
- 2. Brain-type series.
- 3. Spirit-reception series.
- 4. Planetary-mortal epochs.
- 5. Creature-kinship serials.
- 6. Adjuster-fusion series.
- 7. Techniques of terrestrial escape.

The inhabited spheres of the seven super-universes are peopled with mortals who simultaneously classify in some one or more categories of each of these seven generalized classes of evolutionary creature life. But even these general classifications make no provision for such beings as midsoniters nor for certain other forms of intelligent life. The inhabited worlds, as they have been presented in these narratives, are peopled with evolutionary mortal creatures, but there are other life forms.

1. *Adjustment to planetary environment.* There are three general groups of inhabited worlds from the standpoint of the adjustment of creature life to the planetary environment: the normal adjustment group, the radical adjustment group, and the experimental group.

Normal adjustments to planetary conditions follow the general physical patterns previously considered. The worlds of the nonbreathers typify the radical or extreme adjustment, but other types are also included in this group. Experimental worlds are usually ideally adapted to the typical life forms, and on these decimal planets the Life Carriers attempt to produce beneficial variations in the standard life designs. Since your world is an experimental planet, it differs markedly from its sister spheres in Satania;

many forms of life have appeared on Urantia that are not found elsewhere; likewise are many common species absent from your planet.

In the universe of Nebadon, all the life-modification worlds are serially linked together and constitute a special domain of universe affairs which is given attention by designated administrators; and all of these experimental worlds are periodically inspected by a corps of universe directors whose chief is the veteran finaliter known in Satania as Tabamantia.

2. *Brain-type series.* The one physical uniformity of mortals is the brain and nervous system; nevertheless, there are three basic organizations of the brain mechanism: the one-, the two-, and the three-brained types. Urantians are of the two-brained type, somewhat more imaginative, adventurous, and philosophical than the one-brained mortals but somewhat less spiritual, ethical, and worshipful than the three-brained orders. These brain differences characterize even the prehuman animal existences.

From the two-hemisphere type of the Urantian cerebral cortex you can, by analogy, grasp something of the one-brained type. The third brain of the three-brained orders is best conceived as an evolvement of your lower or rudimentary form of brain, which is developed to the point where it functions chiefly in control of physical activities, leaving the two superior brains free for higher engagements: one for intellectual functions and the other for the spiritual-counterparting activities of the Thought Adjuster.

While the terrestrial attainments of the one-brained races are slightly limited in comparison with the two-brained orders, the older planets of the three-brained group exhibit civilizations that would astound Urantians, and which would somewhat shame yours by comparison. In mechanical development and material civilization, even in intellectual progress, the two-brained mortal worlds are able to equal the three-brained spheres. But in the higher control of mind and development of intellectual and spiritual reciprocation, you are somewhat inferior.

All such comparative estimates concerning the intellectual progress or the spiritual attainments of any world or group of worlds should in fairness recognize planetary age; much, very much, depends on age, the help of the biologic uplifters, and the subsequent missions of the various orders of the divine Sons.

While the three-brained peoples are capable of a slightly higher planetary evolution than either the one- or two-brained orders, all have the same type of life plasm and carry on planetary activities in very similar ways, much as do human beings on Urantia. These three types of mortals are distributed throughout the worlds of the local systems. In the majority of cases planetary conditions had very little to do with the decisions of the Life Carriers to project these varied orders of mortals on the different worlds; it is a prerogative of the Life Carriers thus to plan and execute.

These three orders stand on an equal footing in the ascension career. Each must traverse the same intellectual scale of development, and each must master the same spiritual tests of progression. The system administration and the constellation over-control of these different worlds are uniformly free from discrimination; even the regimes of the Planetary Princes are identical.

3. *Spirit-reception series*. There are three groups of mind design as related to contact with spirit affairs. This classification does not refer to the one-, two-, and three-brained orders of mortals; it refers primarily to gland chemistry, more particularly to the organization of certain glands comparable to the pituitary bodies. The races on some worlds have one gland, on others two, as do Urantians, while on still other spheres the races have three of these unique bodies. The inherent imagination and spiritual receptivity is definitely influenced by this differential chemical endowment.

Of the spirit-reception types, sixty-five per cent are of the second group, like the Urantia races. Twelve per cent are of the first type, naturally less receptive, while twenty-three per cent are more spiritually inclined during terrestrial life. But such distinctions do not survive natural death; all of these racial differences pertain only to the life in the flesh.

4. *Planetary-mortal epochs*. This classification recognizes the succession of temporal dispensations as they affect man's terrestrial status and his reception of celestial ministry.

Life is initiated on the planets by the Life Carriers, who watch over its development until sometime after the evolutionary appearance of mortal man. Before the Life Carriers leave a planet, they duly install a Planetary Prince as ruler of the realm. With this ruler there arrives a full quota of subordinate auxiliaries and ministering helpers, and the first adjudication of the living and the dead is simultaneous with his arrival.

With the emergence of human groupings, this Planetary Prince arrives to inaugurate human civilization and to focalize human society. Your world of confusion is no criterion of the early days of the reign of the Planetary Princes, for it was near the beginning of such an administration on Urantia that your Planetary Prince, Caligastia, cast his lot with the rebellion of the System Sovereign, Lucifer. Your planet has pursued a stormy course ever since.

On a normal evolutionary world, biologic progress attains its natural peak during the regime of the Planetary Prince, and shortly thereafter the System Sovereign dispatches a Material Son and Daughter to that planet. These imported beings are of service as biologic uplifters; their default on Urantia further complicated your planetary history.

When the intellectual and ethical progress of a human race has reached the limits of evolutionary development, there comes an Avonal Son of Paradise on a magisterial mission; and later on, when the spiritual status of such a world is nearing its limit of natural attainment, the planet is visited by a Paradise bestowal Son. The chief mission of a bestowal Son is to establish the planetary status, release the Spirit of Truth for planetary function, and thus effect the universal coming of the Thought Adjusters.

Here, again, Urantia deviates: There has never been a magisterial mission on your world, neither was your bestowal Son of the Avonal order; your planet enjoyed the signal honor of becoming the mortal home planet of the Sovereign Son, Michael of Nebadon.

As a result of the ministry of all the successive orders of divine sonship, the inhabited worlds and their advancing races begin to approach the apex of planetary evolution. Such worlds now become ripe for the culminating mission, the arrival of the Trinity Teacher Sons. This epoch of the Teacher Sons is the vestibule to the final planetary age — evolutionary utopia — the age of light and life.

This classification of human beings will receive particular attention in a succeeding paper.

5. *Creature-kinship serials.* Planets are not only organized vertically into systems, constellations, and so on, but the universe administration also

provides for horizontal groupings according to type, series, and other relationships. This lateral administration of the universe pertains more particularly to the co-ordination of activities of a kindred nature which have been independently fostered on different spheres. These related classes of universe creatures are periodically inspected by certain composite corps of high personalities presided over by long-experienced finaliters.

These kinship factors are manifest on all levels, for kinship serials exist among nonhuman personalities as well as among mortal creatures — even between human and superhuman orders. Intelligent beings are vertically related in twelve great groups of seven major divisions each. The co-ordination of these uniquely related groups of living beings is probably effected by some not fully comprehended technique of the Supreme Being.

6. *Adjuster-fusion series.* The spiritual classification or grouping of all mortals during their prefusion experience is wholly determined by the relation of the personality status to the indwelling Mystery Monitor. Almost ninety per cent of the inhabited worlds of Nebadon are peopled with Adjuster-fusion mortals in contrast with a near-by universe where scarcely more than one half of the worlds harbor beings who are Adjuster-indwelt candidates for eternal fusion.

7. *Techniques of terrestrial escape.* There is fundamentally only one way in which individual human life can be initiated on the inhabited worlds, and that is through creature procreation and natural birth; but there are numerous techniques whereby man escapes his terrestrial status and gains access to the inward moving stream of Paradise ascenders.

6. TERRESTRIAL ESCAPE

All of the differing physical types and planetary series of mortals alike enjoy the ministry of Thought Adjusters, guardian angels, and the various orders of the messenger hosts of the Infinite Spirit. All alike are liberated from the bonds of flesh by the emancipation of natural death, and all alike go thence to the morontia worlds of spiritual evolution and mind progress.

From time to time, on motion of the planetary authorities or the system rulers, special resurrections of the sleeping survivors are conducted. Such resurrections occur at least every millennium of planetary time, when not all but "many of those who sleep in the dust awake." These special resurrections are the occasion for mobilizing special groups of ascenders for specific service in the local universe plan of mortal ascension. There are both practical reasons and sentimental associations connected with these special resurrections.

Throughout the earlier ages of an inhabited world, many are called to the mansion spheres at the special and the millennial resurrections, but most survivors are repersonalized at the inauguration of a new dispensation associated with the advent of a divine Son of planetary service.

1. *Mortals of the dispensational or group order of survival.* With the arrival of the first Adjuster on an inhabited world the guardian seraphim also make their appearance; they are indispensable to terrestrial escape. Throughout the life-lapse period of the sleeping survivors the spiritual values and eternal realities of their newly evolved and immortal souls are held as a sacred trust by the personal or by the group guardian seraphim.

The group guardians of assignment to the sleeping survivors always function with the judgment Sons on their world advents. "He shall send his angels, and they shall gather together his elect from the four winds." With each seraphim of assignment to the repersonalization of a sleeping mortal there functions the returned Adjuster, the same immortal Father fragment that lived in him during the days in the flesh, and thus is identity restored and personality resurrected. During the sleep of their subjects these waiting Adjusters serve on Divinington; they never indwell another mortal mind in this interim.

While the older worlds of mortal existence harbor those highly developed and exquisitely spiritual types of human beings who are virtually exempt from the morontia life, the earlier ages of the animal-origin races are characterized by primitive mortals who are so immature that fusion with their Adjusters is impossible. The reawakening of these mortals is accomplished by the guardian seraphim in conjunction with an individualized portion of the immortal spirit of the Third Source and Center.

Thus are the sleeping survivors of a planetary age repersonalized in the dispensational roll calls. But with regard to the non-salvable personalities of a realm, no immortal spirit is present to function with the group guardians of destiny, and this constitutes cessation of creature existence. While some of your records have pictured these events as taking place on the planets of mortal death, they all really occur on the mansion worlds.

2. *Mortals of the individual orders of ascension.* The individual progress of human beings is measured by their successive attainment and traversal (mastery) of the seven cosmic circles. These circles of mortal progression are levels of associated intellectual, social, spiritual, and cosmic-insight values. Starting out in the seventh circle, mortals strive for the first, and all who have attained the third immediately have personal guardians of destiny assigned to them. These mortals may be repersonalized in the morontia life independent of dispensational or other adjudications.

Throughout the earlier ages of an evolutionary world, few mortals go to judgment on the third day. But as the ages pass, more and more the personal guardians of destiny are assigned to the advancing mortals, and thus increasing numbers of these evolving creatures are repersonalized on the first mansion world on the third day after natural death. On such occasions the return of the Adjuster signalizes the awakening of the human soul, and this is the repersonalization of the dead just as literally as when the en masse roll is called at the end of a dispensation on the evolutionary worlds.

There are three groups of individual ascenders: The less advanced land on the initial or first mansion world. The more advanced group may take up the morontia career on any of the intermediate mansion worlds in accordance with previous planetary progression. The most advanced of these orders really begin their morontia experience on the seventh mansion world.

3. *Mortals of the probationary-dependent orders of ascension.* The arrival of an Adjuster constitutes identity in the eyes of the universe, and all indwelt beings are on the roll calls of justice. But temporal life on the evolutionary worlds is uncertain, and many die in youth before choosing the Paradise career. Such Adjuster-indwelt children and youths follow the parent of most advanced spiritual status, thus going to the system finaliter world (the probationary nursery) on the third day, at a special resurrection, or at the regular millennial and dispensational roll calls.

Children who die when too young to have Thought Adjusters are repersonalized on the finaliter world of the local systems concomitant with the arrival of either parent on the mansion worlds. A child acquires physical entity at mortal birth, but in the matter of survival all Adjusterless children are reckoned as still attached to their parents.

In due course Thought Adjusters come to indwell these little ones, while the seraphic ministry to both groups of the probationary-dependent orders of survival is in general similar to that of the more advanced parent or is equivalent to that of the parent in case only one survives. Those attaining the third circle, regardless of the status of their parents, are accorded personal guardians.

Similar probation nurseries are maintained on the finaliter spheres of the constellation and the galaxy headquarters for the Adjusterless children of the primary and secondary modified orders of ascenders.

4. *Mortals of the secondary modified orders of ascension.* These are the progressive human beings of the intermediate evolutionary worlds. As a rule they are not immune to natural death, but they are exempt from passing through the seven mansion worlds.

The less perfected group reawaken on the headquarters of their local system, passing by only the mansion worlds. The intermediate group go to the constellation training worlds; they pass by the entire morontia regime of the local system. Still farther on in the planetary ages of spiritual striving, many survivors awaken on the constellation headquarters and there begin the Paradise ascent.

But before any of these groups may go forward, they must journey back as instructors to the worlds they missed, gaining many experiences as teachers in those realms which they passed by as students. They all subsequently proceed to Paradise by the ordained routes of mortal progression.

5. *Mortals of the primary modified order of ascension.* These mortals belong to the Adjuster-fused type of evolutionary life, but they are most often representative of the final phases of human development on an evolving world. These glorified beings are exempt from passing through the portals of death; they are submitted to Son seizure; they are translated from among the living and appear immediately in the presence of the Secondary Vorondadek Son on the headquarters of the local galaxy.

These are the mortals who fuse with their Adjusters during mortal life, and such Adjuster-fused personalities traverse space freely before being clothed with morontia forms. These fused souls go by direct Adjuster transit to the resurrection halls of the higher morontia spheres, where they receive their initial morontia investiture just as do all other mortals arriving from the evolutionary worlds.

This primary modified order of mortal ascension may apply to individuals in any of the planetary series from the lowest to the highest stages of the Adjuster-fusion worlds, but it more frequently functions on the older of these spheres after they have received the benefits of numerous sojourns of the divine Sons.

With the establishment of the planetary era of light and life, many go to the galaxy morontia worlds by the primary modified order of translation. Further along in the advanced stages of settled existence, when the majority of the mortals leaving a realm are embraced in this class, the planet is regarded as belonging to this series. Natural death becomes decreasingly frequent on these spheres long settled in light and life.

[Presented by a Melchizedek of the Jerusem School of Planetary Administration.]

PAPER 50
THE PLANETARY PRINCES

WHILE BELONGING to the order of Lanonandek Sons, the Planetary Princes are so specialized in service that they are commonly regarded as a distinct group. After their Melchizedek certification as secondary Lanonandeks, these local universe Sons are assigned to the reserves of their order on the constellation headquarters. From here they are assigned to various duties by the System Sovereign and eventually commissioned as Planetary Princes and sent forth to rule the evolving inhabited worlds.

The signal for a System Sovereign to act in the matter of assigning a ruler to a given planet is the reception of a request from the Life Carriers for the dispatch of an administrative head to function on this planet whereon they have established life and developed intelligent evolutionary beings. All planets which are inhabited by evolutionary mortal creatures have assigned to them a planetary ruler of this order of sonship.

1. MISSION OF THE PRINCES

The Planetary Prince and his assistant brethren represent the nearest personalized approach (aside from incarnation) that the Eternal Son of

Paradise can make to the lowly creatures of time and space. True, the Creator Son touches the creatures of the realms through his spirit, but the Planetary Prince is the last of the orders of personal Sons extending out from Paradise to the children of men. The Infinite Spirit comes very near in the persons of the guardians of destiny and other angelic beings; the Universal Father lives in man by the pre-personal presence of the Mystery Monitors; but the Planetary Prince represents the last effort of the Eternal Son and his Sons to draw near you. On a newly inhabited world the Planetary Prince is the sole representative of complete divinity, springing from the Creator Son (the offspring of the Universal Father and the Eternal Son) and the Divine Minister (the universe Daughter of the Infinite Spirit).

The prince of a newly inhabited world is surrounded by a loyal corps of helpers and assistants and by large numbers of the ministering spirits. But the directing corps of such new worlds must be of the lower orders of the administrators of a system in order to be innately sympathetic with, and understanding of, the planetary problems and difficulties. And all of this effort to provide sympathetic rulership for the evolutionary worlds entails the increased liability that these near-human personalities may be led astray by the exaltation of their own minds over and above the will of the Supreme Rulers.

Being quite alone as representatives of divinity on the individual planets, these Sons are tested severely, and Nebadon has suffered the misfortune of several rebellions. In the creation of the System Sovereigns and the Planetary Princes there occurs the personalization of a concept that has been getting farther and farther away from the Universal Father and the Eternal Son, and there is an increasing danger of losing the sense of proportion as to one's self-importance and a greater likelihood of failure to keep a proper grasp of the values and relationships of the numerous orders of divine beings and their gradations of authority. That the Father is not personally present in the local universe also imposes a certain test of faith and loyalty on all these Sons.

But not often do these world princes fail in their missions of organizing and administering the inhabited spheres, and their success greatly facilitates the subsequent missions of the Material Sons, who come to engraft the higher forms of creature life on the primitive men of the worlds. Their rule also does much to prepare the planets for the Paradise Sons of God, who subsequently come to judge the worlds and to inaugurate successive dispensations.

2. PLANETARY ADMINISTRATION

All Planetary Princes are under the universe administrative jurisdiction of Gabriel, the chief executive of Michael, while in immediate authority they are subject to the executive mandates of the System Sovereigns.

The Planetary Princes may at any time seek the counsel of the Melchizedeks, their former instructors and sponsors, but they are not arbitrarily required to ask for such assistance, and if such aid is not voluntarily requested, the Melchizedeks do not interfere with the planetary administration. These world rulers may also avail themselves of the advice of the four and twenty counselors, assembled from the bestowal worlds of the system. In Satania these counselors are at present all natives of Urantia. And there is an analogous council of seventy at the constellation headquarters also selected from the evolutionary beings of the realms.

The rule of the evolutionary planets in their early and unsettled careers is largely autocratic. The Planetary Princes organize their specialized groups of assistants from among their corps of planetary aids. They usually surround themselves with a supreme council of twelve, but this is variously chosen and diversely constituted on the different worlds. A Planetary Prince may also have as assistants one or more of the third order of his own group of sonship and sometimes, on certain worlds, one of his own order, a secondary Lanonandek associate.

The entire staff of a world ruler consists of personalities of the Infinite Spirit and certain types of higher evolved beings and ascending mortals from other worlds. Such a staff averages about one thousand, and as the planet progresses, this corps of helpers may be increased up to one hundred thousand or more. At any time need is felt for more helpers, the Planetary Princes have only to make request of their brothers, the System Sovereigns, and the petition is granted forthwith.

Planets vary greatly in nature and organization and in administration, but all provide for tribunals of justice. The judicial system of the local universe has its beginnings in the tribunals of a Planetary Prince, which are presided over by a member of his personal staff; the decrees of such courts reflect a highly fatherly and discretionary attitude. All problems involving more than the regulation of the planetary inhabitants are subject to appeal to the higher tribunals, but the affairs of his world domain are largely adjusted in accordance with the personal discretion of the prince.

The roving commissions of conciliators serve and supplement the planetary tribunals, and both spirit and physical controllers are subject to the findings of these conciliators. But no arbitrary execution is ever carried out without the consent of the Constellation Father, for the "Most Highs rule in the kingdoms of men."

The controllers and transformers of planetary assignment are also able to collaborate with angels and other orders of celestial beings in rendering these latter personalities visible to mortal creatures. On special occasions the seraphic helpers and even the Melchizedeks can and do make themselves visible to the inhabitants of the evolutionary worlds. The principal reason for bringing mortal ascenders from the system capital as a part of the staff of the Planetary Prince is to facilitate communication with the inhabitants of the realm.

3. THE PRINCE'S CORPOREAL STAFF

On going to a young world, a Planetary Prince usually takes with him a group of volunteer ascending beings from the local system headquarters. These ascenders accompany the prince as advisers and helpers in the work of early race improvement. This corps of material helpers constitutes the connecting link between the prince and the world races. The Urantia Prince, Caligastia, had a corps of one hundred such helpers.

Such volunteer assistants are citizens of a system capital, and none of them have fused with their indwelling Adjusters. The status of the Adjusters of such volunteer servers remains as of the residential standing on the system headquarters while these morontia progressors temporarily revert to a former material state.

The Life Carriers, the architects of form, provide such volunteers with new physical bodies, which they occupy for the periods of their planetary sojourn. These personality forms, while exempt from the ordinary diseases of the realms, are, like the early morontia bodies, subject to certain accidents of a mechanical nature.

The prince's corporeal staff are usually removed from the planet in connection with the next adjudication at the time of the second Son's arrival on the sphere. Before leaving, they customarily assign their various duties to their mutual offspring and to certain superior native volunteers. On those worlds where these helpers of the prince have been permitted to mate with the superior groups of the natives, such offspring usually succeed them.

These assistants to the Planetary Prince seldom mate with the natives, but they do always mate among themselves. Two classes of beings result from these unions: the primary type of midway creatures and certain high types of material beings who remain attached to the prince's staff after their parents have been removed from the planet at the time of the arrival of Adam and Eve. These children do not mate with the mortal races except in certain emergencies and then only by direction of the Planetary Prince. In such an event, their children — the grandchildren of the corporeal staff — are in status as of the superior humans of their day and generation. All the offspring of these semi-material assistants of the Planetary Prince are Adjuster indwelt.

At the end of the prince's dispensation, when the time comes for this "reversion staff" to be returned to the system headquarters for the resumption of the Paradise career, these ascenders present themselves to the Life Carriers for the purpose of yielding up their material bodies. They enter the transition slumber and awaken delivered from their mortal investment and clothed with morontia forms, ready for seraphic transportation back to the system capital, where their detached Adjusters await them. They are a whole dispensation behind their Jerusem class, but they have gained a unique and extraordinary experience, a rare chapter in the career of an ascending mortal.

4. THE PLANETARY HEADQUARTERS AND SCHOOLS

The prince's corporeal staff early organize the planetary schools of training and culture, wherein the cream of the evolutionary races are instructed and then sent forth to teach these better ways to their people. These schools of the prince are located at the material headquarters of the planet.

Much of the physical work connected with the establishment of this headquarters city is performed by the corporeal staff. Such headquarters cities, or settlements, of the early times of the Planetary Prince are very different from what a Urantia mortal might imagine. They are, in comparison with later ages, simple, being characterized by mineral embellishment and by relatively advanced material construction. And all of this stands in contrast with the Adamic regime centering around a garden headquarters, from which their work in behalf of the races is prosecuted during the second dispensation of the universe Sons.

In the headquarters settlement on your world every human habitation was provided with abundance of land. Although the remote tribes continued in hunting and food foraging, the students and teachers in the Prince's schools were all agriculturists and horticulturists. The time was about equally divided between the following pursuits:

1. *Physical labor*. Cultivation of the soil, associated with home building and embellishment.

2. *Social activities*. Play performances and cultural social groupings.

3. *Educational application*. Individual instruction in connection with family-group teaching, supplemented by specialized class training.

4. *Vocational training*. Schools of marriage and homemaking, the schools of art and craft training, and the classes for the training of teachers — secular, cultural, and religious.

5. *Spiritual culture*. The teacher brotherhood, the enlightenment of childhood and youth groups, and the training of adopted native children as missionaries to their people.

A Planetary Prince is not visible to mortal beings; it is a test of faith to believe the representations of the semi-material beings of his staff. But these schools of culture and training are well adapted to the needs of each planet, and there soon develops a keen and laudatory rivalry among the native inhabitants in their efforts to gain entrance to these various institutions of learning.

From such a world center of culture and achievement there gradually radiates to all peoples an uplifting and civilizing influence which slowly and certainly transforms the evolutionary races. Meantime the educated and spiritualized children of the surrounding peoples who have been adopted and trained in the prince's schools are returning to their native groups and, to the best of their ability, are there establishing new and potent centers of learning and culture which they carry on according to the plan of the prince's schools.

On Urantia these plans for planetary progress and cultural advancement were well under way, proceeding most satisfactorily, when the whole enterprise was brought to a rather sudden and most inglorious end by Caligastia's adherence to the Lucifer rebellion.

It was one of the most profoundly shocking episodes of this rebellion for me to learn of the callous perfidy of one of my own order of sonship, Caligastia, who, in deliberation and with malice aforethought, systematically perverted the instruction and poisoned the teaching provided in all the Urantia planetary schools in operation at that time. The wreck of these schools was speedy and complete.

Many of the offspring of the ascenders of the Prince's materialized staff remained loyal, deserting the ranks of Caligastia. These loyalists were encouraged by the Melchizedek receivers of Urantia, and in later times their descendants did much to uphold the planetary concepts of truth and righteousness. The work of these loyal evangels helped to prevent the total obliteration of spiritual truth on Urantia. These courageous souls and their descendants kept alive some knowledge of the Father's rule and preserved for the world races the concept of the successive planetary dispensations of the various orders of divine Sons.

5. PROGRESSIVE CIVILIZATION

The loyal princes of the inhabited worlds are permanently attached to the planets of their original assignment. Paradise Sons and their dispensations may come and go, but a successful Planetary Prince continues on as the ruler of his realm. His work is quite independent of the missions of the higher Sons, being designed to foster the development of planetary civilization.

The progress of civilization is hardly alike on any two planets. The details of the unfoldment of mortal evolution are very different on numerous dissimilar worlds. Notwithstanding these many diversifications of planetary development along physical, intellectual, and social lines, all evolutionary spheres progress in certain well-defined directions.

Under the benign rule of a Planetary Prince, augmented by the Material Sons and punctuated by the periodic missions of the Paradise Sons, the mortal races on an average world of time and space will successively pass through the following seven developmental epochs:

1. *The nutrition epoch.* The prehuman creatures and the dawn races of primitive man are chiefly concerned with food problems. These evolving beings spend their waking hours either in seeking food or in fighting, offensively or defensively. The food quest is paramount in the minds of these early ancestors of subsequent civilization.

2. *The security age.* Just as soon as the primitive hunter can spare any time from the search for food, he turns this leisure to augmenting his security. More and more attention is devoted to the technique of war. Homes are fortified, and the clans are solidified by mutual fear and by the inculcation of hate for foreign groups. Self-preservation is a pursuit which always follows self-maintenance.

3. *The material-comfort era.* After food problems have been partially solved and some degree of security has been attained, the additional leisure is utilized to promote personal comfort. Luxury vies with necessity in occupying the center of the stage of human activities. Such an age is all too often characterized by tyranny, intolerance, gluttony, and drunkenness. The

weaker elements incline towards excesses and brutality. Gradually these pleasure-seeking weaklings are subjugated by the more strong and truth-loving elements of the advancing civilization.

4. *The quest for knowledge and wisdom*. Food, security, pleasure, and leisure provide the foundation for the development of culture and the spread of knowledge. The effort to execute knowledge results in wisdom, and when a culture has learned how to profit and improve by experience, civilization has really arrived. Food, security, and material comfort still dominate society, but many forward-looking individuals are hungering for knowledge and thirsting for wisdom. Every child is provided an opportunity to learn by doing; education is the watchword of these ages.

5. *The epoch of philosophy and brotherhood*. When mortals learn to think and begin to profit by experience, they become philosophical — they start out to reason within themselves and to exercise discriminative judgment. The society of this age becomes ethical, and the mortals of such an era are truly becoming moral beings. Wise moral beings are capable of establishing human brotherhood on such a progressing world. Ethical and moral beings can learn how to live in accordance with the golden rule.

6. *The age of spiritual striving*. When evolving mortals have passed through the physical, intellectual, and social stages of development, sooner or later they attain those levels of personal insight which impel them to seek for spiritual satisfactions and cosmic understandings. Religion is completing the ascent from the emotional domains of fear and superstition to the high levels of cosmic wisdom and personal spiritual experience. Education aspires to the attainment of meanings, and culture grasps at cosmic relationships and true values. Such evolving mortals are genuinely cultured, truly educated, and exquisitely God-knowing.

7. *The era of light and life*. This is the flowering of the successive ages of physical security, intellectual expansion, social culture, and spiritual achievement. These human accomplishments are now blended, associated, and co-ordinated in cosmic unity and unselfish service. Within the limitations of finite nature and material endowments there are no bounds set upon

the possibilities of evolutionary attainment by the advancing generations who successively live upon these supernal and settled worlds of time and space.

After serving their spheres through successive dispensations of world history and the progressing epochs of planetary progress, the Planetary Princes are elevated to the position of Planetary Sovereigns upon the inauguration of the era of light and life.

6. PLANETARY CULTURE

The isolation of Urantia renders it impossible to undertake the presentation of many details of the life and environment of your Satania neighbors. In these presentations we are limited by the planetary quarantine and by the system isolation. We must be guided by these restrictions in all our efforts to enlighten Urantia mortals, but in so far as is permissible, you have been instructed in the progress of an average evolutionary world, and you are able to compare such a world's career with the present state of Urantia.

The development of civilization on Urantia has not differed so greatly from that of other worlds which have sustained the misfortune of spiritual isolation. But when compared with the loyal worlds of the universe, your planet seems most confused and greatly retarded in all phases of intellectual progress and spiritual attainment.

Because of your planetary misfortunes, Urantians are prevented from understanding very much about the culture of normal worlds. But you should not envisage the evolutionary worlds, even the most ideal, as spheres whereon life is a flowery bed of ease. The initial life of the mortal races is always attended by struggle. Effort and decision are an essential part of the acquirement of survival values.

Culture presupposes quality of mind; culture cannot be enhanced unless mind is elevated. Superior intellect will seek a noble culture and find some way to attain such a goal. Inferior minds will spurn the highest culture even when presented to them ready-made. Much depends, also, upon the successive missions of the divine Sons and upon the extent to which enlightenment is received by the ages of their respective dispensations.

You should not forget that for two hundred thousand years all the worlds of Satania have rested under the spiritual ban of Norlatiadek in consequence of the Lucifer rebellion. And it will require age upon age to retrieve the resultant handicaps of sin and secession. Your world still continues to pursue an irregular and checkered career as a result of the double tragedy of a rebellious Planetary Prince and a defaulting Material Son. Even the bestowal of Christ Michael on Urantia did not immediately set aside the temporal consequences of these serious blunders in the earlier administration of the world.

7. THE REWARDS OF ISOLATION

On first thought it might appear that Urantia and its associated isolated worlds are most unfortunate in being deprived of the beneficent presence and influence of such superhuman personalities as a Planetary Prince and a Material Son and Daughter. But isolation of these spheres affords their races a unique opportunity for the exercise of faith and for the development of a peculiar quality of confidence in cosmic reliability which is not dependent on sight or any other material consideration. It may turn out, eventually, that mortal creatures hailing from the worlds quarantined in consequence of rebellion are extremely fortunate. We have discovered that such ascenders are very early intrusted with numerous special assignments to cosmic undertakings where unquestioned faith and sublime confidence are essential to achievement.

On Jerusem the ascenders from these isolated worlds occupy a residential sector by themselves and are known as the *agondonters*, meaning evolutionary will creatures who can believe without seeing, persevere when isolated, and triumph over insuperable difficulties even when alone. This functional grouping of the agondonters persists throughout the ascension of the local universe and the traversal of the super-universe; it disappears during the sojourn in Havona but promptly reappears upon the attainment of Paradise and definitely persists in the Corps of the Mortal Finality. Tabamantia is an *agondonter* of finaliter status, having survived from one of the quarantined spheres involved in the first rebellion ever to take place in the universes of time and space.

All through the Paradise career, reward follows effort as the result of causes. Such rewards set off the individual from the average, provide a differential of creature experience, and contribute to the versatility of ultimate performances in the collective body of the finaliters.

[Presented by a Secondary Lanonandek Son of the Reserve Corps.]

PAPER 51
THE PLANETARY ADAMS

DURING THE DISPENSATION of a Planetary Prince, primitive man reaches the limit of natural evolutionary development, and this biologic attainment signals the System Sovereign to dispatch to such a world the second order of sonship, the biologic uplifters. These Sons, for there are two of them — the Material Son and Daughter — are usually known on a planet as Adam and Eve. The original Material Son of Satania is Adam, and those who go to the system worlds as biologic uplifters always carry the name of this first and original Son of their unique order.

These Sons are the material gift of the Creator Son to the inhabited worlds. Together with the Planetary Prince, they remain on their planet of assignment throughout the evolutionary course of such a sphere. Such an adventure on a world having a Planetary Prince is not much of a hazard, but on an apostate planet, a realm without a spiritual ruler and deprived of interplanetary communication, such a mission is fraught with grave danger.

Although you cannot hope to know all about the work of these Sons on all the worlds of Satania and other systems, other papers depict more fully the life and experiences of the interesting pair, Adam and Eve, who came from the corps of the biologic uplifters of Jerusem to up-step the people of Urantia. While there was a miscarriage of the ideal plans for improving your native inhabitants, still, Adam's mission was not in vain; Urantia has profited immeasurably from the gift of Adam and Eve, and among their fellows and in the councils on high their work is not reckoned as a total loss.

1. ORIGIN AND NATURE OF THE MATERIAL SONS OF GOD

The material or sex Sons and Daughters are the offspring of the Creator Son; the Universe Mother Spirit does not directly participate in the production of these beings who are destined to function as physical uplifters on the evolutionary worlds. However, since the seven adjutant mind spirits of the Universe Mother Spirit in their higher aspects produce the seven ray energies[1], and since our universe is in the seventh super-universe, the Creator Son uses seventh ray energy predominately when producing these Material Sons and Daughters. This order of Sonship, in this universe, are thus very strongly seventh ray beings, and hence have a spiritually visible violet aura and noticeable seventh ray characteristics. Part of their task in acting as physical uplifters is also to impart more seventh ray influences into the intelligent beings of this universe.

The material order of sonship is not uniform throughout the local universe. The Creator Son produces only one pair of these beings in each local system; these original pairs are diverse in nature, being attuned to the life pattern of their respective systems. This is a necessary provision since otherwise the reproductive potential of the Adams would be nonfunctional with that of the evolving mortal beings of the worlds of any one particular system. The Adam and Eve who came to Urantia were descended from the original Satania pair of Material Sons.

Material Sons of your system, as they appear on Jerusem, vary in height from eight to ten feet, and their bodies glow with the brilliance of radiant light of a violet hue, being predominately seventh ray energy. While material blood circulates through their material bodies, they are also surcharged with divine energy and saturated with celestial light. This radiant light is not usually visible to short range physical sight and their height is adjusted on

---

1. JFC Note: the seven ray energies are described in the next paper.

rematerialization so that they will appear as only slightly taller than the native peoples. These Material Sons (the Adams) and Material Daughters (the Eves) are equal to each other, differing only in reproductive nature and in certain chemical endowments. They are equal but differential, male and female — hence complemental — and are designed to serve on almost all assignments in pairs.

The Material Sons enjoy a dual nutrition; they are really dual in nature and constitution, partaking of materialized energy much as do the physical beings of the realm, while their immortal existence is fully maintained by the direct and automatic intake of certain sustaining cosmic energies. Should they fail on some mission of assignment or even consciously and deliberately rebel, this order of Sons becomes isolated, cut off from connection with the universe source of light and life. Thereupon they become practically material beings, destined to take the course of material life on the world of their assignment and compelled to look to the universe magistrates for adjudication. Material death will eventually terminate the planetary career of such an unfortunate and unwise Material Son or Daughter.

An original or directly created Adam and Eve are immortal by inherent endowment just as are all other orders of local universe sonship, but a diminution of immortality potential characterizes their sons and daughters. This original couple cannot transmit unconditioned immortality to their procreated sons and daughters. Their progeny are dependent for continuing life on unbroken intellectual synchrony with the mind-gravity circuit of the Spirit. Since the inception of the system of Satania, thirteen Planetary Adams have been lost in rebellion and default and 681,204 in the subordinate positions of trust. Most of these defections occurred at the time of the Lucifer rebellion.

While living as permanent citizens on the system capitals, even when functioning on descending missions to the evolutionary planets, the Material Sons do not possess Thought Adjusters, but it is through these very services that they acquire experiential capacity for Adjuster indwellment and the Paradise ascension career. These unique and wonderfully useful beings are the connecting links between the spiritual and physical worlds. They are concentrated on the system headquarters, where they reproduce and carry on as material citizens of the realm, and whence they are dispatched to the evolutionary worlds.

Unlike the other created Sons of planetary service, the material order of sonship is not, by nature, invisible to material creatures like the inhabitants of Urantia. These Sons of God can be seen, understood, and can, in turn, actually mingle with the creatures of time, could even procreate with them, though this role of biologic upliftment usually falls to the progeny of the Planetary Adams.

On Jerusem the loyal children of any Adam and Eve are immortal, but the offspring of a Material Son and Daughter procreated subsequent to their arrival on an evolutionary planet are not thus immune to natural death. There occurs a change in the life-transmitting mechanism when these Sons are rematerialized for reproductive function on an evolutionary world. The Life Carriers designedly deprive the Planetary Adams and Eves of the power of begetting undying sons and daughters. If they do not default, an Adam and Eve on a planetary mission can live on indefinitely, but within certain limits their children experience decreasing longevity with each succeeding generation.

2. TRANSIT OF THE PLANETARY ADAMS

Upon receipt of the news that another inhabited world has attained the height of physical evolution, the System Sovereign convenes the corps of Material Sons and Daughters on the system capital; and following the discussion of the needs of such an evolutionary world, two of the volunteering group — an Adam and an Eve of the senior corps of Material Sons — are selected to undertake the adventure, to submit to the deep sleep preparatory to being enseraphimed and transported from their home of associated service to the new realm of new opportunities and new dangers.

Adams and Eves are semi-material creatures and, as such, are not transportable by seraphim. They must undergo dematerialization on the system capital before they can be enseraphimed for transport to the world of assignment. The transport seraphim are able to effect such changes in the Material Sons and in other semi-material beings as enable them to be enseraphimed and thus to be transported through space from one world or system to another. About three days of standard time are consumed in this transport preparation, and it requires the co-operation of a Life Carrier to restore such a dematerialized creature to normal existence upon arrival at the end of the seraphic-transport journey.

While there is this dematerializing technique for preparing the Adams for transit from Jerusem to the evolutionary worlds, there is no equivalent method for taking them away from such worlds unless the entire planet is to be emptied, in which event emergency installation of the dematerialization technique is made for the entire salvable population. If some physical catastrophe should doom the planetary residence of an evolving race, the Melchizedeks and the Life Carriers would install the technique of dematerialization for all survivors, and by seraphic transport these beings would be carried away to the new world prepared for their continuing existence. The evolution of a human race, once initiated on a world of space, must proceed quite independently of the physical survival of that planet, but during the evolutionary ages it is not otherwise intended that a Planetary Adam or Eve shall leave their chosen world.

Upon arrival at their planetary destination the Material Son and Daughter are rematerialized under the direction of the Life Carriers. This entire process takes ten to twenty-eight days of Urantia time. The unconsciousness of the seraphic slumber continues throughout this entire period of reconstruction. When the reassembly of the physical organism is completed, these Material Sons and Daughters stand in their new homes and on their new worlds but in bodies modified for the particular planet. On life experiment worlds, decimal planets like Urantia, this includes modifications necessary to make them consistent with the local genetic adaptations.

3. THE ADAMIC MISSIONS

On the inhabited worlds the Material Sons and Daughters construct their own garden homes, soon being assisted by their own children. Usually the site of the garden has been selected by the Planetary Prince, and his corporeal staff do much of the preliminary work of preparation with the help of many of the higher types of natives.

These Gardens of Eden are so named in honor of Edentia, the constellation capital, and because they are patterned after the botanic grandeur of the headquarters world of the Most High Fathers. Such garden homes are usually located in a secluded section and in a near-tropic zone. They are wonderful creations on an average world. You can judge nothing of these beautiful centers of culture by the fragmentary account of the aborted development of such an undertaking on Urantia.

A Planetary Adam and Eve are, in potential, the full gift of physical grace to the mortal races. The chief business of such an imported pair is to multiply and to uplift the children of time. But there is no immediate interbreeding between the people of the garden and those of the world; for many generations Adam and Eve remain biologically segregated from the evolutionary mortals while they build up a large population of their descendants.

The plans for material up-stepping are prepared by the Planetary Prince and his staff and are executed by Adam and Eve. And this was where your Material Son and his companion were placed at great disadvantage when they arrived on Urantia. Caligastia offered crafty and effective opposition to the Adamic mission; and notwithstanding that the Melchizedek receivers of Urantia had duly warned both Adam and Eve concerning the planetary dangers inherent in the presence of the rebellious Planetary Prince, this archrebel, by a wily stratagem, outmaneuvered the Edenic pair and entrapped them into a violation of the covenant of their trusteeship as the visible rulers of your world. The traitorous Planetary Prince did succeed in compromising your Adam and Eve, but he failed in his effort to involve them in the Lucifer rebellion.

The fifth order of angels, the planetary helpers, are attached to the Adamic mission, always accompanying the Planetary Adams on their world adventures. The corps of initial assignment is usually about one hundred thousand. When the work of the Urantia Adam and Eve was prematurely launched, when they departed from the ordained plan, it was one of the seraphic Voices of the Garden who remonstrated with them concerning their reprehensible conduct. And your narrative of this occurrence well illustrates the manner in which your planetary traditions have tended to ascribe every-thing supernatural to the Lord God. Because of this, Urantians have often become confused concerning the nature of the Universal Father since the words and acts of all his associates and subordinates have been so generally attributed to him. In the case of Adam and Eve, the angel of the Garden was none other than the chief of the planetary helpers then on duty. This seraphim, Solonia, proclaimed the miscarriage of the divine plan and requisitioned the return of the Melchizedek receivers to Urantia.

The secondary midway creatures are indigenous to the Adamic missions. As with the corporeal staff of the Planetary Prince, the descendants of the Material Sons and Daughters are of two orders: their physical children and the secondary order of midway creatures. These material but ordinarily invisible planetary ministers contribute much to the advancement of civilization and even to the subjection of insubordinate minorities who may seek to subvert social development and spiritual progress.

The secondary midwayers should not be confused with the primary order, who date from the near times of the arrival of the Planetary Prince. On Urantia a majority of these earlier midway creatures went into rebellion with Caligastia and have, since Pentecost, been interned. Many of the Adamic group who did not remain loyal to the planetary administration are likewise interned.

On the day of Pentecost the loyal primary and the secondary midwayers effected a voluntary union and have functioned as one unit in world affairs ever since. They serve under the leadership of loyal midwayers alternately chosen from the two groups.

Your world has been visited by four orders of sonship: Caligastia, the Planetary Prince; Adam and Eve of the Material Sons of God; Machiventa Melchizedek, the "sage of Salem" in the days of Abraham; and Christ Michael, who came as the Paradise bestowal Son. How much more effective and beautiful it would have been had Michael, the supreme ruler of the universe of Nebadon, been welcomed to your world by a loyal and efficient Planetary Prince and a devoted and successful Material Son, both of whom could have done so much to enhance the lifework and mission of the bestowal Son! But not all worlds have been so unfortunate as Urantia, neither has the mission of the Planetary Adams always been so difficult or so hazardous. When they are successful, they contribute to the development of a great people, continuing as the visible heads of planetary affairs even far into the age when such a world is settled in light and life.

4. RACIAL AMALGAMATION — BESTOWAL OF THE ADAMIC BLOOD

When a Planetary Adam and Eve arrive on an inhabited world, they have been fully instructed by their superiors as to the best way to effect the improvement of the existing race of intelligent beings. The plan of procedure is not uniform; much is left to the judgment of the ministering pair, and mistakes are not infrequent, especially on disordered, insurrectionary worlds, such as Urantia.

Usually the descendants of Adam and Eve do not begin to amalgamate with the planetary natives until their own group numbers over one million. But in the meantime the staff of the Planetary Prince proclaims that the children of the Gods have come down, as it were, to be one with the race of men; and the people eagerly look forward to the day when announcement will be made that those who have qualified as belonging to the superior types of natives may proceed to the Garden of Eden and be there chosen by the sons and daughters of Adam as the evolutionary fathers and mothers of the new and blended order of mankind.

On normal worlds the Planetary Adam and Eve never mate with the evolutionary race. This work of biologic betterment is a function of the Adamic progeny. But these Adamites do not go out among the natives; the prince's staff bring to the Garden of Eden the superior men and women for voluntary mating with the Adamic offspring. And on most worlds it is considered the highest honor to be selected as a candidate for mating with the sons and daughters of the garden.

For the first time the local wars and other tribal struggles are diminished, while the people of the world increasingly strive to qualify for recognition and admission to the garden. You can at best have but a very meager idea of how this competitive struggle comes to occupy the center of all activities on a normal planet. This whole scheme of native improvement was early wrecked on Urantia.

The Adamites are a monogamous people, and every evolutionary man or woman uniting with the Adamic sons and daughters pledges not to take other mates and to instruct his or her children in single-matedness. The children of each of these unions are educated and trained in the schools of the Planetary Prince and then are permitted to go forth to the people of their evolutionary parent, there to marry among the selected groups of superior mortals.

When this strain of the Material Sons is added to the evolving natives, their descendants are more responsive to the seventh ray energy and a new and greater era of evolutionary progress is initiated. Following this procreative outpouring of imported ability and super-evolutionary traits there ensues a succession of rapid strides in civilization and development; in one hundred thousand years more progress is made than in a million years of former struggle. In your world, even in the face of the miscarriage of the ordained plans, great progress has been made since the gift to your peoples of Adam's life plasm.

5. THE EDENIC REGIME

On most of the inhabited worlds the Gardens of Eden remain as superb cultural centers and continue to function as the social patterns of planetary conduct and usage age after age. Even in early times when the Adamites are relatively segregated, their schools receive suitable candidates from among the natives, while the industrial developments of the garden open up new channels of commercial intercourse. Thus do the Adams and Eves and their progeny contribute to the sudden expansion of culture and to the rapid improvement of the evolutionary people. And all of these relationships are augmented and sealed by the amalgamation of the evolutionary natives and the sons and daughters of Adam, resulting in the immediate up-stepping of biologic status, the quickening of intellectual potential, and the enhancement of spiritual receptivity.

On normal worlds the garden headquarters becomes the second center of world culture and, jointly with the headquarters city of the Planetary Prince, sets the pace for the development of civilization. For centuries the city headquarters schools of the Planetary Prince and the garden schools of Adam and Eve are contemporary. They are usually not very far apart, and they work together in harmonious co-operation.

Think what it would mean on your world if somewhere there were a world center of civilization, a great planetary university of culture, which had functioned uninterruptedly for 37,000 years. And again, pause to consider how the moral authority of even such an ancient center would be reinforced were there situated not far-distant still another and older headquarters of celestial ministry whose traditions would exert a cumulative force of 500,000 years of integrated evolutionary influence. It is custom which eventually spreads the ideals of Eden to a whole world.

The schools of the Planetary Prince are primarily concerned with philosophy, religion, morals, and the higher intellectual and artistic achievements. The garden schools of Adam and Eve are usually devoted to practical arts, fundamental intellectual training, social culture, economic development, trade relations, physical efficiency, and civil government. Eventually these world centers amalgamate, but this actual affiliation sometimes does not occur until the times of the first Magisterial Son.

The continuing existence of the Planetary Adam and Eve, together with their direct descendants, imparts that stability of growth to Edenic culture by virtue of which it comes to act upon the civilization of a world with the compelling force of tradition. In these immortal Material Sons and Daughters we encounter the last and the indispensable link connecting God with man, bridging the almost infinite gulf between the eternal Creator and the lowest finite personalities of time. Here is a being of high origin who is physical, material, even a sex creature like Urantia mortals, one who can see and comprehend the invisible Planetary Prince and interpret him to the mortal creatures of the realm, for the Material Sons and Daughters are able to see all of the lower orders of spirit beings; they visualize the Planetary Prince and his entire staff, visible and invisible.

With the passing of centuries, through the amalgamation of their progeny with the race of men, this same Material Son and Daughter become accepted as the common ancestors of mankind, the common parents of the now blended descendants of the evolutionary race. It is intended that mortals who start out from an inhabited world have the experience of recognizing seven fathers:

1. The biologic father — the father in the flesh.
2. The father of the realm — the Planetary Adam.
3. The father of the spheres — the System Sovereign.
4. The Most High Father — the Constellation Father.
5. The universe Father — the Creator Son and supreme ruler of the local creations.
6. The super-Fathers — the Ancients of Days who govern the super-universe.
7. The spirit or Havona Father — the Universal Father, who dwells on Paradise and bestows his spirit to live and work in the minds of the lowly creatures who inhabit the universe of universes.

6. UNITED ADMINISTRATION

From time to time the Avonal Sons of Paradise come to the inhabited worlds for judicial actions, but the first Avonal to arrive on a magisterial mission inaugurates the fourth dispensation of an evolutionary world of time and space. On some planets where this Magisterial Son is universally accepted, he remains for one age; and thus the planet prospers under the joint rulership of three Sons: the Planetary Prince, the Material Son, and the Magisterial Son, the latter two being visible to all the inhabitants of the realm.

Before the first Magisterial Son concludes his mission on a normal evolutionary world, there has been effected the union of the educational and administrative work of the Planetary Prince and the Material Son. This amalgamation of the dual supervision of a planet brings into existence a new and effective order of world administration. Upon the retirement of the Magisterial Son the Planetary Adam assumes the outward direction of the sphere. The Material Son and Daughter thus act jointly as planetary administrators until the settling of the world in the era of light and life; whereupon the Planetary Prince is elevated to the position of Planetary Sovereign. During this age of advanced evolution, Adam and Eve become what might be called joint prime ministers of the glorified realm.

As soon as the new and consolidated capital of the evolving world has become well established, and just as fast as competent subordinate administrators can be properly trained, sub-capitals are founded on remote land bodies and among the different peoples. Before the arrival of another dispensational Son, from fifty to one hundred of these subcenters will have been organized.

The Planetary Prince and his staff still foster the spiritual and philosophic domains of activity. Adam and Eve pay particular attention to the physical, scientific, and economic status of the realm. Both groups equally devote their energies to the promotion of the arts, social relations, and intellectual achievements.

By the time of the inauguration of the fifth dispensation of world affairs, a magnificent administration of planetary activities has been achieved. Mortal existence on such a well-managed sphere is indeed stimulating and profitable. And if Urantians could only observe life on such a planet, they would immediately appreciate the value of those things which their world has lost.

[Presented by a Secondary Lanonandek Son of the Reserve Corps.]

PAPER 52
PLANETARY MORTAL EPOCHS

From the inception of life on an evolutionary planet to the time of its final flowering in the era of light and life, there appear upon the stage of world action at least seven epochs of human life. These successive ages are determined by the planetary missions of the divine Sons, and on an average inhabited world these epochs appear in the following order:

1. Pre-Planetary Prince Man.
2. Post-Planetary Prince Man.
3. Post-Adamic Man.
4. Post-Magisterial Son Man.
5. Post-Bestowal Son Man.
6. Post-Teacher Son Man.
7. The Era of Light and Life.

The worlds of space, as soon as they are physically suitable for life, are placed on the registry of the Life Carriers, and in due time these Sons are dispatched to such planets for the purpose of initiating life. The entire period from life initiation to the appearance of man is designated the prehuman era and precedes the successive mortal epochs considered in this narrative.

1. PRIMITIVE MAN

From the time of man's emergence from the animal level — when he can choose to worship the Creator — to the arrival of the Planetary Prince, mortal will creatures are called *primitive men*. The seven adjutant mind spirits of the local universe Mother Spirit, in addition to their previously discussed functions, also operate to produce seven qualities or rays which play upon and seek to influence and elevate evolutionary beings. These Seven Rays are:[1]

1. The Ray of Will or Power
2. The Ray of Love – Wisdom
3. The Ray of Abstract Intelligence
4. The Ray of Harmony through Conflict
5. The Ray of Concrete Knowledge
6. The Ray of Devotion
7. The Ray of Ceremonial Order

Primitive men are more strongly responsive to the first six, and each person responds more strongly to one than to the other five, although all people respond to all seven ray influences to some extent. There are thus six basic types of primitive men depending on which of the first six rays dominate in their nature. Viewed from spirit levels these rays each have a color and those beings that are predominately responsive to any one ray are spoken of as being of that color. Ray one is viewed spiritually as red, ray two as orange, ray three yellow, ray four green, ray five blue, and ray six as indigo. Adam and Eve, being Material Sons of this seventh super-universe, are dominated by ray seven, the "violet" ray, and bring to the evolutionary races the ability to respond more strongly to this ray influence.

The evolutionary race of native beings can thus be considered as beings of color — red, orange, yellow, green, blue, and indigo — but this has nothing to do with physical appearance or such things as actual skin pigmen-

---

1. See "Esoteric Psychology" by Alice A. Bailey, Lucis Publishing Company, 1936; pages 163-169.

tation. This responsiveness to the seven rays begins to appear about the time that primitive man was first developing a simple language and was beginning to exercise the creative imagination. The length of time consumed in this early life evolution varies greatly on the different worlds, ranging from one hundred and fifty thousand years to over one million years of Urantia time.

In the light of subsequent civilization, this era of primitive man is a long, dark, and bloody chapter. The ethics of the struggle for survival are not in keeping with the standards of later dispensations of revealed religion and higher spiritual development. On normal and non-experimental worlds this epoch is very different from the prolonged and extraordinarily brutal struggles which characterized this age on Urantia. When you have emerged from your first world experience, you will begin to see why this long and painful struggle on the evolutionary worlds occurs, and as you go forward in the Paradise path, you will increasingly understand the wisdom of these apparently strange doings. But notwithstanding all the vicissitudes of the early ages of human emergence, the performances of primitive man represent a splendid, even a heroic, chapter in the annals of an evolutionary world of time and space.

Before they acquire a high order of intelligence, the planets are sometimes overrun with the larger types of animals. But early in this era mortals learn to kindle and maintain fire, and with the increase of inventive imagination and the improvement in tools, evolving man soon vanquishes the larger and more unwieldy animals.

Man's acquirement of ethical judgment, moral will, is usually coincident with the appearance of early language. Upon attaining the human level, after this emergence of mortal will, these beings become receptive to the temporary indwelling of the divine Adjusters, and upon death many are duly elected as survivors and sealed by the archangels for subsequent resurrection and Spirit fusion. The archangels always accompany the Planetary Princes, and a dispensational adjudication of the realm is simultaneous with the prince's arrival.

All mortals who are indwelt by Thought Adjusters are potential worshipers; they have been "lighted by the true light," and they possess capacity for seeking reciprocal contact with divinity. Nevertheless, the early or biologic religion of primitive man is largely a persistence of animal fear coupled with ignorant awe and tribal superstition. The survival of superstition in the Urantia races is hardly complimentary to your evolutionary development nor compatible with your otherwise splendid achievements in material progress. But this early fear religion serves a very valuable purpose in subduing the fiery tempers of these primitive creatures. It is the forerunner of civilization and the soil for the subsequent planting of the seeds of revealed religion by the Planetary Prince and his ministers.

Within one hundred thousand years from the time man is certified as a creature of will with capacity for worship, the Planetary Prince usually arrives, having been dispatched by the System Sovereign upon the report of the Life Carriers that will is functioning, even though comparatively few individuals have thus developed. Primitive mortals usually welcome the Planetary Prince and his visible staff; in fact, they often look upon them with awe and reverence, almost with worshipfulness, if they are not restrained.

2. POST-PLANETARY PRINCE MAN

With the arrival of the Planetary Prince a new dispensation begins. Government appears on earth, and the advanced tribal epoch is attained. Great social strides are made during a few thousand years of this regime. Under normal conditions mortals attain a high state of civilization during this age. They do not struggle so long in barbarism as Urantia did. But life on an inhabited world is so changed by rebellion that you can have little or no idea of such a regime on a normal planet.

The average length of this dispensation is around five hundred thousand years, some longer, some shorter. During this era the planet is established in the circuits of the system, and a full quota of seraphic and other celestial helpers is assigned to its administration. The Thought Adjusters come in increasing numbers, and the seraphic guardians amplify their regime of mortal supervision.

When the Planetary Prince arrives on a primitive world, the evolved religion of fear and ignorance prevails. The prince and his staff make the first revelations of higher truth and universe organization. These initial presentations of revealed religion are very simple, and they usually pertain to the affairs of the local system. Religion is wholly an evolutionary process prior to the arrival of the Planetary Prince. Subsequently, religion progresses by graduated revelation as well as by evolutionary growth. Each dispensation, each mortal epoch, receives an enlarged presentation of spiritual truth and religious ethics. The evolution of the religious capacity of receptivity in the inhabitants of a world largely determines their rate of spiritual advancement and the extent of religious revelation.

This dispensation witnesses a spiritual dawn, and the different groups and their various tribes tend to develop specialized systems of religious and philosophic thought. There uniformly run through all of these religions two strains: the early fears of primitive men and the later revelations of the Planetary Prince. In some respects Urantians do not seem to have wholly emerged from this stage of planetary evolution. As you pursue this study, you will the more clearly discern how far your world departs from the average course of evolutionary progress and development.

But the Planetary Prince is not "the Prince of Peace." Intergroup struggles and tribal wars continue over into this dispensation but with diminishing frequency and severity. This is the great age of population growth and dispersion, and it culminates in a period of intense nationalism. The different nations often develop separate languages. Each expanding group of mortals tends to seek isolation. This segregation is favored by the existence of many languages. Before the unification of the nations their relentless warfare sometimes results in the obliteration of whole peoples.

On average worlds, during the latter part of the prince's rule, national life begins to replace tribal organization or rather to be superimposed upon the existing tribal groupings. But the great social achievement of the prince's epoch is the emergence of family life. Heretofore, human relationships have been chiefly tribal; now, the home begins to materialize.

This is the dispensation of the realization of sex equality. On some planets the male may rule the female; on others the reverse prevails. During this age normal worlds establish full equality of the sexes, this being preliminary to the fuller realization of the ideals of home life. This is the dawn of the golden age of the home. The idea of tribal rule gradually gives way to the dual concept of national life and family life.

During this age agriculture makes its appearance. The growth of the family idea is incompatible with the roving and unsettled life of the hunter. Gradually the practices of settled habitations and the cultivation of the soil become established. The domestication of animals and the development of home arts proceed apace. Upon reaching the apex of biologic evolution, a high level of civilization has been attained, but there is little development of a mechanical order; invention is the characteristic of the succeeding age.

3. POST-ADAMIC MAN

When the original impetus of evolutionary life has run its biologic course, when man has reached the apex of animal development, there arrives the second order of sonship, and the second dispensation of grace and ministry is inaugurated. This is true on all evolutionary worlds. When the highest possible level of evolutionary life has been attained, when primitive man has ascended as far as possible in the biologic scale, a Material Son and Daughter always appear on the planet, having been dispatched by the System Sovereign.

Thought Adjusters are increasingly bestowed upon the post-Adamic men, and in constantly augmented numbers these mortals attain capacity for subsequent Adjuster fusion. While functioning as descending Sons, the Adams do not possess Adjusters, but their planetary offspring — direct and mixed — become legitimate candidates for the reception, in due time, of the Mystery Monitors. By the termination of the post-Adamic age the planet is in possession of its full quota of celestial ministers; only the fusion Adjusters are not yet universally bestowed.

It is the prime purpose of the Adamic regime to influence evolving man to complete the transit from the hunter and herder stage of civilization to that of the agriculturist and horticulturist, to be later supplemented by the appearance of the urban and industrial adjuncts to civilization. Ten thousand years of this dispensation of the biologic uplifters is sufficient to effect a marvelous transformation. Twenty-five thousand years of such an administration of the conjoint wisdom of the Planetary Prince and the Material Sons usually ripens the sphere for the advent of a Magisterial Son.

The Adamic progeny never amalgamate with the inferior individuals of the evolutionary race. Neither is it the divine plan for the Planetary Adam or Eve to mate, personally, with the evolutionary peoples. This race-improvement project is the task of their progeny. But the offspring of the Material Son and Daughter are mobilized for generations before the racial-amalgamation ministry is inaugurated.

The result of the gift of the Adamic life plasm to the mortal races is an immediate up-stepping of intellectual capacity and an acceleration of spiritual progress. There is usually some physical improvement also. On an average world the post-Adamic dispensation is an age of great invention, energy control, and mechanical development. This is the era of the appearance of multiform manufacture and the control of natural forces; it is the golden age of exploration and the final subduing of the planet. Much of the material progress of a world occurs during this time of the inauguration of the development of the physical sciences, just such an epoch as Urantia is now experiencing. Your world is a full dispensation and more behind the average planetary schedule.

By the end of the Adamic dispensation on a normal planet the natives are practically blended, so that it can be truly proclaimed that "God has made of one blood all the nations."

Primitive man is for the most part carnivorous; the Material Sons and Daughters do not eat meat, but their offspring within a few generations usually gravitate to the omnivorous level, although whole groups of their descendants sometimes remain non-flesh eaters. This double origin of the post-Adamic races explains how such blended human stocks exhibit anatomic vestiges belonging to both the herbivorous and carnivorous animal groups.

Within ten thousand years of racial amalgamation the resultant stocks show varying degrees of anatomic blend, some strains carrying more of the marks of the non flesh-eating ancestry, others exhibiting more of the distinguishing traits and physical characteristics of their carnivorous evolutionary progenitors. The majority of these world races soon become omnivorous, subsisting upon a wide range of viands from both the animal and vegetable kingdoms.

The post-Adamic epoch is the dispensation of internationalism. With the near completion of the task of race blending, nationalism wanes, and the brotherhood of man really begins to materialize. Representative government begins to take the place of the monarchial or paternal form of rulership. The educational system becomes world-wide, and gradually the languages of the nations give way to the tongue of the Adamites. Universal peace and co-operation are seldom attained until the native people are fairly well blended, and until they speak a common language.

During the closing centuries of the post-Adamic age there develops new interest in art, music, and literature, and this world-wide awakening is the signal for the appearance of a Magisterial Son. The crowning development of this era is the universal interest in intellectual realities, true philosophy. Religion becomes less nationalistic, becomes more and more a planetary affair. New revelations of truth characterize these ages, and the Most Highs of the constellations begin to rule in the affairs of men. Truth is revealed up to the administration of the constellations.

Great ethical advancement characterizes this era; the brotherhood of man is the goal of its society. World-wide peace — the cessation of conflict and national animosity — is the indicator of planetary ripeness for the advent of the third order of sonship, the Magisterial Son.

4. POST-MAGISTERIAL SON MAN

On normal and loyal planets this age opens with the mortal natives blended and biologically fit. There are no race or discrimination problems; literally all nations are of one blood. The brotherhood of man flourishes, and the nations are learning to live on earth in peace and tranquillity. Such a world stands on the eve of a great and culminating intellectual development.

When an evolutionary world becomes thus ripe for the magisterial age, one of the high order of Avonal Sons makes his appearance on a magisterial mission. The Planetary Prince and the Material Sons are of local universe origin; the Magisterial Son hails from Paradise.

When the Paradise Avonals come to the mortal spheres on judicial actions, solely as dispensation adjudicators, they are never incarnated. But when they come on magisterial missions, at least the initial one, they are always incarnated, though they do not experience birth, neither do they die the death of the realm. They may live on for generations in those cases where they remain as rulers on certain planets. When their missions are concluded, they yield up their planetary lives and return to their former status of divine sonship.

Each new dispensation extends the horizon of revealed religion, and the Magisterial Sons extend the revelation of truth to portray the affairs of the local galaxy, minor and major sectors, and the universe as a whole.

After the initial visitation of a Magisterial Son the natives soon effect their economic liberation. The daily work required to sustain one's independence would be represented by two and one-half hours of your time. It is perfectly safe to liberate such ethical and intelligent mortals. Such refined peoples well know how to utilize leisure for self-improvement and planetary advancement.

Political government and social administration continue to improve, self-government being fairly well established by the end of this age. By self-government we refer to the highest type of representative government. Such worlds advance and honor only those leaders and rulers who are most fit to bear social and political responsibilities.

During this epoch the majority of the world mortals are Adjuster indwelt. But even yet the bestowal of divine Monitors is not always universal. The Adjusters of fusion destiny are not yet bestowed upon all planetary mortals; it is still necessary for the will creatures to choose the Mystery Monitors.

During the closing ages of this dispensation, society begins to return to more simplified forms of living. The complex nature of an advancing civilization is running its course, and mortals are learning to live more naturally and effectively. And this trend increases with each succeeding epoch. This is the age of the flowering of art, music, and higher learning. The physical sciences have already reached their height of development. The termination of this age, on an ideal world, witnesses the fullness of a great religious awakening, a world-wide spiritual enlightenment. And this extensive arousal of the spiritual natures is the signal for the arrival of the bestowal Son and for the inauguration of the fifth mortal epoch.

On many worlds it develops that the planet is not made ready for a bestowal Son by one magisterial mission; in that event there will be a second, even a succession of Magisterial Sons, each of whom will advance the natives from one dispensation to another until the planet is made ready for the gift of the bestowal Son. On the second and subsequent missions the Magisterial Sons may or may not be incarnated. But no matter how many Magisterial Sons may appear — and they may also come as such after the bestowal Son — the advent of each one marks the end of one dispensation and the beginning of another.

These dispensations of the Magisterial Sons cover anywhere from twenty-five thousand to fifty thousand years of Urantia time. Sometimes such an epoch is much shorter and in rare instances even longer. But in the fullness of time one of these same Magisterial Sons will be born as the Paradise bestowal Son.

5. POST-BESTOWAL SON MAN

When a certain standard of intellectual and spiritual development is attained on an inhabited world, a Paradise bestowal Son always arrives. On normal worlds he does not appear in the flesh until the natives have ascended to the highest levels of intellectual development and ethical attainment. But on Urantia the bestowal Son, even your own Creator Son, appeared at the close of the Adamic dispensation, but that is not the usual order of events on the worlds of space.

When the worlds have become ripe for spiritualization, the bestowal Son arrives. These Sons always belong to the Magisterial or Avonal order except in that case, once in each local universe, when the Creator Son prepares for his terminal bestowal on some evolutionary world, as occurred when Michael of Nebadon appeared on Urantia to bestow himself upon your mortal race. Only one world in the entire universe can enjoy such a gift; all other worlds are spiritually advanced by the bestowal of a Paradise Son of the Avonal order.

The bestowal Son arrives on a world of high educational culture and encounters a people spiritually trained and prepared to assimilate advanced teachings and to appreciate the bestowal mission. This is an age characterized by the world-wide pursuit of moral culture and spiritual truth. The mortal passion of this dispensation is the penetration of cosmic reality and communion with spiritual reality. The revelations of truth are extended to include the super-universe. Entirely new systems of education and government grow up to supplant the crude regimes of former times. The joy of living takes on new color, and the reactions of life are exalted to heavenly heights of tone and timbre.

The bestowal Son lives and dies for the spiritual uplift of the mortal beings of a world. He establishes the "new and living way"; his life is an incarnation of Paradise truth in mortal flesh, that very truth — even the Spirit of Truth — in the knowledge of which men shall be free.

On Urantia the establishment of this "new and living way" was a matter of fact as well as of truth. The isolation of Urantia in the Lucifer rebellion had suspended the procedure whereby mortals can pass, upon death, directly to the shores of the mansion worlds. Before the days of Christ Michael on Urantia all souls slept on until the dispensational or special millennial resurrections. Even Moses was not permitted to go over to the other side until the occasion of a special resurrection, the fallen Planetary Prince, Caligastia, contesting such a deliverance. But ever since the day of Pentecost, Urantia mortals again may proceed directly to the morontia spheres.

Upon the resurrection of a bestowal Son, on the third day after yielding up his incarnated life, he ascends to the right hand of the Universal Father, receives the assurance of the acceptance of the bestowal mission, and returns to the Creator Son at the headquarters of the local universe. Thereupon the bestowal Avonal and the Creator Michael send their joint spirit, the Spirit of Truth, into the bestowal world. This is the occasion when the "spirit of the triumphant Son is poured out upon all flesh." The Universe Mother Spirit also participates in this bestowal of the Spirit of Truth, and concomitant therewith there issues the bestowal edict of the Thought Adjusters. Thereafter all will creatures of that world will receive Adjusters as soon as they attain the age of moral responsibility, of spiritual choice.

If such a bestowal Avonal should return to a world after the bestowal mission, he would not incarnate but would come "in glory with the seraphic hosts."

The post-bestowal Son age may extend from ten thousand to a hundred thousand years. There is no arbitrary time allotted to any of these dispensational eras. This is a time of great ethical and spiritual progress. Under the spiritual influence of these ages, human character undergoes tremendous transformations and experiences phenomenal development. It becomes possible to put the golden rule into practical operation. The teachings of Jesus are really applicable to a mortal world which has had the preliminary training of the pre-bestowal Sons with their dispensations of character ennoblement and culture augmentation.

During this era the problems of disease and disharmony are virtually solved. Disease has been practically mastered through the high resistant qualities of the Adamic strains and by the intelligent and world-wide application of the discoveries of the physical sciences of preceding ages. The average length of life, during this period, climbs well above the equivalent of three hundred years of Urantia time.

Throughout this epoch there is a gradual lessening of governmental supervision. True self-government is beginning to function; fewer and fewer restrictive laws are necessary. The military branches of national resistance are passing away; the era of international cooperation is really arriving. There are many nations, mostly determined by land distribution, but only one people, one language, and one religion. Mortal affairs are almost, but not quite, utopian. This truly is a great and glorious age!

6. URANTIA'S POST-BESTOWAL AGE

The bestowal Son is the Prince of Peace. He arrives with the message,

"Peace on earth and good will among men." On normal worlds this is a dispensation of world-wide peace; the nations no more learn war. But such salutary influences did not attend the coming of your bestowal Son, Christ Michael. Urantia is not proceeding in the normal order. Your world is out of step in the planetary procession. Your Master, when on earth, warned his disciples that his advent would not bring the usual reign of peace on Urantia. He distinctly told them that there would be "wars and rumors of wars," and that nation would rise against nation. At another time he said, "Think not that I have come to bring peace upon earth."

Even on normal evolutionary worlds the realization of the world-wide brotherhood of man is not an easy accomplishment. On a confused and disordered planet like Urantia such an achievement requires a much longer time and necessitates far greater effort. Unaided social evolution can hardly achieve such happy results on a spiritually isolated sphere. Religious revelation is essential to the realization of brotherhood on Urantia. While Jesus has shown the way to the immediate attainment of spiritual brotherhood, the realization of social brotherhood on your world depends much on the achievement of the following personal transformations and planetary adjustments:

1. *Social fraternity.* Multiplication of international and interracial social contacts and fraternal associations through travel, commerce, and competitive play. Development of a common language and the multiplication of multi-linguists. The national interchange of students, teachers, industrialists, and religious philosophers.

2. *Intellectual cross-fertilization.* Brotherhood is impossible on a world whose inhabitants are so primitive that they fail to recognize the folly of unmitigated selfishness. There must occur an exchange of national and group literature. Each group must become familiar with the thought of all groups; each nation must know the feelings of all nations. Ignorance breeds suspicion, and suspicion is incompatible with the essential attitude of sympathy and love.

3. *Ethical awakening.* Only ethical consciousness can unmask the

immorality of human intolerance and the sinfulness of fratricidal strife. Only a moral conscience can condemn the evils of national envy and racial jealousy. Only moral beings will ever seek for that spiritual insight which is essential to living the golden rule.

4. *Political wisdom*. Emotional maturity is essential to self-control. Only emotional maturity will insure the substitution of international techniques of civilized adjudication for the barbarous arbitrament of war. Wise statesmen will sometime work for the welfare of humanity even while they strive to promote the interest of their national or racial groups. Selfish political sagacity is ultimately suicidal — destructive of all those enduring qualities which insure planetary group survival.

5. *Spiritual insight*. The brotherhood of man is, after all, predicated on the recognition of the fatherhood of God. The quickest way to realize the brotherhood of man on Urantia is to effect the spiritual transformation of present-day humanity. The only technique for accelerating the natural trend of social evolution is that of applying spiritual pressure from above, thus augmenting moral insight while enhancing the soul capacity of every mortal to understand and love every other mortal. Mutual understanding and fraternal love are transcendent civilizers and mighty factors in the world-wide realization of the brotherhood of man.

If you could be transplanted from your backward and confused world to some normal planet now in the post-bestowal Son age, you would think you had been translated to the heaven of your traditions. You would hardly believe that you were observing the normal evolutionary workings of a mortal sphere of human habitation. These worlds are in the spiritual circuits of their realm, and they enjoy all the advantages of the universe broadcasts and the reflectivity services of the super-universe.

7. POST-TEACHER SON MAN

The Sons of the next order to arrive on the average evolutionary world are the Trinity Teacher Sons, the divine Sons of the Paradise Trinity. Again we find Urantia out of step with its sister spheres in that your Jesus has promised to return. That promise he will certainly fulfill, but no one knows whether his second coming will precede or follow the appearances of Magisterial or Teacher Sons on Urantia.

The Teacher Sons come in groups to the spiritualizing worlds. A planetary Teacher Son is assisted and supported by seventy primary Sons, twelve secondary Sons, and three of the highest and most experienced of the supreme order of Daynals. This corps will remain for some time on the world, long enough to effect the transition from the evolutionary ages to the era of light and life — not less than one thousand years of planetary time and often considerably longer. This mission is a Trinity contribution to the antecedent efforts of all the divine personalities who have ministered to an inhabited world.

The revelation of truth is now extended to the central universe and to Paradise. The races are becoming highly spiritual. A great people has evolved and a great age is approaching. The educational, economic, and administrative systems of the planet are undergoing radical transformations. New values and relationships are being established. The kingdom of heaven is appearing on earth, and the glory of God is being shed abroad in the world.

This is the dispensation when many mortals are translated from among the living. As the era of Trinity Teacher Sons progresses, the spiritual allegiance of the mortals of time becomes more and more universal. Natural death becomes less frequent as the Adjusters increasingly fuse with their subjects during the lifetime in the flesh. The planet eventually is classed as of the primary modified order of mortal ascension.

Life during this era is pleasant and profitable. Degeneracy and the antisocial end products of the long evolutionary struggle have been virtually obliterated. The length of life approaches five hundred Urantia years, and the reproductive rate of increase is intelligently controlled. An entirely new order of society has arrived. There are still great differences among mortals, but the state of society more nearly approaches the ideals of social brotherhood and spiritual equality. Representative government is vanishing, and the world is passing under the rule of individual self-control. The function of government is chiefly directed to collective tasks of social administration and economic co-ordination. The golden age is coming on apace; the temporal goal of the long and intense planetary evolutionary struggle is in sight. The reward of the ages is soon to be realized; the wisdom of the Gods is about to be manifested.

The physical administration of a world during this age requires about one hour each day on the part of every adult individual; that is, the equivalent of one Urantia hour. The planet is in close touch with universe affairs, and its people scan the latest broadcasts with the same keen interest you now manifest in the latest editions of your daily newspapers. These races are occupied with a thousand things of interest unknown in your world.

Increasingly, true planetary allegiance to the Supreme Being grows. Generation after generation, more and more people step into line with those who practice justice and live mercy. Slowly but surely the world is being won to the joyous service of the Sons of God. The physical difficulties and material problems have been largely solved; the planet is ripening for advanced life and a more settled existence.

From time to time throughout their dispensation, Teacher Sons continue to come to these peaceful worlds. They do not leave a world until they observe that the evolutionary plan, as it concerns that planet, is working smoothly. A Magisterial Son of judgment usually accompanies the Teacher Sons on their successive missions, while another such Son functions at the time of their departure, and these judicial actions continue from age to age throughout the duration of the mortal regime of time and space.

Each recurring mission of the Trinity Teacher Sons successively exalts such a supernal world to ever-ascending heights of wisdom, spirituality, and cosmic illumination. But the noble natives of such a sphere are still finite and mortal. Nothing is perfect; nevertheless, there is evolving a quality of near perfection in the operation of an imperfect world and in the lives of its human inhabitants.

The Trinity Teacher Sons may return many times to the same world. But sooner or later, in connection with the termination of one of their missions, the Planetary Prince is elevated to the position of Planetary Sovereign, and the System Sovereign appears to proclaim the entrance of such a world upon the era of light and life.

It was of the conclusion of the terminal mission of the Teacher Sons (at least that would be the chronology on a normal world) that John wrote: "I saw a new heaven and a new earth and the new Jerusalem coming down from God out of heaven, prepared as a princess adorned for the prince."

This is the same renovated earth, the advanced planetary stage, that the olden seer envisioned when he wrote: "`For, as the new heavens and the new earth, which I will make, shall remain before me, so shall you and your children survive; and it shall come to pass that from one new moon to another and from one Sabbath to another all flesh shall come to worship before me,' says the Lord."

It is the mortals of such an age who are described as "a chosen generation, a royal priesthood, a holy nation, an exalted people; and you shall show forth the praises of Him who has called you out of darkness into this marvelous light."

No matter what the special natural history of an individual planet may be, no difference whether a realm has been wholly loyal, tainted with evil, or cursed by sin — no matter what the antecedents may be — sooner or later the grace of God and the ministry of angels will usher in the day of the advent of the Trinity Teacher Sons; and their departure, following their final mission, will inaugurate this superb era of light and life.

All the worlds of Satania can join in the hope of the one who wrote: "Nevertheless we, according to His promise, look for a new heaven and a new earth, wherein dwells righteousness. Wherefore, beloved, seeing that you look for such things, be diligent that you may be found by Him in peace, without spot and blameless."

The departure of the Teacher Son corps, at the end of their first or some subsequent reign, ushers in the dawn of the era of light and life — the threshold of the transition from time to the vestibule of eternity. The planetary realization of this era of light and life far more than equals the fondest expectations of Urantia mortals who have entertained no more farseeing concepts of the future life than those embraced within religious beliefs which depict heaven as the immediate destiny and final dwelling place of surviving mortals.

[Sponsored by a Mighty Messenger temporarily attached to the staff of Gabriel.]

PAPER 53
THE LUCIFER REBELLION

LUCIFER WAS a brilliant primary Lanonandek Son of Nebadon. He had experienced service in many systems, had been a high counselor of his group, and was distinguished for wisdom, sagacity, and efficiency. Lucifer was number 37 of his order, and when commissioned by the Melchizedeks, he was designated as one of the one hundred most able and brilliant personalities of his kind. From such a magnificent beginning, through evil and error, he embraced sin and now is numbered as one of three System Sovereigns in Nebadon who have succumbed to the urge of self and surrendered to the sophistry of spurious personal liberty — rejection of universe allegiance and disregard of fraternal obligations, blindness to cosmic relationships.

In the universe of Nebadon, the domain of Christ Michael, in all the history of Lanonandek Sons, in all their work throughout these enumerable systems and at the universe headquarters, only three System Sovereigns have ever been found in contempt of the government of the Creator Son.

1. THE LEADERS OF REBELLION

Lucifer was not an ascendant being; he was a created Son of the local universe, and of him it was said: "You were perfect in all your ways from the day you were created till unrighteousness was found in you." Many times had he been in counsel with the Most Highs of Edentia. And Lucifer reigned "upon the holy mountain of God," the administrative mount of Jerusem, for he was the chief executive of a great system of 607 inhabited worlds.

Lucifer was a magnificent being, a brilliant personality; he stood next to the Most High Fathers of the constellations in the direct line of universe authority. Notwithstanding Lucifer's transgression, subordinate intelligences refrained from showing him disrespect and disdain prior to Michael's bestowal on Urantia. Even the archangel of Michael, at the time of Moses' resurrection, "did not bring against him an accusing judgment but simply said, `the Judge rebuke you.'" Judgment in such matters belongs to the Ancients of Days, the rulers of the super-universe.

Lucifer is now the fallen and deposed Sovereign of Satania. Self-contemplation is most disastrous, even to the exalted personalities of the celestial world. Of Lucifer it was said: "Your heart was lifted up because of your beauty; you corrupted your wisdom because of your brightness." Your olden prophet saw his sad estate when he wrote: "How are you fallen from heaven, O Lucifer, son of the morning! How are you cast down, you who dared to confuse the worlds!"

Very little was heard of Lucifer on Urantia owing to the fact that he assigned his first lieutenant, Satan, to advocate his cause on your planet. Satan was a member of the same primary group of Lanonandeks but had never functioned as a System Sovereign; he entered fully into the Lucifer insurrection. The "devil" is none other than Caligastia, the deposed Planetary Prince of Urantia and a Son of the secondary order of Lanonandeks. At the time Michael was on Urantia in the flesh, Lucifer, Satan, and Caligastia were leagued together to effect the miscarriage of his bestowal mission. But they signally failed.

Abaddon was the chief of the staff of Caligastia. He followed his master into rebellion and has ever since acted as chief executive of the Urantia rebels. Beelzebub was the leader of the disloyal midway creatures who allied themselves with the forces of the traitorous Caligastia.

The dragon eventually became the symbolic representation of all these evil personages. Upon the triumph of Michael, "Gabriel came down from Salvington and bound the dragon (all the rebel leaders) for an age." Of the

Jerusem seraphic rebels it is written: "And the angels who kept not their first estate but left their own habitation, he has reserved in sure chains of darkness to the judgment of the great day."

2. THE CAUSES OF REBELLION

Lucifer and his first assistant, Satan, had reigned on Jerusem for more than five hundred thousand years when in their hearts they began to array themselves against the Universal Father and his then vicegerent Son, Michael.

There were no peculiar or special conditions in the system of Satania which suggested or favored rebellion. It is our belief that the idea took origin and form in Lucifer's mind, and that he might have instigated such a rebellion no matter where he might have been stationed. Lucifer first announced his plans to Satan, but it required several months to corrupt the mind of his able and brilliant associate. However, when once converted to the rebel theories, he became a bold and earnest advocate of "self-assertion and liberty."

No one ever suggested rebellion to Lucifer. The idea of self-assertion in opposition to the will of Michael and to the plans of the Universal Father, as they are represented in Michael, had its origin in his own mind. His relations with the Creator Son had been intimate and always cordial. At no time prior to the exaltation of his own mind did Lucifer openly express dissatisfaction about the universe administration. Notwithstanding his silence, for more than one hundred years of standard time the Union of Days on Salvington had been reflectivating to Uversa that all was not at peace in Lucifer's mind. This information was also communicated to the Creator Son and the Constellation Fathers of Norlatiadek.

Throughout this period Lucifer became increasingly critical of the entire plan of universe administration but always professed wholehearted loyalty to the Supreme Rulers. His first outspoken disloyalty was manifested on the occasion of a visit of Gabriel to Jerusem just a few days before the open proclamation of the Lucifer Declaration of Liberty. Gabriel was so profoundly impressed with the certainty of the impending outbreak that he went direct to Edentia to confer with the Constellation Fathers regarding the measures to be employed in case of open rebellion.

It is very difficult to point out the exact cause or causes which finally culminated in the Lucifer rebellion. We are certain of only one thing, and that is: Whatever these first beginnings were, they had their origin in Lucifer's mind. There must have been a pride of self that nourished itself to the point of self-deception, so that Lucifer for a time really persuaded himself that his contemplation of rebellion was actually for the good of the system, if not of the universe. By the time his plans had developed to the point of disillusionment, no doubt he had gone too far for his original and mischief-making pride to permit him to stop. At some point in this experience he became insincere, and evil evolved into deliberate and willful sin. That this happened is proved by the subsequent conduct of this brilliant executive. He was long offered opportunity for repentance, but only some of his subordinates ever accepted the proffered mercy. The Faithful of Days of Edentia, on the request of the Constellation Fathers, in person presented the plan of Michael for the saving of these flagrant rebels, but always was the mercy of the Creator Son rejected and rejected with increasing contempt and disdain.

3. THE LUCIFER MANIFESTO

Whatever the early origins of trouble in the hearts of Lucifer and Satan, the final outbreak took form as the Lucifer Declaration of Liberty. The cause of the rebels was stated under three heads:

1. *The reality of the Universal Father*. Lucifer charged that the Universal Father did not really exist, that physical gravity and space-energy were inherent in the universe, and that the Father was a myth invented by the Paradise Sons to enable them to maintain the rule of the universes in the Father's name. He denied that personality was a gift of the Universal Father. He even intimated that the finaliters were in collusion with the Paradise Sons to foist fraud upon all creation since they never brought back a very clear-cut idea of the Father's actual personality as it is discernible on Paradise. He traded on reverence as ignorance. The charge was sweeping, terrible, and

blasphemous. It was this veiled attack upon the finaliters that no doubt influenced the ascendant citizens then on Jerusem to stand firm and remain steadfast in resistance to all the rebel's proposals.

2. *The universe government of the Creator Son — Michael.* Lucifer contended that the local systems should be autonomous. He protested against the right of Michael, the Creator Son, to assume sovereignty of Nebadon in the name of a hypothetical Paradise Father and require all personalities to acknowledge allegiance to this unseen Father. He asserted that the whole plan of worship was a clever scheme to aggrandize the Paradise Sons. He was willing to acknowledge Michael as his Creator-father but not as his God and rightful ruler.

Most bitterly did he attack the right of the Ancients of Days — "foreign potentates" — to interfere in the affairs of the local systems and universes. These rulers he denounced as tyrants and usurpers. He exhorted his followers to believe that none of these rulers could do aught to interfere with the operation of complete home rule if men and angels only had the courage to assert themselves and boldly claim their rights.

He contended that the executioners of the Ancients of Days could be debarred from functioning in the local systems if the native beings would only assert their independence. He maintained that immortality was inherent in the system personalities, that resurrection was natural and automatic, and that all beings would live eternally except for the arbitrary and unjust acts of the executioners of the Ancients of Days.

3. *The attack upon the universal plan of ascendant mortal training.* Lucifer maintained that far too much time and energy were expended upon the scheme of so thoroughly training ascending mortals in the principles of universe administration, principles which he alleged were unethical and unsound. He protested against the agelong program for preparing the mortals of space for some unknown destiny and pointed to the presence of the finaliter corps on Jerusem as proof that these mortals had spent ages of preparation for some destiny of pure fiction. With derision he pointed out that the finaliters had encountered a destiny no more glorious than to be returned to humble spheres similar to those of their origin. He intimated that they had been debauched by overmuch discipline and prolonged training,

and that they were in reality traitors to their mortal fellows since they were now co-operating with the scheme of enslaving all creation to the fictions of a mythical eternal destiny for ascending mortals. He advocated that ascenders should enjoy the liberty of individual self-determination. He challenged and condemned the entire plan of mortal ascension as sponsored by the Paradise Sons of God and supported by the Infinite Spirit.

And it was with such a Declaration of Liberty that Lucifer launched his orgy of darkness and death.

4. OUTBREAK OF THE REBELLION

The Lucifer manifesto was issued at the annual conclave of Satania on the sea of glass, in the presence of the assembled hosts of Jerusem, on the last day of the year, about two hundred thousand years ago, Urantia time. Satan proclaimed that worship could be accorded the universal forces — physical, intellectual, and spiritual — but that allegiance could be acknowledged only to the actual and present ruler, Lucifer, the "friend of men and angels" and the "God of liberty."

Self-assertion was the battle cry of the Lucifer rebellion. One of his chief arguments was that, if self-government was good and right for the Melchizedeks and other groups, it was equally good for all orders of intelligence. He was bold and persistent in the advocacy of the "equality of mind" and "the brotherhood of intelligence." He maintained that all government should be limited to the local planets and their voluntary confederation into the local systems. All other supervision he disallowed. He promised the Planetary Princes that they should rule the worlds as supreme executives. He denounced the location of legislative activities on the constellation headquarters and the conduct of judicial affairs on the capitals of the galaxy, minor and major sectors, and the universe. He contended that all these functions of government should be concentrated on the system capitals and proceeded to set up his own legislative assembly and organized his own tribunals under the jurisdiction of Satan. And he directed that the princes on the apostate worlds do the same.

The entire administrative cabinet of Lucifer went over in a body and were sworn in publicly as the officers of the administration of the new head of "the liberated worlds and systems."

While there had been two previous rebellions in Nebadon, they were in distant galaxies. Lucifer held that these insurrections were unsuccessful because the majority of the intelligences failed to follow their leaders. He contended that "majorities rule," that "mind is infallible." The freedom allowed him by the universe rulers apparently sustained many of his nefarious contentions. He defied all his superiors; yet they apparently took no note of his doings. He was given a free hand to prosecute his seductive plan without let or hindrance.

All the merciful delays of justice Lucifer pointed to as evidence of the inability of the government of the Paradise Sons to stop the rebellion. He would openly defy and arrogantly challenge Michael, Immanuel, and the Ancients of Days and then point to the fact that no action ensued as positive evidence of the impotency of the universe and the super-universe governments.

Gabriel was personally present throughout all these disloyal proceedings and only announced that he would, in due time, speak for Michael, and that all beings would be left free and unmolested in their choice; that the "government of the Sons for the Father desired only that loyalty and devotion which was voluntary, wholehearted, and sophistry-proof."

Lucifer was permitted fully to establish and thoroughly to organize his rebel government before Gabriel made any effort to contest the right of secession or to counter-work the rebel propaganda. But the Constellation Fathers immediately confined the action of these disloyal personalities to the system of Satania. Nevertheless, this period of delay was a time of great trial and testing to the loyal beings of all Satania. All was chaotic for a few years, and there was great confusion on the mansion worlds.

5. NATURE OF THE CONFLICT

Upon the outbreak of the Satania rebellion, Michael took counsel of his

Paradise brother, Immanuel. Following this momentous conference, Michael announced that he would pursue the same policy which had characterized his dealings with similar upheavals in the past, an attitude of noninterference.

At the time of this rebellion and the two which preceded it there was no absolute and personal sovereign authority in the universe of Nebadon. Michael ruled by divine right, as vicegerent of the Universal Father, but not yet in his own personal right. He had not completed his bestowal career; he had not yet been vested with "all power in heaven and on earth."

From the outbreak of rebellion to the day of his enthronement as sovereign ruler of Nebadon, Michael never interfered with the rebel forces of Lucifer; they were allowed to run a free course for almost two hundred thousand years of Urantia time. Christ Michael now has ample power and authority to deal promptly, even summarily, with such outbreaks of disloyalty, but we doubt that this sovereign authority would lead him to act differently if another such upheaval should occur.

Since Michael elected to remain aloof from the actual warfare of the Lucifer rebellion, Gabriel called his personal staff together on Edentia and, in counsel with the Most Highs, elected to assume command of the loyal hosts of Satania. Michael remained on Salvington while Gabriel proceeded to Jerusem, and establishing himself on the sphere dedicated to the Father — the same Universal Father whose personality Lucifer and Satan had questioned — in the presence of the forgathered hosts of loyal personalities, he displayed the banner of Michael, the material emblem of the Trinity government of all creation, the three azure blue concentric circles on a white background.

The Lucifer emblem was a banner of white with one red circle, in the center of which a black solid circle appeared.

"There was war in heaven; Michael's commander and his angels fought against the dragon (Lucifer, Satan, and the apostate princes); and the dragon and his rebellious angels fought but prevailed not." This "war in heaven" was not a physical battle as such a conflict might be conceived on Urantia. In the early days of the struggle Lucifer held forth continuously in the planetary amphitheater. Gabriel conducted an unceasing exposure of the rebel sophistries from his headquarters taken up near at hand. The various personalities present on the sphere who were in doubt as to their attitude would journey back and forth between these discussions until they arrived at a final decision.

But this war in heaven was very terrible and very real. While displaying none of the barbarities so characteristic of physical warfare on the immature worlds, this conflict was far more deadly; material life is in jeopardy in material combat, but the war in heaven was fought in terms of life eternal.

6. A LOYAL SERAPHIC COMMANDER

There were many noble and inspiring acts of devotion and loyalty which were performed by numerous personalities during the interim between the outbreak of hostilities and the arrival of the new system ruler and his staff. But the most thrilling of all these daring feats of devotion was the courageous conduct of Manotia, the second in command of the Satania headquarters' seraphim.

At the outbreak of rebellion on Jerusem the head of the seraphic hosts joined the Lucifer cause. This no doubt explains why such a large number of the fourth order, the system administrator seraphim, went astray. The seraphic leader was spiritually blinded by the brilliant personality of Lucifer; his charming ways fascinated the lower orders of celestial beings. They simply could not comprehend that it was possible for such a dazzling personality to go wrong.

Not long since, in describing the experiences associated with the onset of the Lucifer rebellion, Manotia said: "But my most exhilarating moment was the thrilling adventure connected with the Lucifer rebellion when, as second seraphic commander, I refused to participate in the projected insult to Michael; and the powerful rebels sought my destruction by means of the liaison forces they had arranged. There was a tremendous upheaval on Jerusem, but not a single loyal seraphim was harmed.

"Upon the default of my immediate superior it devolved upon me to assume command of the angelic hosts of Jerusem as the titular director of the confused seraphic affairs of the system. I was morally upheld by the Melchizedeks, ably assisted by a majority of the Material Sons, deserted by a tremendous group of my own order, but magnificently supported by the ascendant mortals on Jerusem.

"Having been automatically thrown out of the constellation circuits by the secession of Lucifer, we were dependent on the loyalty of our intelligence corps, who forwarded calls for help to Edentia from the near-by system of Rantulia; and we found that the kingdom of order, the intellect of loyalty, and the spirit of truth were inherently triumphant over rebellion, self-assertion, and so-called personal liberty; we were able to carry on until the arrival of the new System Sovereign, the worthy successor of Lucifer. And immediately thereafter I was assigned to the corps of the Melchizedek receivership of Urantia, assuming jurisdiction over the loyal seraphic orders on the world of the traitorous Caligastia, who had proclaimed his sphere a member of the newly projected system of `liberated worlds and emancipated personalities' proposed in the infamous Declaration of Liberty issued by Lucifer in his call to the `liberty-loving, free-thinking, and forward-looking intelligences of the misruled and maladministered worlds of Satania.'"

This angel is still in service on Urantia, functioning as associate chief of seraphim.

7. HISTORY OF THE REBELLION

The Lucifer rebellion was system wide. Thirty-seven seceding Planetary Princes swung their world administrations largely to the side of the archrebel. Only on Panoptia did the Planetary Prince fail to carry his people with him. On this world, under the guidance of the Melchizedeks, the people rallied to the support of Michael. Ellanora, a young woman of that mortal realm, grasped the leadership of the human race, and not a single soul on that strife-torn world enlisted under the Lucifer banner. And ever since have these loyal Panoptians served on the seventh Jerusem transition world as the caretakers and builders on the Father's sphere and its surrounding seven detention worlds. The Panoptians not only act as the literal custodians of these worlds, but they also execute the personal orders of Michael for the embellishment of these spheres for some future and unknown use. They do this work as they tarry en route to Edentia.

Throughout this period Caligastia was advocating the cause of Lucifer on Urantia. The Melchizedeks ably opposed the apostate Planetary Prince, but the sophistries of unbridled liberty and the delusions of self-assertion had every opportunity for deceiving the primitive peoples of a young and undeveloped world.

All secession propaganda had to be carried on by personal effort because the broadcast service and all other avenues of interplanetary communication were suspended by the action of the system circuit supervisors. Upon the actual outbreak of the insurrection the entire system of Satania was isolated in both the constellation, galaxy, and universe circuits. During this time all incoming and outgoing messages were dispatched by seraphic agents and Solitary Messengers. The circuits to the fallen worlds were also cut off, so that Lucifer could not utilize this avenue for the furtherance of his nefarious scheme. And these circuits will not be restored so long as the archrebel lives within the confines of Satania.

This was a Lanonandek rebellion. The higher orders of local universe sonship did not join the Lucifer secession, although a few of the Life Carriers stationed on the rebel planets were somewhat influenced by the rebellion of the disloyal princes. None of the Trinitized Sons went astray. The Melchizedeks, archangels, and the Brilliant Evening Stars were all loyal to Michael and, with Gabriel, valiantly contended for the Father's will and the Son's rule.

No beings of Paradise origin were involved in disloyalty. Together with the Solitary Messengers they took up headquarters on the world of the Spirit and remained under the leadership of the Faithful of Days of Edentia. None of the conciliators apostatized, nor did a single one of the Celestial Recorders go astray. But a heavy toll was taken of the Morontia Companions and the Mansion World Teachers.

Of the supreme order of seraphim, not an angel was lost, but a considerable group of the next order, the superior, were deceived and ensnared. Likewise a few of the third or supervisor order of angels were misled. But the terrible breakdown came in the fourth group, the administrator angels, those seraphim who are normally assigned to the duties of the system capitals. Manotia saved almost two thirds of them, but slightly over one third followed their chief into the rebel ranks. One third of all the Jerusem cherubim attached to the administrator angels were lost with their disloyal seraphim.

Of the planetary angelic helpers, those assigned to the Material Sons, about one third were deceived, and almost ten per cent of the transition ministers were ensnared. In symbol John saw this when he wrote of the great red dragon, saying: "And his tail drew a third part of the stars of heaven and cast them down in darkness."

The greatest loss occurred in the angelic ranks, but most of the lower orders of intelligence were involved in disloyalty. Of the 681,227 Material Sons lost in Satania, ninety-five per cent were casualties of the Lucifer rebellion. Large numbers of midway creatures were lost on those individual planets whose Planetary Princes joined the Lucifer cause.

In many respects this rebellion was the most widespread and disastrous of all such occurrences in Nebadon. More personalities were involved in this insurrection than in both of the others. And it is to their everlasting dishonor that the emissaries of Lucifer and Satan spared not the infant-training schools on the finaliter cultural planet but rather sought to corrupt these developing minds in mercy salvaged from the evolutionary worlds.

The ascending mortals were vulnerable, but they withstood the sophistries of rebellion better than the lower spirits. While many on the lower mansion worlds, those who had not attained final fusion with their Adjusters, fell, it is recorded to the glory of the wisdom of the ascension scheme that not a single member of the Satania ascendant citizenship resident on Jerusem participated in the Lucifer rebellion.

Hour by hour and day by day the broadcast stations of all Nebadon were thronged by the anxious watchers of every imaginable class of celestial intelligence, who intently perused the bulletins of the Satania rebellion and rejoiced as the reports continuously narrated the unswerving loyalty of the ascending mortals who, under their Melchizedek leadership, successfully withstood the combined and protracted efforts of all the subtle evil forces which so swiftly gathered around the banners of secession and sin.

It was over two years of system time from the beginning of the "war in heaven" until the installation of Lucifer's successor. But at last the new Sovereign came, landing on the sea of glass with his staff. I was among the reserves mobilized on Edentia by Gabriel, and I well remember the first message of Lanaforge to the Constellation Father of Norlatiadek. It read: "Not a single Jerusem citizen was lost. Every ascendant mortal survived the fiery trial and emerged from the crucial test triumphant and altogether victorious." And on to Salvington, Uversa, and Paradise went this message of assurance that the survival experience of mortal ascension is the greatest security against rebellion and the surest safeguard against sin. This noble Jerusem band of faithful mortals numbered just 187,432,811.

With the arrival of Lanaforge the archrebels were dethroned and shorn of all governing powers, though they were permitted freely to go about Jerusem, the morontia spheres, and even to the individual inhabited worlds. They continued their deceptive and seductive efforts to confuse and mislead the minds of men and angels. But as concerned their work on the administrative mount of Jerusem, "their place was found no more."

While Lucifer was deprived of all administrative authority in Satania, there then existed no local universe power nor tribunal which could detain or destroy this wicked rebel; at that time Michael was not a sovereign ruler. The Ancients of Days sustained the Constellation Fathers in their seizure of the system government, but they have never handed down any subsequent decisions in the many appeals still pending with regard to the present status and future disposition of Lucifer, Satan, and their associates.

Thus were these archrebels allowed to roam the entire system to seek further penetration for their doctrines of discontent and self-assertion. But in almost two hundred thousand Urantia years they have been unable to deceive another world. No Satania worlds have been lost since the fall of the thirty-seven, not even those younger worlds peopled since that day of rebellion.

8. THE SON OF MAN ON URANTIA

Lucifer and Satan freely roamed the Satania system until the completion of the bestowal mission of Michael on Urantia. They were last on your world together during the time of their combined assault upon the Son of Man.

Formerly, when the Planetary Princes, the "Sons of God," were periodically assembled, "Satan came also," claiming that he represented all of the isolated worlds of the fallen Planetary Princes. But he has not been accorded such liberty on Jerusem since Michael's terminal bestowal. Subsequent to their effort to corrupt Michael when in the bestowal flesh, all sympathy for Lucifer and Satan has perished throughout all Satania, that is, outside the isolated worlds of sin.

The bestowal of Michael terminated the Lucifer rebellion in all Satania aside from the planets of the apostate Planetary Princes. And this was the significance of Jesus' personal experience, just before his death in the flesh, when he one day exclaimed to his disciples, "And I beheld Satan fall as lightning from heaven." He had come with Lucifer to Urantia for the last crucial struggle.

The Son of Man was confident of success, and he knew that his triumph on your world would forever settle the status of his agelong enemies, not only in Satania but also in the other two systems where sin had entered. There was survival for mortals and security for angels when your Master, in reply to the Lucifer proposals, calmly and with divine assurance replied, "Get you behind me, Satan." That was, in principle, the real end of the Lucifer rebellion. True, the Uversa tribunals have not yet rendered the executive decision regarding the appeal of Gabriel praying for the destruction of the rebels, but such a decree will, no doubt, be forthcoming in the fullness of time since the first step in the hearing of this case has already been taken.

Caligastia was recognized by the Son of Man as the technical Prince of Urantia up to near the time of his death. Said Jesus: "Now is the judgment of this world; now shall the prince of this world be cast down." And then still nearer the completion of his lifework he announced, "The prince of this world is judged." And it is this same dethroned and discredited Prince who was once termed "God of Urantia."

The last act of Michael before leaving Urantia was to offer mercy to Caligastia and Daligastia, but they spurned his tender proffer. Caligastia, your apostate Planetary Prince, is still free on Urantia to prosecute his nefarious designs, but he has absolutely no power to enter the minds of men, neither can he draw near to their souls to tempt or corrupt them unless they really desire to be cursed with his wicked presence.

Before the bestowal of Michael these rulers of darkness sought to maintain their authority on Urantia, and they persistently withstood the minor and subordinate celestial personalities. But since the day of Pentecost this traitorous Caligastia and his equally contemptible associate, Daligastia, are servile before the divine majesty of the Paradise Thought Adjusters and the protective Spirit of Truth, the spirit of Michael, which has been poured out upon all flesh.

But even so, no fallen spirit ever did have the power to invade the minds or to harass the souls of the children of God. Neither Satan nor Caligastia could ever touch or approach the faith sons of God; faith is an effective armor against sin and iniquity. It is true: "He who is born of God keeps himself, and the wicked one touches him not."

In general, when weak and dissolute mortals are supposed to be under the influence of devils and demons, they are merely being dominated by their own inherent and debased tendencies, being led away by their own natural propensities. The devil has been given a great deal of credit for evil which does not belong to him. Caligastia has been comparatively impotent since the cross of Christ.

9. PRESENT STATUS OF THE REBELLION

Early in the days of the Lucifer rebellion, salvation was offered all rebels by Michael. To all who would show proof of sincere repentance, he offered, upon his attainment of complete universe sovereignty, forgiveness and reinstatement in some form of universe service. None of the leaders accepted this merciful proffer. But thousands of the angels and the lower orders of celestial beings, including hundreds of the Material Sons and Daughters, accepted the mercy proclaimed by the Panoptians and were given rehabilitation at the time of Jesus' resurrection two thousand years ago. These beings have since been transferred to the Father's world of Jerusem, where they must be held, technically, until the Uversa courts hand down a decision in the matter of Gabriel *vs*. Lucifer. But no one doubts that, when the annihilation verdict is issued, these repentant and salvaged personalities will be exempted from the decree of extinction. These probationary souls now labor with the Panoptians in the work of caring for the Father's world.

The archdeceiver has never been on Urantia since the days when he sought to turn back Michael from the purpose to complete the bestowal and to establish himself finally and securely as the unqualified ruler of Nebadon. Upon Michael's becoming the settled head of the universe of Nebadon, Lucifer was taken into custody by the agents of the Uversa Ancients of Days and has since been a prisoner on satellite number one of the Father's group of the transition spheres of Jerusem. And here the rulers of other worlds and systems behold the end of the unfaithful Sovereign of Satania. Paul knew of the status of these rebellious leaders following Michael's bestowal, for he wrote of Caligastia's chiefs as "spiritual hosts of wickedness in the heavenly places."

Michael, upon assuming the supreme sovereignty of Nebadon, petitioned the Ancients of Days for authority to intern all personalities concerned in the Lucifer rebellion pending the rulings of the super-universe tribunals in the case of Gabriel *vs*. Lucifer, placed on the records of the Uversa supreme court almost two hundred thousand years ago, as you reckon time. Concerning the system capital group, the Ancients of Days granted the Michael petition with but a single exception: Satan was allowed to make periodic visits to the apostate princes on the fallen worlds until another Son of God should be accepted by such apostate worlds, or until such time as the courts of Uversa should begin the adjudication of the case of Gabriel *vs*. Lucifer.

Satan could come to Urantia because you had no Son of standing in residence — neither Planetary Prince nor Material Son. Machiventa Melchizedek has since been proclaimed vicegerent Planetary Prince of Urantia, and the opening of the case of Gabriel *vs*. Lucifer has signalized the inauguration of temporary planetary regimes on all the isolated worlds. It is true that Satan did periodically visit Caligastia and others of the fallen princes right up to the time of the presentation of these revelations, when there occurred the first hearing of Gabriel's plea for the annihilation of the archrebels. Satan is now unqualifiedly detained on the Jerusem prison worlds.

Since Michael's final bestowal no one in all Satania has desired to go to the prison worlds to minister to the interned rebels. And no more beings have been won to the deceiver's cause. For two thousand years the status has been unchanged.

We do not look for a removal of the present Satania restrictions until the Ancients of Days make final disposition of the archrebels. The system circuits will not be reinstated so long as Lucifer lives. Meantime, he is wholly inactive.

The rebellion has ended on Jerusem. It ends on the fallen worlds as fast as divine Sons arrive. We believe that all rebels who will ever accept mercy have done so. We await the flashing broadcast that will deprive these traitors of personality existence. We anticipate the verdict of Uversa will be announced by the executionary broadcast which will effect the annihilation of these interned rebels. Then will you look for their places, but they shall not be found. "And they who know you among the worlds will be astonished at you; you have been a terror, but never shall you be any more." And thus shall all of these unworthy traitors "become as though they had not been." All await the Uversa decree.

But for ages the seven prison worlds of spiritual darkness in Satania have constituted a solemn warning to all Nebadon, eloquently and effectively proclaiming the great truth "that the way of the transgressor is hard"; "that within every sin is concealed the seed of its own destruction"; that "the wages of sin is death."

[Presented by Manovandet Melchizedek, onetime attached to the receivership of Urantia.]

PAPER 54
PROBLEMS OF THE LUCIFER REBELLION

Evolutionary man finds it difficult fully to comprehend the significance and to grasp the meanings of evil, error, sin, and iniquity. Man is slow to perceive that contrastive perfection and imperfection produce potential evil; that conflicting truth and falsehood create confusing error; that the divine endowment of freewill choice eventuates in the divergent realms of sin and righteousness; that the persistent pursuit of divinity leads to the kingdom of God as contrasted with its continuous rejection, which leads to the domains of iniquity.

The Gods neither create evil nor permit sin and rebellion. Potential evil is time-existent in a universe embracing differential levels of perfection meanings and values. Sin is potential in all realms where imperfect beings are endowed with the ability to choose between good and evil. The very conflicting presence of truth and untruth, fact and falsehood, constitutes the potentiality of error. The deliberate choice of evil constitutes sin; the willful rejection of truth is error; the persistent pursuit of sin and error is iniquity.

1. TRUE AND FALSE LIBERTY

Of all the perplexing problems growing out of the Lucifer rebellion, none has occasioned more difficulty than the failure of immature evolutionary mortals to distinguish between true and false liberty.

True liberty is the quest of the ages and the reward of evolutionary progress. False liberty is the subtle deception of the error of time and the evil of space. Enduring liberty is predicated on the reality of justice — intelligence, maturity, fraternity, and equity.

Liberty is a self-destroying technique of cosmic existence when its motivation is unintelligent, unconditioned, and uncontrolled. True liberty is progressively related to reality and is ever regardful of social equity, cosmic fairness, universe fraternity, and divine obligations.

Liberty is suicidal when divorced from material justice, intellectual fairness, social forbearance, moral duty, and spiritual values. Liberty is nonexistent apart from cosmic reality, and all personality reality is proportional to its divinity relationships.

Unbridled self-will and unregulated self-expression equal unmitigated selfishness, the acme of ungodliness. Liberty without the associated and ever-increasing conquest of self is a figment of egoistic mortal imagination. Self-motivated liberty is a conceptual illusion, a cruel deception. License masquerading in the garments of liberty is the forerunner of abject bondage.

True liberty is the associate of genuine self-respect; false liberty is the consort of self-admiration. True liberty is the fruit of self-control; false liberty, the assumption of self-assertion. Self-control leads to altruistic service; self-admiration tends towards the exploitation of others for the selfish aggrandizement of such a mistaken individual as is willing to sacrifice righteous attainment for the sake of possessing unjust power over his fellow beings.

Even wisdom is divine and safe only when it is cosmic in scope and spiritual in motivation.

There is no error greater than that species of self-deception which leads intelligent beings to crave the exercise of power over other beings for the purpose of depriving these persons of their natural liberties. The golden rule of human fairness cries out against all such fraud, unfairness, selfishness, and unrighteousness. Only true and genuine liberty is compatible with the reign of love and the ministry of mercy.

How dare the self-willed creature encroach upon the rights of his fellows in the name of personal liberty when the Supreme Rulers of the universe stand back in merciful respect for these prerogatives of will and potentials of personality! No being, in the exercise of his supposed personal liberty, has a right to deprive any other being of those privileges of existence conferred by the Creators and duly respected by all their loyal associates, subordinates, and subjects.

Evolutionary man may have to contend for his material liberties with tyrants and oppressors on a world of sin and iniquity or during the early times of a primitive evolving sphere, but not so on the morontia worlds or on the spirit spheres. War is the heritage of early evolutionary man, but on worlds of normal advancing civilization physical combat as a technique of adjusting misunderstandings has long since fallen into disrepute.

2. THE THEFT OF LIBERTY

With the Son and in the Spirit did God project eternal Havona, and ever since has there obtained the eternal pattern of co-ordinate participation in creation — sharing. This pattern of sharing is the master design for every one of the Sons and Daughters of God who go out into space to engage in the attempt to duplicate in time the central universe of eternal perfection.

Every creature of every evolving universe who aspires to do the Father's will is destined to become the partner of the time-space Creators in this magnificent adventure of experiential perfection attainment. Were this not true, the Father would have hardly endowed such creatures with creative free will, neither would he indwell them, actually go into partnership with them by means of his own spirit.

Lucifer's folly was the attempt to do the non-doable, to short-circuit time in an experiential universe. Lucifer's crime was the attempted creative disenfranchisement of every personality in Satania, the unrecognized abridgment of the creature's personal participation — freewill participation — in the long evolutionary struggle to attain the status of light and life both individually and collectively. In so doing this onetime Sovereign of your system set the temporal purpose of his own will directly athwart the eternal purpose of God's will as it is revealed in the bestowal of free will upon all personal creatures. The Lucifer rebellion thus threatened the maximum possible infringement of the freewill choice of the ascenders and servers of the system of Satania — a threat forevermore to deprive every one of these beings of the thrilling experience of contributing something personal and unique to the slowly erecting monument to experiential wisdom which will sometime exist as the perfected system of Satania. Thus does the Lucifer manifesto, masquerading in the habiliments of liberty, stand forth in the clear light of reason as a monumental threat to consummate the theft of personal liberty and to do it on a scale that has been approached only twice in all the history of Nebadon.

In short, what God had given men and angels Lucifer would have taken away from them, that is, the divine privilege of participating in the creation of their own destinies and of the destiny of this local system of inhabited worlds.

No being in all the universe has the rightful liberty to deprive any other being of true liberty, the right to love and be loved, the privilege of worshiping God and of serving his fellows.

3. THE TIME LAG OF JUSTICE

The moral will creatures of the evolutionary worlds are always bothered with the unthinking question as to why the all-wise Creators permit evil and sin. They fail to comprehend that both are inevitable if the creature is to be truly free. The free will of evolving man or exquisite angel is not a mere philosophic concept, a symbolic ideal. Man's ability to choose good or evil is a universe reality. This liberty to choose for oneself is an endowment of the Supreme Rulers, and they will not permit any being or group of beings to deprive a single personality in the wide universe of this divinely bestowed liberty — not even to satisfy such misguided and ignorant beings in the enjoyment of this misnamed personal liberty.

Although conscious and wholehearted identification with evil (sin) is the equivalent of nonexistence (annihilation), there must always intervene between the time of such personal identification with sin and the execution of the penalty — the automatic result of such a willful embrace of evil — a period of time of sufficient length to allow for such an adjudication of such an individual's universe status as will prove entirely satisfactory to all related universe personalities, and which will be so fair and just as to win the approval of the sinner himself.

But if this universe rebel against the reality of truth and goodness refuses to approve the verdict, and if the guilty one knows in his heart the justice of his condemnation but refuses to make such confession, then must the execution of sentence be delayed in accordance with the discretion of the Ancients of Days. And the Ancients of Days refuse to annihilate any being until all moral values and all spiritual realities are extinct, both in the evildoer and in all related supporters and possible sympathizers.

4. THE MERCY TIME LAG

Another problem somewhat difficult of explanation in the constellation of Norlatiadek pertains to the reasons for permitting Lucifer, Satan, and the fallen princes to work mischief so long before being apprehended, interned, and adjudicated.

Parents, those who have borne and reared children, are better able to understand why Michael, a Creator-father, might be slow to condemn and destroy his own Sons. Jesus' story of the prodigal son well illustrates how a loving father can long wait for the repentance of an erring child.

The very fact that an evil-doing creature can actually choose to do wrong — commit sin — establishes the fact of free-wiliness and fully justifies any length delay in the execution of justice provided the extended mercy might conduce to repentance and rehabilitation.

Most of the liberties which Lucifer sought he already had; others he was to receive in the future. All these precious endowments were lost by giving way to impatience and yielding to a desire to possess what one craves now and to possess it in defiance of all obligation to respect the rights and liberties of all other beings composing the universe of universes. Ethical obligations are innate, divine, and universal.

There are many reasons known to us why the Supreme Rulers did not immediately destroy or intern the leaders of the Lucifer rebellion. There are no doubt still other and possibly better reasons unknown to us. The mercy features of this delay in the execution of justice were extended personally by Michael of Nebadon. Except for the affection of this Creator-father for his erring Sons, the supreme justice of the super-universe would have acted. If such an episode as the Lucifer rebellion had occurred in Nebadon while Michael was incarnated on Urantia, the instigators of such evil might have been instantly and absolutely annihilated.

Supreme justice can act instantly when not restrained by divine mercy. But the ministry of mercy to the children of time and space always provides for this time lag, this saving interval between seedtime and harvest. If the seed sowing is good, this interval provides for the testing and upbuilding of character; if the seed sowing is evil, this merciful delay provides time for repentance and rectification. This time delay in the adjudication and execution of evildoers is inherent in the mercy ministry of the seven super-universes. This restraint of justice by mercy proves that God is love, and that such a God of love dominates the universes and in mercy controls the fate and judgment of all his creatures.

The mercy delays of time are by the mandate of the free will of the Creators. There is good to be derived in the universe from this technique of patience in dealing with sinful rebels. While it is all too true that good cannot come of evil to the one who contemplates and performs evil, it is equally true that all things (including evil, potential and manifest) work together for good to all beings who know God, love to do his will, and are ascending Paradiseward according to his eternal plan and divine purpose.

But these mercy delays are not interminable. Notwithstanding the long delay (as time is reckoned on Urantia) in adjudicating the Lucifer rebellion, we may record that, during the time of effecting this revelation, the first hearing in the pending case of Gabriel *vs.* Lucifer was held on Uversa, and soon thereafter there issued the mandate of the Ancients of Days directing that Satan be henceforth confined to the prison world with Lucifer. This ends the ability of Satan to pay further visits to any of the fallen worlds of Satania. Justice in a mercy-dominated universe may be slow, but it is certain.

5. THE WISDOM OF DELAY

Of the many reasons known to me as to why Lucifer and his confederates were not sooner interned or adjudicated, I am permitted to recite the following:

1. Mercy requires that every wrongdoer have sufficient time in which to formulate a deliberate and fully chosen attitude regarding his evil thoughts and sinful acts.
2. Supreme justice is dominated by a Father's love; therefore will justice never destroy that which mercy can save. Time to accept salvation is vouchsafed every evildoer.
3. No affectionate father is ever precipitate in visiting punishment upon an erring member of his family. Patience cannot function independently of time.
4. While wrongdoing is always deleterious to a family, wisdom and love admonish the upright children to bear with an erring brother during the time granted by the affectionate father in which the sinner may see the error of his way and embrace salvation.
5. Regardless of Michael's attitude toward Lucifer, notwithstanding his being Lucifer's Creator-father, it was not in the province of the Creator Son to exercise summary jurisdiction over the apostate System Sovereign because he had not then completed his bestowal career, thereby attaining unqualified sovereignty of Nebadon.
6. The Ancients of Days could have immediately annihilated these rebels, but they seldom execute wrongdoers without a full hearing. In this instance they refused to overrule the Michael decisions.
7. It is evident that Immanuel counseled Michael to remain aloof from the rebels and allow rebellion to pursue a natural course of

self-obliteration. And the wisdom of the Union of Days is the time reflection of the united wisdom of the Paradise Trinity.

8. The Faithful of Days on Edentia advised the Constellation Fathers to allow the rebels free course to the end that all sympathy for these evildoers should be the sooner uprooted in the hearts of every present and future citizen of Norlatiadek — every mortal, morontia, or spirit creature.

9. On Jerusem the personal representative of the Supreme Executive of Orvonton counseled Gabriel to foster full opportunity for every living creature to mature a deliberate choice in those matters involved in the Lucifer Declaration of Liberty. The issues of rebellion having been raised, the Paradise emergency adviser of Gabriel portrayed that, if such full and free opportunity were not given all Norlatiadek creatures, then would the Paradise quarantine against all such possible halfhearted or doubt-stricken creatures be extended in self-protection against the entire constellation. To keep open the Paradise doors of ascension to the beings of Norlatiadek, it was necessary to provide for the full development of rebellion and to insure the complete determination of attitude on the part of all beings in any way concerned therewith.

10. The Divine Minister of Salvington issued as her third independent proclamation a mandate directing that nothing be done to half cure, cowardly suppress, or otherwise hide the hideous visage of rebels and rebellion. The angelic hosts were directed to work for full disclosure and unlimited opportunity for sin-expression as the quickest technique of achieving the perfect and final cure of the plague of evil and sin.

11. An emergency council of ex-mortals consisting of Mighty Messengers, glorified mortals who had had personal experience with like situations, together with their colleagues, was organized on Jerusem. They advised Gabriel that at least three times the number of beings would be led astray if arbitrary or summary methods of suppression were attempted. The entire Uversa corps of counselors concurred in advising Gabriel to permit the

rebellion to take its full and natural course, even if it should require a million years to wind up the consequences.

12. Time, even in a universe of time, is relative: If a Urantia mortal of average length of life should commit a crime which precipitated world-wide pandemonium, and if he were apprehended, tried, and executed within two or three days of the commission of the crime, would it seem a long time to you? And yet that would be nearer a comparison with the length of Lucifer's life even if his adjudication, now begun, should not be completed for a hundred thousand Urantia years. The relative lapse of time from the viewpoint of Uversa, where the litigation is pending, could be indicated by saying that the crime of Lucifer was being brought to trial within two and a half seconds of its commission. From the Paradise viewpoint, the adjudication is simultaneous with the enactment.

There are an equal number of reasons for not arbitrarily stopping the Lucifer rebellion which would be partially comprehensible to you, but which I am not permitted to narrate. I may inform you that on Uversa we teach forty-eight reasons for permitting evil to run the full course of its own moral bankruptcy and spiritual extinction. I doubt not that there are just as many additional reasons not known to me.

6. THE TRIUMPH OF LOVE

Whatever the difficulties evolutionary mortals may encounter in their efforts to understand the Lucifer rebellion, it should be clear to all reflective thinkers that the technique of dealing with the rebels is a vindication of divine love. The loving mercy extended to the rebels does seem to have involved many innocent beings in trials and tribulations, but all these distraught personalities may securely depend upon the all-wise Judges to adjudicate their destinies in mercy as well as justice.

In all their dealings with intelligent beings, both the Creator Son and his Paradise Father are love dominated. It is impossible to comprehend many phases of the attitude of the universe rulers toward rebels and rebellion —

sin and sinners — unless it be remembered that God as a Father takes precedence over all other phases of Deity manifestation in all the dealings of divinity with humanity. It should also be recalled that the Paradise Creator Sons are all mercy motivated.

If an affectionate father of a large family chooses to show mercy to one of his children guilty of grievous wrongdoing, it may well be that the extension of mercy to this misbehaving child will work a temporary hardship upon all the other and well-behaved children. Such eventualities are inevitable; such a risk is inseparable from the reality situation of having a loving parent and of being a member of a family group. Each member of a family profits by the righteous conduct of every other member; likewise must each member suffer the immediate time-consequences of the misconduct of every other member. Families, groups, nations, races, worlds, systems, constellations, and universes are relationships of association which possess individuality; and therefore does every member of any such group, large or small, reap the benefits and suffer the consequences of the rightdoing and the wrongdoing of all other members of the group concerned.

But one thing should be made clear: If you are made to suffer the evil consequences of the sin of some member of your family, some fellow citizen or fellow mortal, even rebellion in the system or elsewhere — no matter what you may have to endure because of the wrongdoing of your associates, fellows, or superiors — you may rest secure in the eternal assurance that such tribulations are transient afflictions. None of these fraternal consequences of misbehavior in the group can ever jeopardize your eternal prospects or in the least degree deprive you of your divine right of Paradise ascension and God attainment.

And there is compensation for these trials, delays, and disappointments which invariably accompany the sin of rebellion. Of the many valuable repercussions of the Lucifer rebellion which might be named, I will only call attention to the enhanced careers of those mortal ascenders, the Jerusem citizens, who, by withstanding the sophistries of sin, placed themselves in line for becoming future Mighty Messengers, fellows of my own order. Every being who stood the test of that evil episode thereby immediately advanced his administrative status and enhanced his spiritual worth.

At first the Lucifer upheaval appeared to be an unmitigated calamity to the system and to the universe. Gradually benefits began to accrue. With the passing of twenty-five thousand years of system time (twenty thousand years of Urantia time), the Melchizedeks began to teach that the good resulting from Lucifer's folly had come to equal the evil incurred. The sum of evil had by that time become almost stationary, continuing to increase only on certain isolated worlds, while the beneficial repercussions continued to multiply and extend out through the universe and super-universe, even to Havona. The Melchizedeks now teach that the good resulting from the Satania rebellion is more than a thousand times the sum of all the evil.

But such an extraordinary and beneficent harvest of wrongdoing could only be brought about by the wise, divine, and merciful attitude of all of Lucifer's superiors, extending from the Constellation Fathers on Edentia to the Universal Father on Paradise. The passing of time has enhanced the consequential good to be derived from the Lucifer folly; and since the evil to be penalized was quite fully developed within a comparatively short time, it is apparent that the all-wise and farseeing universe rulers would be certain to extend the time in which to reap increasingly beneficial results. Regardless of the many additional reasons for delaying the apprehension and adjudication of the Satania rebels, this one gain would have been enough to explain why these sinners were not sooner interned, and why they have not been adjudicated and destroyed.

Shortsighted and time-bound mortal minds should be slow to criticize the time delays of the farseeing and all-wise administrators of universe affairs.

One error of human thinking respecting these problems consists in the idea that all evolutionary mortals on an evolving planet would choose to enter upon the Paradise career if sin had not cursed their world. The ability to decline survival does not date from the times of the Lucifer rebellion. Mortal man has always possessed the endowment of freewill choice regarding the Paradise career.

As you ascend in the survival experience, you will broaden your universe concepts and extend your horizon of meanings and values; and thus will you be able the better to understand why such beings as Lucifer and Satan are permitted to continue in rebellion. You will also better comprehend how ultimate (if not immediate) good can be derived from time-limited evil. After you attain Paradise, you will really be enlightened and comforted when you listen to the superaphic philosophers discuss and explain these profound problems of universe adjustment. But even then, I doubt that you will be fully satisfied in your own minds. At least I was not even when I had thus attained the acme of universe philosophy. I did not achieve a full comprehension of these complexities until after I had been assigned to administrative duties in the super-universe, where by actual experience I have acquired conceptual capacity adequate for the comprehension of such many-sided problems in cosmic equity and spiritual philosophy. As you ascend Paradiseward, you will increasingly learn that many problematic features of universe administration can only be comprehended subsequent to the acquirement of increased experiential capacity and to the achievement of enhanced spiritual insight. Cosmic wisdom is essential to the understanding of cosmic situations.

[Presented by a Mighty Messenger of experiential survival in the first system rebellion in the universes of time now attached to the super-universe government of Orvonton and acting in this matter by request of Gabriel of Salvington.]

PAPER 55
THE SPHERES OF LIGHT AND LIFE

THE AGE of light and life is the final evolutionary attainment of a world of time and space. From the early times of primitive man, such an inhabited world has passed through the successive planetary ages — the pre- and the post-Planetary Prince ages, the post-Adamic age, the post-Magisterial Son age, and the post-bestowal Son age. And then is such a world made ready for the culminating evolutionary attainment, the settled status of light and life, by the ministry of the successive planetary missions of the Trinity Teacher Sons with their ever-advancing revelations of divine truth and cosmic wisdom. In these endeavors the Teacher Sons enjoy the assistance of the Brilliant Evening Stars always, and the Melchizedeks sometimes, in establishing the final planetary age.

This era of light and life, inaugurated by the Teacher Sons at the conclusion of their final planetary mission, continues indefinitely on the inhabited worlds. Each advancing stage of settled status may be segregated by the judicial actions of the Magisterial Sons into a succession of dispensations; but all such judicial actions are purely technical, in no way modifying the course of planetary events.

Only those planets whose galaxies attain existence in the main circuits of the universe are assured of continuous survival, and as far as we know, these worlds settled in light and life are destined to go on throughout the eternal ages of all future time.

There are seven stages in the unfoldment of the era of light and life on an evolutionary world, and in this connection it should be noted that the worlds of the Spirit-fused mortals evolve along lines identical with those of the Adjuster-fusion series. These seven stages of light and life are:

1. The first or planetary stage.
2. The second or system stage.
3. The third or constellation stage.
4. The fourth or local galaxy stage.
5. The fifth or minor sector stage.
6. The sixth or major sector stage.
7. The seventh or universe stage.

At the conclusion of this narrative these stages of advancing development are described as they relate to the universe organization, but the planetary values of any stage may be attained by any world quite independent of the development of other worlds or of the super-planetary levels of universe administration.

1. THE MORONTIA TEMPLE

The presence of a morontia temple at the capital of an inhabited world is the certificate of the admission of such a sphere to the settled ages of light and life. Before the Teacher Sons leave a world at the conclusion of their terminal mission, they inaugurate this final epoch of evolutionary attainment; they preside on that day when the "holy temple comes down upon earth." This event, signalizing the dawn of the era of light and life, is always honored by the personal presence of the Paradise bestowal Son of that planet, who comes to witness this great day. There in this temple of unparalleled beauty, this bestowal Son of Paradise proclaims the long-time Planetary Prince as the new Planetary Sovereign and invests such a faithful

Lanonandek Son with new powers and extended authority over planetary affairs. The System Sovereign is also present and speaks in confirmation of these pronouncements.

A morontia temple has three parts: Centermost is the sanctuary of the Paradise bestowal Son. On the right is the seat of the former Planetary Prince, now Planetary Sovereign; and when present in the temple, this Lanonandek Son is visible to the more spiritual individuals of the realm. On the left is the seat of the acting chief of finaliters attached to the planet.

Although the planetary temples have been spoken of as "coming down from heaven," in reality no actual material is transported from the system headquarters. The architecture of each is worked out in miniature on the system capital, and the Morontia Power Supervisors subsequently bring these approved plans to the planet. Here, in association with the Master Physical Controllers, they proceed to build the morontia temple according to specifications.

The average morontia temple seats about three hundred thousand spectators. These edifices are not used for worship, play, or for receiving broadcasts; they are devoted to the special ceremonies of the planet, such as: communications with the System Sovereign or with the Most Highs, special visualization ceremonies designed to reveal the personality presence of spirit beings, and silent cosmic contemplation. The schools of cosmic philosophy here conduct their graduation exercises, and here also do the mortals of the realm receive planetary recognition for achievements of high social service and for other outstanding attainments.

Such a morontia temple also serves as the place of assembly for witnessing the translation of living mortals to the morontia existence. It is because the translation temple is composed of morontia material that it is not destroyed by the blazing glory of the consuming fire which so completely obliterates the physical bodies of those mortals who therein experience final fusion with their divine Adjusters. On a large world these departure flares are almost continuous, and as the number of translations increases, subsidiary morontia life shrines are provided in different areas of the planet. Not long since I sojourned on a world in the far north whereon twenty-five morontia shrines were functioning.

On pre-settled worlds, planets without morontia temples, these fusion flashes many times occur in the planetary atmosphere, where the material body of a translation candidate is elevated by the midway creatures and the physical controllers.

2. DEATH AND TRANSLATION

Natural, physical death is not a mortal inevitability. The majority of advanced evolutionary beings, citizens on worlds existing in the final era of light and life, do not die; they are translated directly from the life in the flesh to the morontia existence.

This experience of translation from the material life to the morontia state — fusion of the immortal soul with the indwelling Adjuster — increases in frequency commensurate with the evolutionary progress of the planet. At first only a few mortals in each age attain translation levels of spiritual progress, but with the onset of the successive ages of the Teacher Sons, more and more Adjuster fusions occur before the termination of the lengthening lives of these progressing mortals; and by the time of the terminal mission of the Teacher Sons, approximately one quarter of these superb mortals are exempt from natural death.

Farther along in the era of light and life the midway creatures or their associates sense the approaching status of probable soul-Adjuster union and signify this to the destiny guardians, who in turn communicate these matters to the finaliter group under whose jurisdiction this mortal may be functioning; then there is issued the summons of the Planetary Sovereign for such a mortal to resign all planetary duties, bid farewell to the world of his origin, and repair to the inner temple of the Planetary Sovereign, there to await morontia transit, the translation flash, from the material domain of evolution to the morontia level of prespirit progression.

When the family, friends, and working group of such a fusion candidate have forgathered in the morontia temple, they are distributed around the central stage whereon the fusion candidates are resting, meantime freely conversing with their assembled friends. A circle of intervening celestial personalities is arranged to protect the material mortals from the action of the energies manifest at the instant of the "life flash" which delivers the ascension candidate from the bonds of material flesh, thereby doing for such an evolutionary mortal everything that natural death does for those who are thereby delivered from the flesh.

Many fusion candidates may be assembled in the spacious temple at the same time. And what a beautiful occasion when mortals thus forgather to witness the ascension of their loved ones in spiritual flames, and what a contrast to those earlier ages when mortals must commit their dead to the embrace of the terrestrial elements! The scenes of weeping and wailing characteristic of earlier epochs of human evolution are now replaced by ecstatic joy and the sublimest enthusiasm as these God-knowing mortals bid their loved ones a transient farewell as they are removed from their material associations by the spiritual fires of consuming grandeur and ascending glory. On worlds settled in light and life, "funerals" are occasions of supreme joy, profound satisfaction, and inexpressible hope.

The souls of these progressing mortals are increasingly filled with faith, hope, and assurance. The spirit permeating those gathered around the translation shrine resembles that of the joyful friends and relatives who might assemble at a graduating exercise for one of their group, or who might come together to witness the conferring of some great honor upon one of their number. And it would be decidedly helpful if less advanced mortals could only learn to view natural death with something of this same cheerfulness and lightheartedness.

Mortal observers can see nothing of their translated associates subsequent to the fusion flash. Such translated souls proceed by Adjuster transit direct to the resurrection hall of the appropriate morontia-training world. These transactions concerned with the translation of living human beings to the morontia world are supervised by an archangel who was assigned to such a world on the day when it was first settled in light and life.

By the time a world attains the fourth stage of light and life, more than half the mortals leave the planet by translation from among the living. Such diminishment of death continues on and on, but I know of no system whose inhabited worlds, even though long settled in life, are entirely free from natural death as the technique of escape from the bonds of flesh. And until such a high state of planetary evolution is uniformly attained, the morontia-training worlds of the local universe must continue in service as educational and cultural spheres for the evolving morontia progressors. The elimination of death is theoretically possible, but it has not yet occurred according to my observation. Perhaps such a status may be attained during the faraway stretches of the succeeding epochs of the seventh stage of settled planetary life.

The translated souls of the flowering ages of the settled spheres do not pass through the mansion worlds. Neither do they sojourn, as students, on the morontia worlds of the system or constellation. They do not pass through any of the earlier phases of morontia life. They are the only ascending mortals who so nearly escape the morontia transition from material existence to semi-spirit status. The initial experience of such *Son-seized* mortals in the ascension career is in the services of the progression worlds of the galaxy headquarters. And from these study worlds of Zion they go back as teachers to the very worlds they passed by, subsequently going on inward to Paradise by the established route of mortal ascension.

Could you but visit a planet in an advanced stage of development, you would quickly grasp the reasons for providing for the differential reception of ascending mortals on the mansion and higher morontia worlds. You would readily understand that beings passing on from such highly evolved spheres are prepared to resume their Paradise ascent far in advance of the average mortal arriving from a disordered and backward world like Urantia.

No matter from what level of planetary attainment human beings may ascend to the morontia worlds, the seven mansion spheres afford them ample opportunity to gain in experience as teacher-students all of everything which they failed to pass through because of the advanced status of their native planets.

The universe is unfailing in the application of these equalizing techniques designed to insure that no ascender shall be deprived of aught which is essential to his ascension experience.

3. THE GOLDEN AGES

During this age of light and life the world increasingly prospers under the fatherly rule of the Planetary Sovereign. By this time the worlds are progressing under the momentum of one language and one religion. But this age is not perfect. These worlds still have well-appointed hospitals, homes for the care of the sick. There still remain the problems of caring for accidental injuries and other inescapable infirmities. Disease has not been entirely vanquished but such worlds are like Paradise in comparison with the early times of primitive man during the pre-Planetary Prince age. You would instinctively describe such a realm — could you be suddenly transported to a planet in this stage of development — as heaven on earth.

Human government in the conduct of material affairs continues to function throughout this age of relative progress and perfection. The public activities of a world in the first stage of light and life which I recently visited were financed by the tithing technique. Every adult worker — and all able-bodied citizens worked at something — paid ten per cent of his income or increase to the public treasury, and it was disbursed as follows:

1. Three percent was expended in the promotion of truth — science, education, and philosophy.
2. Three percent was devoted to beauty — play, social leisure, and art.
3. Three percent was dedicated to goodness — social service, altruism, and religion.
4. One percent was assigned to the insurance reserves against the risk of incapacity for labor resultant from accident, disease, old age, or unpreventable disasters.

The natural resources of this planet were administered as social possessions, community property.

On this world the highest honor conferred upon a citizen was the order of "supreme service," being the only degree of recognition ever to be granted in the morontia temple. This recognition was bestowed upon those who had long distinguished themselves in some phase of super-material discovery or planetary social service.

The majority of social and administrative posts were held jointly by men and women. Most of the teaching was also done jointly; likewise all judicial trusts were discharged by similar associated couples.

On these superb worlds the childbearing period is not greatly prolonged. It is not best for too many years to intervene between the ages of a family of children. When close together in age, children are able to contribute much more to their mutual training. And on these worlds they are magnificently trained by the competitive systems of keen striving in the advanced domains and divisions of diverse achievement in the mastery of truth, beauty, and goodness. Never fear but that even such glorified spheres present plenty of evil, real and potential, which is stimulative of the choosing between truth and error, good and evil, sin and righteousness.

Nevertheless, there is a certain, inevitable penalty attaching to mortal existence on such advanced evolutionary planets. When a settled world progresses beyond the third stage of light and life, all ascenders are destined, before attaining the minor sector, to receive some sort of transient assignment on a planet passing through the earlier stages of evolution.

Each of these successive ages represents advancing achievements in all phases of planetary attainment. In the initial age of light the revelation of truth was enlarged to embrace the workings of the universe of universes, while the Deity study of the second age is the attempt to master the protean concept of the nature, mission, ministry, associations, origin, and destiny of the Creator Sons, the first level of God the Sevenfold.

A planet the size of Urantia, when fairly well settled, would have about one hundred sub-administrative centers. These subordinate centers would be presided over by one of the following groups of qualified administrators:

1. Young Material Sons and Daughters brought from the system headquarters to act as assistants to the ruling Adam and Eve.
2. The progeny of the semi-mortal staff of the Planetary Prince who were procreated on certain worlds for this and other similar responsibilities.

3. The direct planetary progeny of Adam and Eve.
4. Materialized and humanized midway creatures.
5. Mortals of Adjuster-fusion status who, upon their own petition, are temporarily exempted from translation by the order of the Personalized Adjuster of universe chieftainship in order that they may continue on the planet in certain important administrative posts.
6. Specially trained mortals of the planetary schools of administration who have also received the order of supreme service of the morontia temple.
7. Certain elective commissions of three properly qualified citizens who are sometimes chosen by the citizenry by direction of the Planetary Sovereign in accordance with their special ability to accomplish some definite task which is needful in that particular planetary sector.

The great handicap confronting Urantia in the matter of attaining the high planetary destiny of light and life is embraced in the problems of disease, war, religious fanaticism, racial inequalities and discrimination, and multilingualism.

No evolutionary world can hope to progress beyond the first stage of settledness in light until it has achieved one language, one religion, and one philosophy.

4. ADMINISTRATIVE READJUSTMENTS

In the successive stages of settled existence the inhabited worlds make marvelous progress under the wise and sympathetic administration of the volunteer Corps of the Finality, ascenders of Paradise attainment who have come back to minister to their brethren in the flesh. These finaliters are active in co-operation with the Trinity Teacher Sons, but they do not begin their real participation in world affairs until the morontia temple appears on earth.

Upon the formal inauguration of the planetary ministry of the Corps of the Finality, the majority of the celestial hosts withdraw. But the seraphic guardians of destiny continue their personal ministry to the progressing mortals in light; indeed such angels come in ever-increasing numbers throughout the settled ages since larger and larger groups of human beings reach the third cosmic circle of co-ordinate mortal attainment during the planetary life span.

This is merely the first of the successive administrative adjustments which attend the unfolding of the successive ages of increasingly brilliant attainment on the inhabited worlds as they pass from the first to the seventh stage of settled existence.

1. *The first stage of light and life.* A world in this initial settled stage is being administered by three rulers:

a. The Planetary Sovereign, presently to be advised by a counseling Trinity Teacher Son, in all probability the chief of the terminal corps of such Sons to function on the planet.

b. The chief of the planetary corps of finaliters.

c. Adam and Eve, who function jointly as the unifiers of the dual leadership of the Prince-Sovereign and the chief of finaliters.

Acting as interpreters for the seraphic guardians and the finaliters are the exalted and liberated midway creatures. One of the last acts of the Trinity Teacher Sons on their terminal mission is to liberate the midwayers of the realm and to promote (or restore) them to advanced planetary status, assigning them to responsible places in the new administration of the settled sphere. Such changes have already been made in the range of human vision as enable mortals to recognize these heretofore invisible cousins of the early Adamic regime. This is made possible by the final discoveries of physical science in liaison with the enlarged planetary functions of the Master Physical Controllers.

The System Sovereign has authority to release midway creatures any time after the first settled stage so that they may humanize in the morontia by the aid of the Life Carriers and the physical controllers and, after receiving Thought Adjusters, start out on their Paradise ascension.

In the third and subsequent stages, some of the midwayers are still functioning, chiefly as contact personalities for the finaliters, but as each stage of light and life is entered, new orders of liaison ministers largely replace the midwayers; very few of them ever remain beyond the fourth stage of light. The seventh stage will witness the coming of the first absonite ministers from Paradise to serve in the places of certain universe creatures.

2. *The second stage of light and life.* This epoch is signalized on the worlds by the arrival of a Life Carrier who becomes the volunteer adviser of the planetary rulers regarding the further efforts to eradicate all disease and stabilize the health of the mortal population.

3. *The third stage of light and life.* During this epoch the inhabited worlds arrive at a new appreciation of the Ancients of Days, the second phase of God the Sevenfold, and the representatives of these super-universe rulers enter into new relationships with the planetary administration.

In each succeeding age of settled existence the finaliters function in ever-increasing capacities. There exists a close working connection between the finaliters, the Evening Stars (the super-angels), and the Trinity Teacher Sons.

During this or the following age a Teacher Son, assisted by the ministering-spirit quartette, becomes attached to the elective mortal chief executive, who now becomes associated with the Planetary Sovereign as joint administrator of world affairs. These mortal chief executives serve for twenty-five years of planetary time, and it is this new development that makes it easy for the Planetary Adam and Eve to secure release from their world of long-time assignment during the following ages.

The ministering-spirit quartettes consist of: the seraphic chief of the sphere, the super-universe secoraphic counselor, the archangel of translations, and the omniaphim who functions as the personal representative of the Assigned Sentinel stationed on the system headquarters. But these advisers never proffer counsel unless it is asked for.

4. *The fourth stage of light and life.* On the worlds the Trinity Teacher Sons appear in new roles. Assisted by the creature-trinitized sons so long associated with their order, they now come to the worlds as volunteer counselors and advisers to the Planetary Sovereign and his associates. Such

couples — Paradise-Havona-trinitized sons and ascender-trinitized sons — represent differing universe viewpoints and diverse personal experiences which are highly serviceable to the planetary rulers.

At any time after this age the Planetary Adam and Eve can petition the Sovereign Creator Son for release from planetary duties in order to begin their Paradise ascent; or they can remain on the planet as directors of the newly appearing order of increasingly spiritual society composed of advanced mortals striving to comprehend the philosophic teachings of the finaliters portrayed by the Brilliant Evening Stars, who are now assigned to these worlds to collaborate in pairs with the seconaphim from the headquarters of the super-universe.

The finaliters are chiefly engaged in initiating the new and super-material activities of society — social, cultural, philosophic, cosmic, and spiritual. As far as we can discern, they will continue this ministry far into the seventh epoch of evolutionary stability, when, possibly, they may go forth to minister in outer space; whereupon we conjecture their places may be taken by absonite beings from Paradise.

5. *The fifth stage of light and life.* The readjustments of this stage of settled existence pertain almost entirely to the physical domains and are of primary concern to the Master Physical Controllers.

6. *The sixth stage of light and life* witnesses the development of new functions of the mind circuits of the realm. Cosmic wisdom seems to become constitutive in the universe ministry of mind.

7. *The seventh stage of light and life.* Early in the seventh epoch the Trinity Teacher counselor of the Planetary Sovereign is joined by a volunteer adviser sent by the Ancients of Days, and later on they will be augmented by a third counselor coming from the super-universe Supreme Executive.

During this epoch, if not before, Adam and Eve are always relieved of planetary duties. If there is a Material Son in the finaliter corps, he may become associated with the mortal chief executive, and sometimes it is a Melchizedek who volunteers to function in this capacity. If a midwayer is among the finaliters, all of that order remaining on the planet are immediately released.

Upon obtaining release from their agelong assignment, a Planetary Adam and Eve may select careers as follows:

1. They can secure planetary release and from the universe headquarters start out immediately on the Paradise career, receiving Thought Adjusters at the conclusion of the morontia experience.
2. Very often a Planetary Adam and Eve will receive Adjusters while yet serving on a world settled in light concomitant with the receiving of Adjusters by some of their imported pure-line children who have volunteered for a term of planetary service. Subsequently they may all go to universe headquarters and there begin the Paradise career.
3. A Planetary Adam and Eve may elect — as do Material Sons and Daughters from the system capital — to go direct to the midsonite world for a brief sojourn, there to receive their Adjusters.
4. They may decide to return to the system headquarters, there for a time to occupy seats on the supreme court, after which service they will receive Adjusters and begin the Paradise ascent.
5. They may choose to go from their administrative duties back to their native world to serve as teachers for a season and to become Adjuster indwelt at the time of transfer to the galactic headquarters.

Throughout all of these epochs the imported assisting Material Sons and Daughters exert a tremendous influence on the progressing social and economic orders. They are potentially immortal, at least until such time as they elect to humanize, receive Adjusters, and start for Paradise.

On the evolutionary worlds a being must humanize to receive a Thought Adjuster. All ascendant members of the Mortal Corps of Finaliters have been Adjuster indwelt and fused except seraphim, and they are Father indwelt by another type of spirit at the time of being mustered into this corps.

5. THE ACME OF MATERIAL DEVELOPMENT

Mortal creatures living on a sin-stricken, evil-dominated, self-seeking, isolated world, such as Urantia, can hardly conceive of the physical perfection, the intellectual attainment, and the spiritual development which characterize these advanced epochs of evolution on a sinless sphere.

The advanced stages of a world settled in light and life represent the acme of evolutionary material development. On these cultured worlds, gone are the idleness and friction of the earlier primitive ages. Poverty and social inequality have all but vanished.

The economic, social, and administrative status of these worlds is of a high and perfected order. Science, art, and industry flourish, and society is a smoothly working mechanism of high material, intellectual, and cultural achievement. Industry has been largely diverted to serving the higher aims of such a superb civilization. The economic life of such a world has become ethical.

War has become a matter of history, and there are no more armies or police forces. Government is gradually disappearing. Self-control is slowly rendering laws of human enactment obsolete. The extent of civil government and statutory regulation, in an intermediate state of advancing civilization, is in inverse proportion to the morality and spirituality of the citizenship.

Schools are vastly improved and are devoted to the training of mind and the expansion of soul. The art centers are exquisite and the musical organizations superb. The temples of worship with their associated schools of philosophy and experiential religion are creations of beauty and grandeur. The open-air arenas of worship assembly are equally sublime in the simplicity of their artistic appointment.

The provisions for competitive play, humor, and other phases of personal and group achievement are ample and appropriate. A special feature of the competitive activities on such a highly cultured world concerns the efforts of individuals and groups to excel in the sciences and philosophies of cosmology. Literature and oratory flourish, and language is so improved as to be symbolic of concepts as well as to be expressive of ideas. Life is refreshingly simple; man has at last co-ordinated a high state of mechanical development with an inspiring intellectual attainment and has overshadowed both with an exquisite spiritual achievement. The pursuit of happiness is an experience of joy and satisfaction.

6. THE INDIVIDUAL MORTAL

As worlds advance in the settled status of light and life, society becomes increasingly peaceful. The individual, while no less independent and devoted to his family, has become more altruistic and fraternal. But such beings are still mortal; they continue to breathe, eat, sleep, and drink. This great evolution is not heaven, but it is a sublime foreshadowing of the divine worlds of the Paradise ascent.

The Adjusters continue to come as in former evolutionary eras, and as the epochs pass, these mortals are increasingly able to commune with the indwelling Father fragment. During the embryonic and pre-spiritual stages of development the adjutant mind-spirits are still functioning, but as the world advances the seven ray energies become more influential and aid mankind in developing enhanced capabilities. The Holy Spirit and the ministry of angels are even more effective as the successive epochs of settled life are experienced. In the fourth stage of light and life the advanced mortals seem to experience considerable conscious contact with the spirit presence of the Master Spirit of super-universe jurisdiction, while the philosophy of such a world is focused upon the attempt to comprehend the new revelations of God the Supreme. More than one half of the human inhabitants on planets of this advanced status experience translation to the morontia state from among the living. Even so, "old things are passing away; behold, all things are becoming new."

We conceive that physical evolution will have attained its full development by the end of the fifth epoch of the light-and-life era. We observe that the upper limits of spiritual development associated with evolving human mind are determined by the Adjuster-fusion level of conjoint morontia values and cosmic meanings. But concerning wisdom: While we do not really know, we conjecture that there can never be a limit to intellectual evolution and the attainment of wisdom. On a seventh-stage world, wisdom can exhaust the material potentials, enter upon mota insight, and eventually even taste of absonite grandeur.

We observe that on these highly evolved and long seventh-stage worlds human beings fully learn the local universe language before they are translated; and I have visited a few very old planets where abandonters were teaching the older mortals the tongue of the super-universe. And on these worlds I have observed the technique whereby the absonite personalities reveal the presence of the finaliters in the morontia temple.

This is the story of the magnificent goal of mortal striving on the evolutionary worlds; and it all takes place even before human beings enter upon their morontia careers; all of this splendid development is attainable by material mortals on the inhabited worlds, the very first stage of that endless and incomprehensible career of Paradise ascension and divinity attainment.

But can you possibly imagine what sort of evolutionary mortals are now coming up from worlds long existing in the seventh epoch of settled light and life? It is such as these who go on to the morontia worlds of the local universe capital to begin their ascension careers.

If the mortals of distraught Urantia could only view one of these more advanced worlds long settled in light and life, they would nevermore question the wisdom of the evolutionary scheme of creation. Were there no future of eternal creature progression, still the superb evolutionary attainments of the mortal races on such settled worlds of perfected achievement would amply justify man's creation on the worlds of time and space.

We often ponder: If the grand universe should be settled in light and life, would the ascending exquisite mortals still be destined to the Corps of the Finality? But we do not know.

7. THE FIRST OR PLANETARY STAGE

This epoch extends from the appearance of the morontia temple at the new planetary headquarters to the time of the settling of the entire system in light and life. This age is inaugurated by the Trinity Teacher Sons at the close of their successive world missions when the Planetary Prince is elevated to the status of Planetary Sovereign by the mandate and personal presence of the Paradise bestowal Son of that sphere. Concomitant therewith the finaliters inaugurate their active participation in planetary affairs.

To outward and visible appearances the actual rulers, or directors, of such a world settled in light and life are the Material Son and Daughter, the Planetary Adam and Eve. The finaliters are invisible, as also is the Prince-Sovereign except when in the morontia temple. The actual and literal heads of the planetary regime are therefore the Material Son and Daughter. It is the knowledge of these arrangements that has given prestige to the idea of kings and queens throughout the universe realms. And kings and queens are a great success under these ideal circumstances, when a world can command such high personalities to act in behalf of still higher but invisible rulers.

When such an era is attained on your world, no doubt Machiventa Melchizedek, now the vicegerent Planetary Prince of Urantia, will occupy the seat of the Planetary Sovereign; and it has long been conjectured on Jerusem that he will be accompanied by a son and daughter of the Urantia Adam and Eve who are now held on Edentia as wards of the Most Highs of Norlatiadek. These children of Adam might so serve on Urantia in association with the Melchizedek-Sovereign since they were deprived of procreative powers almost 37,000 years ago at the time they gave up their material bodies on Urantia in preparation for transit to Edentia.

This settled age continues on and on until every inhabited planet in the system attains the era of stabilization; and then, when the youngest world — the last to achieve light and life — has experienced such settledness for one millennium of system time, the entire system enters the stabilized status, and the individual worlds are ushered into the system epoch of the era of light and life.

8. THE SECOND OR SYSTEM STAGE

When an entire system becomes settled in life, a new order of government is inaugurated. The Planetary Sovereigns become members of the system conclave, and this new administrative body, subject to the veto of the Constellation Fathers, is supreme in authority. Such a system of inhabited worlds becomes virtually self-governing. The system legislative assembly is constituted on the headquarters world, and each planet sends its ten representatives thereto. Courts are now established on the system capitals, and only appeals are taken to the galaxy headquarters.

With the settling of the system the Assigned Sentinel, representative of the super-universe Supreme Executive, becomes the volunteer adviser to the system supreme court and actual presiding officer of the new legislative assembly.

After the settling of an entire system in light and life the System Sovereigns will no more come and go. Such a sovereign remains perpetually at the head of his system. The assistant sovereigns continue to change as in former ages.

During this epoch of stabilization, for the first time midsoniters come from the universe headquarters worlds of their sojourn to act as counselors to the legislative assemblies and advisers to the adjudicational tribunals. These midsoniters also carry on certain efforts to inculcate new mota meanings of supreme value into the teaching enterprises which they sponsor jointly with the finaliters. What the Material Sons did for the mortal races biologically, the midsonite creatures now do for these unified and glorified humans in the ever-advancing realms of philosophy and spiritualized thinking.

On the inhabited worlds the Teacher Sons become voluntary collaborators with the finaliters, and these same Teacher Sons also accompany the finaliters to the mansion worlds when those spheres are no longer to be utilized as differential receiving worlds after an entire system is settled in light and life; at least this is true by the time the entire constellation has thus evolved. But there are no groups that far advanced in Nebadon.

We are not permitted to reveal the nature of the work of the finaliters who will supervise such rededicated mansion worlds. You have, however, been informed that there are throughout the universes various types of intelligent creatures who have not been portrayed in these narratives.

And now, as the systems one by one become settled in light by virtue of the progress of their component worlds, the time comes when the last system in a given constellation attains stabilization, and the galaxy administrators — the Secondary Vorondadek Son, and the Recents of Days, arrive on the capital of the constellation to proclaim the Most Highs the unqualified rulers of the newly perfected family of settled systems of inhabited worlds.

9. THE THIRD OR CONSTELLATION STAGE

The unification of a whole constellation of settled systems is attended by new distributions of executive authority and additional readjustments of universe administration. This epoch witnesses advanced attainment on every inhabited world but is particularly characterized by readjustments on the constellation headquarters, with marked modification of relationships with both the system supervision and the local universe government. During this age many constellation and galaxy activities are transferred to the system capitals, and the representatives of the minor sector assume new and more intimate relations with the planetary, system, constellation, and galaxy rulers. Concomitant with these new associations, certain universe and superuniverse administrators establish themselves on the constellation and galaxy capitals as volunteer advisers to the Most High Fathers.

When a constellation is thus settled in light, the legislative function ceases, and the house of System Sovereigns, presided over by the Most Highs, functions instead. Now, for the first time, such administrative groups deal directly with the minor sector government in matters pertaining to universe and Paradise relationships. Otherwise the constellation remains related to the local galaxy as before. From stage to stage in the settled life the univitatia continue to administer the constellation morontia worlds.

As the ages pass, the Constellation Fathers take over more and more of the detailed administrative or supervising functions which were formerly centered on the galaxy headquarters. By the attainment of the sixth stage of stabilization these unified constellations will have reached the position of well-nigh complete autonomy. Entrance upon the seventh stage of settledness will no doubt witness the exaltation of these rulers to the true dignity signified by their names, the Most Highs. To all intents and purposes the constellations will then deal directly with the major sector rulers.

10. THE FOURTH OR LOCAL GALAXY STAGE

When a galaxy becomes settled in light and life, it soon swings into the established minor sector circuits, and the Perfections of Days proclaim the establishment of the *supreme council of unlimited authority*. This new governing body consists of the Faithfuls of Days, presided over by the Recents of Days, and the first act of this supreme council is to acknowledge the continued sovereignty of the Master Creator Son.

The settling of an entire galaxy in light and life inaugurates profound readjustments in the entire scheme of administration, from the individual inhabited worlds to the minor sector headquarters. New relationships extend down to the constellations and systems.

During this and subsequent ages the Magisterial Sons continue to function as dispensational adjudicators. Later on, and as requested by the System Sovereigns, one of these Magisterial Sons will become the supreme counselor stationed on the headquarters world of each local system until the seventh stage of unity is attained.

11. THE MINOR AND MAJOR SECTOR STAGES

The minor sector age. The fifth or minor sector stage of stabilization has to do with physical, morontial, and spiritual status and with the co-ordinate settling of all of the associated local galaxies and galactic clusters into the established circuits of the universe.

The major sector age. Concerning the sixth stage, or major sector stabilization, we can only conjecture since none of us have witnessed such an event. Nevertheless, we can postulate much concerning the administrative and other readjustments which would probably accompany such an advanced status of inhabited worlds and their universe groupings.

We infer that major sector unification will be concerned with certain new intellectual levels of attainment, possibly some advanced achievements in the supreme realization of cosmic wisdom.

We arrive at conclusions regarding the readjustments which would probably attend the realization of hitherto unattained levels of evolutionary progress by observing the results of such achievements on the individual worlds and in the experiences of individual mortals living on these older and highly developed spheres.

Let it be made clear that the administrative mechanisms and governmental techniques of a universe or a super-universe cannot in any manner limit or retard the evolutionary development or spiritual progress of an individual inhabited planet or of any individual mortal on such a sphere.

In some of the older universes we find worlds settled in the fifth and the sixth stages of light and life — even far extended into the seventh epoch — whose local systems are not yet settled in light. Younger planets may delay system unification, but this does not in the least handicap the progress of an older and advanced world. Neither can environmental limitations, even on an isolated world, thwart the personal attainment of the individual mortal; Jesus of Nazareth, as a man among men, personally achieved the status of light and life over two thousand years ago on Urantia.

It is by observing what takes place on long-settled worlds that we arrive at fairly reliable conclusions as to what will happen when a whole major sector or a whole universe is settled in light.

12. THE SEVENTH OR UNIVERSE STAGE

When a universe becomes settled in light and life it swings into the established circuits of the super-universe. The Union of Days now presides over the supreme council of unlimited authority. The finaliter corps now, for the first time, acknowledges the jurisdiction of an extra-Paradise authority, the supreme council. Heretofore the finaliters have recognized no supervision this side of Paradise.

The universe administration, as far as concerns Gabriel and the Father Melchizedek, is quite unchanged. This council of unlimited authority is chiefly concerned with the new problems and the new conditions arising out of the advanced status of light and life.

The Creator Sons of such settled universes spend much of their time on

Paradise and its associated worlds and in counseling the numerous finaliter groups serving throughout the local creation. In this way the man of Michael will find a fuller fraternity of association with the glorified finaliter mortals.

The local universe Mother Spirit experiences new liaison relations with the Master Spirit of the super-universe, and Gabriel establishes direct contact with the Ancients of Days to be effective when and as the Master Son may be absent from the headquarters world.

Speculation concerning the function of these Creator Sons in connection with the outer universes now in process of preliminary assembly is wholly futile. But we all engage in such postulations from time to time. On attaining this stage of development the Creator Son becomes administratively free; the Divine Minister is progressively blending her ministry with that of the super-universe Master Spirit and the Infinite Spirit. There seems to be evolving a new and sublime relationship between the Creator Son, the Creative Spirit, the Evening Stars, the Teacher Sons, and the ever-increasing finaliter corps.

If Michael should ever leave Nebadon, Gabriel would undoubtedly become chief administrator with the Father Melchizedek as his associate. At the same time new status would be imparted to all orders of permanent citizenship, such as Material Sons, univitatia, midsoniters, susatia, and Spirit-fused mortals. But as long as evolution continues, the seraphim and the archangels will be required in universe administration.

We are, however, satisfied regarding two features of our speculations: If the Creator Sons are destined to the outer universes, the Divine Ministers will undoubtedly accompany them. We are equally sure that the Melchizedeks are to remain with the universes of their origin. We hold that the Melchizedeks are destined to play ever-increasingly responsible parts in local universe government and administration.

13. FUTURE SUPERUNIVERSE STAGES

We cannot positively forecast what would occur when a super-universe became settled in light because such an event has never factualized. From the teachings of the Melchizedeks, which have never been contradicted, we infer that sweeping changes would be made in the entire organization and administration of every unit of the creations of time and space extending from the inhabited worlds to the super-universe headquarters.

It is generally believed that large numbers of the otherwise unattached creature-trinitized sons are to be assembled on the headquarters and divisional capitals of the settled super-universes. This may be in anticipation of the sometime arrival of outer-spacers on their way in to Havona and Paradise; but we really do not know.

If and when a super-universe should be settled in light and life, we believe that the now advisory Unqualified Supervisors of the Supreme would become the high administrative body on the headquarters world of the super-universe. These are the personalities who are able to contact directly with the absonite administrators, who will forthwith become active in the settled super-universe. Although these Unqualified Supervisors have long functioned as advisers and counselors in advanced evolutionary units of creation, they do not assume administrative responsibilities until the authority of the Supreme Being becomes sovereign.

The Unqualified Supervisors of the Supreme, who function more extensively during this epoch, are not finite, absonite, ultimate, or infinite; they *are* supremacy and only represent God the Supreme. They are the personalization of time-space supremacy and therefore do not function in Havona. They function only as supreme unifiers. They may possibly be involved in the technique of universe reflectivity, but we are not certain.

None of us entertain a satisfactory concept of what will happen when the grand universe (the seven super-universes as dependent on Havona) becomes entirely settled in light and life. That event will undoubtedly be the most profound occurrence in the annals of eternity since the appearance of the central universe. There are those who hold that the Supreme Being himself will emerge from the Havona mystery enshrouding his spirit person and will become residential on the headquarters of the seventh super-universe as the almighty and experiential sovereign of the perfected creations of time and space. But we really do not know.

[Presented by a Mighty Messenger temporarily assigned to the Archangel Council on Urantia.]

PAPER 56
UNIVERSAL UNITY

GOD IS UNITY. Deity is universally co-ordinated. The universe of universes is one vast integrated mechanism which is absolutely controlled by one infinite mind. The physical, intellectual, and spiritual domains of universal creation are divinely correlated. The perfect and imperfect are truly interrelated, and therefore may the finite evolutionary creature ascend to Paradise in obedience to the Universal Father's mandate: "Be you perfect, even as I am perfect."

The diverse levels of creation are all unified in the plans and administration of the Architects of the Master Universe. To the circumscribed minds of time-space mortals the universe may present many problems and situations which apparently portray disharmony and indicate absence of effective co-ordination; but those of us who are able to observe wider stretches of universal phenomena, and who are more experienced in this art of detecting the basic unity which underlies creative diversity and of discovering the divine oneness which overspreads all this functioning of plurality, better perceive the divine and single purpose exhibited in all these manifold manifestations of universal creative energy.

1. PHYSICAL CO-ORDINATION

The physical or material creation is not infinite, but it is perfectly co-ordinated. There are force, energy, and power, but they are all one in origin. The seven super-universes are seemingly dual; the central universe, triune; but Paradise is of single constitution. And Paradise is the actual source of all material universes — past, present, and future. But this cosmic derivation is an *eternity* event; at no *time* — past, present, or future — does either space or the material cosmos come forth from the nuclear Isle of Light. As the cosmic source, Paradise functions prior to space and before time; hence would its derivations seem to be orphaned in time and space did they not emerge through the Unqualified Absolute, their ultimate repository in space and their revealer and regulator in time.

The Unqualified Absolute upholds the physical universe, while the Deity Absolute motivates the exquisite over-control of all material reality; and both Absolutes are functionally unified by the Universal Absolute. This cohesive correlation of the material universe is best understood by all personalities — material, morontia, absonite, or spiritual — by the observation of the gravity response of all bona fide material reality to the gravity centering on nether Paradise.

Gravity unification is universal and unvarying; pure-energy response is likewise universal and inescapable. Pure energy (primordial force) and pure spirit are wholly pre-responsive to gravity. These primal forces, inhering in the Absolutes, are personally controlled by the Universal Father; hence does all gravity center in the personal presence of the Paradise Father of pure energy and pure spirit and in his super-material abode.

Pure energy is the ancestor of all relative, non-spirit functional realities, while pure spirit is the potential of the divine and directive over-control of all basic energy systems. And these realities, so diverse as manifested throughout space and as observed in the motions of time, are both centered in the person of the Paradise Father. In him they are one — must be unified — because God is one. The Father's personality is absolutely unified.

In the infinite nature of God the Father there could not possibly exist duality of reality, such as physical and spiritual; but the instant we look aside from the infinite levels and absolute reality of the personal values of the Paradise Father, we observe the existence of these two realities and recognize that they are fully responsive to his personal presence; in him all things consist.

The moment you depart from the unqualified concept of the infinite personality of the Paradise Father, you must postulate MIND as the inevitable technique of unifying the ever-widening divergence of these dual universe manifestations of the original monothetic Creator personality, the First Source and Center — the I AM.

2. INTELLECTUAL UNITY

The Thought-Father realizes spirit expression in the Word-Son and attains reality expansion through Paradise in the far-flung material universes. The spiritual expressions of the Eternal Son are correlated with the material levels of creation by the functions of the Infinite Spirit, by whose spirit-responsive ministry of mind, and in whose physical-directive acts of mind, the spiritual realities of Deity and the material repercussions of Deity are correlated the one with the other.

Mind is the functional endowment of the Infinite Spirit, therefore infinite in potential and universal in bestowal. The primal thought of the Universal Father eternalizes in dual expression: the Isle of Paradise and his Deity equal, the spiritual and Eternal Son. Such duality of eternal reality renders the mind God, the Infinite Spirit, inevitable. Mind is the indispensable channel of communication between spiritual and material realities. The material evolutionary creature can conceive and comprehend the indwelling spirit only by the ministry of mind.

This infinite and universal mind is ministered in the universes of time and space as the cosmic mind; and though extending from the primitive ministry of the adjutant spirits up to the magnificent mind of the chief executive of a universe, even this cosmic mind is adequately unified in the supervision of the Seven Master Spirits, who are in turn co-ordinated with the Supreme Mind of time and space and perfectly correlated with the all-embracing mind of the Infinite Spirit.

3. SPIRITUAL UNIFICATION

As the universal mind gravity is centered in the Paradise personal presence of the Infinite Spirit, so does the universal spirit gravity center in the Paradise personal presence of the Eternal Son. The Universal Father is one, but to time-space he is revealed in the dual phenomena of pure energy and pure spirit.

Paradise spirit realities are likewise one, but in all time-space situations and relations this single spirit is revealed in the dual phenomena of the spirit personalities and emanations of the Eternal Son and the spirit personalities and influences of the Infinite Spirit and associated creations; and there is yet a third — pure-spirit fragmentations — the Father's bestowal of the Thought Adjusters and other spirit entities which are pre-personal.

No matter on what level of universe activities you may encounter spiritual phenomena or contact with spirit beings, you may know that they are all derived from the God who is spirit by the ministry of the Spirit Son and the Infinite Mind Spirit. And this far-flung spirit functions as a phenomenon on the evolutionary worlds of time as it is directed from the headquarters of the local universes. From these capitals of the Creator Sons come the Holy Spirit and the Spirit of Truth, together with the ministry of the adjutant mind-spirits, to the lower and evolving levels of material minds, and the Seven Ray energies to the higher minds.

While mind is more unified on the level of the Master Spirits in association with the Supreme Being and as the cosmic mind in subordination to the Absolute Mind, the spirit ministry to the evolving worlds is more directly unified in the personalities resident on the headquarters of the local universes and in the persons of the presiding Divine Ministers, who are in turn well-nigh perfectly correlated with the Paradise gravity circuit of the Eternal Son, wherein occurs final unification of all time-space spirit manifestations.

Perfected creature existence can be attained, sustained, and eternalized by the fusion of self-conscious mind with a fragment of the pre-Trinity spirit endowment of some one of the persons of the Paradise Trinity. The mortal mind is the creation of the Sons and Daughters of the Eternal Son and the Infinite Spirit and, when fused with the Thought Adjuster from the Father, partakes of the threefold spirit endowment of the evolutionary realms. But these three spirit expressions become perfectly unified in the finaliters, even as they were in eternity so unified in the Universal I AM ere he ever became the Universal Father of the Eternal Son and the Infinite Spirit.

Spirit must always and ultimately become threefold in expression and Trinity-unified in final realization. Spirit originates from one source through a threefold expression; and in finality it must and does attain its full realization in that divine unification which is experienced in finding God — oneness with divinity — in eternity, and by means of the ministry of the cosmic mind of the infinite expression of the eternal word of the Father's universal thought.

4. PERSONALITY UNIFICATION

The Universal Father is a divinely unified personality; hence will all his ascendant children who are carried to Paradise by the rebound momentum of the Thought Adjusters, who went forth from Paradise to indwell material mortals in obedience to the Father's mandate, likewise be fully unified personalities ere they reach Havona.

Personality inherently reaches out to unify all constituent realities. The infinite personality of the First Source and Center, the Universal Father, unifies all seven constituent Absolutes of Infinity; and the personality of mortal man, being an exclusive and direct bestowal of the Universal Father, likewise possesses the potential of unifying the constituent factors of the mortal creature. Such unifying creativity of all creature personality is a birth-mark of its high and exclusive source and is further evidential of its unbroken contact with this same source through the personality circuit, by means of which the personality of the creature maintains direct and sustaining contact with the Father of all personality on Paradise.

Notwithstanding that God is manifest from the domains of the Sevenfold up through supremacy and ultimacy to God the Absolute, the personality circuit, centering on Paradise and in the person of God the Father, provides for the complete and perfect unification of all these diverse expressions of divine personality so far as concerns all creature personalities on all levels of intelligent existence and in all the realms of the perfect, perfected, and perfecting universes.

While God is to and in the universes all that we have portrayed, nevertheless, to you and to all other God-knowing creatures he is one, your Father and their Father. To personality God cannot be plural. God is Father to each of his creatures.

Philosophically, cosmically, and with reference to differential levels and locations of manifestation, you may and perforce must conceive of the functioning of plural Deities and postulate the existence of plural Trinities; but in the worshipful experience of the personal contact of every worshiping personality throughout the master universe, God is one; and that unified and personal Deity is our Paradise parent, God the Father, the bestower, conservator, and Father of all personalities from mortal man on the inhabited worlds to the Eternal Son on the central Isle of Light.

5. DEITY UNITY

The oneness, the indivisibility, of Paradise Deity is existential and absolute. There are three eternal personalizations of Deity — the Universal Father, the Eternal Son, and the Infinite Spirit — but in the Paradise Trinity they are *actually* one Deity, undivided and indivisible.

From the original Paradise-Havona level of existential reality, two subabsolute levels have differentiated, and thereon have the Father, Son, and Spirit engaged in the creation of numerous personal associates and subordinates. And while it is inappropriate in this connection to undertake the consideration of absonite deity unification on transcendental levels of ultimacy, it is feasible to look at some features of the unifying function of the various Deity personalizations in whom divinity is functionally manifest to the diverse sectors of creation and to the different orders of intelligent beings.

The present functioning of divinity in the super-universes is actively manifest in the operations of the Supreme Creators — the local universe

Creator Sons and Spirits, the super-universe Ancients of Days, and the Seven Master Spirits of Paradise. These beings constitute the first three levels of God the Sevenfold leading inward to the Universal Father, and this entire domain of God the Sevenfold is co-ordinating on the first level of experiential deity in the evolving Supreme Being.

On Paradise and in the central universe, Deity unity is a fact of existence. Throughout the evolving universes of time and space, Deity unity is an achievement.

6. UNIFICATION OF EVOLUTIONARY DEITY

When the three eternal persons of Deity function as undivided Deity in the Paradise Trinity, they achieve perfect unity; likewise, when they create, either associatively or severally, their Paradise progeny exhibit the characteristic unity of divinity. And this divinity of purpose manifested by the Supreme Creators and Rulers of the time-space domains eventuates in the unifying power potential of the sovereignty of experiential supremacy which, in the presence of the impersonal energy unity of the universe, constitutes a reality tension that can be resolved only through adequate unification with the experiential personality realities of experiential Deity.

The personality realities of the Supreme Being come forth from the Paradise Deities and on the pilot world of the outer Havona circuit unify with the power prerogatives of the Almighty Supreme coming up from the Creator divinities of the grand universe. God the Supreme as a person existed in Havona before the creation of the seven super-universes, but he functioned only on spiritual levels. The evolution of the Almighty power of Supremacy by diverse divinity synthesis in the evolving universes eventuated in a new power presence of Deity which co-ordinated with the spiritual person of the Supreme in Havona by means of the Supreme Mind, which concomitantly translated from the potential resident in the infinite mind of the Infinite Spirit to the active functional mind of the Supreme Being.

The material-minded creatures of the evolutionary worlds of the seven super-universes can comprehend Deity unity only as it is evolving in this power-personality synthesis of the Supreme Being. On any level of existence God cannot exceed the conceptual capacity of the beings who live on such a level. Mortal man must, through the recognition of truth, the appreciation of beauty, and the worship of goodness, evolve the recognition of a God of love and then progress through ascending deity levels to the comprehension of the Supreme. Deity, having been thus grasped as unified in power, can then be personalized in spirit to creature understanding and attainment.

While ascending mortals achieve power comprehension of the Almighty on the capitals of the super-universes and personality comprehension of the Supreme on the outer circuits of Havona, they do not actually find the Supreme Being as they are destined to find the Paradise Deities. Even the finaliters, sixth-stage spirits, have not found the Supreme Being, nor are they likely to until they have achieved seventh-stage-spirit status, and until the Supreme has become actually functional in the activities of the future outer universes.

But when ascenders find the Universal Father as the seventh level of God the Sevenfold, they have attained the personality of the First Person of *all* deity levels of personal relationships with universe creatures.

7. UNIVERSAL EVOLUTIONARY REPERCUSSIONS

The steady progress of evolution in the time-space universes is accompanied by ever-enlarging revelations of Deity to all intelligent creatures. The attainment of the height of evolutionary progress on a world, in a system, constellation, galaxy, universe, super-universe, or in the grand universe signalizes corresponding enlargements of deity function to and in these progressive units of creation. And every such local enhancement of divinity realization is accompanied by certain well-defined repercussions of enlarged deity manifestation to all other sectors of creation. Extending outward from Paradise, each new domain of realized and attained evolution constitutes a new and enlarged revelation of experiential Deity to the universe of universes.

As the components of a local universe are progressively settled in light and life, God the Sevenfold is increasingly made manifest. Time-space evolution begins on a planet with the first expression of God the Sevenfold

— the Creator Son-Creative Spirit association — in control. With the settling of a system in light, this Son-Spirit liaison attains the fullness of function; and when an entire constellation is thus settled, the second phase of God the Sevenfold becomes more active throughout such a realm. The completed administrative evolution of a local universe is attended by new and more direct ministrations of the super-universe Master Spirits; and at this point there also begins that ever-expanding revelation and realization of God the Supreme which culminates in the ascender's comprehension of the Supreme Being while passing through the worlds of the sixth Havona circuit.

The Universal Father, the Eternal Son, and the Infinite Spirit are existential deity manifestations to intelligent creatures and are not, therefore, similarly expanded in personality relations with the mind and spirit creatures of all creation.

It should be noted that ascending mortals may experience the impersonal presence of successive levels of Deity long before they become sufficiently spiritual and adequately educated to attain experiential personal recognition of, and contact with, these Deities as personal beings.

Each new evolutionary attainment within a sector of creation, as well as every new invasion of space by divinity manifestations, is attended by simultaneous expansions of Deity functional-revelation within the then existing and previously organized units of all creation. This new invasion of the administrative work of the universes and their component units may not always appear to be executed exactly in accordance with the technique herewith outlined because it is the practice to send forth advance groups of administrators to prepare the way for the subsequent and successive eras of new administrative over-control. Even God the Ultimate foreshadows his transcendental over-control of the universes during the later stages of a local universe settled in light and life.

It is a fact that, as the creations of time and space are progressively settled in evolutionary status, there is observed a new and fuller functioning of God the Supreme concomitant with a corresponding withdrawing of the first three manifestations of God the Sevenfold. If and when the grand universe becomes settled in light and life, what then will be the future function of the Creator-Creative manifestations of God the Sevenfold if God the Supreme assumes direct control of these creations of time and space? Are these organizers and pioneers of the time-space universes to be liberated for similar activities in outer space? We do not know, but we speculate much concerning these and related matters.

As the frontiers of experiential Deity are extended out into the domains of the Unqualified Absolute, we envision the activity of God the Sevenfold during the earlier evolutionary epochs of these creations of the future. We are not all in agreement respecting the future status of the Ancients of Days and the super-universe Master Spirits. Neither do we know whether or not the Supreme Being will therein function as in the seven super-universes. But we all conjecture that the Michaels, the Creator Sons, are destined to function in these outer universes. Some hold that the future ages will witness some closer form of union between the associated Creator Sons and Divine Ministers; it is even possible that such a creator union might eventuate in some new expression of associate-creator identity of an ultimate nature. But we really know nothing about these possibilities of the unrevealed future.

We do know, however, that in the universes of time and space, God the Sevenfold provides a progressive approach to the Universal Father, and that this evolutionary approach is experientially unified in God the Supreme. We might conjecture that such a plan must prevail in the outer universes; on the other hand the new orders of beings that may sometime inhabit these universes may be able to approach Deity on ultimate levels and by absonite techniques. In short, we have not the slightest concept of what technique of deity approach may become operative in the future universes of outer space.

Nevertheless, we deem that the perfected super-universes will in some way become a part of the Paradise-ascension careers of those beings who may inhabit these outer creations. It is quite possible that in that future age we may witness outer-spacers approaching Havona through the seven super-universes, administered by God the Supreme with or without the collaboration of the Seven Master Spirits.

8. THE SUPREME UNIFIER

The Supreme Being has a threefold function in the experience of mortal man: First, he is the unifier of time-space divinity, God the Sevenfold; second, he is the maximum of Deity which finite creatures can actually comprehend; third, he is mortal man's only avenue of approach to the transcendental experience of consorting with absonite mind, eternal spirit, and Paradise personality.

Ascendant finaliters, having been born in the local universes, nurtured in the super-universes, and trained in the central universe, embrace in their personal experiences the full potential of the comprehension of the time-space divinity of God the Sevenfold unifying in the Supreme. Finaliters serve successively in super-universes other than those of nativity, thereby superimposing experience upon experience until the fullness of the sevenfold diversity of possible creature experience has been encompassed. Through the ministry of the indwelling Adjusters the finaliters are enabled to *find* the Universal Father, but it is by these techniques of experience that such finaliters come really to *know* the Supreme Being, and they are destined to the service and the *revelation* of this Supreme Deity in and to the future universes of outer space.

Bear in mind, all that God the Father and his Paradise Sons do for us, we in turn and in spirit have the opportunity to do for and in the emerging Supreme Being. The experience of love, joy, and service in the universe is mutual. God the Father does not need that his sons should return to him all that he bestows upon them, but they do (or may) in turn bestow all of this upon their fellows and upon the evolving Supreme Being.

All creational phenomena are reflective of antecedent creator-spirit activities. Said Jesus, and it is literally true, "The Son does only those things which he sees the Father do." In time you mortals may begin the revelation of the Supreme to your fellows, and increasingly may you augment this revelation as you ascend Paradiseward. In eternity you may be permitted to make increasing revelations of this God of evolutionary creatures on supreme levels — even ultimate — as seventh-stage finaliters.

9. UNIVERSAL ABSOLUTE UNITY

The Unqualified Absolute and the Deity Absolute are unified in the Universal Absolute. The Absolutes are co-ordinated in the Ultimate, conditioned in the Supreme, and time-space modified in God the Sevenfold. On sub-infinite levels there are *three* Absolutes, but in infinity they appear to be *one*. On Paradise there are three personalizations of Deity, but in the Trinity they *are* one.

The major philosophic proposition of the master universe is this: Did the Absolute (the three Absolutes as one in infinity) exist before the Trinity? and is the Absolute ancestral to the Trinity? or is the Trinity antecedent to the Absolute?

Is the Unqualified Absolute a force presence independent of the Trinity? Does the presence of the Deity Absolute connote the unlimited function of the Trinity? and is the Universal Absolute the final function of the Trinity, even a Trinity of Trinities?

On first thought, a concept of the Absolute as ancestor to all things — even the Trinity — seems to afford transitory satisfaction of consistency gratification and philosophic unification, but any such conclusion is invalidated by the actuality of the eternity of the Paradise Trinity. We are taught, and we believe, that the Universal Father and his Trinity associates are eternal in nature and existence. There is, then, but one consistent philosophic conclusion, and that is: The Absolute is, to all universe intelligences, the impersonal and co-ordinate reaction of the Trinity (of Trinities) to all basic and primary space situations, intrauniversal and extra-universal. To all personality intelligences of the grand universe the Paradise Trinity forever stands in finality, eternity, supremacy, and ultimacy and, for all practical purposes of personal comprehension and creature realization, as absolute.

As creature minds may view this problem, they are led to the final postulate of the Universal I AM as the primal cause and the unqualified source of both the Trinity and the Absolute. When, therefore, we crave to entertain a personal concept of the Absolute, we revert to our ideas and ideals of the Paradise Father. When we desire to facilitate comprehension or to augment consciousness of this otherwise impersonal Absolute, we revert to the fact that the Universal Father is the existential Father of absolute personality; the Eternal Son is the Absolute Person, though not, in the experiential sense, the personalization of the Absolute. And then we go on to envisage the experiential Trinities as culminating in the experiential personalization of the Deity Absolute, while conceiving the Universal Absolute as constituting the universe and the extra-universe phenomena of the manifest presence of the impersonal activities of the unified and co-ordinated Deity associations of supremacy, ultimacy, and infinity — the Trinity of Trinities.

God the Father is discernible on all levels from the finite to the infinite, and though his creatures from Paradise to the evolutionary worlds have variously perceived him, only the Eternal Son and the Infinite Spirit know him as an infinity.

Spiritual personality is absolute only on Paradise, and the concept of the Absolute is unqualified only in infinity. Deity presence is absolute only on Paradise, and the revelation of God must always be partial, relative, and progressive until his power becomes experientially infinite in the space potency of the Unqualified Absolute, while his personality manifestation becomes experientially infinite in the manifest presence of the Deity Absolute, and while these two potentials of infinity become reality-unified in the Universal Absolute.

But beyond sub-infinite levels the three Absolutes *are* one, and thereby is infinity Deity-realized regardless of whether any other order of existence ever self-realizes consciousness of infinity.

Existential status in eternity implies existential self-consciousness of infinity, even though another eternity may be required to experience self-realization of the experiential potentialities inherent in an infinity eternity — an eternal infinity.

And God the Father is the personal source of all manifestations of Deity and reality to all intelligent creatures and spirit beings throughout all the universe of universes. As personalities, now or in the successive universe experiences of the eternal future, no matter if you achieve the attainment of God the Sevenfold, comprehend God the Supreme, find God the Ultimate, or attempt to grasp the concept of God the Absolute, you will discover to your eternal satisfaction that in the consummation of each adventure you have, on new experiential levels, rediscovered the eternal God — the Paradise Father of all universe personalities.

The Universal Father is the explanation of universal unity as it must be supremely, even ultimately, realized in the post-ultimate unity of absolute values and meanings — unqualified Reality.

The Master Force Organizers go out into space and mobilize its energies to become gravity responsive to the Paradise pull of the Universal Father; and subsequently there come the Creator Sons, who organize these gravity-responding forces into inhabited universes and therein evolve intelligent creatures who receive unto themselves the spirit of the Paradise Father and subsequently ascend to the Father to become like him in all possible divinity attributes.

The ceaseless and expanding march of the Paradise creative forces through space seems to presage the ever-extending domain of the gravity grasp of the Universal Father and the never-ending multiplication of varied types of intelligent creatures who are able to love God and be loved by him, and who, by thus becoming God-knowing, may choose to be like him, may elect to attain Paradise and find God.

The universe of universes is altogether unified. God is one in power and personality. There is co-ordination of all levels of energy and all phases of personality. Philosophically and experientially, in concept and in reality, all things and beings center in the Paradise Father. God is all and in all, and no things or beings exist without him.

10. TRUTH, BEAUTY, AND GOODNESS

As the worlds settled in life and light progress from the initial stage to the seventh epoch, they successively grasp for the realization of the reality of God the Sevenfold, ranging from the adoration of the Creator Son to the worship of his Paradise Father. Throughout the continuing seventh stage of such a world's history the ever-progressing mortals grow in the knowledge of God the Supreme, while they vaguely discern the reality of the overshadowing ministry of God the Ultimate.

Throughout this glorious age the chief pursuit of the ever-advancing mortals is the quest for a better understanding and a fuller realization of the comprehensible elements of Deity — truth, beauty, and goodness. This represents man's effort to discern God in mind, matter, and spirit. And as the mortal pursues this quest, he finds himself increasingly absorbed in the experiential study of philosophy, cosmology, and divinity.

Philosophy you somewhat grasp, and divinity you comprehend in worship, social service, and personal spiritual experience, but the pursuit of beauty — cosmology — you all too often limit to the study of man's crude artistic endeavors. Beauty, art, is largely a matter of the unification of contrasts. Variety is essential to the concept of beauty. The supreme beauty, the height of finite art, is the drama of the unification of the vastness of the cosmic extremes of Creator and creature. Man finding God and God finding man — the creature becoming perfect as is the Creator — that is the supernal achievement of the supremely beautiful, the attainment of the apex of cosmic art.

Hence materialism, atheism, is the maximation of ugliness, the climax of the finite antithesis of the beautiful.[1] Highest beauty consists in the panorama of the unification of the variations which have been born of pre-existent harmonious reality.

The attainment of cosmologic levels of thought includes:

1. *Curiosity.* Hunger for harmony and thirst for beauty. Persistent attempts to discover new levels of harmonious cosmic relationships.

2. *Aesthetic appreciation.* Love of the beautiful and ever-advancing appreciation of the artistic touch of all creative manifestations on all levels of reality.

3. *Ethic sensitivity.* Through the realization of truth the appreciation of

---

1. *JFC Note: What's said above is true for the era of Light, but for us, it can sometimes happen that belief becomes too dogmatic, too literal, too small minded and restrictive. When this happens, the spiritual life becomes barren. Going through a materialistic or atheistic phase can be a positive step at these times and free the mind; allowing a more complete and expanded religious life to re-develop later. In such a situation, I disagree with the previous statement, as then these atheism phases can be a necessary process, beautiful in their own way, leading eventually to a new beginning.*

beauty leads to the sense of the eternal fitness of those things which impinge upon the recognition of divine goodness in Deity relations with all beings; and thus even cosmology leads to the pursuit of divine reality values — to God-consciousness.

The worlds settled in light and life are so fully concerned with the comprehension of truth, beauty, and goodness because these quality values embrace the revelation of Deity to the realms of time and space. The meanings of eternal truth make a combined appeal to the intellectual and spiritual natures of mortal man. Universal beauty embraces the harmonious relations and rhythms of the cosmic creation; this is more distinctly the intellectual appeal and leads towards unified and synchronous comprehension of the material universe. Divine goodness represents the revelation of infinite values to the finite mind, therein to be perceived and elevated to the very threshold of the spiritual level of human comprehension.

Truth is the basis of science and philosophy, presenting the intellectual foundation of religion. Beauty sponsors art, music, and the meaningful rhythms of all human experience. Goodness embraces the sense of ethics, morality, and religion — experiential perfection-hunger.

The existence of beauty implies the presence of appreciative creature mind just as certainly as the fact of progressive evolution indicates the dominance of the Supreme Mind. Beauty is the intellectual recognition of the harmonious time-space synthesis of the far-flung diversification of phenomenal reality, all of which stems from pre-existent and eternal oneness.

Goodness is the mental recognition of the relative values of the diverse levels of divine perfection. The recognition of goodness implies a mind of moral status, a personal mind with ability to discriminate between good and evil. But the possession of goodness, greatness, is the measure of real divinity attainment.

The recognition of *true relations* implies a mind competent to discriminate between truth and error. The bestowal Spirit of Truth which invests the human minds of Urantia is unerringly responsive to truth — the living spirit relationship of all things and all beings as they are co-ordinated in the eternal ascent Godward.

Every impulse of every electron, thought, or spirit is an acting unit in the whole universe. Only sin is isolated and evil gravity resisting on the mental and spiritual levels. The universe is a whole; no thing or being exists or lives in isolation. Self-realization is potentially evil if it is antisocial. It is literally true: "No man lives by himself." Cosmic socialization constitutes the highest form of personality unification. Said Jesus: "He who would be greatest among you, let him become server of all."

Even truth, beauty, and goodness — man's intellectual approach to the universe of mind, matter, and spirit — must be combined into one unified concept of a divine and supreme *ideal*. As mortal personality unifies the human experience with matter, mind, and spirit, so does this divine and supreme ideal become power-unified in Supremacy and then personalized as a God of fatherly love.

All insight into the relations of the parts to any given whole requires an understanding grasp of the relation of all parts to that whole; and in the universe this means the relation of created parts to the Creative Whole. Deity thus becomes the transcendental, even the infinite, goal of universal and eternal attainment.

Universal beauty is the recognition of the reflection of the Isle of Paradise in the material creation, while eternal truth is the special ministry of the Paradise Sons who not only bestow themselves upon the mortal races but even pour out their Spirit of Truth upon all peoples. Divine goodness is more fully shown forth in the loving ministry of the manifold personalities of the Infinite Spirit. But love, the sum total of these three qualities, is man's perception of God as his spirit Father.

Physical matter is the time-space shadow of the Paradise energy-shining of the absolute Deities. Truth meanings are the mortal-intellect repercussions of the eternal word of Deity — the time-space comprehension of supreme concepts. The goodness values of divinity are the merciful ministries of the spirit personalities of the Universal, the Eternal, and the Infinite to the time-space finite creatures of the evolutionary spheres.

These meaningful reality values of divinity are blended in the Father's relation with each personal creature as divine love. They are co-ordinated in the Son and his Sons as divine mercy. They manifest their qualities through the Spirit and his spirit children as divine ministry, the portrayal of loving mercy to the children of time. These three divinities are primarily manifested by the Supreme Being as power-personality synthesis. They are variously shown forth by God the Sevenfold in seven differing associations of divine meanings and values on seven ascending levels.

To finite man truth, beauty, and goodness embrace the full revelation of divinity reality. As this love-comprehension of Deity finds spiritual expression in the lives of God-knowing mortals, there are yielded the fruits of divinity: intellectual peace, social progress, moral satisfaction, spiritual joy, and cosmic wisdom. The advanced mortals on a world in the seventh stage of light and life have learned that love is the greatest thing in the universe — and they know that God is love.

Love is the desire to do good to others.

[Presented by a Mighty Messenger visiting on Urantia, by request of the Nebadon Revelatory Corps and in collaboration with a certain Melchizedek, the vicegerent Planetary Prince of Urantia.]

This paper on Universal Unity is the twenty-fifth of a series of presentations by various authors, having been sponsored as a group by a commission of Nebadon personalities numbering twelve and acting under the direction of Mantutia Melchizedek. We indited these narratives and put them in the English language, by a technique authorized by our superiors, in the year 1934 of Urantia time.

Our Local Cosmology Summary

Type of unit	Name	Capital	Paradise Representative
Planet	Urantia		
System	Satania	Jerusem	none
Constellation	Norlatiadek	Edentia	Faithful of Days
Galaxy	Milky Way	Zion	Recents of Days
Minor Sector	Uminor the Third	Ensa	Recents of Days
Major Sector	Umajor the Fifth	Splandon	Perfections of Days
Universe	Nebadon	Salvington	Union of Days
Superuniverse	Orvonton	Uversa	Ancient of Days